The 80s Music Compendium

by Dave Kinzer

The 80s Music Compendium

First Edition
Printed in the United States of America

ISBN-13: 978-1515287766
ISBN-10: 1515287769

Publisher's Cataloging-in-Publication data

Kinzer, Dave.
    The 80s Music Compendium / by Dave Kinzer.
    pages cm
    ISBN 978-1515287766 (pbk.)
    ISBN 978-1310027222 (ebook)
    Includes bibliographical references.

1. Rock music --1980-1989 --Discography. 2. Rock music --United States --1980-1989 --History and criticism. 3. Alternative rock music --United States --1980-1989 --History and criticism. 4. Alternative rock music --1980-1989 – Discography. 5. Popular culture --United States. I. The Eighties Music Compendium. II. Title.

ML156.4.R6 K56 2015
016.78166/0266 --dc23   2015912968

Library of Congress Control Number: 2015912968

To contact the author, and to receive a discount coupon for an ebook version, email him at davekinzerbooks@gmail.com.

Also by the author:

Pranked!

INTRODUCTION

There were 4,172 songs that made the Billboard Hot 100 chart in the 80s. Recently, I listened to all of them. Every. Single. One. I know you're thinking, "Yeah, the 80s had some amazing music, but still... are you nuts?"

Well, it all started when I discovered that many of my music students couldn't correctly identify instruments by their sound. To help them, I decided to play as many different musical clips for them from modern music that featured all kinds of instruments. This proved to be a difficult task.

I started looking for a resource that listed a bunch of hit songs that featured these instruments. I found a few, but not everything I was looking for. So, I decided to make my own resource.

Since everybody knows that the 80s had the best music (right?), I decided to select all my musical examples from that decade. At first, I was just compiling lists of songs that featured certain instruments.

Then, as I was listening to all these pop songs, I started noticing other interesting things, like the number of hit songs that have been written (at least partially) in a foreign language. Or songs that have countermelodies, or lots of syncopation. And what about songs that tell stories? There's another list. The more songs I listened to, the more lists I made.

By the time I listened to all 4,172 songs, I had 113 lists- Songs with flutes. Songs with steel drums. Songs in German. Songs with the longest saxophone solos. Medleys. The shortest songs, the longest songs, songs that deserved to be in the top 40, songs with fake endings, Christmas songs- the list(s) goes on and on.

Over 3,600 songs are part of at least one list. What happened to the other 572 songs? Those songs, frankly, weren't unique or interesting. They didn't have any unusual instruments, didn't have any words in Swahili, and didn't even have Michael McDonald singing backup (and he sang backup for everybody in the 80s).

But you don't have to be a music teacher to enjoy this book. If you're in a cover band and need some new material to feature your gifted accordion player, I've got a list of accordion hit songs for you. What if you really want to show off your skills on the oboe or glockenspiel? I've got lists of hit songs for those, and dozens of other instruments as well. Or, if you're a music nerd, 80s music fan, or just someone who would love to be on a game show so you can answer questions like, "What number one song from the 80s had a gong in it?", then you'll find this book fascinating as well.

Oh, and one more thing. I freely admit that there may be a mistake or two in here. Sorry about that. I may have mis-identified an instrument, or omitted a song that did, indeed, have a marimba. Your mind tends to go to mush sometimes after listening to thousands of 80s songs. It is a good kind of mush, though.

If you find a mistake, feel free to email me at davekinzerbooks@gmail.com. Include a link to a resource that will confirm my error. For example, instead of simply saying, "There isn't a flute in that song!", send me a link to an interview where the artist confirms your point.

Remember, only songs that made Billboard's Hot 100 list will be included in this book. The songs are always listed in the year that they peaked on the charts. So, if you're wondering why, for example, Janet Jackson's "Rhythm Nation" isn't listed in this compendium even though it was released in 1989, it's because it peaked at #2 in January of 1990. Likewise, a song that peaked on the charts in December of 1979 wouldn't be listed in this book even though it remained on the charts in 1980.

For added enjoyment, I've created several YouTube videos to accompany some of the lists in this book. To find those, just search for "Dave Kinzer" at YouTube.

Also, if you've got a strong opinion on which decade my next compendium should be about, please email me at the above email address. A lot of support for a particular decade will definitely influence my decision.

Thanks for reading. Enjoy.

Table of Contents

GENRES

The first few sections list songs in several different genres: Instrumental, "Live" songs, Country crossover hits, Medleys, Novelty and Comedy hits, Remakes, and songs that charted on the Hot 100 chart twice (rap songs are included in a later section).

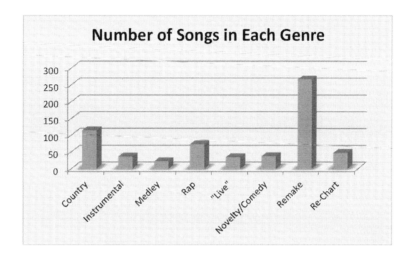

INSTRUMENTAL SONGS

Instrumental songs (songs without singing) were quite popular at the beginning of the 80s. The first three years of the decade produced 22 instrumental hits. The public soon had enough, though. The last seven years of the 80s produced only 14 more. While 36 is a decent number of hits for this style, it was never incredibly popular. Nineteen of the thirty-six songs peaked no higher then number fifty on the charts.

INSTRUMENTAL SONGS (cont'd)

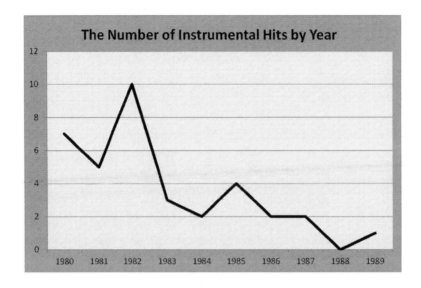

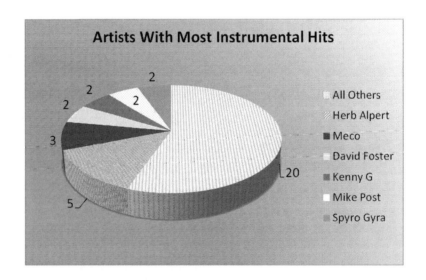

SONG	ARTIST	HOT 100 CHART
1980		
Give It All You Got	Chuck Mangione	#18
Empire Strikes Back (Medley)	Meco	#18
The Seduction (Love Theme)	James Last Band	#28
Rotation	Herb Alpert	#30
Computer Game "Theme From The Circus"	Yellow Magic Orchestra	#60
Catching The Sun	Spyro Gyra	#68
Love Theme From Shogun (Mariko's Theme)	Meco	#70

The 80s Music Compendium

INSTRUMENTAL SONGS (cont'd)

1981		
Theme From Hill Street Blues	Mike Post w/Larry Carlton	#10
Seasons	Charles Fox	#75
Café Amore	Spyro Gyra	#77
Theme From Raging Bull (Cavalleria Rusticana)	Joel Diamond	#82
Toccata	Sky	#83

1982		
Chariots Of Fire- Titles	Vangelis	#1
Hooked On Classics	Royal Philharmonic Orchestra	#10
(Theme From) Magnum P.I.	Mike Post	#25
Hooked On Swing	Larry Elgart	#31
Pop Goes The Movies (Part 1)	Meco	#35
Route 101	Herb Alpert	#37
Theme From E.T. (The Extra-Terrestrial)	Walter Murphy	#47
Theme From Dynasty	Bill Conti	#52
Hooked On Big Bands	Frank Barber Orchestra	#61
Sleepwalk	Larry Carlton	#74

1983		
Rockit	Herbie Hancock	#71
Red Hot	Herb Alpert	#77
Garden Party	Herb Alpert	#81

1984		
Theme From "Terms Of Endearment"	Michael Gore	#84
Bullish	Herb Alpert Tijuana Brass	#90

1985		
Miami Vice Theme	Jan Hammer	#1
Axel F	Harold Faltermeyer	#3
Love Theme From St. Elmo's Fire	David Foster	#15
Rain Forest	Paul Hardcastle	#57

1986		
Peter Gunn	Art Of Noise w/ Duane Eddy	#50
Winter Games	David Foster	#85

1987		
Songbird	Kenny G	#4
Oh Yeah	Yello	#51

INSTRUMENTAL SONGS (cont'd)

1989		
Silhouette	Kenny G	#13

"LIVE" SONGS

Much like the instrumental hit song, the popularity of the "live" hit song also declined dramatically during the 80s (see chart). Twenty-two of the thirty-four "live" songs hit the chart between 1980-1982. The last two years of the decade didn't even have one "live" hit song.

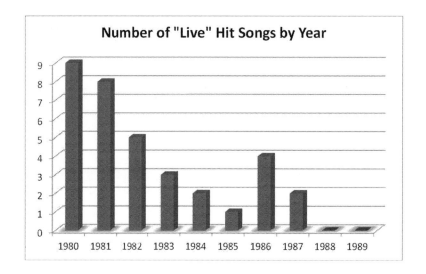

SONG	ARTIST	HOT 100 CHART
1980		
Tulsa Time	Eric Clapton	#30
When A Man Loves A Woman	Bette Midler	#35
One-Trick Pony	Paul Simon	#40
It's Hard To Be Humble	Mac Davis	#43
It's Not A Wonder	Little River Band	#51
Breakfast In America	Supertramp	#62
Blues Power	Eric Clapton	#76
Lola	The Kinks	#81
Spend The Night In Love	The Four Seasons	#91

1981		
Tryin' To Live My Life Without You	Bob Seger	#5

"LIVE" SONGS (cont'd)

Say Goodbye To Hollywood	Billy Joel	#17
Seven Bridges Road	Eagles	#21
I Can Take Care Of Myself	Billy Vera & The Beaters	#39
My Mother's Eyes	Bette Midler	#39
Who's Making Love	Blues Brothers	#39
At This Moment	Billy Vera & The Beaters	#79
Unchained Melody	Heart	#83

1982		
She's Got A Way	Billy Joel	#23
Going To A Go-Go	The Rolling Stones	#25
Wake Up Little Susie	Simon & Garfunkel	#27
Feel Like A Number	Bob Seger	#48
Closer To The Heart	Rush	#69

1983		
Land Of A Thousand Dances	J. Geils Band	#60
You Belong To Me	The Doobie Brothers	#79
Solsbury Hill	Peter Gabriel	#84

1984		
Encore	Cheryl Lynn	#69
I Will Follow	U2	#81

1985		
A Nite At The Apollo Live! The Way You Do The Things You Do/ My Girl	Daryl Hall & John Oates w/ David Ruffin & Eddie Kendrick	#20

1986		
War	Bruce Springsteen	#8
Live Is Life	Opus	#32
Needles And Pins	Tom Petty w/ Stevie Nicks	#37
Once In A Lifetime	Talking Heads	#91

1987		
Mony Mony "Live"	Billy Idol	#1
Fire	Bruce Springsteen	#46

COUNTRY SONGS

The country music industry enjoyed quite a run on the pop charts between 1980-1983. Each of those four years saw more than twenty country songs cross over to the Hot 100. Then, the bottom fell out- only six country songs made the Hot 100 in 1984, and the number steadily declined until 1988 and 1989, when there wasn't a single country song that made the pop charts.

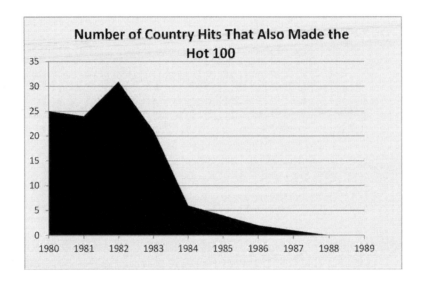

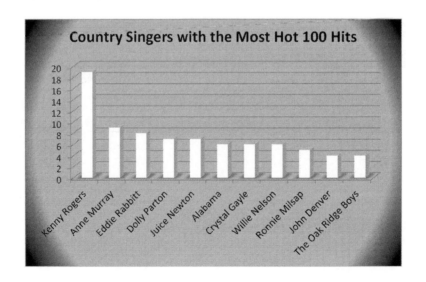

SONG	ARTIST	COUNTRY CHART	HOT 100 CHART
1980			
Lady	Kenny Rogers	#1	#1
Longer	Dan Fogelberg	#85	#2

COUNTRY SONGS (cont'd)

Coward Of The County	Kenny Rogers	#1	#3
Don't Fall In Love With A Dreamer	Kenny Rogers	#3	#4
Drivin' My Life Away	Eddie Rabbitt	#1	#5
Lookin' For Love	Johnny Lee	#1	#5
Daydream Believer	Anne Murray	#3	#12
Love The World Away	Kenny Rogers	#4	#14
Why Not Me	Fred Knobloch	#30	#18
On The Road Again	Willie Nelson	#1	#20
Stand By Me	Mickey Gilley	#1	#22
I Believe In You	Don Williams	#1	#24
Could I Have This Dance	Anne Murray	#1	#33
Starting Over Again	Dolly Parton	#1	#36
Lucky Me	Anne Murray	#9	#42
It's Hard To Be Humble	Mac Davis	#10	#43
My Heroes Have Always Been Cowboys	Willie Nelson	#1	#44
Texas In My Rear View Mirror	Mac Davis	#9	#51
Autograph	John Denver	#84	#52
That Lovin' You Feelin' Again	Emmylou Harris	#6	#55
It's Like We Never Said Goodbye	Crystal Gayle	#1	#63
I'm Happy Just To Dance With You	Anne Murray	#23	#64
A Lesson In Leavin'	Dottie West	#1	#73
The Blue Side	Crystal Gayle	#8	#81
Gone Too Far	Eddie Rabbitt	#1	#82

1981			
I Love A Rainy Night	Eddie Rabbitt	#1	#1
9 To 5	Dolly Parton	#1	#1
Queen Of Hearts	Juice Newton	#14	#2
I Don't Need You	Kenny Rogers	#1	#3
Angel Of The Morning	Juice Newton	#22	#4
Step By Step	Eddie Rabbitt	#1	#5
Elvira	The Oak Ridge Boys	#1	#5
Somebody's Knockin'	Terri Gibbs	#8	#13
What Are We Doin' In Love	Dottie West w/Kenny Rogers	#1	#14
Share Your Love With Me	Kenny Rogers	#5	#14
Feels So Right	Alabama	#1	#20
Seven Year Ache	Rosanne Cash	#1	#22
Blessed Are The Believers	Anne Murray	#1	#34
Some Days Are Diamonds (Some Days Are Stones)	John Denver	#10	#36
Mister Sandman	Emmylou Harris	#10	#37
But You Know I Love You	Dolly Parton	#1	#41

COUNTRY SONGS (cont'd)

It's All I Can Do	Anne Murray	#9	#53
Bet Your Heart On Me	Johnny Lee	#1	#54
The Cowboy And The Lady	John Denver	#50	#66
Secrets	Mac Davis	#47	#76
The Woman In Me	Crystal Gayle	#3	#76
House Of The Rising Sun	Dolly Parton	#14	#77
Rich Man	Terri Gibbs	#19	#89
1982			
Always On My Mind	Willie Nelson	#1	#5
Love's Been A Little Bit Hard On Me	Juice Newton	#30	#7
The Sweetest Thing (I've Ever Known)	Juice Newton	#1	#7
Break It To Me Gently	Juice Newton	#2	#11
Bobbie Sue	The Oak Ridge Boys	#1	#12
Through The Years	Kenny Rogers	#5	#13
Love Will Turn You Around	Kenny Rogers	#1	#13
Any Day Now	Ronnie Milsap	#1	#14
Someone Could Lose A Heart Tonight	Eddie Rabbitt	#1	#15
Nobody	Sylvia	#1	#15
Take Me Down	Alabama	#1	#18
What's Forever For	Michael Murphey	#1	#19
I Wouldn't Have Missed It For The World	Ronnie Milsap	#1	#20
After The Glitter Fades	Stevie Nicks	#70	#32
I Don't Know Where To Start	Eddie Rabbitt	#2	#35
Let It Be Me	Willie Nelson	#2	#40
Another Sleepless Night	Anne Murray	#4	#44
Dreamin'	John Schneider	#32	#45
Could It Be Love	Jennifer Warnes	#57	#47
A Love Song	Kenny Rogers	#3	#47
Just To Satisfy You	Waylon Jennings & Willie Nelson	#1	#52
Autograph	John Denver	#84	#52
I Will Always Love You	Dolly Parton	#1	#53
She Got The Goldmine (I Got The Shaft)	Jerry Reed	#1	#57
Finally	T.G. Sheppard	#1	#58
He Got You	Ronnie Milsap	#1	#59
Close Enough To Perfect	Alabama	#1	#65
Natural Love	Petula Clark	#20	#66
Only One You	T.G. Sheppard	#1	#68
So Fine	The Oak Ridge Boys	#22	#76

COUNTRY SONGS (cont'd)

1983			
Islands In The Stream	Kenny Rogers & Dolly Parton	#1	#1
We've Got Tonight	Kenny Rogers	#1	#6
You And I	Crystal Gayle	#1	#7
Stranger In My House	Ronnie Milsap	#5	#23
Heart Of The Night	Juice Newton	#53	#25
All My Life	Kenny Rogers	#13	#37
The Closer You Get	Alabama	#1	#38
Swingin'	John Anderson	#1	#43
Save The Last Dance For Me	Dolly Parton	#3	#45
You Can't Run From Love	Eddie Rabbitt	#1	#55
Don't You Know How Much I Love You	Ronnie Milsap	#1	#58
American Made	The Oak Ridge Boys	#1	#72
A Little Good News	Anne Murray	#1	#74
Lady Down On Love	Alabama	#1	#76
Still Taking Chances	Michael Murphey	#3	#76
You Put The Beat In My Heart	Eddie Rabbitt	#10	#81
Baby, What About You	Crystal Gayle	#1	#83
The Sound Of Goodbye	Crystal Gayle	#1	#84
Whatever Happened To Old Fashioned Love	B.J. Thomas	#1	#93
Scarlet Fever	Kenny Rogers	#5	#94
Somebody's Gonna Love You	Lee Greenwood	#1	#96

1984			
What About Me?	Kenny Rogers	#70	#15
Baby I Lied	Deborah Allen	#4	#26
A Little Love	Juice Newton	#64	#44
When We Make Love	Alabama	#1	#72
Eyes That See In The Dark	Kenny Rogers	#30	#79
The Greatest Gift Of All	Kenny Rogers & Dolly Parton	#53	#81

1985			
Morning Desire	Kenny Rogers	#1	#72
Crazy	Kenny Rogers	#1	#79
Go Down Easy	Dan Fogelberg	#56	#85
Real Love	Dolly Parton w/ Kenny Rogers	#1	#91

1986			
Bop	Dan Seals	#1	#42
Now And Forever (You And Me)	Anne Murray	#1	#92

1987			
I'll Still Be Loving You	Restless Heart	#1	#33

MEDLEYS

A medley is a song that consists of parts of several other songs. All the parts are put together to form a new song, called a medley. Usually, the medley will use the catchiest parts of other songs, like the chorus.

For example, the music in "Beach Boys Medley" from 1981 is taken from nine different Beach Boys songs from the 60s. If you want to hear basically just the choruses from a bunch of different Beach Boys songs, then that's the song for you.

A European group called "Stars On 45" helped popularize the medley. One of their records, simply titled "Medley", hit number one- eight of the songs in the medley were Beatles hits.

Some medleys only combined two songs, like Journey's medley in 1980. Others combined a bunch of hit songs from the 60s ("Back To The 60s"), classical tunes from composers like Mozart and Bach ("Hooked On Classics"), or songs of Elvis Presley ("The Elvis Medley").

The medley craze really only lasted for two years: 1981-1982. Fifteen of the twenty-two medleys from the 80s came from those two years.

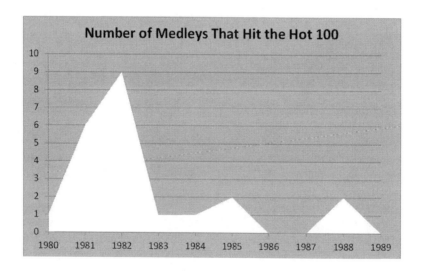

SONG	ARTIST	HOT 100 CHART	NOTES
1980			
Good Morning Girl/Stay Awhile	Journey	#55	

SONG	ARTIST	HOT 100 CHART	NOTES
1981			
Medley	Stars On 45	#1	8 Beatles songs, "Venus", and "Sugar, Sugar" (41 word title)
The Beach Boys Medley	The Beach Boys	#12	
More Stars	Stars On 45	#55	Bunch of hit songs by America, Simon & Garfunkel, Mamas and Papas and others
Medley II	Stars On 45	#67	Beatles songs

MEDLEYS (cont'd)

Summer '81 Medley	The Cantina Band	#81	Beach Boys songs
Back To The 60's	Tight Fit	#89	Bunch of 60s songs

1982			
Hooked On Classics	Royal Philharmonic Orchestra	#10	Classical music
The Beatles' Movie Medley	The Beatles	#12	Beatles songs
Stars On 45 III	Stars On	#28	
Hooked On Swing	Larry Elgart	#31	Big Band/Swing
Pop Goes The Movies (Part 1)	Meco	#35	Movie theme songs
Hooked On Big Bands	Frank Barber Orchestra	#61	Big Bands
Memories Of Days Gone By	Fred Parris/ Five Satins	#71	50s Doo Wop
The Elvis Medley	Elvis Presley	#71	Elvis Presley songs
Seasons Of Gold	Gidea Park	#82	Four Seasons songs

1983			
Do It Again/Billie Jean	Club House	#75	Mix of "Do It Again" by Steely Dan and "Billie Jean" by Michael Jackson

1984			
Medley: Love Songs Are Back Again	Band Of Gold	#64	Old love songs

1985			
Just A Gigolo/ I Ain't Got Nobody	David Lee Roth	#12	
A Nite At The Apollo Live! The Way You Do The Things You Do/ My Girl	Daryl Hall & John Oates w/ David Ruffin & Eddie Kendrick	#20	

1988			
Baby, I Love Your Way/ Freebird Medley (Free Baby)	Will To Power	#1	
Route 66/ Behind The Wheel	Depeche Mode	#61	

NOVELTY/COMEDY SONGS

The 1980s saw quite a few novelty songs hit the Hot 100. Like medleys, instrumental songs, "live" songs, and country songs that hit the pop charts, the novelty genre saw a steep decline in popularity. Sixty-eight percent of the novelty songs charted in 1980-1984.

The charts did not give novelty songs much respect- the highest charting novelty hit was a song about a video game character ("Pac-Man Fever", by Buckner & Garcia)! It made it all the way to number nine. It would be the only novelty hit to break inside the top ten. The average charting position of the 37 hits was #53.

It's not too surprising when you consider the topic matter of these songs, however. We've got corny songs about television shows, two songs about the Star Wars movies, one song that narrates a rap battle with Superman, one song about the Three Stooges, and one song about beating Mike Tyson in the ring, among others.

Who was responsible for these songs? We have singers with quite a range of backgrounds. Several were established and well-respected actors: Rodney Dangerfield, Cheech & Chong, Clint Eastwood, and Billy Crystal. There were also songs by athletes, radio DJs, and movie characters.

Sometimes you could tell a song might be a little weird, just based on the name of the performer. Really, how could you expect a "normal" hit song from The Star Wars Intergalactic Droid Choir & Chorale? What about "Weird Al" Yankovic? We've also got songs by The American Comedy Network, The Chicago Bears Shufflin' Crew, and The Flying Lizards.

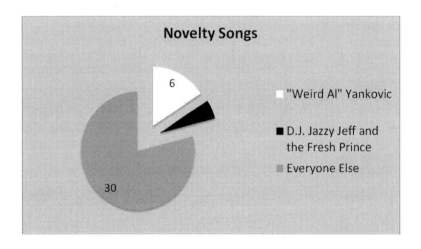

SONG	ARTIST	HOT 100 CHART	NOTES
1980			
It's Hard To Be Humble	Mac Davis	#43	
Money	The Flying Lizards	#50	
Rock Lobster	B-52s	#56	
Who Shot J.R. ?	Gary Burbank	#67	About TV show, "Dallas"
What Do You Get A Wookiee For Christmas (When He Already Owns A Comb?)	Star Wars Intergalactic Droid Choir & Chorale	#69	By the artist Meco
1981			
Double Dutch Bus	Frankie Smith	#30	
General Hospi-Tale	The Afternoon Delights	#33	About TV show, "General Hospital"
Shaddap You Face	Joe Dolce	#53	
1982			
Pac-Man Fever	Buckner & Garcia	#9	Every song on album was about video games

The 80s Music Compendium

NOVELTY/COMEDY SONGS (cont'd)

Take Off	Bob & Doug McKenzie w/Geddy Lee	#16	
Valley Girl	Frank Zappa	#32	
Murphy's Law	Cheri	#39	
She Got The Goldmine (I Got The Shaft)	Jerry Reed	#57	
Attack Of The Name Game	Stacy Lattisaw	#70	

1983			
The Clapping Song	Pia Zadora	#36	
Ewok Celebration	Meco	#60	Star Wars reference
Ricky	"Weird Al" Yankovic	#63	Parody of "Mickey", by Tony Basil

1984			
Eat It	"Weird Al" Yankovic	#12	Parody of "Beat It by Michael Jackson
The Curly Shuffle	Jump 'N The Saddle	#15	The Three Stooges
Jam On It	Newcleus	#56	
Make My Day	T.G. Sheppard w/ Clint Eastwood	#62	
King Of Suede	"Weird Al" Yankovic	#62	Parody of "King Of Pain", by Police
Breaking Up Is Hard On You (A/K/A Don't Take Ma Bell Away From Me)	The American Comedy Network	#70	Parody of "Breaking Up Is Hard To Do", by Neil Sedaka
Eat My Shorts	Rick Dees	#75	
I Lost On Jeopardy	"Weird Al" Yankovic	#81	Parody of "I Was In Jeopardy"
Rappin' Rodney	Rodney Dangerfield	#83	

1985			
Bruce	Rick Springfield	#27	About fans confusing him with Bruce Springsteen
Like A Surgeon	"Weird Al" Yankovic	#47	Parody of "Like A Virgin", by Madonna
Born In East L.A.	Cheech & Chong	#48	Parody of "Born in USA", by Bruce Springsteen
My Toot	Jean Knight	#50	
You Look Marvelous	Billy Crystal	#58	
Basketball	Kurtis Blow	#71	

1986			
Superbowl Shuffle	The Chicago Bears Shufflin' Crew	#41	Rapped by Chicago Bears

1987			
Oh Yeah	Yello	#51	
Ronnie's Rap	Ron & The D.C Crew	#93	"Ronald Reagan" rapping

NOVELTY/COMEDY SONGS (cont'd)

1988			
Girls Ain't Nothing But Trouble	D.J. Jazzy Jeff and the Fresh Prince	#57	
Fat	"Weird Al" Yankovic	#99	Parody of "Bad", by Michael Jackson

1989			
I Think I Can Beat Mike Tyson	D.J. Jazzy Jeff and the Fresh Prince	#58	

CHRISTMAS SONGS

You'd think there'd be more Christmas songs that made the Hot 100, but only six songs from the decade are classified as a Christmas song.

The artists responsible are as varied as they could possibly be. You've got Star Wars characters, a duo best known for a song about a video game, a bona fide pop/rock singer-songwriter, an all-star collection of European pop stars, a country duo, and a boy band.

One note about "Same Old Lang Syne"- I debated whether or not I should include this song in this category. The song tells a story that takes place on Christmas Eve, and at the very end, a snippet of "Auld Lang Syne" is played on the saxophone. It is for those reasons that I believe this song gets played every Christmas season. So because of the regular airplay it receives around Christmastime, I included it in this list.

		HOT 100
SONG	**ARTIST**	**CHART**
1980		
What Can You Get A Wookiee For Christmas (When He Already Owns A Comb?)	Star Wars Intergalactic Droid Choir & Chorale	#69
Merry Christmas In The NFL	Willis "The Guard & Vigorish	#82

1981		
Same Old Lang Syne	Dan Fogelberg	#9

1984		
Do They Know It's Christmas?	Band Aid	#13
The Greatest Gift Of All	Kenny Rogers & Dolly Parton	#81

1989		
This One's For The Children	New Kids On The Block	#7

REMAKES

Of the 4172 hits in the 80s, 266 (about 6.4%) were remakes, or covers. Nostalgia for the 60s must've been rampant, because 58% of the remakes were hits from that decade. Somewhat surprisingly, there were a decent number of covers of hits from the 80s, including two remakes from 1981.

In the case of a song that has been covered multiple times, the "original artist" listed is the first artist to chart with the song. That is why the original artist listed for "I Heard It Through The Grapevine" is Gladys Knight & The Pips (from 1967), not Marvin Gaye (1968), even though it was a bigger hit for him.

It was interesting to see how each version charted. Sometimes, the results were drastically different. For instance, "Cum On Feel The Noize" barely squeaked into the Top 100 for Slade in 1973. It peaked at #98. Ten years later, Quiet Riot made it the biggest hit of their career, taking it all the way to #5. Luis Cardenas wasn't so lucky. He covered Del Shannon's "Runaway" in 1986. It peaked at #83, while Shannon's version hit #1 in 1961.

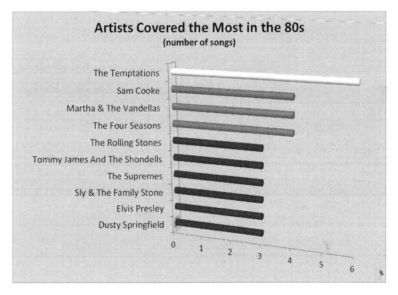

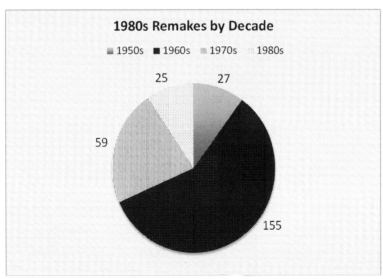

1950s REMAKES

SONG	ARTIST	80s CHART	50s ARTIST	YEAR	50s CHART
1980					
Don't Let Go	Isaac Hayes	#18	Roy Hamilton	1958	#13
My Prayer	Ray, Goodman & Brown	#47	Platters	1956	#1
1981					
Why Do Fools Fall In Love	Diana Ross	#7	Frankie Lymon	1956	#6
Since I Don't Have You	Don McLean	#23	Skyliners	1959	#12
Mister Sandman	Emmylou Harris	#37	Four Aces	1955	#5
All I Have To Do Is Dream	Andy Gibb & Victoria Principal	#51	Everly Brothers	1958	#1
You Don't Know Me	Mickey Gilley	#55	Jerry Vale	1956	#14
Dedicated To The One I Love	Bernadette Peters	#65	Shirelles	1959	#83
Unchained Melody	Heart	#83	Les Baxter	1955	#1
1982					
Come Go With Me	The Beach Boys	#18	Dell-Vikings	1957	#4
Wake Up Little Susie	Simon & Garfunkel	#27	The Everly Brothers	1957	#1
Sea Of Love	Del Shannon	#33	Phil Phillips	1959	#2
Let It Be Me	Willie Nelson	#40	Jill Corey w/ Jimmy Carroll	1957	#57
Teach Me Tonight	Al Jarreau	#70	Decastro Sisters	1955	#2
Sleepwalk	Larry Carlton	#74	Santo & Johnny	1959	#1
So Fine	The Oak Ridge Boys	#76	The Fiestas	1959	#11
1983					
Johnny B. Goode	Peter Tosh	#84	Chuck Berry	1958	#8
1984					
There Goes My Baby	Donna Summer	#21	Drifters	1959	#2
1985					
Sea Of Love	Honeydrippers	#3	Phil Phillips	1959	#2
Willie And The Hand Jive	George Thorogood	#63	Johnny Otis Show	1958	#9

1950s REMAKES (cont'd)

You Send Me	The Manhattans	#81	Sam Cooke	1957	#1

1986					
Peter Gunn	Art Of Noise w/ Duane Eddy	#50	Ray Anthony	1959	#8

1986					
Earth Angel	New Edition	#21	Penguins	1955	#3

1987					
La Bamba	Los Lobos	#1	Ritchie Valens	1959	#22
Come On, Let's Go	Los Lobos	#21	Ritchie Valens	1958	#42
Young Blood	Bruce Willis	#68	Coasters	1957	#8

1988					
Don't Be Cruel	Cheap Trick	#4	Elvis Presley	1956	#1

1960s REMAKES

SONGS	ARTIST	80s CHART	60s ARTIST	YEAR	60s CHART
1980					
Yes, I'm Ready	Teri Desario w/ K.C.	#2	Barbara Mason	1965	#5
More Than I Can Say	Leo Sayer	#2	Bobby Vee	1961	#61
Working My Way Back To You	Spinners	#2	The Four Seasons	1966	#9
Cupid	Spinners	#4	Sam Cooke	1961	#17
Hurt So Bad	Linda Ronstadt	#8	Little Anthony & The Imperials	1965	#10
More Love	Kim Carnes	#10	Miracles	1967	#23
Daydream Believer	Anne Murray	#12	Monkees	1967	#1
You've Lost That Lovin' Feelin'	Daryl Hall & John Oates	#12	Righteous Brothers	1965	#1
Gimme Some Lovin'	Blues Brothers	#18	Spencer Davis Group	1967	#7
Stand By Me	Mickey Gilley	#22	Ben E. King	1961	#4
Gee Whiz	Bernadette Peters	#31	Carla Thomas	1961	#10
Hey There Lonely Girl (Boy)	Robert John	#31	Ruby & The Romantics	1963	#27
I Can't Let Go	Linda Ronstadt	#31	Hollies	1966	#42
I Thank You	ZZ Top	#34	Sam & Dave	1968	#9

1960s REMAKES (cont'd)

When A Man Loves A Woman	Bette Midler	#35	Percy Sledge	1966	#1
I Don't Want To Walk Without You	Barry Manilow	#36	Phyllis McGuire	1964	#79
I Can't Help Myself	Bonnie Pointer	#40	The Four Tops	1965	#1
You Better Run	Pat Benatar	#42	Young Rascals	1966	#20
Cry Like A Baby	Kim Carnes	#44	Box Tops	1968	#2
Money (That's What I Want)	The Flying Lizards	#50	Barrett Strong	1960	#23
Dirty Water	Inmates	#51	Standells	1966	#11
Happy Together (A Fantasy)	Captain & Tennille	#53	Turtles	1967	#1
A Certain Girl	Warren Zevon	#57	Ernie K-Doe	1961	#71
My Guy/My Girl	Amii Stewart & Johnny Bristol	#63	Mary Wells	1964	#1
I'm Happy Just To Dance With You	Anne Murray	#64	Beatles	1964	#95
True Love Ways	Mickey Gilley	#66	Peter & Gordon	1965	#14
Dancin' In The Streets	Teri Desario w/ K.C. And The Sunshine Band	#66	Martha & The Vandellas	1964	#2
Don't Make Me Over	Jennifer Warnes	#67	Dionne Warwick	1963	#21
Remember (Walking In The Sand)	Aerosmith	#67	The Shangri-Las	1964	#5
Darlin'	Yipes!!	#68	The Beach Boys	1968	#19
Sherry	Robert John	#70	Frankie Valli & The Four Seasons	1962	#1
When We Get Married	Larry Graham	#76	Dreamlovers	1961	#10
I Only Want To Be With You	The Tourists	#83	Dusty Springfield	1964	#12

1981					
Sukiyaki	Taste Of Honey	#3	Kyu Sakamoto	1963	#1
Angel Of The Morning	Juice Newton	#4	Merrilee Rush & The Turnabouts	1968	#7
Crying	Don McLean	#5	Roy Orbison	1961	#2
Elvira	The Oak Ridge Boys	#5	Dallas Frazier	1966	#72
Boy From New York City	Manhattan Transfer	#7	Ad Libs	1965	#8
Tell It Like It Is	Heart	#8	Aaron Neville	1967	#2
It's Now Or Never	John Schneider	#14	Elvis Presley	1960	#1
Share Your Love With Me	Kenny Rogers	#14	Bobby Bland	1964	#42
Together	Tierra	#18	The Intruders	1967	#48
(Ghost) Riders In The Sky	Outlaws	#31	Ramrods	1961	#30
Everlasting Love	Rex Smith/ Rachel Sweet	#32	Robert Knight	1967	#13
Who's Making Love	Blues Brothers	#39	Johnnie Taylor	1968	#5
But You Know I Love You	Dolly Parton	#41	First Edition	1969	#19
Working In The Coal Mine	Devo	#43	Lee Dorsey	1966	#8
Running Scared	The Fools	#50	Roy Orbison	1961	#1

1960s REMAKES (cont'd)

The Sun Ain't Gonna Shine Anymore	Nielsen/Pearson	#56	Walker Bros.	1966	#13
96 Tears	Garland Jeffreys	#66	? And The Mysterians	1966	#1
Pay You Back With Interest	Gary O'	#70	The Hollies	1967	#28
La La Means I Love You	Tierra	#72	The Delfonics	1968	#4
It Hurts To Be In Love	Dan Hartman	#72	Gene Pitney	1964	#7
Not Fade Away	Eric Hine	#73	The Rolling Stones	1964	#48
Winkin', Blinkin', And Nod	The Doobie Brothers	#76	Simon Sisters	1964	#73
House Of The Rising Sun	Dolly Parton	#77	Animals	1964	#1
I Heard It Through The Grapevine (Part One)	Roger	#79	Gladys Knight & The Pips	1967	#2

1982					
I Keep Forgettin'	Michael McDonald	#4	Chuck Jackson	1962	#55
Crimson And Clover	Joan Jett & The Blackhearts	#7	Tommy James & The Shondells	1969	#1
It's Gonna Take A Miracle	Deniece Williams	#10	The Royalettes	1965	#41
Break It To Me Gently	Juice Newton	#11	Brenda Lee	1962	#4
(Oh) Pretty Woman	Van Halen	#12	Roy Orbison w/ The Candy Men	1964	#1
Any Day Now	Ronnie Milsap	#14	Chuck Jackson	1962	#23
My Guy	Sister Sledge	#23	Mary Wells	1964	#1
Daddy's Home	Cliff Richard	#23	Shep & The Limelites	1961	#2
Going To A Go-Go	The Rolling Stones	#25	The Miracles	1966	#11
Let's Hang On!	Barry Manilow	#32	The Four Seasons	1965	#3
Dancing In The Street	Van Halen	#38	Martha & The Vandellas	1964	#2
I'll Try Something New	Taste Of Honey	#41	Miracles	1962	#39
Dreamin'	John Schneider	#45	Johnny Burnette	1960	#11
On A Carousel	Glass Moon	#50	The Hollies	1967	#11
I Only Want To Be With You	Nicolette Larson	#53	Dusty Springfield	1964	#12
Apache	The Sugarhill Gang	#53	Jorgen Ingmann	1961	#2
(Sittin' On) The Dock Of The Bay	The Reddings	#55	Otis Redding	1968	#1
Havin A Party	Luther Vandross	#55	Sam Cooke	1962	#17
Hot Fun In The Summertime	Dayton	#58	Sly & The Family Stone	1969	#2
So Much In Love	Timothy B. Schmit	#59	Tymes	1963	#1
I Want Candy	Bow Wow Wow	#62	Strangeloves	1965	#11
It's My Party	Dave Stewart & Barbara Gaskin	#72	Lesley Gore	1963	#1
Piece Of My Heart	Sammy Hagar	#73	Erma Franklin	1967	#62
Beechwood 4-5789	Carpenters	#74	Marvelettes	1962	#17

1960s REMAKES (cont'd)

Ain't Nothing Like The Real Thing	Chris Christian w/ Amy Holland	#88	Marvin Gaye & Tammi Terrell	1968	#8
You're All I Need To Get By	Chris Christian w/ Amy Holland	#88	Marvin Gaye & Tammi Terrell	1968	#7
Sing A Simple Song	West Street Mob	#89	Sly & The Family Stone	1969	#89
Sad Girl	GQ	#93	Intruders	1969	#47

1983					
Always Something There To Remind Me	Naked Eyes	#8	Lou Johnson	1964	#49
You Can't Hurry Love	Phil Collins	#10	The Supremes	1966	#1
I Do	J. Geils Band	#24	Marvelows	1965	#37
Tell Her No	Juice Newton	#27	Zombies	1965	#6
Stop In The Name Of Love	The Hollies	#29	The Supremes	1965	#1
Clapping Song (Clap Pat Clap Slap)	Pia Zadora	#36	Shirley Ellis	1965	#8
Everyday People	Joan Jett & The Blackhearts	#37	Sly & The Family Stone	1969	#1
I Knew You When	Linda Ronstadt	#37	Billy Joe Royal	1965	#14
Doggin' Around	Klique	#50	Jackie Wilson	1960	#15
Land Of A Thousand Dances	J. Geils Band	#60	Chris Kenner	1963	#77
Funny How Time Slips Away	Spinners	#67	Jimmy Elledge	1962	#22
The Monkey Time	The Tubes	#68	Major Lance	1963	#8
Bread And Butter	Robert John	#68	The Newbeats	1964	#2
Please Mr. Postman	Gentle Persuasion	#82	The Marvelettes	1961	#1

1984					
Red Red Wine	UB40	#34	Neil Diamond	1968	#62
Save The Last Dance For Me	Dolly Parton w/ The Jordanaires	#45	The Drifters	1960	#1
Love Of The Common People	Paul Young	#45	Winstons	1969	#54
Gloria	Doors	#71	Them	1965	#93
Downtown	Dolly Parton	#80	Petula Clark	1965	#1
Do You Love Me	Andy Fraser	#82	Contours	1962	#3
Whiter Shade Of Pale	Hagar, Schon, Aaronson, Shrieve	#94	Procol Harum	1967	#5

1985					
California Girls	David Lee Roth	#3	The Beach Boys	1965	#3
Dancing In The Street	Mick Jagger/ David Bowie	#7	Martha & The Vandellas	1964	#2

1960s REMAKES (cont'd)

Way You Do The Things You Do	Daryl Hall & John Oates w/ David Ruffin & Eddie Kendrick	#20	The Temptations	1964	#11
My Girl	Daryl Hall & John Oates w/ David Ruffin & Eddie Kendrick	#20	The Temptations	1965	#1
I Got You Babe	UB40 w/ Chrissie Hynde	#28	Sonny & Cher	1965	#1
People Get Ready	Jeff Beck & Rod Stewart	#48	Impressions	1965	#14
Stand By Me	Maurice White	#50	Ben E. King	1961	#4
I'll Be Around	What Is This	#62	Spinners	1972	#3

1986					
Harlem Shuffle	The Rolling Stones	#5	Bob & Earl	1964	#44
To Be A Lover	Billy Idol	#6	William Bell	1969	#45
Jumpin' Jack Flash	Aretha Franklin	#21	The Rolling Stones	1968	#3
Twist And Shout	The Beatles	#23	Isley Brothers	1962	#17
Needles And Pins	Tom Petty w/ Stevie Nicks	#37	Jackie Deshannon	1963	#84
Walk Like A Man	Mary Jane Girls	#41	The Four Seasons	1963	#1
Somewhere	Barbra Streisand	#43	P.J. Proby	1965	#91
Leader Of The Pack	Twisted Sister	#53	Shangri-Las	1964	#1
California Dreamin'	The Beach Boys	#57	Mamas & Papas	1966	#4
Jimmy Mack	Sheena Easton	#65	Martha & The Vandellas	1967	#10
Runaway	Luis Cardenas	#83	Del Shannon	1961	#1
That's Life	David Lee Roth	#85	Frank Sinatra	1966	#4
Walk Away Renee	Southside Johnny & The Jukes	#98	Left Banke	1966	#5

1987					
Mony Mony "Live	Billy Idol	#1	Tommy James & The Shondells	1968	#3
I Think We're Alone Now	Tiffany	#1	Tommy James & The Shondells	1967	#4
You Keep Me Hangin' On	Kim Wilde	#1	The Supremes	1966	#1
Kiss Him Goodbye	The Nylons	#12	Steam	1969	#1
Wipeout	The Fat Boys w/ The Beach Boys	#12	Surfaris	1963	#2
Can't Help Falling In Love	Corey Hart	#24	Elvis Presley	1962	#2
Under The Boardwalk	Bruce Willis	#59	Drifters	1964	#4
Happy Together	The Nylons	#75	Turtles	1967	#1
Twistin' The Night Away	Rod Stewart	#80	Sam Cooke	1962	#9
(I Know) I'm Losing You	Uptown	#80	The Temptations	1966	#8

1988					
Red Red Wine	UB40	#1	Neil Diamond	1968	#62

1970s REMAKES (cont'd)

1987					
Lean On Me	Club Nouveau	#1	Bill Withers	1972	#1
Respect Yourself	Bruce Willis	#5	Staple Singers	1971	#12
What's Going On	Cyndi Lauper	#12	Marvin Gaye	1971	#2
Don't Leave Me This Way	Communards	#40	Thelma Houston	1977	#1
Fire	Bruce Springsteen	#46	The Pointer Sisters	1979	#2
Black Dog	Newcity Rockers	#80	Led Zeppelin	1972	#15
Montego Bay	Amazulu	#90	Bobby Bloom	1970	#8

1988					
Baby, I Love Your Way/ Freebird Medley (Free Baby)	Will To Power	#1	Peter Frampton	1976	#12
Never Can Say Goodbye	Communards	#51	Jackson 5	1971	#2
Play That Funky Music	Roxanne	#63	Wild Cherry	1976	#1
All Right Now	Pepsi & Shirlie	#66	Free	1970	#4
Cecilia	Times Two	#79	Simon & Garfunkel	1970	#4
Killing Me Softly	Al B. Sure!	#80	Roberta Flack	1973	#1

1989					
If You Don't Know Me By Now	Simply Red	#1	Harold Melvin	1972	#3
Rock On	Michael Damian	#1	David Essex	1974	#5
Baby, I Love Your Way/ Freebird Medley (Free Baby)	Will To Power	#2	Lynyrd Skynyrd	1975	#19
Didn't I (Blow Your Mind This Time)	New Kids On The Block	#8	The Delfonics	1970	#10
Your Mama Don't Dance	Poison	#10	Loggins & Messina	1973	#4
Wild World	Maxi Priest	#25	Cat Stevens	1971	#11
Radar Love	White Lion	#59	Golden Earring	1974	#13
You Ain't Seen Nothing Yet	Figures On A Beach	#67	Bachman-Turner Overdrive	1974	#1
For The Love Of Money	Bulletboys	#78	O'Jays	1974	#9
Right Back Where We Started From	Sinitta	#84	Maxine Nightingale	1976	#2
Imagine	Tracie Spencer	#85	John Lennon	1971	#3
500 Miles	Hooters	#97	Heaven Bound	1972	#72

1980s REMAKES

SONG	(Remake) ARTIST	80s CHART	(Original) 80s ARTIST	YEAR	(Original) CHART
1981					
Shotgun Rider	Delbert McClinton	#70	Joe Sun	1980	#71
All I Need To Know (Don't Know Much)	Bette Midler	#77	Bill Medley	1981	#88
1982					
Someday, Someway*	Marshall Crenshaw	#36	Robert Gordon	1981	#76
	*Not sure if this should be classified as a remake. Crenshaw wrote it, but Gordon released it first.				
If I Were You	Lulu	#44	Toby Beau	1980	#70
Fly Away	Stevie Woods	#84	Peter Allen	1981	#55
1983					
Memory	Barry Manilow	#39	Barbra Streisand	1982	#52
You Are In My System	Robert Palmer	#78	The System	1983	#64
1985					
One Night In Bangkok	Robey	#77	Murray Head	1985	#3
1986					
I Didn't Mean To Turn You On	Robert Palmer	#2	Cherrelle	1984	#79
Don't Stand So Close To Me '86	The Police	#46	The Police	1981	#10
The Power Of Love	Jennifer Rush	#57	Air Supply	1985	#68
1987					
Funky Town	Pseudo Echo	#6	Lipps, Inc.	1980	#1
I Wanna Go Back	Eddie Money	#14	Billy Satellite	1984	#78
Weatherman	Jack Wagner	#67	Nick Jameson	1986	#95
1988					
Always On My Mind	Pet Shop Boys	#4	Willie Nelson	1982	#5
I Found Someone	Cher	#10	Laura Branigan	1986	#90
Early In The Morning	Robert Palmer	#19	The Gap Band	1982	#24
The Power Of Love	Laura Branigan	#26	Air Supply	1985	#68
Route 66/ Behind The Wheel	Depeche Mode	#61	Manhattan Transfer	1982	#78
Don't Look Any Further	Kane Gang	#64	Dennis Edwards w/ Siedah Garrett	1984	#72

1980s Remakes (cont'd)

1989					
Wind Beneath My Wings	Bette Midler	#1	Lou Rawls	1983	#65
What I Like About You	Michael Morales	#28	Romantics	1980	#49
Kiss	Art Of Noise/Tom Jones	#31	Prince	1986	#1
Foolish Heart	Sharon Bryant	#90	Steve Perry	1985	#18

SONGS THAT HIT THE HOT 100 TWICE

Every now and then, a song will drop off the Hot 100 chart, and then return to the chart for a second time. Sometimes only a year or two pass between both chart appearances; other times, decades will pass. The reasons for re-charting vary.

In some instances, an old song is included on a popular new movie's soundtrack, and this new exposure results in a flood of new sales and airplay that send it up the charts again. This happened in 1986. "Stand By Me", by Ben E. King, was included on the soundtrack for the movie of the same name, and "Twist And Shout" by The Beatles was included on the "Ferris Bueller's Day Off" soundtrack. They both reached the top five in the 1960s, and returned to the charts in 1986, though they didn't chart quite as high.

Exposure from being played on a television show can be equally as helpful to a song's popularity. "At This Moment" by Billy Vera and the Beaters originally peaked at #79 in 1981. After being featured on the popular show "Family Ties", it ran all the way to #1 in 1987.

Other songs will usually re-enter the chart because a DJ somewhere starts playing the song again, and enough radio stations get requests for it, so more radio stations start playing it again, so more people buy and request the song, etc.

SONG	ARTIST	HOT 100 CHART	YEAR SONG PREVIOUSLY CHARTED	PREVIOUS CHART POSITION
1980				
Time For Me To Fly	REO Speedwagon	#77	1978	#56
Lola (Live)	The Kinks	#81	1970	#9
1981				
Guitar Man	Elvis Presley	#28	1968	#43
No Time To Lose	Tarney/Spencer Band	#74	1979	#84

SONGS THAT HIT THE HOT 100 TWICE (cont'd)

1982				
I've Never Been To Me	Charlene	#3	1977	#97
Closer To The Heart	Rush	#69	1977	#76

1983				
Baby, Come To Me	Pattie Austin w/ James Ingram	#1	1982	#73
Stray Cat Strut	Stray Cats	#3	1982	#102
1999	Prince	#12	1982	#44
White Wedding	Billy Idol	#36	1982	#108
Old Time Rock & Roll	Bob Seger	#48	1979	#28
Should I Stay Or Should I Go	The Clash	#50	1982	#45
Every Home Should Have One	Pattie Austin	#69	1982	#62
Solsbury Hill	Peter Gabriel	#84	1977	#68

1984				
On The Dark Side	John Cafferty*	#7	1983	#64
	*As Eddie And The Cruisers			
I'm So Excited	The Pointer Sisters	#9	1982	#30
Thin Line Between Love & Hate	Persuaders	#83	1971	#15

1985				
Relax	Frankie Goes To Hollywood	#10	1984	#67
Tender Years	John Cafferty	#31	1984	#78

1986				
Stand By Me	Ben E. King	#9	1961	#4
Twist And Shout	The Beatles	#23	1964	#2
25 Or 6 To 4	Chicago	#48	1970	#4
Chain Reaction (Special New Mix)	Diana Ross	#66	1985	#95
Daydream Believer	The Monkees	#79	1967	#1
The Men All Pause	Klymaxx	#80	1985	#105
Once In A Lifetime	Talking Heads	#91	1981	#103

1987				
At This Moment	Billy Vera & The Beaters	#1	1981	#79
Valerie	Steve Winwood	#9	1982	#70
Every Little Kiss	Bruce Hornsby and the Range	#14	1986	#72
You Can Call Me Al	Paul Simon	#23	1986	#44
Twistin' The Night Away	Rod Stewart	#80	1973	#59

SONGS THAT HIT THE HOT 100 TWICE (cont'd)

1988				
Red Red Wine*	UB40	#1	1984	#34
	*Slightly different version			
Do You Love Me	The Contours	#11	1962	#3
What A Wonderful World	Louis Armstrong	#32	1968	#116
Hot In The City	Billy Idol	#48	1982	#23
Strangelove	Depeche Mode	#50	1987	#76
Forever Young	Alphaville	#65	1985	#93

1989				
When I'm With You	Sheriff	#1	1983	#61
(It's Just) The Way That You Love Me	Paula Abdul	#3	1988	#88
Where Are You Now?	Jimmy Harnen w/Synch	#10	1986	#77
Into The Night	Benny Mardones	#20	1980	#11
Hooked On You	Sweet Sensation	#23	1987	#64
Send Me An Angel '89	Real Life	#26	1984	#29
Fool For Your Loving	Whitesnake	#37	1980	#53
In Your Eyes	Peter Gabriel	#41	1986	#26
What About Me	Moving Pictures	#46	1983	#29
Dancing In Heaven (Orbital Be-Bop)	Q-Feel	#75	1983	#110

INSTRUMENTS

Each section below contains a list of songs that feature a particular instrument. You'll be surprised at the wide variety of instruments used in the hits from the 80s.

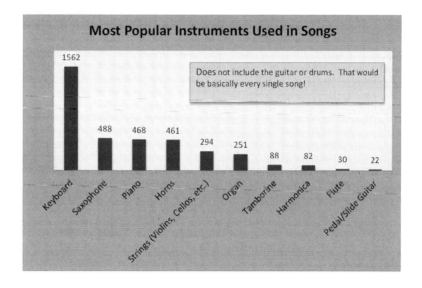

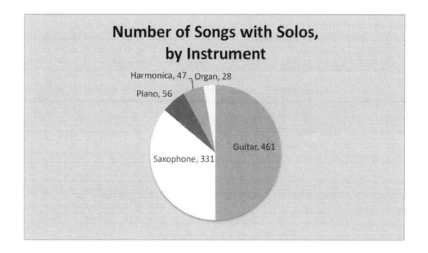

ACCORDION

The main thing I learned from compiling this list is that John Cougar Mellencamp really likes the accordion. That's about it.

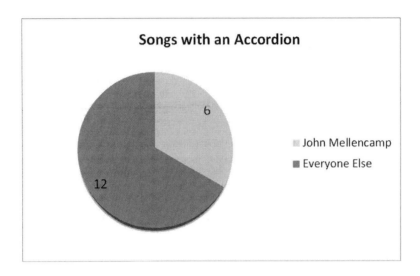

SONG	ARTIST	HOT 100 CHART
1980		
What Can You Get A Wookiee For Christmas (When He Already Owns A Comb?)	Star Wars Intergalactic Droid Choir & Chorale	#69
1981		
Shaddap You Face	Joe Dolce	#53
Jole Blon	Gary U.S. Bonds	#65
1983		
Come On Eileen	Dexys Midnight Runners	#1
Ricky	"Weird Al" Yankovic	#63
The Celtic Soul Brothers	Dexys Midnight Runners	#86
1986		
The Love Parade	The Dream Academy	#36
1987		
La Bamba	Los Lobos	#1
Paper In Fire	John Cougar Mellencamp	#9
Boy In The Bubble	Paul Simon	#86

ACCORDION (cont'd)

1988		
Kokomo	The Beach Boys	#1
Check It Out	John Cougar Mellencamp	#14
Peek-A-Boo	Siouxsie & The Banshees	#53
Rooty Toot Toot	John Cougar Mellencamp	#61

1989		
Cherry Bomb	John Cougar Mellencamp	#9
Pop Singer	John Cougar Mellencamp	#15
Jackie Brown	John Cougar Mellencamp	#48
Crossroads	Tracy Chapman	#90

BAGPIPES

SONG	ARTIST	HOT 100 CHART
1986		
Every Beat Of My Heart	Rod Stewart	#83

1988		
Broken Land*	The Adventures	#95
	*Uilleann pipes	

HONORABLE MENTIONS

These songs sound as if they have bagpipes, but they don't. In some of these songs, the musicians are using an E-Bow, a device used with electric guitars that make it sound like bagpipes. So if you like the sound of bagpipes in pop songs, you might like these songs, just realize that you aren't actually hearing bagpipes!

SONG	ARTIST	HOT 100 CHART
1983		
In A Big Country*	Big Country	#17
	*E-Bow	

1984		
Run Runaway	Slade	#20

1988		
Under The Milky Way*	The Church	#24
	*E-Bow	

BANJO

SONG	ARTIST	HOT 100 CHART
1980		
Volcano*	Jimmy Buffett	#66
	*Banjo-Uke	

1981		
Seduced	Leon Redbone	#72

1983		
Come On Eileen	Dexys Midnight Runners	#1
Still Taking Chances	Michael Murphey	#76

1987		
Paper In Fire	John Cougar Mellencamp	#9

BASS LINE

The songs in the section all have notable bass lines. The bass line may be technically difficult, interesting, or maybe it simply dominates the musical texture of the song. This list is not limited to songs with bass lines played on bass guitar. The bass line could be played on any instrument.

Two examples of songs with bass lines that make the whole song worth listening to are "Rio" by Duran Duran, and "Too Shy" by Kajagoogoo, both from 1983.

SONGS	ARTIST	HOT 100 CHART
1980		
Another One Bites The Dust	Queen	#1
Stomp!	The Brothers Johnson	#7
Ladies Night	Kool & The Gang	#8
And The Beat Goes On	The Whispers	#19
Old-Fashion Love	Commodores	#20
Train In Vain (Stand By Me)	The Clash	#23
Rappers Delight	The Sugarhill Gang	#36
Atomic	Blondie	#39
A Lover's Holiday	Change	#40
Red Light	Linda Clifford	#41
Don't Push It Don't Force It	Leon Haywood	#49

BASS LINE (cont'd)

Could I Be Dreaming	The Pointer Sisters	#52
Glide	Pleasure	#55
Back Together Again	Roberta Flack & Donny Hathaway	#56
Rock Lobster	B-52s	#56
I Shoulda Loved Ya	Narada Michael Walden	#66
High On Your Love	Debbie Jacobs	#70
Bounce, Rock, Skate, Roll Pt. 1	Vaughan Mason	#81
Peanut Butter	Twennynine Feat. Lenny White	#83

1981		
Just The Two Of Us	Grover Washington Jr. w/Bill Withers	#2
Let's Groove	Earth, Wind & Fire	#3
Who's Crying Now	Journey	#4
Passion	Rod Stewart	#5
Why Do Fools Fall In Love	Diana Ross	#7
Too Much Time On My Hands	Styx	#9
This Little Girl	Gary U.S. Bonds	#11
I Ain't Gonna Stand For It	Stevie Wonder	#11
Super Freak (Part 1)	Rick James	#16
Don't Stop The Music	Yarbrough & Peoples	#19
She's A Bad Mama Jama (She's Built, She's Stacked)	Carl Carlton	#22
Sausalito Summernight	Diesel	#25
Never Too Much	Luther Vandross	#33
I'm In Love	Evelyn King	#40
Stranger	Jefferson Starship	#48
Fantastic Voyage	Lakeside	#55
Walking On Thin Ice	Yoko Ono	#58
Hurry Up And Wait	Isley Brothers	#58
Make That Move	Shalamar	#60
Lately	Stevie Wonder	#64
WKRP In Cincinnati	Steve Carlisle	#65
Why You Wanna Try Me	Commodores	#66
She Did It	Michael Damian	#69
Shake It Up Tonight	Cheryl Lynn	#70
All American Girls	Sister Sledge	#79
Paradise	Change	#80
Burn Rubber (Why You Wanna Hurt Me)	The Gap Band	#84
Snap Shot	Slave	#91

1982		
I Keep Forgettin' (Every Time You're Near)	Michael McDonald	#4
Spirits In The Material World	The Police	#11

BASS LINE (cont'd)

Body Language	Queen	#11
Forget Me Nots	Patrice Rushen	#23
Under Pressure	Queen & David Bowie	#29
Shine On	George Duke	#41
Work That Body	Diana Ross	#44
A Night To Remember	Shalamar	#44
Street Corner	Ashford & Simpson	#56
Cross My Heart	Lee Ritenour	#69
Make Up Your Mind	Aurra	#71
Route 66	Manhattan Transfer	#78

1983		
Billie Jean	Michael Jackson	#1
Too Shy	Kajagoogoo	#5
Rio	Duran Duran	#14
Ain't Nobody	Rufus/Chaka Khan	#22
Lies	Thompson	#30
I Like It	Debarge	#31
When The Lights Go Out	Naked Eyes	#37
Tip Of My Tongue	The Tubes	#52
Just Be Good To Me	The S.O.S. Band	#55
Get It Right	Aretha Franklin	#61
Bang The Drum All Day	Todd Rundgren	#63
Young Love	Janet Jackson	#64
Painted Picture	Commodores	#70
Wherever I Lay My Hat (That's My Home)	Paul Young	#70
For The Love Of Money	Bulletboys	#78
Drop The Pilot	Joan Armatrading	#78
Tonight	The Whispers	#84

1984		
Breakdance	Irene Cara	#8
You Can't Get What You Want (Till You Know What You Want)	Joe Jackson	#15
Bop 'Til You Drop	Rick Springfield	#20
17	Rick James	#36
You Make My Heart Beat Faster (And That's All That Matters)	Kim Carnes	#54
Jam On It	Newcleus	#56
Black Stations/White Stations	M+M	#63
Give	Missing Persons	#67
Don't Look Any Further	Dennis Edwards w/Siedah Garrett	#72
Somebody Else's Guy	Jocelyn Brown	#75

BASS LINE (cont'd)

I Send A Message	INXS	#77
Gotta Give A Little Love (Ten Years After)	Timmy Thomas	#80
Shooting Shark	Blue Oyster Cult	#83
Bullish	Herb Alpert Tijuana Brass	#90

1985		
Axel F	Harold Faltermeyer	#3
Lovergirl	Teena Marie	#4
I'm Gonna Tear Your Playhouse Down	Paul Young	#13
Wild And Crazy Love	Mary Jane Girls	#42
You Wear It Well	El Debarge w/ Debarge	#46
I'll Be Good	Rene & Angela	#47
Be Your Man	Jesse Johnson	#61
Go For It	Kim Wilde	#65
Dancin' In The Key Of Life	Steve Arrington	#68
You Send Me	The Manhattans	#81

1986		
When I Think Of You	Janet Jackson	#1
I Can't Wait	Nu Shooz	#3
Your Wildest Dreams	The Moody Blues	#9
Jumpin' Jack Flash	Aretha Franklin	#21
A Kind Of Magic	Queen	#42
The Finest	The S.O.S. Band	#44
You Can Call Me Al	Paul Simon	#44
Love Is The Hero	Billy Squier	#80

1987		
Lost In Emotion	Lisa Lisa & Cult Jam	#1
I Think We're Alone Now	Tiffany	#1
Jam Tonight	Freddie Jackson	#32
Oh Yeah	Yello	#51
Criticize	Alexander O'Neal	#70
Strangelove	Depeche Mode	#76
Showing Out (Get Fresh At The Weekend)	Mel & Kim	#78
He's My Girl	David Hallyday	#79
I'm Bad	L.L. Cool J	#84
He Wants My Body	Starpoint	#89
Certain Things Are Likely	KTP	#97

1988		
Simply Irresistible	Robert Palmer	#2

BASS LINE (cont'd)

The Loco-Motion	Kylie Minogue	#3
Don't Be Cruel	Bobby Brown	#8
Paradise	Sade	#16
Early In The Morning	Robert Palmer	#19
Push It	Salt-N-Pepa	#19
Downtown Life	Daryl Hall & John Oates	#31
Stand Up	David Lee Roth	#64
Turn Off The Lights	The World Class Wreckin Cru	#84
Fat	"Weird Al" Yankovic	#99

1989		
Bust A Move	Young MC	#7
Dial My Heart	The Boys	#13
Fascination Street	The Cure	#46

BELLS

SONG	ARTIST	HOT 100 CHART
1980		
(Just Like) Starting Over	John Lennon	#1

1982		
Tell Me Tomorrow- Part 1	Smokey Robinson	#33
Old Fashioned Love	Smokey Robinson	#60

CELLO

SONG	ARTIST	HOT 100 CHART
1985		
Raspberry Beret	Prince	#2
Don't Come Around Here No More	Tom Petty And The Heartbreakers	#13

1988		
When We Was Fab	George Harrison	#23
The Dead Heart	Midnight Oil	#53

FLUTE

Thirty songs from the decade used the flute.

A few notes about some of these songs: "Next Love", by Deniece Williams, features a 30 second flute solo at the very beginning. Both "Sledgehammer (Peter Gabriel) and "But You Know I Love You" (Dolly Parton) feature a synthesized flute, not a real flute. "The Sound Of Goodbye", by Crystal Gayle, features a "piccolo flute".

SONG	ARTIST	HOT 100 CHART
1980		
Sexy Eyes	Dr. Hook	#5
Off The Wall	Michael Jackson	#10
Do You Love What You Feel	Rufus & Chaka	#30
Dig The Gold	Joyce Cobb	#42
Love That Got Away	Firefall	#50
Autograph	John Denver	#52
Love X Love	George Benson	#61
Dancing With The Mountains	John Denver	#97
1981		
A Woman Needs Love (Just Like You Do)	Ray Parker Jr. & Raydio	#4
Just Once	Quincy Jones & James Ingram	#17
But You Know I Love You	Dolly Parton	#41
What Cha' Gonna Do For Me	Chaka Khan	#53
Playing With Lightning	Shot In The Dark	#71
Winkin', Blinkin', And Nod	The Doobie Brothers	#76
1982		
John Denver	Shanghai Breezes	#31
Let Me Go	Ray Parker Jr.	#38
Loveline	Dr. Hook	#60
1983		
Down Under	Men At Work	#1
Tied Up	Olivia Newton-John	#38
Memory	Barry Manilow	#39
Crazy	Manhattans	#72
The Sound Of Goodbye	Crystal Gayle	#84

FLUTE (cont'd)

1984		
Next Love	Deniece Williams	#81

1985		
One Night In Bangkok	Murray Head	#3
Oo-Ee-Diddley-Bop!	Peter Wolf	#61

1986		
Sledgehammer	Peter Gabriel	#1
Vienna Calling	Falco	#18
Say It, Say It	E.G. Daily	#70

1987		
Johnny B	Hooters	#61

1989		
The Different Story (World Of Lust And Crime)	Peter Schilling	#61

GLOCKENSPIEL

SONG	ARTIST	HOT 100 CHART
1980		
Take Your Time (Do It Right) Part 1	S.O.S. Band	#3

1982		
Call Me	Skyy	#26

1983		
You Can't Hurry Love	Phil Collins	#10

1989		
Veronica	Elvis Costello	#19

GUITAR (Slide/Pedal)

SONG	ARTIST	HOT 100 CHART
1980		
Jesse	Carly Simon	#11
That Girl Could Sing	Jackson Browne	#22
Texas In My Rear View Mirror	Mac Davis	#51
True Love Ways	Mickey Gilley	#66
Midnight Rain	Poco	#74
Let's Do Something Cheap And Superficial	Burt Reynolds	#88
1981		
I Ain't Gonna Stand For It	Stevie Wonder	#11
Seven Year Ache	Roseanne Cash	#22
Bet Your Heart On Me	Johnny Lee	#54
Right Away	Hawks	#63
Pay The Devil (Ooo, Baby, Ooo)	The Knack	#67
House Of The Rising Sun	Dolly Parton	#77
Leila	ZZ Top	#77
At This Moment	Billy Vera & The Beaters	#79
Long Time Lovin' You	McGuffey Lane	#85
1982		
Run For The Roses	Dan Fogelberg	#18
After The Glitter Fades	Stevie Nicks	#32
Those Good Old Dreams	Carpenters	#63
Loving You	Chris Rea	#88
1983		
American Made	The Oak Ridge Boys	#72
1986		
Everything Must Change	Paul Young	#56
1989		
Leave A Light On	Belinda Carlisle	#11

SONGS WITH GUITAR SOLOS

There are three lists for this section. The first lists every song that featured a guitar solo*. It's organized by year. The second list has all the songs that have more than one solo. The last list contains the same songs as the first list, but it's organized according to length of solo.

* Only guitar solos twenty seconds or longer are included in this book.

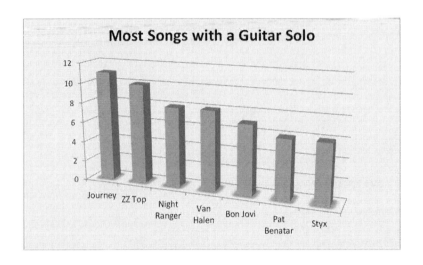

SONG	ARTIST	HOT 100 CHART	LENGTH OF SOLO
1980			
Breakdown Dead Ahead	Boz Scaggs	#15	26 seconds
Fool In The Rain	Led Zeppelin	#21	63 seconds
Third Time Lucky (First Time I Was A Fool)	Foghat	#23	34 seconds
Heartbreaker	Pat Benatar	#23	46 seconds
This Time	John Cougar	#27	26 seconds
Who'll Be The Fool Tonight	Larsen-Feiten Band	#29	22 seconds
Twilight Zone/Twilight Tone	Manhattan Transfer	#30	27 seconds
We Were Meant To Be Lovers	Photoglo	#31	30 seconds
Walks Like A Lady	Journey	#32	37 seconds
Voices	Cheap Trick	#32	21 seconds
Savannah Nights	Tom Johnston	#34	32 seconds
You Shook Me All Night Long	AC/DC	#35	29 seconds
Touch And Go	The Cars	#37	39 seconds
New Romance (It's A Mystery)	Spider	#39	21 seconds
Atomic*	Blondie	#39	16 seconds
	*Included because bass guitar solos of this length are rare		

SONGS WITH GUITAR SOLOS (cont'd)

Hold On	Kansas	#40	39 seconds
You Better Run	Pat Benatar	#42	30 seconds
Somethin' 'Bout You Baby I Like	Glen Campbell & Rita Coolidge	#42	21 seconds
Flirtin' With Disaster	Molly Hatchet	#42	41 seconds
Is This Love	Pat Travers Band	#50	20 seconds
Dirty Water	The Inmates	#51	38 seconds
It's Not A Wonder	Little River Band	#51	55 seconds
I Could Be Good For You	707	#52	30 seconds
Free Me	Roger Daltrey	#53	34 seconds
Fool For Your Loving	Whitesnake	#53	29 seconds
Girl With The Hungry Eyes	Jefferson Starship	#55	27 seconds
A Certain Girl	Warren Zevon	#57	30 seconds
Angeline	Allman Brothers Band	#58	25 seconds
Stargazer	Peter Brown	#59	30 seconds
I'm Alive	Gamma	#60	30 seconds
Rebels Are We	Chic	#61	31 seconds
Borrowed Time	Styx	#64	34 seconds
Brite Eyes	Robbin Thompson Band	#66	78 seconds
Don't Make Me Over	Jennifer Warnes	#67	22 seconds
Somewhere In America	Survivor	#70	24 seconds
Too Late	Journey	#70	35 seconds
Blues Power	Eric Clapton	#76	49 seconds
The Very Last Time	Utopia	#76	37 seconds
I Can't Stop This Feelin'	Pure Prairie League	#77	22 seconds
Back Of My Hand (I've Got Your Number)	The Jags	#84	24 seconds
Wango Tango	Ted Nugent	#86	24 seconds
I Like To Rock	April Wine	#86	32 seconds
Cheap Sunglasses	ZZ Top	#89	24 seconds
What's Your Hurry Darlin'	Ironhorse	#89	47 seconds
I Can Survive	Triumph	#91	38 seconds

1981			
Rapture	Blondie	#1	25 seconds
Keep On Loving You	REO Speedwagon	#1	22 seconds
Physical	Olivia Newton-John	#1	30 seconds
Kiss On My List	Daryl Hall & John Oates	#1	30 seconds
The Best Of Times	Styx	#3	38 seconds
Who's Crying Now	Journey	#4	87 seconds
Young Turks	Rod Stewart	#5	24 seconds
Take It On The Run	REO Speedwagon	#5	48 seconds
Too Much Time On My Hands	Styx	#9	29 seconds
Cool Love	Pablo Cruise	#13	27 seconds

SONGS WITH GUITAR SOLOS (cont'd)

Games People Play	Alan Parsons Project	#16	27 seconds
Fire And Ice	Pat Benatar	#17	20 seconds
Winning	Santana	#17	40 seconds
Treat Me Right	Pat Benatar	#18	20 seconds
Hearts On Fire	Randy Meisner	#18	28 seconds
The Waiting	Tom Petty And The Heartbreakers	#19	23 seconds
Just Between You And Me	April Wine	#21	23 seconds
Love You Like I Never Loved Before	John O'Banion	#24	20 seconds
Juke Box Hero	Foreigner	#26	34 seconds
Hold On Loosely	.38 Special	#27	40 seconds
Draw Of The Cards	Kim Carnes	#28	37 seconds
(Ghost) Riders In The Sky	Outlaws	#31	22 seconds
Chloe*	Elton John	#34	27 seconds
	*Acoustic guitar		
Back In Black	AC/DC	#37	30 seconds
Promises In The Dark	Pat Benatar	#38	35 seconds
Nicole	Point Blank	#39	34 seconds
Burnin' For You	Blue Oyster Cult	#40	28 seconds
Tom Sawyer	Rush	#44	26 seconds
Games	Phoebe Snow	#46	22 seconds
Stranger	Jefferson Starship	#48	27 seconds
When She Dances	Joey Scarbury	#49	24 seconds
Fantasy Girl	.38 Special	#52	60 seconds
Nothing Ever Goes As Planned	Styx	#54	33 seconds
Limelight	Rush	#55	35 seconds
The Sensitive Kind	Santana	#56	65 seconds
Sign Of The Gypsy Queen	April Wine	#57	51 seconds
Yearning For Your Love	The Gap Band	#60	22 seconds
Fireflies	Fleetwood Mac	#60	26 seconds
Playing With Lightning	Shot In The Dark	#71	23 seconds
Leila	ZZ Top	#77	37 seconds
Café Amore	Spyro Gyra	#77	46 seconds
La-Di-Da	Sad Café	#78	24 seconds
Sweet Merilee	Donnie Iris	#80	23 seconds

1982			
Shake It Up	The Cars	#4	25 seconds
Heat Of The Moment	Asia	#4	28 seconds
Sweet Dreams	Air Supply	#5	30 seconds
Love's Been A Little Bit Hard On Me	Juice Newton	#7	25 seconds
I Ran (So Far Away)	A Flock Of Seagulls	#9	25 seconds
Pac-Man Fever	Buckner & Garcia	#9	27 seconds

SONGS WITH GUITAR SOLOS (cont'd)

Think I'm In Love	Eddie Money	#16	24 seconds
You Don't Want Me Anymore	Steel Breeze	#16	27 seconds
Don't Fight It	Kenny Loggins w/Steve Perry	#17	25 seconds
Still They Ride	Journey	#19	40 seconds
All Our Tomorrows	Eddie Schwartz	#28	34 seconds
Be My Lady	Jefferson Starship	#28	35 seconds
I Believe	Chilliwack	#33	20 seconds
Oh Julie	Barry Manilow	#38	23 seconds
Dancing In The Street	Van Halen	#38	31 seconds
Stone Cold	Rainbow	#40	32 seconds
Whatcha Gonna Do	Chilliwack	#41	31 seconds
Crazy (Keep On Falling)	The John Hall Band	#42	45 seconds
Another Sleepless Night	Anne Murray	#44	20 seconds
Let's Get It Up	AC/DC	#44	32 seconds
How Long	Rod Stewart	#49	33 seconds
Enough Is Enough	April Wine	#50	26 seconds
I'll Drink To You	Duke Jupiter	#58	22 seconds
Night Shift	Quarterflash	#60	30 seconds
Mega Force	707	#62	24 seconds
Don't Let Me In	Sneaker	#63	35 seconds
Now Or Never	Axe	#64	28 seconds
You've Got Another Thing Comin'	Judas Priest	#67	29 seconds
Electricland	Bad Company	#74	52 seconds
Too Good To Turn Back Now	Rick Bowles	#77	22 seconds
When I'm Holding You Tight	Michael Stanley Band	#78	20 seconds
Perfect	Fairground Attraction	#80	25 seconds

1983			
Beat It	Michael Jackson	#1	28 seconds
Maniac	Michael Sembello	#1	24 seconds
Making Love Out Of Nothing At All	Air Supply	#2	23 seconds
Cum On Feel The Noize	Quiet Riot	#5	38 seconds
(She's) Sexy + 17	Stray Cats	#5	31 seconds
Don't Let It End	Styx	#6	36 seconds
Separate Ways (Worlds Apart)	Journey	#8	27 seconds
Undercover Of The Night	The Rolling Stones	#9	30 seconds
China Girl	David Bowie	#10	28 seconds
I Won't Hold You Back	Toto	#10	37 seconds
Twilight Zone	Golden Earring	#10	25 seconds
Photograph	Def Leppard	#12	22 seconds
How Am I Supposed To Live Without You	Laura Branigan	#12	26 seconds
Cuts Like A Knife	Bryan Adams	#15	20 seconds

SONGS WITH GUITAR SOLOS (cont'd)

Rock Of Ages	Def Leppard	#16	27 seconds
All This Love*	Debarge	#17	40 seconds
	*Acoustic guitar		
Dead Giveaway	Shalamar	#22	25 seconds
Send Her My Love	Journey	#23	28 seconds
Kiss The Bride	Elton John	#25	24 seconds
Dreamin' Is Easy	Steel Breeze	#30	22 seconds
Does It Make You Remember	Kim Carnes	#36	40 seconds
Gimme All Your Lovin	ZZ Top	#37	52 seconds
My Town	Michael Stanley Band	#39	24 seconds
Burning Heart	Vandenberg	#39	61 seconds
Don't Tell Me You Love Me	Night Ranger	#40	44 seconds
Allergies	Paul Simon	#44	21 seconds
High Time	Styx	#48	27 seconds
New Year's Day	U2	#53	30 seconds
Sharp Dressed Man	ZZ Top	#56	53 seconds
Take Another Picture	Quarterflash	#58	38 seconds
Come Give Your Love To Me	Janet Jackson	#58	40 seconds
Love Me Again	The John Hall Band	#64	22 seconds
Too Much Love To Hide	Crosby, Stills & Nash	#69	22 seconds
Don't Make Me Do It	Patrick Simmons	#75	30 seconds
Caught In The Game	Survivor	#77	29 seconds
For The Love Of Money	Bulletboys	#78	20 seconds
You Put The Beat In My Heart	Eddie Rabbitt	#81	25 seconds
Johnny B. Goode	Peter Tosh	#84	26 seconds
Guns For Hire	AC/DC	#84	29 seconds
Lucky	Eye To Eye	#88	32 seconds

1984			
Hello*	Lionel Richie	#1	25 seconds
	*Acoustic guitar		
Owner Of A Lonely Heart	Yes	#1	29 seconds
Oh Sherrie	Steve Perry	#3	24 seconds
Sister Christian	Night Ranger	#5	35 seconds
If This Is It	Huey Lewis & The News	#6	20 seconds
Infatuation	Rod Stewart	#6	26 seconds
I Can Dream About You	Dan Hartman	#6	34 seconds
No More Lonely Nights	Paul McCartney	#6	50 seconds
The Warrior	Scandal Featuring Patty Smyth	#7	31 seconds
Legs	ZZ Top	#8	28 seconds
Eat It	Weird Al Yankovic	#12	22 seconds
Round And Round	Ratt	#12	29 seconds

SONGS WITH GUITAR SOLOS (cont'd)

Panama	Van Halen	#13	29 seconds
Authority Song	John Cougar Mellencamp	#15	26 seconds
Torture	Jacksons	#17	28 seconds
Walking On A Thin Line	Huey Lewis & The News	#18	26 seconds
We're Not Gonna Take It	Twisted Sister	#21	25 seconds
She's Mine	Steve Perry	#21	21 seconds
No Way Out	Jefferson Starship	#23	25 seconds
Rock You Like A Hurricane	Scorpions	#25	33 seconds
Romancing The Stone	Eddy Grant	#26	26 seconds
Love Will Show Us How	Christine McVie	#30	22 seconds
Bang Your Head (Metal Health)	Quiet Riot	#31	24 seconds
Turn To You	The Go-Go's	#32	24 seconds
Prime Time	Alan Parsons Project	#34	24 seconds
Runaway	Bon Jovi	#39	25 seconds
Strung Out	Steve Perry	#40	26 seconds
Don't Stop	Jeffrey Osborne	#44	26 seconds
She Was Hot	The Rolling Stones	#44	24 seconds
For A Rocker	Jackson Browne	#45	25 seconds
Rebel Yell	Billy Idol	#46	23 seconds
(You Can Still) Rock In America	Night Ranger	#51	47 seconds
Mama Weer All Crazee Now	Quiet Riot	#51	30 seconds
The Allnighter	Glenn Frey	#54	46 seconds
You Make My Heart Beat Faster (And That's All That Matters)	Kim Carnes	#54	26 seconds
Sweetheart Like You*	Bob Dylan	#55	31 seconds
	*Acoustic guitar		
Hot For Teacher	Van Halen	#56	29 seconds
New Girl Now	Honeymoon Suite	#57	20 seconds
This Could Be The Right One	April Wine	#58	25 seconds
So You Ran	Orion The Hunter	#58	27 seconds
Love Has Taken Its Toll	Saraya	#64	20 seconds
Club Michelle	Eddie Money	#66	23 seconds
Little Lady	Duke Jupiter	#68	24 seconds
Headpins	Just One More Time	#70	30 seconds
Midnite Maniac	Krokus	#71	26 seconds
All Night Long	Billy Squier	#75	23 seconds
Flashes	Tiggi Clay	#86	40 seconds
Thief Of Hearts	Melissa Manchester	#86	25 seconds
Wanted Man	Ratt	#87	33 seconds
Taxi	J. Blackfoot	#90	57 seconds
Whiter Shade Of Pale	Hagar, Schon, Aaronson, Shrieve	#94	27 seconds

SONGS WITH GUITAR SOLOS (cont'd)

1985			
Power Of Love	Huey Lewis & The News	#1	32 seconds
Money For Nothing	Dire Straits	#1	29 seconds
Can't Fight This Feeling	REO Speedwagon	#1	24 seconds
Easy Lover	Philip Bailey w/ Phil Collins	#2	27 seconds
Sea Of Love	Honeydrippers	#3	23 seconds
Don't Lose My Number	Phil Collins	#4	35 seconds
Lovergirl	Teena Marie	#4	33 seconds
Private Dancer	Tina Turner	#7	32 seconds
Sleeping Bag	ZZ Top	#8	60 seconds
Sentimental Street	Night Ranger	#8	37 seconds
Only The Young	Journey	#9	24 seconds
What About Love?	Heart	#10	23 seconds
One Night Love Affair	Bryan Adams	#13	32 seconds
C-I-T-Y	John Cafferty	#18	25 seconds
Sisters Are Doin' It For Themselves	Eurythmics & Aretha Franklin	#18	25 seconds
Four In The Morning (I Can't Take Any More)	Night Ranger	#19	31 seconds
One Lonely Night	REO Speedwagon	#19	33 seconds
Just As I Am	Air Supply	#19	23 seconds
Rockin' At Midnight	The Honeydrippers	#25	35 seconds
Take Me With U	Prince	#25	115 seconds
Vox Humana	Kenny Loggins	#29	21 seconds
Turn Up The Radio	Autograph	#29	35 seconds
Live Every Moment	REO Speedwagon	#34	24 seconds
Oh Girl	Boy Meets Girl	#39	24 seconds
Lay It Down	Ratt	#40	22 seconds
You Wear It Well	El Debarge w/ Debarge	#46	33 seconds
Say It Again	Santana	#46	27 seconds
Can't Stop	Rick James	#50	28 seconds
Tears Are Falling	Kiss	#51	28 seconds
Reaction To Action	Foreigner	#54	23 seconds
Restless Heart	John Waite	#59	29 seconds
Lonely School	Tommy Shaw	#60	20 seconds
Alone Again	Dokken	#64	28 seconds
In And Out Of Love	Bon Jovi	#69	33 seconds
Que Te Quiero	Katrina & The Waves	#71	30 seconds
Sweet, Sweet Baby (I'm Falling)	Lone Justice	#73	28 seconds
One Foot Back In Your Door	Roman Holliday	#76	22 seconds
Remo's Theme (What If)	Tommy Shaw	#81	27 seconds
Welcome To Paradise	John Waite	#85	27 seconds
Go For Soda	Kim Mitchell	#86	20 seconds
You're In Love	Ratt	#89	25 seconds

SONGS WITH GUITAR SOLOS (cont'd)

Home Sweet Home	Motley Crue	#89	23 seconds
Too Much Ain't Enough Love	Jimmy Barnes	#91	37 seconds

1986			
Walk Like An Egyptian	Bangles	#1	27 seconds
Burning Heart	Survivor	#2	23 seconds
Silent Running (On Dangerous Ground)	Mike + The Mechanics	#6	29 seconds
Spies Like Us	Paul McCartney	#7	21 seconds
Tonight She Comes	The Cars	#7	30 seconds
Be Good To Yourself	Journey	#9	77 seconds
Nothin' At All	Heart	#10	22 seconds
Like A Rock	Bob Seger	#12	60 seconds
Like No Other Night	38 Special	#14	30 seconds
Suzanne	Journey	#17	24 seconds
Goodbye	Night Ranger	#17	25 seconds
All The Love In The World	The Outfield	#19	29 seconds
That Was Then, This Is Now	The Monkees	#20	21 seconds
Stages	ZZ Top	#21	32 seconds
Dreams	Van Halen	#22	32 seconds
Love Walks In	Van Halen	#22	44 seconds
What About Love	Til Tuesday	#26	38 seconds
Tomorrow Doesn't Matter Tonight	Starship	#26	24 seconds
Night Moves	Marilyn Martin	#28	29 seconds
For America	Jackson Browne	#30	22 seconds
Everything In My Heart	Corey Hart	#30	22 seconds
Velcro Fly	ZZ Top	#35	23 seconds
25 Or 6 To 4	Chicago	#48	77 seconds
What Does It Take	Honeymoon Suite	#52	22 seconds
If Looks Could Kill	Heart	#54	24 seconds
Voice Of America's Sons	John Cafferty	#62	29 seconds
Goin' Crazy!	David Lee Roth	#66	21 seconds
Everytime You Cry	The Outfield	#66	20 seconds
Shot In The Dark	Ozzy Osbourne	#68	31 seconds
Lead A Double Life	Loverboy	#68	31 seconds
Lying	Peter Frampton	#74	25 seconds
If Anybody Had A Heart	John Waite	#76	21 seconds
Lonely Is The Night	Air Supply	#76	21 seconds
In My Dreams	Dokken	#77	30 seconds
Where Are You Now?	Synch	#77	30 seconds
Eye Of The Zombie	John Fogerty	#81	30 seconds
Runaway	Luis Cardenas	#83	28 seconds
Now And Forever (You And Me)	Anne Murray	#92	20 seconds

SONGS WITH GUITAR SOLOS (cont'd)

1987			
Faith	George Michael	#1	20 seconds
Shakedown	Bob Seger	#1	30 seconds
Alone	Heart	#1	21 seconds
Somewhere Out There	Linda Ronstadt & James Ingram	#2	23 seconds
Is This Love	Whitesnake	#2	45 seconds
Carrie	Europe	#3	28 seconds
Big Love	Fleetwood Mac	#5	31 seconds
Doing It All For My Baby	Huey Lewis & The News	#6	20 seconds
Heat Of The Night	Bryan Adams	#6	33 seconds
Wanted Dead Or Alive	Bon Jovi	#7	24 seconds
The Final Countdown	Europe	#8	33 seconds
Love You Down	Ready For The World	#9	28 seconds
Talk Dirty To Me	Poison	#9	27 seconds
Meet Me Half Way	Kenny Loggins	#11	21 seconds
Girls, Girls, Girls	Motley Crue	#12	33 seconds
Nobody's Fool	Cinderella	#13	30 seconds
I'll Be Alright Without You	Journey	#14	53 seconds
Dude (Looks Like A Lady)	Aerosmith	#14	30 seconds
Stop To Love	Luther Vandross	#15	25 seconds
This Is The Time	Billy Joel	#18	30 seconds
Come On, Let's Go	Los Lobos	#21	21 seconds
Smoking Gun	Robert Cray Band	#22	80 seconds
Never Say Goodbye	Bon Jovi	#28	28 seconds
Holiday	The Other Ones	#29	21 seconds
Light Of Day	The Barbusters (Joan Jett & The Blackhearts)	#33	23 seconds
I'll Still Be Loving You	Restless Heart	#33	25 seconds
I Will Be There	Glass Tiger	#34	31 seconds
We Connect	Stacey Q	#35	30 seconds
Without Your Love	Toto	#38	27 seconds
Back To Paradise	38 Special	#41	20 seconds
I'm No Angel	The Gregg Allman Band	#49	28 seconds
I Want Action	Poison	#50	30 seconds
How Much Love	Survivor	#51	20 seconds
Why Can't This Night Go On Forever	Journey	#60	45 seconds
Rock Me	Great White	#60	29 seconds
Johnny B	Hooters	#61	31 seconds
Throwaway	Mick Jagger	#67	30 seconds
Hold Me	Sheila E.	#68	25 seconds
Learning To Fly	Pink Floyd	#70	30 seconds
Primitive Love Rites	Mondo Rock	#71	25 seconds

SONGS WITH GUITAR SOLOS (cont'd)

True To You	Ric Ocasek	#75	22 seconds
Jane's Getting Serious	Jon Astley	#77	30 seconds
Women	Def Leppard	#80	21 seconds
You're All I Need	Motley Crue	#83	31 seconds
Do Ya Do Ya (Wanna Please Me)	Samantha Fox	#87	24 seconds
Hearts Away	Night Ranger	#90	26 seconds
Little Suzi	Tesla	#91	21 seconds
One Simple Thing	Stabilizers	#93	21 seconds

1988			
The Flame	Cheap Trick	#1	20 seconds
Sweet Child O' Mine	Guns N' Roses	#1	64 seconds
Every Rose Has Its Thorn	Poison	#1	30 seconds
Devil Inside	INXS	#2	22 seconds
I Don't Wanna Live Without Your Love	Chicago	#3	26 seconds
Make It Real	The Jets	#4	23 seconds
When It's Love	Van Halen	#5	20 seconds
Just Like Paradise	David Lee Roth	#6	23 seconds
Nothin' But A Good Time	Poison	#6	29 seconds
Wait	White Lion	#8	27 seconds
Tunnel Of Love	Bruce Springsteen	#9	41 seconds
Rush Hour	Jane Wiedlin	#9	26 seconds
Hysteria	Def Leppard	#10	27 seconds
(Sittin' On) The Dock Of The Bay	Michael Bolton	#11	22 seconds
Fallen Angel	Poison	#12	40 seconds
Don't Know What You Got (Till It's Gone)	Cinderella	#12	35 seconds
Rag Doll	Aerosmith	#17	26 seconds
A Word In Spanish	Elton John	#19	32 seconds
All Fired Up	Pat Benatar	#19	27 seconds
Under The Milky Way*	The Church	#24	28 seconds
	*E-Bow		
Small World	Huey Lewis & The News	#25	36 seconds
Edge Of A Broken Heart	Vixen	#26	31 seconds
Superstitious	Europe	#31	43 seconds
I'm Still Searching	Glass Tiger	#31	28 seconds
Black And Blue	Van Halen	#34	37 seconds
Just Like Heaven	The Cure	#40	23 seconds
Give Me All Your Love	Whitesnake	#48	31 seconds
Save Your Love	Great White	#57	27 seconds
Tell Me	White Lion	#58	27 seconds
Heart Don't Fail Me Now	Holly Knight w/ Daryl Hall	#59	31 seconds
Reason To Live	Kiss	#64	22 seconds

SONGS WITH GUITAR SOLOS (cont'd)

Powerful Stuff	The Fabulous Thunderbirds	#65	40 seconds
Get It On	Kingdom Come	#69	28 seconds
Always There For You	Stryper	#71	32 seconds
Burning Like A Flame	Dokken	#72	28 seconds
Don't Be Afraid Of The Dark	Robert Cray Band	#74	34 seconds
I Did It For Love	Night Ranger	#75	21 seconds
Rhythm Of Love	Scorpions	#75	23 seconds
Love Struck	Jesse Johnson	#78	30 seconds
Ship Of Fools*	Robert Plant	#84	41 seconds
	*Acoustic guitar		
I Feel Free	Belinda Carlisle	#88	21 seconds
Without You	Peabo Bryson & Regina Belle	#89	25 seconds
Love Changes Everything	Honeymoon Suite	#91	35 seconds
Black Leather	Kings Of The Sun	#98	31 seconds
Long Way To Love	Britny Fox	#100	50 seconds

1989			
Hangin' Tough	New Kids On The Block	#1	20 seconds
I'll Be There For You	Bon Jovi	#1	26 seconds
Listen To Your Heart	Roxette	#1	22 seconds
Right Here Waiting*	Richard Marx	#1	20 seconds
	*Acoustic guitar		
Don't Rush Me	Taylor Dayne	#2	30 seconds
Heaven	Warrant	#2	23 seconds
When The Children Cry	White Lion	#3	31 seconds
Born To Be My Baby	Bon Jovi	#3	30 seconds
*Patience	Guns N' Roses	#4	30 seconds
	*Finger-picking		
18 And Life	Skid Row	#4	20 seconds
Love In An Elevator	Aerosmith	#5	36 seconds
Angel Eyes	The Jeff Healey Band	#5	35 seconds
Once Bitten Twice Shy	Great White	#5	56 seconds
Dr. Feelgood	Motley Crue	#6	22 seconds
Surrender To Me	Ann Wilson & Robin Zander	#6	29 seconds
All This Time	Tiffany	#6	23 seconds
What I Am	Edie Brickell	#7	31 seconds
Close My Eyes Forever	Lita Ford w/ Ozzy Osbourne	#8	30 seconds
Living In Sin	Bon Jovi	#9	25 seconds
Leave A Light On	Belinda Carlisle	#11	31 seconds
Don't Close Your Eyes	Kix	#11	26 seconds
Thinking Of You	Sa-Fire	#12	24 seconds
Cult Of Personality	Living Colour	#13	53 seconds

SONGS WITH GUITAR SOLOS (cont'd)

Runnin' Down A Dream	Tom Petty	#23	73 seconds
Seventeen	Winger	#26	29 seconds
Down Boys	Warrant	#27	21 seconds
What I Like About You	Michael Morales	#28	23 seconds
The Angel Song	Great White	#30	35 seconds
Feels So Good	Van Halen	#35	26 seconds
Forget Me Not	Bad English	#45	27 seconds
Love Cries	Stage Dolls	#46	31 seconds
If We Never Meet Again	Tommy Conwell	#48	20 seconds
I Want It All	Queen	#50	29 seconds
Sold Me Down The River	The Alarm	#50	37 seconds
Let The Day Begin	The Call	#51	31 seconds
Little Fighter	White Lion	#52	32 seconds
I Wanna Be Loved	House Of Lords	#58	22 seconds
Over And Over	Pajama Party	#59	31 seconds
Radar Love	White Lion	#59	47 seconds
Somebody Like You*	Robbie Nevil	#63	33 seconds
	*Acoustic fade out		
Praying To A New God	Wang Chung	#63	23 seconds
Hide Your Heart	Kiss	#66	20 seconds
On The Line	Tangier	#67	20 seconds
Comin' Down Tonight	Thirty Eight Special	#67	28 seconds
Stand Up	Underworld	#67	31 seconds
When Love Comes To Town	U2 w/ B.B. King	#68	45 seconds
Smooth Up	Bulletboys	#71	41 seconds
Across The Miles	Survivor	#74	33 seconds
Way Cool Jr.	Ratt	#75	26 seconds
Halleluiah Man	Love & Money	#75	20 seconds
Come Out Fighting	Easterhouse	#82	22 seconds
Gimme Your Good Lovin'	Diving For Pearls	#84	29 seconds
Big Talk	Warrant	#93	31 seconds
Dear God	Midge Ure	#95	37 seconds
500 Miles	Hooters	#97	34 seconds

SONGS WITH MULTIPLE GUITAR SOLOS

SONG	ARTIST	HOT 100 CHART	LENGTH OF SOLOS
1980			
All Night Long	Joe Walsh	#19	26s, 26s
You Know That I Love You	Santana	#35	31s (Intro), 30s
Horizontal Bop	Bob Seger	#42	24s, 84s
I Thank You	ZZ Top	#34	30s + (Outro)
Alabama Getaway	Grateful Dead	#68	25s, 24s
1981			
The Night Owls	Little River Band	#6	27s, 33s
I Love You	Climax Blues Band	#12	30s, 29s
It Didn't Take Long	Spider	#43	24s, 23s
1982			
No One Like You	Scorpions	#65	Intro 35s, 31s
1983			
Dirty Laundry	Don Henley	#3	41s, 41s
Big Log	Robert Plant	#20	22s, 40s
1985			
People Get Ready	Jeff Beck & Rod Stewart	#48	25s, 40s
1986			
Rough Boy	ZZ Top	#22	24s, 50s + Fade out
1987			
La Bamba	Los Lobos	#1	30s, 20s + Fade out
Keep Your Hands To Yourself	Georgia Satellites	#2	50s, 40s, + Fade out
Big Mistake	Peter Cetera	#61	28s, 30s + Fade out
Right Next Door (Because Of Me)	Robert Cray Band	#80	39s, 33s Fade out
She Don't Look Back	Dan Fogelberg	#84	26s, 30s + Fade out
1988			
Stand Up	David Lee Roth	#64	25s, Fade out
Family Man	Fleetwood Mac	#90	48s + Fade out acoustic

SONGS WITH MULTIPLE GUITAR SOLOS (cont'd)

1989			
Headed For A Heartbreak	Winger	#19	31s, Outro
One	Metallica	#35	31s, 22s, 37s
Night Train	Guns N' Roses	#93	46, 25s Fade out
Edie (Ciao Baby)	The Cult	#93	40s

THE LONGEST GUITAR SOLOS OF THE 80s

YEAR	SONG	ARTIST	HOT 100 CHART	LENGTH OF SOLO
1985	Take Me With U	Prince	#25	115 seconds
1981	Who's Crying Now	Journey	#4	87 seconds
1980	Horizontal Bop	Bob Seger	#42	84, 24 seconds
1987	Smoking Gun	Robert Cray Band	#22	80 seconds
1980	Brite Eyes	Robbin Thompson Band	#66	78 seconds
1986	Be Good To Yourself	Journey	#9	77 seconds
1986	25 Or 6 To 4	Chicago	#48	77 seconds
1989	Runnin' Down A Dream	Tom Petty	#23	73 seconds
1981	The Sensitive Kind	Santana	#56	65 seconds
1988	Sweet Child O' Mine	Guns N' Roses	#1	64 seconds
1980	Fool In The Rain	Led Zeppelin	#21	63 seconds
1983	Burning Heart	Vandenberg	#39	61 seconds
1981	Fantasy Girl	.38 Special	#52	60 seconds
1985	Sleeping Bag	ZZ Top	#8	60 seconds
1986	Like A Rock	Bob Seger	#12	60 seconds
1989	Once Bitten Twice Shy	Great White	#5	59 seconds
1984	Taxi	J. Blackfoot	#90	57 seconds
1980	It's Not A Wonder	Little River Band	#51	55 seconds
1983	Sharp Dressed Man	ZZ Top	#56	53 seconds
1989	Cult Of Personality	Living Colour	#13	53 seconds
1987	I'll Be Alright Without You	Journey	#14	53 seconds
1982	Electricland	Bad Company	#74	52 seconds
1983	Gimme All Your Lovin	ZZ Top	#37	52 seconds
1981	Sign Of The Gypsy Queen	April Wine	#57	51 seconds
1987	Keep Your Hands To Yourself	Georgia Satellites	#2	50, 40 seconds
1986	Rough Boy	ZZ Top	#22	50, 24 seconds
1984	No More Lonely Nights	Paul McCartney	#6	50 seconds
1988	Long Way To Love	Britny Fox	#100	50 seconds
1980	Blues Power	Eric Clapton	#76	49 seconds
1988	Family Man	Fleetwood Mac	#90	48 seconds

THE LONGEST GUITAR SOLOS OF THE 80s (cont'd)

1981	Take It On The Run	REO Speedwagon	#5	48 seconds
1980	What's Your Hurry Darlin'	Ironhorse	#89	47 seconds
1984	(You Can Still) Rock In America	Night Ranger	#51	47 seconds
1989	Radar Love	White Lion	#59	47 seconds
1980	Heartbreaker	Pat Benatar	#23	46 seconds
1981	Café Amore	Spyro Gyra	#77	46 seconds
1984	The Allnighter	Glenn Frey	#54	46 seconds
1989	Night Train	Guns N' Roses	#93	46, 25 seconds
1982	Crazy (Keep On Falling)	The John Hall Band	#42	45 seconds
1987	Why Can't This Night Go On Forever	Journey	#60	45 seconds
1987	Is This Love	Whitesnake	#2	45 seconds
1983	Don't Tell Me You Love Me	Night Ranger	#40	44 seconds
1986	Love Walks In	Van Halen	#22	44 seconds
1988	Superstitious	Europe	#31	43 seconds
1983	Dirty Laundry	Don Henley	#3	41, 41 seconds
1988	Ship Of Fools	Robert Plant	#84	41 seconds
1980	Flirtin' With Disaster	Molly Hatchet	#42	41 seconds
1988	Tunnel Of Love	Bruce Springsteen	#9	41 seconds
1989	Smooth Up	Bulletboys	#71	41 seconds
1985	People Get Ready	Jeff Beck & Rod Stewart	#48	40, 25 seconds
1983	Big Log	Robert Plant	#20	40, 22 seconds
1989	Edie (Ciao Baby)	The Cult	#93	40 seconds
1981	Hold On Loosely	.38 Special	#27	40 seconds
1983	Come Give Your Love To Me	Janet Jackson	#58	40 seconds
1983	Does It Make You Remember	Kim Carnes	#36	40 seconds
1984	Flashes	Tiggi Clay	#86	40 seconds
1988	Powerful Stuff	The Fabulous Thunderbirds	#65	40 seconds
1988	Fallen Angel	Poison	#12	40 seconds
1981	Winning	Santana	#17	40 seconds
1982	Still They Ride	Journey	#19	40 seconds
1983	All This Love	Debarge	#17	40 seconds
1987	Right Next Door (Because Of Me)	Robert Cray Band	#80	39, 33 seconds
1980	Touch And Go	The Cars	#37	39 seconds
1980	Hold On	Kansas	#40	39 seconds
1980	Dirty Water	The Inmates	#51	38 seconds
1980	I Can Survive	Triumph	#91	38 seconds
1983	Take Another Picture	Quarterflash	#58	38 seconds
1983	Cum On Feel The Noize	Quiet Riot	#5	38 seconds
1986	What About Love	Til Tuesday	#26	38 seconds
1981	The Best Of Times	Styx	#3	38 seconds
1989	One	Metallica	#35	37, 31, 22 seconds
1980	Walks Like A Lady	Journey	#32	37 seconds

THE LONGEST GUITAR SOLOS OF THE 80s (cont'd)

1980	The Very Last Time	Utopia	#76	37 seconds
1981	Draw Of The Cards	Kim Carnes	#28	37 seconds
1981	Leila	ZZ Top	#77	37 seconds
1983	I Won't Hold You Back	Toto	#10	37 seconds
1985	Too Much Ain't Enough Love	Jimmy Barnes	#91	37 seconds
1985	Sentimental Street	Night Ranger	#8	37 seconds
1988	Black And Blue	Van Halen	#34	37 seconds
1989	Sold Me Down The River	The Alarm	#50	37 seconds
1989	Dear God	Midge Ure	#95	37 seconds
1983	Don't Let It End	Styx	#6	36 seconds
1988	Small World	Huey Lewis & The News	#25	36 seconds
1989	Love In An Elevator	Aerosmith	#5	36 seconds
1982	No One Like You	Scorpions	#65	35, 31 seconds
1989	Angel Eyes	The Jeff Healey Band	#5	35 seconds
1980	Too Late	Journey	#70	35 seconds
1981	Limelight	Rush	#55	35 seconds
1982	Don't Let Me In	Sneaker	#63	35 seconds
1982	Be My Lady	Jefferson Starship	#28	35 seconds
1984	Sister Christian	Night Ranger	#5	35 seconds
1985	Don't Lose My Number	Phil Collins	#4	35 seconds
1985	Turn Up The Radio	Autograph	#29	35 seconds
1985	Rockin' At Midnight	The Honeydrippers	#25	35 seconds
1988	Love Changes Everything	Honeymoon Suite	#91	35 seconds
1988	Don't Know What You Got (Till It's Gone)	Cinderella	#12	35 seconds
1989	The Angel Song	Great White	#30	35 seconds
1981	Promises In The Dark	Pat Benatar	#38	35 seconds
1980	Third Time Lucky (First Time I Was A Fool)	Foghat	#23	34 seconds
1980	Free Me	Roger Daltrey	#53	34 seconds
1980	Borrowed Time	Styx	#64	34 seconds
1981	Nicole	Point Blank	#39	34 seconds
1982	All Our Tomorrows	Eddie Schwartz	#28	34 seconds
1984	I Can Dream About You	Dan Hartman	#6	34 seconds
1988	Don't Be Afraid Of The Dark	Robert Cray Band	#74	34 seconds
1989	500 Miles	Hooters	#97	34 seconds
1981	Juke Box Hero	Foreigner	#26	34 seconds
1981	The Night Owls	Little River Band	#6	33, 27 seconds
1989	Somebody Like You	Robbie Nevil	#63	33 seconds
1984	Wanted Man	Ratt	#87	33 seconds
1984	Rock You Like A Hurricane	Scorpions	#25	33 seconds
1985	In And Out Of Love	Bon Jovi	#69	33 seconds
1985	Lovergirl	Teena Marie	#4	33 seconds
1985	You Wear It Well	El Debarge w/ Debarge	#46	33 seconds

THE LONGEST GUITAR SOLOS OF THE 80s (cont'd)

1985	One Lonely Night	REO Speedwagon	#19	33 seconds
1987	Girls, Girls, Girls	Motley Crue	#12	33 seconds
1987	The Final Countdown	Europe	#8	33 seconds
1987	Heat Of The Night	Bryan Adams	#6	33 seconds
1989	Across The Miles	Survivor	#74	33 seconds
1981	Nothing Ever Goes As Planned	Styx	#54	33 seconds
1982	How Long	Rod Stewart	#49	33 seconds
1980	Savannah Nights	Tom Johnston	#34	32 seconds
1980	I Like To Rock	April Wine	#86	32 seconds
1982	Let's Get It Up	AC/DC	#44	32 seconds
1982	Stone Cold	Rainbow	#40	32 seconds
1983	Lucky	Eye To Eye	#88	32 seconds
1985	One Night Love Affair	Bryan Adams	#13	32 seconds
1985	Private Dancer	Tina Turner	#7	32 seconds
1985	Power Of Love	Huey Lewis & The News	#1	32 seconds
1986	Dreams	Van Halen	#22	32 seconds
1986	Stages	ZZ Top	#21	32 seconds
1988	Always There For You	Stryper	#71	32 seconds
1988	A Word In Spanish	Elton John	#19	32 seconds
1989	Little Fighter	White Lion	#52	32 seconds
1989	Headed For A Heartbreak	Winger	#19	31 seconds
1984	Sweetheart Like You	Bob Dylan	#55	31 seconds
1980	You Know That I Love You	Santana	#35	31, 30 seconds
1980	Rebels Are We	Chic	#61	31 seconds
1982	Whatcha Gonna Do	Chilliwack	#41	31 seconds
1982	Dancing In The Street	Van Halen	#38	31 seconds
1983	(She's) Sexy + 17	Stray Cats	#5	31 seconds
1984	The Warrior	Scandal Featuring Patty Smyth	#7	31 seconds
1985	Four In The Morning (I Can't Take Any More)	Night Ranger	#19	31 seconds
1986	Shot In The Dark	Ozzy Osbourne	#68	31 seconds
1986	Lead A Double Life	Loverboy	#68	31 seconds
1987	You're All I Need	Motley Crue	#83	31 seconds
1987	Johnny B	Hooters	#61	31 seconds
1987	I Will Be There	Glass Tiger	#34	31 seconds
1987	Big Love	Fleetwood Mac	#5	31 seconds
1988	Heart Don't Fail Me Now	Holly Knight w/ Daryl Hall	#59	31 seconds
1988	Give Me All Your Love	Whitesnake	#48	31 seconds
1988	Edge Of A Broken Heart	Vixen	#26	31 seconds
1988	Black Leather	Kings Of The Sun	#98	31 seconds
1989	Over And Over	Pajama Party	#59	31 seconds
1989	Let The Day Begin	The Call	#51	31 seconds

THE LONGEST GUITAR SOLOS OF THE 80s (cont'd)

1989	Love Cries	Stage Dolls	#46	31 seconds
1989	Stand Up	Underworld	#67	31 seconds
1989	When The Children Cry	White Lion	#3	31 seconds
1989	Leave A Light On	Belinda Carlisle	#11	31 seconds
1989	What I Am	Edie Brickell	#7	31 seconds
1989	Big Talk	Warrant	#93	31 seconds
1981	I Love You	Climax Blues Band	#12	30, 29 seconds
1987	Big Mistake	Peter Cetera	#61	30, 28 seconds
1987	She Don't Look Back	Dan Fogelberg	#84	30, 26 seconds
1987	La Bamba	Los Lobos	#1	30, 20 seconds
1989	Patience	Guns N' Roses	#4	30 seconds
1988	Love Struck	Jesse Johnson	#78	30 seconds
1986	Like No Other Night	38 Special	#14	30 seconds
1987	Learning To Fly	Pink Floyd	#70	30 seconds
1987	This Is The Time	Billy Joel	#18	30 seconds
1980	I Thank You	ZZ Top	#34	30 seconds
1980	We Were Meant To Be Lovers	Photoglo	#31	30 seconds
1980	You Better Run	Pat Benatar	#42	30 seconds
1980	I Could Be Good For You	707	#52	30 seconds
1980	A Certain Girl	Warren Zevon	#57	30 seconds
1980	Stargazer	Peter Brown	#59	30 seconds
1980	I'm Alive	Gamma	#60	30 seconds
1981	Back In Black	AC/DC	#37	30 seconds
1982	Night Shift	Quarterflash	#60	30 seconds
1983	New Year's Day	U2	#53	30 seconds
1983	Undercover Of The Night	The Rolling Stones	#9	30 seconds
1983	Don't Make Me Do It	Patrick Simmons	#75	30 seconds
1984	Headpins	Just One More Time	#70	30 seconds
1984	Mama Weer All Crazee Now	Quiet Riot	#51	30 seconds
1985	Que Te Quiero	Katrina & The Waves	#71	30 seconds
1986	Eye Of The Zombie	John Fogerty	#81	30 seconds
1986	In My Dreams	Dokken	#77	30 seconds
1986	Where Are You Now?	Synch	#77	30 seconds
1986	Tonight She Comes	The Cars	#7	30 seconds
1987	Dude (Looks Like A Lady)	Aerosmith	#14	30 seconds
1987	Nobody's Fool	Cinderella	#13	30 seconds
1987	Jane's Getting Serious	Jon Astley	#77	30 seconds
1987	Throwaway	Mick Jagger	#67	30 seconds
1987	I Want Action	Poison	#50	30 seconds
1987	We Connect	Stacey Q	#35	30 seconds
1987	Shakedown	Bob Seger	#1	30 seconds
1988	Every Rose Has Its Thorn	Poison	#1	30 seconds

THE LONGEST GUITAR SOLOS OF THE 80s (cont'd)

1989	Close My Eyes Forever	Lita Ford w/ Ozzy Osbourne	#8	30 seconds
1989	Born To Be My Baby	Bon Jovi	#3	30 seconds
1989	Don't Rush Me	Taylor Dayne	#2	30 seconds
1981	Physical	Olivia Newton-John	#1	30 seconds
1981	Kiss On My List	Daryl Hall & John Oates	#1	30 seconds
1982	Sweet Dreams	Air Supply	#5	30 seconds
1980	You Shook Me All Night Long	AC/DC	#35	29 seconds
1980	Fool For Your Loving	Whitesnake	#53	29 seconds
1982	You've Got Another Thing Comin'	Judas Priest	#67	29 seconds
1983	Guns For Hire	AC/DC	#84	29 seconds
1983	Caught In The Game	Survivor	#77	29 seconds
1984	Owner Of A Lonely Heart	Yes	#1	29 seconds
1984	Hot For Teacher	Van Halen	#56	29 seconds
1984	Panama	Van Halen	#13	29 seconds
1984	Round And Round	Ratt	#12	29 seconds
1985	Restless Heart	John Waite	#59	29 seconds
1985	Money For Nothing	Dire Straits	#1	29 seconds
1986	Voice Of America's Sons	John Cafferty	#62	29 seconds
1986	Night Moves	Marilyn Martin	#28	29 seconds
1986	All The Love In The World	The Outfield	#19	29 seconds
1986	Silent Running (On Dangerous Ground)	Mike + The Mechanics	#6	29 seconds
1987	Rock Me	Great White	#60	29 seconds
1988	Nothin' But A Good Time	Poison	#6	29 seconds
1989	I Want It All	Queen	#50	29 seconds
1989	Seventeen	Winger	#26	29 seconds
1989	Surrender To Me	Ann Wilson & Robin Zander	#6	29 seconds
1989	Gimme Your Good Lovin'	Diving For Pearls	#84	29 seconds
1981	Too Much Time On My Hands	Styx	#9	29 seconds
1988	Under The Milky Way	The Church	#24	28 seconds
1981	Burnin' For You	Blue Oyster Cult	#40	28 seconds
1982	Heat Of The Moment	Asia	#4	28 seconds
1982	Now Or Never	Axe	#64	28 seconds
1983	Beat It	Michael Jackson	#1	28 seconds
1983	Send Her My Love	Journey	#23	28 seconds
1983	China Girl	David Bowie	#10	28 seconds
1984	Torture	Jacksons	#17	28 seconds
1984	Legs	ZZ Top	#8	28 seconds
1985	Sweet, Sweet Baby (I'm Falling)	Lone Justice	#73	28 seconds
1985	Alone Again	Dokken	#64	28 seconds
1985	Tears Are Falling	Kiss	#51	28 seconds
1985	Can't Stop	Rick James	#50	28 seconds
1986	Runaway	Luis Cardenas	#83	28 seconds

THE LONGEST GUITAR SOLOS OF THE 80s (cont'd)

1987	Love You Down	Ready For The World	#9	28 seconds
1987	I'm No Angel	The Gregg Allman Band	#49	28 seconds
1987	Never Say Goodbye	Bon Jovi	#28	28 seconds
1987	Carrie	Europe	#3	28 seconds
1988	Burning Like A Flame	Dokken	#72	28 seconds
1988	Get It On	Kingdom Come	#69	28 seconds
1988	I'm Still Searching	Glass Tiger	#31	28 seconds
1989	Comin' Down Tonight	Thirty Eight Special	#67	28 seconds
1981	Hearts On Fire	Randy Meisner	#18	28 seconds
1981	Chloe	Elton John	#34	27 seconds
1980	Twilight Zone/Twilight Tone	Manhattan Transfer	#30	27 seconds
1980	Girl With The Hungry Eyes	Jefferson Starship	#55	27 seconds
1981	Stranger	Jefferson Starship	#48	27 seconds
1982	Pac-Man Fever	Buckner & Garcia	#9	27 seconds
1982	You Don't Want Me Anymore	Steel Breeze	#16	27 seconds
1983	Rock Of Ages	Def Leppard	#16	27 seconds
1983	High Time	Styx	#48	27 seconds
1983	Separate Ways (Worlds Apart)	Journey	#8	27 seconds
1984	Whiter Shade Of Pale	Hagar, Schon, Aaronson, Shrieve	#94	27 seconds
1984	So You Ran	Orion The Hunter	#58	27 seconds
1985	Welcome To Paradise	John Waite	#85	27 seconds
1985	Remo's Theme (What If)	Tommy Shaw	#81	27 seconds
1985	Say It Again	Santana	#46	27 seconds
1985	Easy Lover	Philip Bailey w/ Phil Collins	#2	27 seconds
1986	Walk Like An Egyptian	Bangles	#1	27 seconds
1987	Without Your Love	Toto	#38	27 seconds
1987	Talk Dirty To Me	Poison	#9	27 seconds
1988	Tell Me	White Lion	#58	27 seconds
1988	Save Your Love	Great White	#57	27 seconds
1988	All Fired Up	Pat Benatar	#19	27 seconds
1988	Hysteria	Def Leppard	#10	27 seconds
1988	Wait	White Lion	#8	27 seconds
1989	Forget Me Not	Bad English	#45	27 seconds
1981	Cool Love	Pablo Cruise	#13	27 seconds
1981	Games People Play	Alan Parsons Project	#16	27 seconds
1980	All Night Long	Joe Walsh	#19	26, 26 seconds
1980	Breakdown Dead Ahead	Boz Scaggs	#15	26 seconds
1980	This Time	John Cougar	#27	26 seconds
1981	Tom Sawyer	Rush	#44	26 seconds
1981	Fireflies	Fleetwood Mac	#60	26 seconds
1982	Enough Is Enough	April Wine	#50	26 seconds

THE LONGEST GUITAR SOLOS OF THE 80s (cont'd)

1983	Johnny B. Goode	Peter Tosh	#84	26 seconds
1983	How Am I Supposed To Live Without You	Laura Branigan	#12	26 seconds
1984	Midnite Maniac	Krokus	#71	26 seconds
1984	You Make My Heart Beat Faster (And That's All That Matters)	Kim Carnes	#54	26 seconds
1984	Don't Stop	Jeffrey Osborne	#44	26 seconds
1984	Strung Out	Steve Perry	#40	26 seconds
1984	Romancing The Stone	Eddy Grant	#26	26 seconds
1984	Walking On A Thin Line	Huey Lewis & The News	#18	26 seconds
1984	Authority Song	John Cougar Mellencamp	#15	26 seconds
1984	Infatuation	Rod Stewart	#6	26 seconds
1987	Hearts Away	Night Ranger	#90	26 seconds
1988	I Don't Wanna Live Without Your Love	Chicago	#3	26 seconds
1988	Rag Doll	Aerosmith	#17	26 seconds
1988	Rush Hour	Jane Wiedlin	#9	26 seconds
1989	Feels So Good	Van Halen	#35	26 seconds
1989	Don't Close Your Eyes	Kix	#11	26 seconds
1989	I'll Be There For You	Bon Jovi	#1	26 seconds
1989	Way Cool Jr.	Ratt	#75	26 seconds
1988	Stand Up	David Lee Roth	#64	25 seconds
1980	Alabama Getaway	Grateful Dead	#68	25, 24 seconds
1984	Hello	Lionel Richie	#1	25 seconds
1980	Angeline	Allman Brothers Band	#58	25 seconds
1982	Shake It Up	The Cars	#4	25 seconds
1982	Love's Been A Little Bit Hard On Me	Juice Newton	#7	25 seconds
1982	I Ran (So Far Away)	A Flock Of Seagulls	#9	25 seconds
1982	Don't Fight It	Kenny Loggins w/Steve Perry	#17	25 seconds
1982	Perfect	Fairground Attraction	#80	25 seconds
1983	Dead Giveaway	Shalamar	#22	25 seconds
1983	Twilight Zone	Golden Earring	#10	25 seconds
1983	You Put The Beat In My Heart	Eddie Rabbitt	#81	25 seconds
1984	Thief Of Hearts	Melissa Manchester	#86	25 seconds
1984	This Could Be The Right One	April Wine	#58	25 seconds
1984	For A Rocker	Jackson Browne	#45	25 seconds
1984	Runaway	Bon Jovi	#39	25 seconds
1984	No Way Out	Jefferson Starship	#23	25 seconds
1984	We're Not Gonna Take It	Twisted Sister	#21	25 seconds
1985	You're In Love	Ratt	#89	25 seconds
1985	C-I-T-Y	John Cafferty	#18	25 seconds
1985	Sisters Are Doin' It For Themselves	Eurythmics & Aretha Franklin	#18	25 seconds
1986	Lying	Peter Frampton	#74	25 seconds
1986	Goodbye	Night Ranger	#17	25 seconds

THE LONGEST GUITAR SOLOS OF THE 80s (cont'd)

1987	Primitive Love Rites	Mondo Rock	#71	25 seconds
1987	I'll Still Be Loving You	Restless Heart	#33	25 seconds
1987	Stop To Love	Luther Vandross	#15	25 seconds
1987	Hold Me	Sheila E.	#68	25 seconds
1988	Without You	Peabo Bryson & Regina Belle	#89	25 seconds
1989	Living In Sin	Bon Jovi	#9	25 seconds
1981	Rapture	Blondie	#1	25 seconds
1981	It Didn't Take Long	Spider	#43	24, 23 seconds
1980	Somewhere In America	Survivor	#70	24 seconds
1980	Back Of My Hand (I've Got Your Number)	The Jags	#84	24 seconds
1980	Wango Tango	Ted Nugent	#86	24 seconds
1980	Cheap Sunglasses	ZZ Top	#89	24 seconds
1981	When She Dances	Joey Scarbury	#49	24 seconds
1981	La-Di-Da	Sad Café	#78	24 seconds
1982	Mega Force	707	#62	24 seconds
1982	Think I'm In Love	Eddie Money	#16	24 seconds
1983	Maniac	Michael Sembello	#1	24 seconds
1983	My Town	Michael Stanley Band	#39	24 seconds
1983	Kiss The Bride	Elton John	#25	24 seconds
1984	Little Lady	Duke Jupiter	#68	24 seconds
1984	She Was Hot	The Rolling Stones	#44	24 seconds
1984	Prime Time	Alan Parsons Project	#34	24 seconds
1984	Turn To You	The Go-Go's	#32	24 seconds
1984	Bang Your Head (Metal Health)	Quiet Riot	#31	24 seconds
1984	Oh Sherrie	Steve Perry	#3	24 seconds
1985	Oh Girl	Boy Meets Girl	#39	24 seconds
1985	Live Every Moment	REO Speedwagon	#34	24 seconds
1985	Only The Young	Journey	#9	24 seconds
1985	Can't Fight This Feeling	REO Speedwagon	#1	24 seconds
1986	Tomorrow Doesn't Matter Tonight	Starship	#26	24 seconds
1986	Suzanne	Journey	#17	24 seconds
1987	Do Ya Do Ya (Wanna Please Me)	Samantha Fox	#87	24 seconds
1987	Wanted Dead Or Alive	Bon Jovi	#7	24 seconds
1989	Thinking Of You	Sa-Fire	#12	24 seconds
1981	Young Turks	Rod Stewart	#5	24 seconds
1986	If Looks Could Kill	Heart	#54	24 seconds
1986	Burning Heart	Survivor	#2	23 seconds
1981	Just Between You And Me	April Wine	#21	23 seconds
1981	Playing With Lightning	Shot In The Dark	#71	23 seconds
1981	Sweet Merilee	Donnie Iris	#80	23 seconds
1982	Oh Julie	Barry Manilow	#38	23 seconds
1983	Making Love Out Of Nothing At All	Air Supply	#2	23 seconds

THE LONGEST GUITAR SOLOS OF THE 80s (cont'd)

1984	All Night Long	Billy Squier	#75	23 seconds
1984	Club Michelle	Eddie Money	#66	23 seconds
1984	Rebel Yell	Billy Idol	#46	23 seconds
1985	Home Sweet Home	Motley Crue	#89	23 seconds
1985	Reaction To Action	Foreigner	#54	23 seconds
1985	Just As I Am	Air Supply	#19	23 seconds
1985	What About Love?	Heart	#10	23 seconds
1985	Sea Of Love	Honeydrippers	#3	23 seconds
1986	Velcro Fly	ZZ Top	#35	23 seconds
1987	Light Of Day	The Barbusters (Joan Jett & The Blackhearts)	#33	23 seconds
1987	Somewhere Out There	Linda Ronstadt & James Ingram	#2	23 seconds
1988	Rhythm Of Love	Scorpions	#75	23 seconds
1988	Just Like Heaven	The Cure	#40	23 seconds
1988	Just Like Paradise	David Lee Roth	#6	23 seconds
1988	Make It Real	The Jets	#4	23 seconds
1989	Praying To A New God	Wang Chung	#63	23 seconds
1989	What I Like About You	Michael Morales	#28	23 seconds
1989	All This Time	Tiffany	#6	23 seconds
1989	Heaven	Warrant	#2	23 seconds
1981	The Waiting	Tom Petty And The Heartbreakers	#19	23 seconds
1980	I Can't Stop This Feelin'	Pure Prairie League	#77	22 seconds
1980	Who'll Be The Fool Tonight	Larsen-Feiten Band	#29	22 seconds
1980	Don't Make Me Over	Jennifer Warnes	#67	22 seconds
1981	(Ghost) Riders In The Sky	Outlaws	#31	22 seconds
1981	Games	Phoebe Snow	#46	22 seconds
1981	Yearning For Your Love	The Gap Band	#60	22 seconds
1982	Too Good To Turn Back Now	Rick Bowles	#77	22 seconds
1982	I'll Drink To You	Duke Jupiter	#58	22 seconds
1983	Too Much Love To Hide	Crosby, Stills & Nash	#69	22 seconds
1983	Love Me Again	The John Hall Band	#64	22 seconds
1983	Dreamin' Is Easy	Steel Breeze	#30	22 seconds
1983	Photograph	Def Leppard	#12	22 seconds
1984	Love Will Show Us How	Christine McVie	#30	22 seconds
1984	Eat It	Weird Al Yankovic	#12	22 seconds
1985	One Foot Back In Your Door	Roman Holliday	#76	22 seconds
1985	Lay It Down	Ratt	#40	22 seconds
1986	What Does It Take	Honeymoon Suite	#52	22 seconds
1986	For America	Jackson Browne	#30	22 seconds
1986	Everything In My Heart	Corey Hart	#30	22 seconds
1986	Nothin' At All	Heart	#10	22 seconds

THE LONGEST GUITAR SOLOS OF THE 80s (cont'd)

1987	True To You	Ric Ocasek	#75	22 seconds
1988	Reason To Live	Kiss	#64	22 seconds
1988	(Sittin' On) The Dock Of The Bay	Michael Bolton	#11	22 seconds
1988	Devil Inside	INXS	#2	22 seconds
1989	I Wanna Be Loved	House Of Lords	#58	22 seconds
1989	Dr. Feelgood	Motley Crue	#6	22 seconds
1989	Listen To Your Heart	Roxette	#1	22 seconds
1989	Come Out Fighting	Easterhouse	#82	22 seconds
1981	Keep On Loving You	REO Speedwagon	#1	22 seconds
1980	Voices	Cheap Trick	#32	21 seconds
1980	New Romance (It's A Mystery)	Spider	#39	21 seconds
1980	Somethin' 'Bout You Baby I Like	Glen Campbell & Rita Coolidge	#42	21 seconds
1983	Allergies	Paul Simon	#44	21 seconds
1984	She's Mine	Steve Perry	#21	21 seconds
1985	Vox Humana	Kenny Loggins	#29	21 seconds
1986	If Anybody Had A Heart	John Waite	#76	21 seconds
1986	Lonely Is The Night	Air Supply	#76	21 seconds
1986	Goin' Crazy!	David Lee Roth	#66	21 seconds
1986	That Was Then, This Is Now	The Monkees	#20	21 seconds
1986	Spies Like Us	Paul McCartney	#7	21 seconds
1987	One Simple Thing	Stabilizers	#93	21 seconds
1987	Little Suzi	Tesla	#91	21 seconds
1987	Women	Def Leppard	#80	21 seconds
1987	Meet Me Half Way	Kenny Loggins	#11	21 seconds
1987	Holiday	The Other Ones	#29	21 seconds
1987	Come On, Let's Go	Los Lobos	#21	21 seconds
1987	Alone	Heart	#1	21 seconds
1988	I Feel Free	Belinda Carlisle	#88	21 seconds
1988	I Did It For Love	Night Ranger	#75	21 seconds
1989	Down Boys	Warrant	#27	21 seconds
1989	Right Here Waiting	Richard Marx	#1	20 seconds
1980	Is This Love	Pat Travers Band	#50	20 seconds
1981	Love You Like I Never Loved Before	John O'Banion	#24	20 seconds
1982	When I'm Holding You Tight	Michael Stanley Band	#78	20 seconds
1982	Another Sleepless Night	Anne Murray	#44	20 seconds
1982	I Believe	Chilliwack	#33	20 seconds
1983	For The Love Of Money	Bulletboys	#78	20 seconds
1983	Cuts Like A Knife	Bryan Adams	#15	20 seconds
1984	If This Is It	Huey Lewis & The News	#6	20 seconds
1984	Love Has Taken Its Toll	Saraya	#64	20 seconds
1984	New Girl Now	Honeymoon Suite	#57	20 seconds

THE LONGEST GUITAR SOLOS OF THE 80s (cont'd)

1985	Go For Soda	Kim Mitchell	#86	20 seconds
1985	Lonely School	Tommy Shaw	#60	20 seconds
1986	Now And Forever (You And Me)	Anne Murray	#92	20 seconds
1986	Everytime You Cry	The Outfield	#66	20 seconds
1987	How Much Love	Survivor	#51	20 seconds
1987	Doing It All For My Baby	Huey Lewis & The News	#6	20 seconds
1987	Faith	George Michael	#1	20 seconds
1988	When It's Love	Van Halen	#5	20 seconds
1988	The Flame	Cheap Trick	#1	20 seconds
1989	If We Never Meet Again	Tommy Conwell	#48	20 seconds
1989	On The Line	Tangier	#67	20 seconds
1989	18 And Life	Skid Row	#4	20 seconds
1989	Hangin' Tough	New Kids On The Block	#1	20 seconds
1989	Halleluiah Man	Love & Money	#75	20 seconds
1989	Hide Your Heart	Kiss	#66	20 seconds
1981	Fire And Ice	Pat Benatar	#17	20 seconds
1981	Treat Me Right	Pat Benatar	#18	20 seconds
1987	Back To Paradise	38 Special	#41	20 seconds

HARMONICA

The first list has all the songs that used a harmonica, not including the songs with a harmonica solo. The second list includes the songs that featured one harmonica solo, while the next list includes the songs that had multiple harmonica solos. The last list shows all the songs with harmonica solos, but this time they are organized by length of solo.

SONG	ARTIST	HOT 100 CHART
1980		
You May Be Right	Billy Joel	#7
Train In Vain (Stand By Me)	The Clash	#23
Make A Little Magic	The Dirt Band	#25
My Heroes Have Always Been Cowboys	Willie Nelson	#44
Heroes	Commodores	#54
Angeline	Allman Brothers Band	#58
Take You Tonight	Ozark Mountain Daredevils	#67
I Get Off On It	Tony Joe White	#79

HARMONICA (cont'd)

1981		
Somebody's Knockin'	Terri Gibbs	#13
It's My Job	Jimmy Buffett	#57
Fire In The Sky	The Dirt Band	#76
Rich Man	Terri Gibbs	#89
I Love My Truck	Glen Campbell	#94

1982		
I Wouldn't Have Missed It For The World	Ronnie Milsap	#20
Used To Be	Charlene & Stevie Wonder	#46
I Will Always Love You	Dolly Parton	#53

1983		
Say Say Say	Paul McCartney & Michael Jackson	#1
Europa And The Pirate Twins	Thomas Dolby	#67
New Frontier	Donald Fagen	#70

1984		
Karma Chameleon	Culture Club	#1
The Heart Of Rock & Roll	Huey Lewis & The News	#6
Unfaithfully Yours (One Love)	Stephen Bishop	#87

1985		
Small Town	John Cougar Mellencamp	#6

1986		
Sara	Starship	#1
Face The Face	Pete Townshend	#26
Every Little Kiss	Bruce Hornsby and the Range	#72
I Knew The Bride (When She Use To Rock And Roll)	Nick Lowe	#77

1987		
Respect Yourself	Bruce Willis	#5
Wild Horses	Gino Vannelli	#55
Rock Me	Great White	#60
Johnny B	Hooters	#61

1988		
Handle Me With Care	Traveling Wilburys	#45

HARMONICA (cont'd)

1989		
I Don't Want A Lover	Texas	#77
This One	Paul McCartney	#94

SONGS WITH HARMONICA SOLOS

Only harmonica solos lasting ten seconds or longer are included in this book.

SONG	ARTIST	HOT 100 CHART	LENGTH OF SOLO
1980			
An American Dream	The Dirt Band (Linda Ronstadt)	#13	12 seconds
On The Road Again	Willie Nelson	#20	15 seconds
What I Like About You	The Romantics	#49	23 seconds
Leaving L.A.	Deliverance	#71	10 seconds
Survive	Jimmy Buffett	#77	12 seconds
1981			
When She Was My Girl	The Four Tops	#11	21 seconds
You Like Me Don't You	Jermaine Jackson	#50	44 seconds
One Day In Your Life	Michael Jackson	#55	13 seconds
I'm Just Too Shy	Jermaine Jackson	#60	22 seconds
Long Time Lovin' You	McGuffey Lane	#85	13 seconds
1982			
That Girl	Stevie Wonder	#4	35 seconds
Run For The Roses	Dan Fogelberg	#18	30 seconds
Turn On Your Radar	Prism	#64	14 seconds
1983			
I Do	J. Geils Band	#24	16 seconds
Spice Of Life	Manhattan Transfer	#40	17 seconds
Mexican Radio	Wall Of Voodoo	#58	14 seconds
Love Is The Key	Maze Feat. Frankie Beverly	#80	31 seconds
1984			
I Guess That's Why They Call It The Blues	Elton John	#4	28 seconds
Middle Of The Road	The Pretenders	#19	40 seconds
Bop 'Til You Drop	Rick Springfield	#20	15 seconds

SONGS WITH HARMONICA SOLOS (cont'd)

Leave A Tender Moment Alone	Billy Joel	#27	17 seconds
You Take Me Up	Thompson Twins	#44	19 seconds
Love Me In A Special Way	Debarge	#45	15 seconds

1985			
Too Late For Goodbyes	Julian Lennon	#5	14 seconds
Smokin' In The Boys Room	Motley Crue	#16	15 seconds
Ooh Ooh Song	Pat Benatar	#36	22 seconds

1987			
Shake You Down	Gregory Abbott	#1	16 seconds
Wot's It To Ya	Robbie Nevil	#10	19 seconds
Moonlighting (Theme)	Al Jarreau	#23	33 seconds
Never Let Me Down	David Bowie	#27	17 seconds
Love Will Find A Way	Yes	#30	8 seconds
Notorious	Loverboy	#38	24 seconds
Primitive Love Rites	Mondo Rock	#71	21 seconds

1988			
Desire	U2	#3	13 seconds
Strange But True	Times Two	#21	18 seconds
My Love	Julio Iglesias w/ Stevie Wonder	#80	26 seconds

1989			
No Big Deal	Love & Rockets	#82	34 seconds

*HONORABLE MENTIONS

These songs sound like they have harmonicas, but they don't. They're using a synthesizer. The first two songs are using a Yamaha DX7.

SONG	ARTIST	HOT 100 CHART	LENGTH OF SOLO
1984			
What's Love Got To Do With It	Tina Turner	#1	14 seconds

1986			
Sweet Freedom	Michael McDonald	#7	14 seconds

1988			
Century's End	Donald Fagen	#83	38 seconds

SONGS WITH MULTIPLE HARMONICA SOLOS

SONG	ARTIST	HOT 100 CHART	LENGTH OF SOLOS
1980			
Texas In My Rear View Mirror	Mac Davis	#51	12s, 10s
1981			
Steal The Night	Stevie Woods	#25	18s, 15s
Pay The Devil (Ooo, Baby, Ooo)	The Knack	#67	11s, 12s, 22s
1982			
Workin' For A Livin'	Huey Lewis & The News	#41	23s, 16s
Fool For Your Love	Jimmy Hall	#77	15s, 14s
1983			
Church Of The Poison Mind	Culture Club	#10	14s, 14s
1984			
I Feel For You	Chaka Khan	#3	14s, 15s
1985			
There Must Be An Angel (Playing With My Heart)	Eurythmics	#22	31s, 16s
1986			
That's What Friends Are For	Dionne Warwick And Friends	#1	16s, 38s
Missionary Man	Eurythmics	#14	14s, 30s, 12s
The Future's So Bright, I Gotta Wear Shades	Timbuk 3	#19	11s, 23s, 30s

THE LONGEST HARMONICA SOLOS OF THE 80s

YEAR	SONG	ARTIST	HOT 100 CHART	LENGTH OF SOLO(S)
1981	You Like Me Don't You	Jermaine Jackson	#50	44 seconds
1984	Middle Of The Road	The Pretenders	#19	40 seconds
1986	That's What Friends Are For	Dionne Warwick And Friends	#1	38, 16 seconds
1982	That Girl	Stevie Wonder	#4	35 seconds
1989	No Big Deal	Love & Rockets	#82	34 seconds
1987	Moonlighting (Theme)	Al Jarreau	#23	33 seconds

THE LONGEST HARMONICA SOLOS OF THE 80s (cont'd)

1985	There Must Be An Angel (Playing With My Heart)	Eurythmics	#22	31, 16 seconds
1983	Love Is The Key	Maze Feat. Frankie Beverly	#80	31 seconds
1982	Run For The Roses	Dan Fogelberg	#18	30 seconds
1986	The Future's So Bright, I Gotta Wear Shades	Timbuk 3	#19	11, 23, 30 seconds
1986	Missionary Man	Eurythmics	#14	14, 30, 12 seconds
1984	I Guess That's Why They Call It The Blues	Elton John	#4	28 seconds
1988	My Love	Julio Iglesias w/ Stevie Wonder	#80	26 seconds
1987	Notorious	Loverboy	#38	24 seconds
1982	Workin' For A Livin'	Huey Lewis & The News	#41	23, 16 seconds
1980	What I Like About You	The Romantics	#49	23 seconds
1981	I'm Just Too Shy	Jermaine Jackson	#60	22 seconds
1985	Ooh Ooh Song	Pat Benatar	#36	22 seconds
1981	Pay The Devil (Ooo, Baby, Ooo)	The Knack	#67	11, 12, 22 seconds
1981	When She Was My Girl	The Four Tops	#11	21 seconds
1987	Primitive Love Rites	Mondo Rock	#71	21 seconds
1984	You Take Me Up	Thompson Twins	#44	19 seconds
1987	Wot's It To Ya	Robbie Nevil	#10	19 seconds
1981	Steal The Night	Stevie Woods	#25	18, 15 seconds
1988	Strange But True	Times Two	#21	18 seconds
1983	Spice Of Life	Manhattan Transfer	#40	17 seconds
1984	Leave A Tender Moment Alone	Billy Joel	#27	17 seconds
1987	Never Let Me Down	David Bowie	#27	17 seconds
1983	I Do	J. Geils Band	#24	16 seconds
1987	Shake You Down	Gregory Abbott	#1	16 seconds
1982	Fool For Your Love	Jimmy Hall	#77	15, 14 seconds
1980	On The Road Again	Willie Nelson	#20	15 seconds
1984	Bop 'Til You Drop	Rick Springfield	#20	15 seconds
1984	Love Me In A Special Way	Debarge	#45	15 seconds
1985	Smokin' In The Boys Room	Motley Crue	#16	15 seconds
1984	I Feel For You	Chaka Khan	#3	14, 15 seconds
1983	Church Of The Poison Mind	Culture Club	#10	14, 14 seconds
1982	Turn On Your Radar	Prism	#64	14 seconds
1983	Mexican Radio	Wall Of Voodoo	#58	14 seconds
1985	Too Late For Goodbyes	Julian Lennon	#5	14 seconds
1981	One Day In Your Life	Michael Jackson	#55	13 seconds
1981	Long Time Lovin' You	McGuffey Lane	#85	13 seconds
1988	Desire	U2	#3	13 seconds
1980	Texas In My Rear View Mirror	Mac Davis	#51	12, 10 seconds
1980	An American Dream	The Dirt Band (Linda Ronstadt)	#13	12 seconds
1980	Survive	Jimmy Buffett	#77	12 seconds
1980	Leaving L.A.	Deliverance	#71	10 seconds

HARP

SONG	ARTIST	HOT 100 CHART
1981		
Touch Me (When We're Dancing)	Carpenters	#16
United Together	Aretha Franklin	#56
1982		
Those Good Old Dreams	Carpenters	#63
Beechwood 4-5789	Carpenters	#74
1988		
Seasons Change	Expose	#1

HORNS (excluding the saxophone)

SONG	ARTIST	HOT 100 CHART
1980		
Rock With You	Michael Jackson	#1
Longer	Dan Fogelberg	#2
Take Your Time (Do It Right) Part 1	S.O.S. Band	#3
Cupid/I've Loved You For A Long Time	Spinners	#4
Give Me The Night	George Benson	#4
I'm Comin' Out	Diana Ross	#5
On The Radio	Donna Summer	#5
Hungry Heart	Bruce Springsteen	#5
Master Blaster (Jammin')	Stevie Wonder	#5
Special Lady	Ray, Goodman & Brown	#5
Late In The Evening	Paul Simon	#6
Stomp!	The Brothers Johnson	#7
Ladies Night	Kool & The Gang	#8
Lets Get Serious	Jermaine Jackson	#9
Off The Wall	Michael Jackson	#10
Daydream Believer	Anne Murray	#12
Better Love Next Time	Dr. Hook	#12
Lovely One	The Jacksons	#12
September Morn'	Neil Diamond	#17
Give It All You Got	Chuck Mangione	#18

HORNS (excluding the saxophone) (cont'd)

Don't Let Go	Isaac Hayes	#18
Gimme Some Lovin'	Blues Brothers	#18
I Pledge My Love	Peaches & Herb	#19
Old-Fashion Love	Commodores	#20
How Do I Survive	Amy Holland	#22
Wonderland	Commodores	#25
Forever Mine	O'Jays	#28
Who'll Be The Fool Tonight	Larsen-Feiten Band	#29
Rotation	Herb Alpert	#30
Tulsa Time	Eric Clapton	#30
Theme From New York, New York	Frank Sinatra	#32
Even It Up	Heart	#33
Savannah Nights	Tom Johnston	#34
When A Man Loves A Woman	Bette Midler	#35
If You Should Sail	Nielsen/Pearson	#38
I Can't Help Myself (Sugar Pie, Honey Bunch)	Bonnie Pointer	#40
A Lover's Holiday	Change	#40
Red Light	Linda Clifford	#41
Haven't You Heard	Patrice Rushen	#42
Power	The Temptations	#43
Let Me Talk	Earth, Wind & Fire	#44
All Night Thing	Invisible Man Band	#45
Landlord	Gladys Knight & The Pips	#46
My Prayer	Ray, Goodman & Brown	#47
Bad Times	Tavares	#47
You	Earth, Wind & Fire	#48
Don't Push It Don't Force It	Leon Haywood	#49
Beyond	Herb Alpert	#50
Sweet Sensation	Stephanie Mills	#52
Could I Be Dreaming	The Pointer Sisters	#52
First... Be A Woman	Lenore O'Malley	#53
Free Me	Roger Daltrey	#53
Let's Go 'Round Again	Average White Band	#53
Thunder And Lightning	Chicago	#56
Back Together Again	Roberta Flack & Donny Hathaway	#56
Today Is The Day	Bar-Kays	#60
Love X Love	George Benson	#61
Star	Earth, Wind & Fire	#64
Got To Love Somebody	Sister Sledge	#64
After You	Dionne Warwick	#65
Dancin' In The Streets	Teri Desario w/ K.C. And The Sunshine Band	#66

HORNS (excluding the saxophone) (cont'd)

I Shoulda Loved Ya	Narada Michael Walden	#66
Don't Cry For Me Argentina	Festival	#72
Inside Of You	Ray, Goodman & Brown	#76
The Waiting Game	Swing Out Sister	#86
Remote Control	The Reddings	#89
I Love Women	Jim Hurt	#90
The Part Of Me That Needs You Most	Jay Black	#98

1981		
Physical	Olivia Newton-John	#1
9 To 5	Dolly Parton	#1
The Tide Is High	Blondie	#1
Celebration	Kool & The Gang	#1
Woman In Love	Barbra Streisand	#1
Let's Groove	Earth, Wind & Fire	#3
Elvira	The Oak Ridge Boys	#5
Tryin' To Live My Life Without You	Bob Seger	#5
Why Do Fools Fall In Love	Diana Ross	#7
Boy From New York City	Manhattan Transfer	#7
Lady (You Bring Me Up)	Commodores	#8
Tell It Like It Is	Heart	#8
Watching The Wheels	John Lennon	#10
What Kind Of Fool	Barbra Streisand And Barry Gibb	#10
I Made It Through The Rain	Barry Manilow	#10
When She Was My Girl	The Four Tops	#11
The Old Songs	Barry Manilow	#15
Is It You	Lee Ritenour w/Eric Tagg	#15
Just Once	Quincy Jones & James Ingram	#17
I Missed Again	Phil Collins	#19
Time Out Of Mind	Steely Dan	#22
Heartbreak Hotel	The Jacksons	#22
It's A Love Thing	The Whispers	#28
Ai No Corrida	Quincy Jones & James Ingram	#28
No Reply At All*	Genesis	#29
	*Earth, Wind, and Fire horn section	
General Hospi-Tale	The Afternoon Delights	#33
Never Too Much	Luther Vandross	#33
A Life Of Illusion*	Joe Walsh	#34
	*In the style of a mariachi band	
I Need Your Lovin'	Teena Marie	#37
Wrack My Brain*	Ringo Starr	#38
	*Tuba	

HORNS (excluding the saxophone) (cont'd)

Jones Vs. Jones	Kool & The Gang	#39
My Mother's Eyes	Bette Midler	#39
Who's Making Love	Blues Brothers	#39
Give It To Me Baby	Rick James	#40
Too Tight	Con Funk Shun	#40
Me (Without You)	Andy Gibb	#40
Backfired	Debbie Harry	#43
Lonely Together	Barry Manilow	#45
Square Biz	Teena Marie	#50
Yesterday Once More/Nothing Remains The Same	Spinners	#52
Silly	Deniece Williams	#53
What Cha' Gonna Do For Me	Chaka Khan	#53
Nothing Ever Goes As Planned	Styx	#54
Fly Away	Peter Allen	#55
One Day In Your Life	Michael Jackson	#55
Full Of Fire	Shalamar	#55
Glide	Pleasure	#55
Walking On Thin Ice	Yoko Ono	#58
And Love Goes On	Earth, Wind & Fire	#59
Memories	Tierra	#62
Bon Bon Vie (Gimme The Good Life)	T.S. Monk	#63
The Real Thing	The Brothers Johnson	#67
Michael Damian	She Did It	#69
Seduced*	Leon Redbone	#72
	*Tuba, trombone	
Walk Right Now	The Jacksons	#73
I Heard It Through The Grapevine (Part One)	Roger	#79
Magic Man	Herb Alpert	#79
8th Wonder	The Sugarhill Gang	#82
Let's Dance (Make Your Body Move)	West Street Mob	#88
Very Special	Debra Laws w/Ronnie Laws	#90
Sharing The Love	Rufus Feat. Chaka Khan	#91

1982		
Truly*	Lionel Richie	#1
	*French Horn	
Rosanna	Toto	#2
Freeze-Frame	J. Geils Band	#4
The Other Woman	Ray Parker Jr.	#4
Turn Your Love Around	George Benson	#5
Mirror, Mirror	Diana Ross	#8

HORNS (excluding the saxophone) (cont'd)

Leader Of The Band*	Dan Fogelberg	#9
	*Brass quintet	
Get Down On It	Kool & The Gang	#10
Take It Away	Paul McCartney	#10
Love Is In Control (Finger On The Trigger)	Donna Summer	#10
Bobbie Sue	The Oak Ridge Boys	#12
Do I Do	Stevie Wonder	#13
One Hundred Ways	Quincy Jones & James Ingram	#14
Find Another Fool	Quarterflash	#16
Somewhere Down The Road	Barry Manilow	#21
Big Fun	Kool & The Gang	#21
And I Am Telling You I'm Not Going	Jennifer Holliday	#22
My Guy	Sister Sledge	#23
Daddy's Home	Cliff Richard	#23
I.G.Y. (What A Beautiful World)	Donald Fagen	#26
If The Love Fits Wear It	Leslie Pearl	#28
Paperlate	Genesis	#32
Hope You Love Me Like You Say You Do	Huey Lewis & The News	#36
Island Of Lost Souls	Blondie	#37
Route 101	Herb Alpert	#37
Angel In Blue	J. Geils Band	#40
Shine On	George Duke	#41
Let The Feeling Flow	Peabo Bryson	#42
Breakin' Away	Al Jarreau	#43
Work That Body	Diana Ross	#44
A Night To Remember	Shalamar	#44
(You're So Square) Baby, I Don't Care	Joni Mitchell	#47
Wanna Be With You	Earth, Wind & Fire	#51
Never Give Up On A Good Thing	George Benson	#52
(Sittin' On) The Dock Of The Bay	The Reddings	#55
Tonight Tonight	Bill Champlin	#55
Street Corner	Ashford & Simpson	#56
The Gigolo	O'Bryan	#57
He Got You	Ronnie Milsap	#59
Cutie Pie	One Way	#61
Standing On The Top- Part 1	The Temptations w/ Rick James	#66
You Got The Power	War	#66
Nowhere To Run	Santana	#66
Cross My Heart	Lee Ritenour	#69
Happy Hour	Deodato	#70
Back To School Again	The Four Tops	#71
Right Away	Kansas	#73

HORNS (excluding the saxophone) (cont'd)

So Fine	The Oak Ridge Boys	#76
Fool For Your Love	Jimmy Hall	#77
Seasons Of The Heart	John Denver	#78
Fly Away	Stevie Woods	#84
Steppin' Out	Kool & The Gang	#89
Outlaw	War	#94
Never Thought I'd Fall In Love	The Spinners	#95

1983		
Say Say Say	Paul McCartney & Michael Jackson	#1
All Night Long (All Night)	Lionel Richie	#1
Islands In The Stream	Kenny Rogers & Dolly Parton	#1
Let's Dance	David Bowie	#1
Tell Her About It	Billy Joel	#1
She Works Hard For The Money	Donna Summer	#3
Union Of The Snake	Duran Duran	#3
You Are	Lionel Richie	#4
Wanna Be Startin' Somethin'	Michael Jackson	#5
Come Dancing	The Kinks	#6
Our House	Madness	#7
I'll Tumble 4 Ya	Culture Club	#9
Far From Over	Frank Stallone	#10
Goody Two Shoes	Adam Ant	#12
Fall In Love With Me	Earth, Wind & Fire	#17
All This Love	Debarge	#17
I Do	J. Geils Band	#24
Poison Arrow	ABC	#25
Let's Go Dancin' (Ooh La, La, La)	Kool & The Gang	#30
I Like It	Debarge	#31
You're Driving Me Out Of My Mind	Little River Band	#35
The Clapping Song	Pia Zadora	#36
Just Got Lucky	Joboxers	#36
Tied Up	Olivia Newton-John	#38
Memory	Barry Manilow	#39
So Close	Diana Ross	#40
Spice Of Life	Manhattan Transfer	#40
Put It In A Magazine	Sonny Charles	#40
The Way He Makes Me Feel	Barbra Streisand	#40
Take The Short Way Home	Dionne Warwick w/Barry Gibb	#41
Nice Girls	Melissa Manchester	#42
Swingin'	John Anderson	#43

HORNS (excluding the saxophone) (cont'd)

Allergies	Paul Simon	#44
High Time	Styx	#48
After I Cry	Lanier & Co.	#48
I Am Love	Jennifer Holliday	#49
Outstanding	The Gap Band	#51
Tip Of My Tongue	The Tubes	#52
What's New	Linda Ronstadt	#53
Stand By	Roman Holliday	#54
Only You	Commodores	#54
Take Another Picture	Quarterflash	#58
Always	Firefall	#59
Land Of A Thousand Dances	J. Geils Band	#60
Trouble In Paradise	Al Jarreau	#63
Forever	Little Steven	#63
Young Love	Janet Jackson	#64
Are You Getting Enough Happiness	Hot Chocolate	#65
Desperate But Not Serious	Adam Ant	#66
Funny How Time Slips Away	Spinners	#67
The Monkey Time	The Tubes	#68
Don't Try To Stop It	Roman Holliday	#68
Ship To Shore	Chris DeBurgh	#71
Don't Make Me Do It	Patrick Simmons	#75
Side By Side	Earth, Wind & Fire	#76
Boogie Down	Al Jarreau	#77
Red Hot	Herb Alpert	#77
The Devil Made Me Do It	Golden Earring	#79
I Cannot Believe It's True	Phil Collins	#79
What You're Missing	Chicago	#81
Take The Time	Michael Stanley Band	#81
Garden Party	Herb Alpert	#81
Johnny B. Goode	Peter Tosh	#84
Maybe This Day	Kissing The Pink	#87

1984		
Wake Me Up Before You Go-Go	Wham!	#1
Joanna	Kool & The Gang	#2
Hard Habit To Break	Chicago	#3
Thriller	Michael Jackson	#4
Infatuation	Rod Stewart	#6
Strut	Sheena Easton	#7
Lights Out	Peter Wolf	#12
It's A Miracle	Culture Club	#13

HORNS (excluding the saxophone) (cont'd)

The Curly Shuffle	Jump 'N The Saddle	#15
You Can't Get What You Want (Till You Know What You Want)	Joe Jackson	#15
Give It Up	KC	#18
Centipede	Rebbie Jackson	#24
Right By Your Side	Eurythmics	#29
My Ever Changing Moods	The Style Council	#29
Holding Out For A Hero	Bonnie Tyler	#34
Shine Shine	Barry Gibb	#37
Love Of The Common People	Paul Young	#45
Wouldn't It Be Good	Nik Kershaw	#46
In The Name Of Love	Ralph Macdonald w/ Bill Withers	#58
Blue Light	David Gilmour	#62
Hyperactive	Thomas Dolby	#62
Black Stations/White Stations	M+M	#63
Vitamin L	B.E. Taylor Group	#66
Cleanin' Up The Town	The Bus Boys	#68
Look At That Cadillac	Stray Cats	#68
The Sun And The Rain	Madness	#72
Someone Like You	Michael Stanley Band	#75
Downtown	Dolly Parton	#80
Darlin'	Frank Stallone	#81
Simple	Johnny Mathis	#81
The Real End	Rickie Lee Jones	#83
Bullish	Herb Alpert Tijuana Brass	#90

1985		
Sussudio	Phil Collins	#1
St. Elmo's Fire (Man In Motion)	John Parr	#1
Things Can Only Get Better	Howard Jones	#5
Would I Lie To You?	Eurythmics	#5
Some Like It Hot	Power Station	#6
Dancing In The Street	Mick Jagger/ David Bowie	#7
Fortress Around Your Heart	Sting	#8
Walking On Sunshine	Katrina & The Waves	#9
You're Only Human (Second Wind)	Billy Joel	#9
Just A Gigolo/ I Ain't Got Nobody	David Lee Roth	#12
Solid	Ashford & Simpson	#12
Along Comes A Woman	Chicago	#14
Love Is The Seventh Wave	Sting	#17
Keeping The Faith	Billy Joel	#18
Emergency	Kool & The Gang	#18

HORNS (excluding the saxophone) (cont'd)

A Nite At The Apollo Live! The Way You Do The Things You Do/ My Girl	Daryl Hall & John Oates w/ David Ruffin & Eddie Kendrick	#20
Wrap Her Up	Elton John	#20
Say You're Wrong	Julian Lennon	#21
Rockin' At Midnight	The Honeydrippers	#25
Tenderness	General Public	#27
I Got You Babe	UB40 w/ Chrissie Hynde	#28
Cannonball	Supertramp	#28
Second Nature	Dan Hartman	#39
Weird Science	Oingo Boingo	#45
Walking On The Chinese Wall	Phillip Bailey	#46
Born In East L.A.	Cheech & Chong	#48
Make It Better (Forget About Me)	Tom Petty And The Heartbreakers	#54
Your Love Is King	Sade	#54
All Fall Down	Five Star	#65
Holyanna	Toto	#71
All Right Now	Rod Stewart	#72
Rebels	Tom Petty And The Heartbreakers	#74
Mathematics	Melissa Manchester	#74
Frankie	Sister Sledge	#75
It's Gettin' Late	The Beach Boys	#82
Discipline Of Love (Why Did You Do It)	Robert Palmer	#82
Bong Bongo	Steve Miller Band	#84

1986		
Higher Love	Steve Winwood	#1
Holding Back The Years	Simply Red	#1
West End Girls	Pet Shop Boys	#1
Sledgehammer	Peter Gabriel	#1
Don't Forget Me (When I'm Gone)	Glass Tiger	#2
Everybody Have Fun Tonight	Wang Chung	#2
I Can't Wait	Nu Shooz	#3
Hip To Be Square	Huey Lewis & The News	#3
Living In America	James Brown	#4
The Sweetest Taboo	Sade	#5
We Don't Have To Take Our Clothes Off	Jermaine Stewart	#5
Word Up	Cameo	#6
Sweet Freedom	Michael McDonald	#7
Sweet Love	Anita Baker	#8
Bad Boy	Miami Sound Machine	#8
Go Home	Stevie Wonder	#10
The Edge Of Heaven	Wham!	#10
Conga	Miami Sound Machine	#10

HORNS (excluding the saxophone) (cont'd)

Man Size Love	Klymaxx	#15
I Think It's Love	Jermaine Jackson	#16
You Know I Love You… Don't You?	Howard Jones	#17
Freedom Overspill	Steve Winwood	#20
Mountains	Prince	#23
Face The Face	Pete Townshend	#26
You Be Illin'	Run-D.M.C.	#29
You Can Call Me Al	Paul Simon	#44
25 Or 6 To 4	Chicago	#48
Ruthless People	Mick Jagger	#51
Absolute Beginners	David Bowie	#53
Anotherloverholenyohead	Prince	#63
Jimmy Mack	Sheena Easton	#65
Rock 'N' Roll To The Rescue	The Beach Boys	#68
Is That It?	Katrina & The Waves	#70
Say It, Say It	E.G. Daily	#70
Johnny Come Home*	Fine Young Cannibals	#76
	*Muted trumpet	
It's Alright (Baby's Coming Back)	Eurythmics	#78
Daydream Believer	The Monkees	#79
That's Life	David Lee Roth	#85
No Frills Love	Jennifer Holliday	#87
Hot Water	Level 42	#87
Vanity Kills	ABC	#91
Gravity	James Brown	#93

1987		
Who's That Girl	Madonna	#1
Bad	Michael Jackson	#1
Notorious	Duran Duran	#2
Respect Yourself	Bruce Willis	#5
Diamonds	Herb Alpert w/ Janet Jackson	#5
Rhythm Is Gonna Get You	Gloria Estefan/Miami Sound Machine	#5
Doing It All For My Baby	Huey Lewis & The News	#6
Breakout	Swing Out Sister	#6
What's Going On	Cyndi Lauper	#12
Dude (Looks Like A Lady)	Aerosmith	#14
Hourglass	Squeeze	#15
If She Would Have Been Faithful	Chicago	#17
Serious	Donna Allen	#21
Lies	Jonathan Butler	#27

HORNS (excluding the saxophone) (cont'd)

The Right Thing	Simply Red	#27
Jimmy Lee	Aretha Franklin	#28
Holiday	The Other Ones	#29
Making Love In The Rain	Herb Alpert w/ Lisa Keith	#35
Betcha Say That	Gloria Estefan/Miami Sound Machine	#36
Skin Trade	Duran Duran	#39
Don't Leave Me This Way	Communards	#40
No One In The World	Anita Baker	#44
Keep Your Eye On Me	Herb Alpert	#46
Brass Monkey	Beastie Boys	#48
System Of Survival	Earth, Wind & Fire	#60
If I Was Your Girlfriend	Prince	#67
Young Blood	Bruce Willis	#68
If You Let Me Stay	Terence Trent D'Arby	#68
Meet El Presidente	Duran Duran	#70
Stand Back	The Fabulous Thunderbirds	#76
What's Too Much	Smokey Robinson	#79
He's My Girl	David Hallyday	#79
Let's Dance	Chris Rea	#81
Montego Bay	Amazulu	#90
Niagara Falls	Chicago	#91
Hold Me	Colin James Hay	#99

1988		
The Way You Make Me Feel	Michael Jackson	#1
Wild, Wild West	The Escape Club	#1
Got My Mind Set On You	George Harrison	#1
Get Outta My Dreams, Get Into My Car	Billy Ocean	#1
Roll With It	Steve Winwood	#1
Perfect World	Huey Lewis & The News	#3
I Don't Want Your Love	Duran Duran	#4
Kissing A Fool	George Michael	#5
One Moment In Time	Whitney Houston	#5
Pink Cadillac	Natalie Cole	#5
Alphabet St.	Prince	#8
It Would Take A Strong Strong Man	Rick Astley	#10
(Sittin' On) The Dock Of The Bay	Michael Bolton	#11
Parents Just Don't Understand	D.J. Jazzy Jeff and the Fresh Prince	#12
True Love	Glenn Frey	#13
Spy In The House Of Love	Was (Not Was)	#16
Rag Doll	Aerosmith	#17

HORNS (excluding the saxophone) (cont'd)

Beds Are Burning	Midnight Oil	#17
Rock Of Life	Rick Springfield	#22
Pamela	Toto	#22
Small World	Huey Lewis & The News	#25
Say It Again	Jermaine Stewart	#27
Dance Little Sister (Part One)	Terence Trent D'Arby	#30
Twilight World	Swing Out Sister	#31
Going Back To Cali	L.L. Cool J	#31
Yeah, Yeah, Yeah	Judson Spence	#32
Hot Hot Hot	Buster Poindexter	#45
Never Can Say Goodbye	The Communards	#51
The Dead Heart	Midnight Oil	#53
Jackie	Blue Zone U.K.	#54
Most Of All	Jody Watley	#60
I Can't Wait	Deniece Williams	#66
Thinking Of You	Earth, Wind & Fire	#67
Dancing Under A Latin Moon	Candi	#68
Don't Walk Away	Toni Childs	#72
Don't Be Afraid Of The Dark	Robert Cray Band	#74
Joy	Teddy Pendergrass	#77
Wait On Love	Michael Bolton	#79
Century's End	Donald Fagen	#83
You Make Me Work	Cameo	#85
Got A New Love	Good Question	#86
(It's Just) The Way That You Love Me	Paula Abdul	#88
Hey Mambo	Barry Manilow w/ Kid Creole	#90
Sweet Lies	Robert Palmer	#94
Fat	"Weird Al" Yankovic	#99

1989		
Love Shack	The B-52s	#3
Heaven Help Me	Deon Estus & George Michael	#5
With Every Beat Of My Heart	Taylor Dayne	#5
Walk The Dinosaur	Was (Not Was)	#7
Smooth Criminal	Michael Jackson	#7
What You Don't Know	Expose	#8
Get On Your Feet	Gloria Estefan	#11
Holding On	Steve Winwood	#11
Angel Of Harlem	U2	#14
Rock And A Hard Place	The Rolling Stones	#23
Kiss	Art Of Noise/Tom Jones	#31
Giving Up On Love	Rick Astley	#38

HORNS (excluding the saxophone) (cont'd)

The Way To Your Heart	Soulsister	#41
Give Me The Keys (And I'll Drive You Crazy)	Huey Lewis & The News	#47
Talk To Myself	Christopher Williams	#49
Tribute (Right On)	The Pasadenas	#52
Pretending	Eric Clapton w/ Chaka Khan	#55
We Can Last Forever	Chicago	#55
It's Only Love	Simply Red	#57
We Could Be Together	Debbie Gibson	#71
Darlin, I	Vanessa Williams	#88
Livin' Right	Glenn Frey	#90
My One Temptation	Micah Paris	#97

JINGLE BELLS

SONG	ARTIST	HOT 100 CHART
1983		
Total Eclipse Of The Heart	Bonnie Tyler	#1

1986		
I Feel The Magic	Belinda Carlisle	#82

1988		
Hazy Shade Of Winter	Bangles	#2

KEYBOARDS

This section lists songs that feature keyboard instruments (with the exception of the piano and organ, both of which get their own section). So here you'll find songs that feature the synthesizer and electric piano.

I debated whether or not to even include this list. I mean, a list of songs from the 80s that use the synthesizer? Wouldn't that be every single song? Well, not quite, but at times it sure felt like it. At 1562 songs, it is by far the longest instrument list in this book.

Cover bands with a talented keyboardist, or someone who simply enjoys the musical textures a synthesizer can add to a song may enjoy perusing this list.

SONG	ARTIST	HOT 100 CHART
1980		
Funkytown	Lipps, Inc.	#1
Rock With You	Michael Jackson	#1
Ride Like The Wind	Christopher Cross	#2
The Wanderer	Donna Summer	#3
He's So Shy	The Pointer Sisters	#3
Little Jeannie	Elton John	#3
Fame	Irene Cara	#4
Too Hot	Kool & The Gang	#5
Stomp!	The Brothers Johnson	#7
Let My Love Open The Door	Pete Townshend	#9
Cars	Gary Numan	#9
Off The Wall	Michael Jackson	#10
More Love	Kim Carnes	#10
She's Out Of My Life	Michael Jackson	#10
Into The Night	Benny Mardones	#11
I Wanna Be Your Lover	Prince	#11
You've Lost That Lovin' Feelin'	Daryl Hall & John Oates	#12
Whip It	Devo	#14
Dreamer	Supertramp	#15
Never Be The Same	Christopher Cross	#15
Breakdown Dead Ahead	Boz Scaggs	#15
Déjà Vu	Dionne Warwick	#15
Ali Thompson	Take A Little Rhythm	#15
I'm Alive	Electric Light Orchestra	#16
Wait For Me	Daryl Hall & John Oates	#18
Everybody's Got To Learn Sometime	The Korgis	#18
And The Beat Goes On	The Whispers	#19
Without Your Love	Roger Daltrey	#20
That Girl Could Sing	Jackson Browne	#22

KEYBOARDS (cont'd)

Stand By Me	Mickey Gilley	#22
How Do I Survive	Amy Holland	#22
99	Toto	#26
Why Me	Styx	#26
I'm Happy That Love Has Found You	Jimmy Hall	#27
The Seduction (Love Theme)	James Last Band	#28
Do You Love What You Feel	Rufus & Chaka	#30
Rotation	Herb Alpert	#30
Come Back	J. Geils Band	#32
Back On My Feet Again	The Babys	#33
Savannah Nights	Tom Johnston	#34
I'm Almost Ready	Pure Prairie League	#34
You Know That I Love You	Santana	#35
Sometimes A Fantasy	Billy Joel	#36
Touch And Go	The Cars	#37
Love Stinks	J. Geils Band	#38
Atomic	Blondie	#39
Last Train To London	Electric Light Orchestra	#39
Clones (We're All)	Alice Cooper	#40
One-Trick Pony	Paul Simon	#40
Red Light	Linda Clifford	#41
Live Every Minute	Ali Thomson	#42
Haven't You Heard	Patrice Rushen	#42
Turn And Walk Away	The Babys	#42
Switchin' To Glide	The Kings	#43
When The Feeling Comes Around	Jennifer Warnes	#45
Bad Times	Tavares	#47
Gotta Have More Love	Climax Blues Band	#47
My Prayer	Ray, Goodman & Brown	#47
You Are My Heaven	Roberta Flack & Donny Hathaway	#47
Games Without Frontiers	Peter Gabriel	#48
Red Rider	White Hot	#48
Beyond	Herb Alpert	#50
Outside My Window	Stevie Wonder	#52
I Got You	Split Enz	#53
Happy Together (A Fantasy)	Captain & Tennille	#53
You Might Need Somebody	Turley Richards	#54
I Hear You Now	Jon & Vangelis	#58
Honey, Honey	David Hudson	#59
Computer Game "Theme From The Circus"	Yellow Magic Orchestra	#60
I'm Alive	Gamma	#60
Today Is The Day	Bar-Kays	#60

KEYBOARDS (cont'd)

Love X Love	George Benson	#61
Rock It	Lipps, Inc.	#64
Borrowed Time	Styx	#64
(Call Me) When The Spirit Moves You	Touch	#65
Morning Man	Rupert Holmes	#68
Catching The Sun	Spyro Gyra	#68
Sherry	Robert John	#70
High On Your Love	Debbie Jacobs	#70
If I Were You	Toby Beau	#70
A Little Is Enough	Pete Townshend	#72
Treasure	The Brothers Johnson	#73
Shooting Star	Dollar	#74
Holdin' On For Dear Love	Lobo	#75
In It For Love	England Dan & John Ford Coley	#75
You've Got What I Need	Shooting Star	#76
Love And Loneliness	The Motors	#78
Just Can't Wait	J. Geils Band	#78
Cry Just A Little	Paul Davis	#78
Real Love	The Cretones	#79
Over You	Roxy Music	#80
Merry Christmas In The NFL	Willis "The Guard" & Vigorish	#82
Just For The Moment	Ray Kennedy	#82
I Call Your Name	Switch	#83
Blondie	The Hardest Part	#84
More Bounce To The Ounce (Part 1)	Zapp	#86
I've Just Begun To Love You	Dynasty	#87
Gypsy Spirit	Pendulum	#89
Remote Control	The Reddings	#89
Only The Lonely (Have A Reason To Be Sad)	La Flavour	#91

1981		
Bette Davis Eyes	Kim Carnes	#1
Kiss On My List	Daryl Hall & John Oates	#1
Slow Hand	The Pointer Sisters	#2
Just The Two Of Us	Grover Washington Jr. w/Bill Withers	#2
Waiting For A Girl Like You	Foreigner	#2
All Those Years Ago	George Harrison	#2
Theme From Greatest American Hero (Believe It Or Not)	Joey Scarbury	#2
Being With You	Smokey Robinson	#2
Guilty	Barbra Streisand And Barry Gibb	#3

KEYBOARDS (cont'd)

The Best Of Times	Styx	#3
Every Little Thing She Does Is Magic	The Police	#3
A Woman Needs Love (Just Like You Do)	Ray Parker Jr. & Raydio	#4
You Make My Dreams	Daryl Hall & John Oates	#5
Young Turks	Rod Stewart	#5
The Night Owls	Little River Band	#6
While You See A Chance	Steve Winwood	#7
Too Much Time On My Hands	Styx	#9
Sweetheart	Franke And The Knockouts	#10
I Can't Stand It	Eric Clapton	#10
What Kind Of Fool	Barbra Streisand And Barry Gibb	#10
Hey Nineteen	Steely Dan	#10
I Ain't Gonna Stand For It	Stevie Wonder	#11
Her Town Too	James Taylor & J.D. Souther	#11
Gemini Dream	The Moody Blues	#12
The Voice	The Moody Blues	#15
We're In This Love Together	Al Jarreau	#15
Games People Play	Alan Parsons Project	#16
Really Wanna Know You	Gary Wright	#16
Just Once	Quincy Jones & James Ingram	#17
Winning	Santana	#17
Modern Girl	Sheena Easton	#18
In The Air Tonight	Phil Collins	#19
Don't Stop The Music	Yarbrough & Peoples	#19
Suddenly	Olivia Newton-John & Cliff Richard	#21
That Old Song	Ray Parker Jr. & Raydio	#21
Nobody Wins	Elton John	#21
Heartbreak Hotel	The Jacksons	#22
Ai No Corrida	Quincy Jones & James Ingram	#28
It's A Love Thing	The Whispers	#28
No Reply At All	Genesis	#29
Find Your Way Back	Jefferson Starship	#29
Alien	Atlanta Rhythm Section	#29
Stronger Than Before	Carole Bayer Sager	#30
He's A Liar	Bee Gees	#30
Poor Man's Son	Survivor	#33
In The Dark	Billy Squier	#35
Don't Want To Wait Anymore	The Tubes	#35
Turn Me Loose	Loverboy	#35
Mister Sandman	Emmylou Harris	#37

KEYBOARDS (cont'd)

I Want You, I Need You	Chris Christian	#37
Twilight	Electric Light Orchestra	#38
Just So Lonely	Get Wet	#39
Straight From The Heart	Allman Brothers Band	#39
Who Do You Think You're Foolin'	Donna Summer	#40
Me (Without You)	Andy Gibb	#40
She's In Love With You	Suzi Quatro	#41
Working In The Coal Mine	Devo	#43
Tom Sawyer	Rush	#44
Games	Phoebe Snow	#46
Love All The Hurt Away	Aretha Franklin & George Benson	#46
Games	Phoebe Snow	#46
Arc Of A Diver	Steve Winwood	#48
Promises	Barbra Streisand	#48
When She Dances	Joey Scarbury	#49
Silly	Deniece Williams	#53
What Cha' Gonna Do For Me	Chaka Khan	#53
Ch Ch Cherie	Johnny Average Band	#53
Fly Away	Peter Allen	#55
Fantastic Voyage	Lakeside	#55
The Kid Is Hot Tonite	Loverboy	#55
Glide	Pleasure	#55
I Don't Need You	Rupert Holmes	#56
You Are Forever	Smokey Robinson	#59
Mistaken Identity	Kim Carnes	#60
I'm Just Too Shy	Jermaine Jackson	#60
Make That Move	Shalamar	#60
Yearning For Your Love	The Gap Band	#60
I Have The Skill	The Sherbs	#61
What She Does To Me (The Diana Song)	The Producers	#61
We Can Get Together	Icehouse	#62
Talking Out Of Turn	The Moody Blues	#65
WKRP In Cincinnati	Steve Carlisle	#65
I Don't Want To Know Your Name	Glen Campbell	#65
Dreamer	The Association	#66
Aiming At Your Heart	The Temptations	#67
Just Be My Lady	Larry Graham	#67
You're Mine Tonight	Pure Prairie League	#68
Don't You Know What Love Is	Touch	#69
That Didn't Hurt Too Bad	Dr. Hook	#69
Controversy	Prince	#70
I Surrender	Arlan Day	#71

KEYBOARDS (cont'd)

Want You Back In My Life Again	Carpenters	#72
It Hurts To Be In Love	Dan Hartman	#72
Walk Right Now	The Jacksons	#73
Not Fade Away	Eric Hine	#73
House Of The Rising Sun	Dolly Parton	#77
All American Girls	Sister Sledge	#79
Don't Want No-Body	J.D. Drews	#79
Love Light	Yutaka w/Patti Austin	#81
Toccata	Sky	#83
Come To Me	Aretha Franklin	#84
Burn Rubber (Why You Wanna Hurt Me)	The Gap Band	#84
Where's Your Angel	Lani Hall	#88
Snap Shot	Slave	#91
Once A Night	Jackie English	#94

1982		
Ebony And Ivory	Paul McCartney & Stevie Wonder	#1
Don't You Want Me	The Human League	#1
Abracadabra	Steve Miller Band	#1
I Can't Go For That (No Can Do)	Daryl Hall & John Oates	#1
Chariots Of Fire- Titles	Vangelis	#1
Rosanna	Toto	#2
Gloria	Laura Branigan	#2
Axel F	Harold Faltermeyer	#3
I Keep Forgettin' (Every Time You're Near)	Michael McDonald	#4
Shake It Up	The Cars	#4
Make A Move On Me	Olivia Newton-John	#5
You Should Hear How She Talks About You	Melissa Manchester	#5
Heartlight	Neil Diamond	#5
Let It Whip	Dazz Band	#5
Leather And Lace	Stevie Nicks w/ Don Henley	#6
Steppin' Out	Joe Jackson	#6
65 Love Affair	Paul Davis	#6
Love's Been A Little Bit Hard On Me	Juice Newton	#7
Tainted Love	Soft Cell	#8
Only The Lonely	The Motels	#9
Did It In A Minute	Daryl Hall & John Oates	#9
I Ran (So Far Away)	A Flock Of Seagulls	#9
Get Down On It	Kool & The Gang	#10
Muscles	Diana Ross	#10
It's Gonna Take A Miracle	Deniece Williams	#10
It's Raining Again	Supertramp	#11

KEYBOARDS (cont'd)

Break It To Me Gently	Juice Newton	#11
Making Love	Roberta Flack	#13
Shadows Of The Night	Pat Benatar	#13
Making Love	Roberta Flack	#13
Empty Garden (Hey Hey Johnny)	Elton John	#13
One Hundred Ways	Quincy Jones & James Ingram	#14
Nobody	Sylvia	#15
The One You Love	Glenn Frey	#15
American Music	The Pointer Sisters	#16
You Don't Want Me Anymore	Steel Breeze	#16
American Heartbeat	Survivor	#17
Love Come Down	Evelyn King	#17
Let Me Tickle Your Fancy	Jermaine Jackson	#18
Tonight I'm Yours (Don't Hurt Me)	Rod Stewart	#20
Pressure	Billy Joel	#20
Love Me Tomorrow	Chicago	#22
Hot In The City	Billy Idol	#23
Forget Me Nots	Patrice Rushen	#23
Fantasy	Aldo Nova	#23
Daddy's Home	Cliff Richard	#23
Early In The Morning	The Gap Band	#24
Jump To It	Aretha Franklin	#24
Kids In America	Kim Wilde	#25
Baby Makes Her Blue Jeans Talk	Dr. Hook	#25
(Theme From) Magnum P.I.	Mike Post	#25
Abacab	Genesis	#26
When It's Over	Loverboy	#26
Break It Up	Foreigner	#26
When All Is Said And Done	Abba	#27
Never Been In Love	Randy Meisner	#28
All Our Tomorrows	Eddie Schwartz	#28
Voyeur	Kim Carnes	#29
Working For The Weekend	Loverboy	#29
When He Shines	Sheena Easton	#30
Mama Used To Say	Junior	#30
You Dropped A Bomb On Me	The Gap Band	#31
John Denver	Shanghai Breezes	#31
The Woman In Me	Donna Summer	#33
A Penny For Your Thoughts	Tavares	#33
Your Imagination	Daryl Hall & John Oates	#33
If I Had My Wish Tonight	David Lasley	#36

KEYBOARDS (cont'd)

Nice Girls	Eye To Eye	#37
Route 101	Herb Alpert	#37
Holdin' On	Tane Cain	#37
Just Can't Win 'Em All	Stevie Woods	#38
Let Me Go	Ray Parker Jr.	#38
Circles	Atlantic Starr	#38
Murphy's Law	Cheri	#39
Man On The Corner	Genesis	#40
Let It Be Me	Willie Nelson	#40
State Of Independence	Donna Summer	#41
Since You're Gone	The Cars	#41
Words	Missing Persons	#42
I'm The One	Roberta Flack	#42
Johnny Can't Read	Don Henley	#42
Destination Unknown	Missing Persons	#42
Breakin' Away	Al Jarreau	#43
You're My Latest, My Greatest Inspiration	Teddy Pendergrass	#43
I Gotta Try	Michael McDonald	#44
If I Were You	Lulu	#44
A Night To Remember	Shalamar	#44
1999	Prince	#44
Secret Journey	Police	#46
Used To Be	Charlene & Stevie Wonder	#46
Still In The Game	Steve Winwood	#47
If It Ain't One Thing… It's Another	Richard "Dimples" Fields	#47
Planet Rock	Afrika Bambaataa	#48
On A Carousel	Glass Moon	#50
Wanna Be With You	Earth, Wind & Fire	#51
I'll Find My Way Home	Jon & Vangelis	#51
Wake Up My Love	George Harrison	#53
Apache	The Sugarhill Gang	#53
Bad Boy/ Having A Party	Luther Vandross	#55
Street Corner	Ashford & Simpson	#56
Machinery	Sheena Easton	#57
The Gigolo	O'Bryan	#57
Psychobabble	Alan Parsons Project	#57
Hot Fun In The Summertime	Dayton	#58
Right Here And Now	Bill Medley	#58
What Do All The People Know	The Monroes	#59
Forever Mine	The Motels	#60
Night Shift	Quarterflash	#60
Cutie Pie	One Way	#61

KEYBOARDS (cont'd)

The Message	Grand Master Flash	#62
Every Home Should Have One	Pattie Austin	#62
Please Be The One	Karla Bonoff	#63
Don't Let Me In	Sneaker	#63
The Visitors	Abba	#63
Now Or Never	Axe	#64
The Only Way Out	Cliff Richard	#64
Dance Wit' Me - Part 1	Rick James	#64
Foolin' Yourself	Aldo Nova	#65
Goodbye To You	Scandal	#65
Standing On The Top- Part 1	The Temptations w/ Rick James	#66
Nowhere To Run	Santana	#66
She Looks A Lot Like You	Clocks	#67
All Night With Me	Laura Branigan	#69
Valerie	Steve Winwood	#70
Happy Hour	Deodato	#70
Attack Of The Name Game	Stacy Lattisaw	#70
Put Away Your Love	Alessi	#71
How Can I Live Without Her	Christopher Atkins	#71
It's My Party	Dave Stewart & Barbara Gaskin	#72
Situation	Yaz	#73
Right Away	Kansas	#73
Sleepwalk	Larry Carlton	#74
Why	Carly Simon	#74
He Could Be The One	Josie Cotton	#74
Talk Talk	Talk Talk	#75
You Can	Madleen Kane	#77
Right The First Time	Gamma	#77
The Last Safe Place On Earth	Le Roux	#77
All Of My Love	Bobby Caldwell	#77
Opposites Do Attract	All Sports Band	#78
This Time	Kiara w/Shanice Wilson	#78
Soup For One	Chic	#80
Younger Days	Joe Fagin	#80
Don't Run My Life	Spys	#82
Don't Stop Trying	Rodway	#83
Loving You	Chris Rea	#88
Ain't Nothing Like The Real Thing/ You're All I Need To Get By	Chris Christian w/ Amy Holland	#88
Cool (Part 1)	The Time	#90
Be Mine (Tonight)	Grover Washington, Jr. (Grady Tate)	#92

KEYBOARDS (cont'd)

1983		
Billie Jean	Michael Jackson	#1
Flashdance… What A Feeling	Irene Cara	#1
Total Eclipse Of The Heart	Bonnie Tyler	#1
Maniac	Michael Sembello	#1
Sweet Dreams (Are Made Of This)	Eurythmics	#1
Africa	Toto	#1
Say It Isn't So	Daryl Hall & John Oates	#2
The Girl Is Mine	Michael Jackson & Paul McCartney	#2
The Safety Dance	Men Without Hats	#3
She Works Hard For The Money	Donna Summer	#3
Union Of The Snake	Duran Duran	#3
Mr. Roboto	Styx	#3
True	Spandau Ballet	#4
Puttin' On The Ritz	Taco	#4
She Blinded Me With Science	Thomas Dolby	#5
Wanna Be Startin' Somethin'	Michael Jackson	#5
Der Kommissar	After The Fire	#5
Stand Back	Stevie Nicks	#5
Too Shy	Kajagoogoo	#5
Little Red Corvette	Prince	#6
Don't Let It End	Styx	#6
Human Nature	Michael Jackson	#7
Solitaire	Laura Branigan	#7
(Keep Feeling) Fascination	The Human League	#8
Delirious	Prince	#8
Separate Ways (Worlds Apart)	Journey	#8
Burning Down The House	Talking Heads	#9
Affair Of The Heart	Rick Springfield	#9
Telefone (Long Distance Love Affair)	Sheena Easton	#9
P.Y.T. (Pretty Young Thing)	Michael Jackson	#10
China Girl	David Bowie	#10
Hot Girls In Love	Loverboy	#11
Promises, Promises	Naked Eyes	#11
Your Love Is Driving Me Crazy	Sammy Hagar	#13
Why Me?	Irene Cara	#13
I Know There's Something Going On	Frida	#13
If Anyone Falls	Stevie Nicks	#14
Rio	Duran Duran	#14
Heart To Heart	Kenny Loggins	#15
Tonight, I Celebrate My Love	Peabo Bryson/ Roberta Flack	#16
Fall In Love With Me	Earth, Wind & Fire	#17

KEYBOARDS (cont'd)

All This Love	Debarge	#17
The Look Of Love (Part One)	ABC	#18
Big Log	Robert Plant	#20
You Got Lucky	Tom Petty And The Heartbreakers	#20
Mornin'	Al Jarreau	#21
Dead Giveaway	Shalamar	#22
Ain't Nobody	Rufus/Chaka Khan	#22
Love Is A Stranger	Eurythmics	#23
Stranger In My House	Ronnie Milsap	#23
Send Her My Love	Journey	#23
Don't You Get So Mad	Jeffrey Osborne	#25
It Might Be You	Stephen Bishop	#25
Poison Arrow	ABC	#25
Wishing (If I Had A Photograph Of You)	A Flock Of Seagulls	#26
Some Kind Of Friend	Barry Manilow	#26
On The Loose	Saga	#26
Tell Her No	Juice Newton	#27
Whirly Girl	Oxo	#28
That's Love	Jim Capaldi	#28
Mirror Man	The Human League	#30
Lady Love Me (One More Time)	George Benson	#30
Lies	Thompson	#30
I Like It	Debarge	#31
No Time For Talk	Christopher Cross	#33
Automatic Man	Michael Sembello	#34
Queen Of The Broken Hearts	Loverboy	#34
Don't Pay The Ferryman	Chris DeBurgh	#34
The Smile Has Left Your Eyes	Asia	#34
I'm Alive	Neil Diamond	#35
Bad Boy	Ray Parker Jr.	#35
Everyday I Write The Book	Elvis Costello	#36
When The Lights Go Out	Naked Eyes	#37
Looking For A Stranger	Pat Benatar	#39
I Don't Care Anymore	Phil Collins	#39
Spice Of Life	Manhattan Transfer	#40
Invisible Hands	Kim Carnes	#40
The Way He Makes Me Feel	Barbra Streisand	#40
Don't Tell Me You Love Me	Night Ranger	#40
Nice Girls	Melissa Manchester	#42
Unconditional Love	Donna Summer w/Musical Youth	#43
Allergies	Paul Simon	#44

KEYBOARDS (cont'd)

Love My Way	The Psychedelic Furs	#44
Love On Your Side	Thompson Twins	#45
War Games	Crosby, Stills & Nash	#45
Juicy Fruit	Mtume	#45
Right Before Your Eyes	America	#45
Candy Girl	New Edition	#46
Midnight Blue	Louise Tucker w/Charlie Skarbek	#46
It's Raining Men	The Weather Girls	#46
The Night	The Animals	#48
Cool Places	Sparks & Jane Wiedlin	#49
Smiling Islands	Robbie Patton	#52
Easy For You To Say	Linda Ronstadt	#54
You Don't Believe	Alan Parsons Project	#54
Papa Was A Rollin' Stone	Wolf	#55
Magnetic	Earth, Wind & Fire	#57
Take Another Picture	Quarterflash	#58
Don't You Know How Much I Love You	Ronnie Milsap	#58
All Touch	Rough Trade	#58
Escalator Of Life	Robert Hazard	#58
The Metro	Berlin	#58
Theme From Doctor Detroit	Devo	#59
Give It Up	Steve Miller Band	#60
Bad Boys	Wham!	#60
Street Of Dreams	Rainbow	#60
When I'm With You	Sheriff	#61
This Must Be The Place (Naïve Melody)	Talking Heads	#62
Words	F.R. David	#62
Blue World	The Moody Blues	#62
Sex (I'm A…)	Berlin	#62
Trouble In Paradise	Al Jarreau	#63
What Love Is	Marty Balin	#63
Do You Compute?	Donnie Iris	#64
Wind Him Up	Saga	#64
Young Love	Janet Jackson	#64
You Are In My System	The System	#64
Front Page Story	Neil Diamond	#65
Freak-A-Zoid	Midnight Star	#66
I Eat Cannibals	Total Coelo	#66
Europa And The Pirate Twins	Thomas Dolby	#67
If You Wanna Get Back Your Lady	The Pointer Sisters	#67
Got To Be There	Chaka Khan	#67
Only You	Yaz	#67

KEYBOARDS (cont'd)

Eminence Front	The Who	#68
Don't Girls Get Lonely	Glenn Shorrock	#69
Wherever I Lay My Hat (That's My Home)	Paul Young	#70
Reap The Wild Wind	Ultravox	#71
Rockit	Herbie Hancock	#71
Crazy	Manhattans	#72
Voo Doo	Rachel Sweet	#72
Waiting For Your Love	Toto	#73
Change	Tears For Fears	#73
Mama	Genesis	#73
The Walls Came Down	The Call	#74
Let Me Go	Heaven 17	#74
Living On The Edge	Jim Capaldi	#75
Yo No Se'	Pajama Party	#75
Anything Can Happen	Was (Not Was)	#75
Serious Kinda Girl	Christopher Max	#75
Owwww!	Chunky A	#77
Boogie Down	Al Jarreau	#77
No One Can Love You More Than Me	Melissa Manchester	#78
You Are In My System	Robert Palmer	#78
I Melt With You	Modern English	#78
You Belong To Me	The Doobie Brothers	#79
Beg, Borrow Or Steal	Hughes/Thrall	#79
Don't Change	INXS	#80
Love Is The Key	Maze Feat. Frankie Beverly	#80
Legal Tender	The B-52s	#81
Carrie's Gone	Le Roux	#81
State Of The Nation	Industry	#81
Garden Party	Herb Alpert	#81
Masquerade	Berlin	#82
Should I Love You	Cee Farrow	#82
Fools Game	Michael Bolton	#82
Please Mr. Postman	Gentle Persuasion	#82
He's A Pretender	High Inergy	#82
You Know What To Do	Carly Simon	#83
Where Everybody Knows Your Name (The Theme From "Cheers")	Gary Portnoy	#83
I Like	Men Without Hats	#84
Solsbury Hill	Peter Gabriel	#84
Tonight	The Whispers	#84
The Sound Of Goodbye	Crystal Gayle	#84
Memphis	Joe Jackson	#85

KEYBOARDS (cont'd)

All The Right Moves	Jennifer Warnes/ Christ Thompson	#85
Lady, Lady, Lady	Joe "Bean" Esposito	#86
Four Little Diamonds	Electric Light Orchestra	#86
What's She Got	Liquid Gold	#86
Maybe This Day	Kissing The Pink	#87
Touch A Four Leaf Clover	Atlantic Starr	#87
Love On My Mind Tonight	The Temptations	#88
Dirty Looks	Juice Newton	#90
Take Away	Big Ric	#91
Canvas Of Life	Minor Detail	#92
Scarlet Fever	Kenny Rogers	#94
Night Pulse	Double Image	#94
Somebody's Gonna Love You	Lee Greenwood	#96

1984		
Like A Virgin	Madonna	#1
Jump	Van Halen	#1
When Doves Cry	Prince	#1
I Just Called To Say I Love You	Stevie Wonder	#1
Ghostbusters	Ray Parker Jr.	#1
Out Of Touch	Daryl Hall & John Oates	#1
Let's Hear It For The Boy	Deniece Williams	#1
Let's Go Crazy	Prince	#1
Caribbean Queen (No More Love On The Run)	Billy Ocean	#1
Somebody's Watching Me	Rockwell	#2
Girls Just Want To Have Fun	Cyndi Lauper	#2
99 Luftballons	Nena	#2
She Bop	Cyndi Lauper	#3
Drive	The Cars	#3
Jump (For My Love)	The Pointer Sisters	#3
Hard Habit To Break	Chicago	#3
Thriller	Michael Jackson	#4
Here Comes The Rain Again	Eurythmics	#4
Break My Stride	Matthew Wilder	#5
Sad Songs (Say So Much)	Elton John	#5
All Through The Night	Cyndi Lauper	#5
To All The Girls I've Loved Before	Julio Iglesias & Willie Nelson	#5
Automatic	The Pointer Sisters	#5
That's All!	Genesis	#6
I Can Dream About You	Dan Hartman	#6
I Want A New Drug	Huey Lewis & The News	#6
Sunglasses At Night	Corey Hart	#7

KEYBOARDS (cont'd)

Running With The Night	Lionel Richie	#7
You Might Think	The Cars	#7
Breakdance	Irene Cara	#8
Let The Music Play	Shannon	#8
Breakin' … There's No Stopping Us	Ollie & Jerry	#9
Cruel Summer	Bananarama	#9
Got A Hold On Me	Christine McVie	#10
Desert Moon	Dennis DeYoung	#10
Borderline	Madonna	#10
Doctor! Doctor!	Thompson Twins	#11
Magic	The Cars	#12
Do They Know It's Christmas?	Band Aid	#13
I'll Wait	Van Halen	#13
What About Me?	Kenny Rogers With Kim Carnes & James Ingram	#15
Rock Me Tonite	Billy Squier	#15
Stay The Night	Chicago	#16
Holiday	Madonna	#16
Torture	Jacksons	#17
Dancing In The Sheets	Shalamar	#17
Time Will Reveal	Debarge	#18
Yah Mo B There	James Ingram w/ Michael McDonald	#19
Swept Away	Diana Ross	#19
The Lucky One	Laura Branigan	#20
Sexy Girl	Glenn Frey	#20
Hello Again	The Cars	#20
There Goes My Baby	Donna Summer	#21
Who's That Girl	Eurythmics	#21
Go Insane	Lindsey Buckingham	#23
No Way Out	Jefferson Starship	#23
So Bad	Paul McCartney	#23
No More Words	Berlin	#23
Leave It	Yes	#24
Centipede	Rebbie Jackson	#24
Let's Stay Together	Tina Turner	#26
White Horse	Laid Back	#26
Don't Walk Away	Rick Springfield	#26
New Song	Howard Jones	#27
Right By Your Side	Eurythmics	#29
Send Me An Angel	Real Life	#29
Alibis	Sergio Mendes	#29
Stranger In Town	Toto	#30

KEYBOARDS (cont'd)

Stay With Me Tonight	Jeffrey Osborne	#30
Livin' In Desperate Times	Olivia Newton-John	#31
It's My Life	Talk Talk	#31
Girls With Guns	Tommy Shaw	#33
The Kid's American	Matthew Wilder	#33
A Girl In Trouble (Is A Temporary Thing)	Romeo Void	#35
Obscene Phone Caller	Rockwell	#35
I Need You Tonight	Peter Wolf	#36
Sugar Don't Bite	Sam Harris	#36
17	Rick James	#36
Boys Do Fall In Love	Robin Gibb	#37
Runaway	Bon Jovi	#39
(What) In The Name Of Love	Naked Eyes	#39
Catch Me I'm Falling	Real Life	#40
The Last Time I Made Love	Joyce Kennedy & Jeffrey Osborne	#40
Two Tribes	Frankie Goes To Hollywood	#43
Don't Stop	Jeffrey Osborne	#44
I Want To Break Free	Queen	#45
What The Big Girls Do	Van Stephenson	#45
Save The Last Dance For Me	Dolly Parton w/ The Jordanaires	#45
For A Rocker	Jackson Browne	#45
If Only You Knew	Patti Labelle	#46
Wouldn't It Be Good	Nik Kershaw	#46
Give Me Tonight	Shannon	#46
Rebel Yell	Billy Idol	#46
Don't Waste Your Time	Yarbrough & Peoples	#48
Taking It All Too Hard	Genesis	#50
(You Can Still) Rock In America	Night Ranger	#51
Let's Pretend We're Married	Prince	#52
Strangers In A Strange World	Jenny Burton & Patrick Jude	#54
Ti Amo	Laura Branigan	#55
Jam On It	Newcleus	#56
Olympia	Sergio Mendes	#58
There's No Easy Way	James Ingram	#58
You're Looking Like Love To Me	Peabo Bryson/ Roberta Flack	#58
In The Name Of Love	Ralph Macdonald w/ Bill Withers	#58
Communication	Spandau Ballet	#59
The Ghost In You	The Psychedclic Furs	#59
Stranger	Stephen Stills	#61
Joystick	Dazz Band	#61
Wet My Whistle	Midnight Star	#61
The Moment Of Truth	Survivor	#63

KEYBOARDS (cont'd)

Just The Way You Like It	The S.O.S. Band	#64
She's Trouble	Musical Youth	#65
Fading Away	Will To Power	#65
Vitamin L	B.E. Taylor Group	#66
Straight From The Heart (Into Your Life)	Coyote Sisters	#66
Give	Missing Persons	#67
Relax	Frankie Goes To Hollywood	#67
Can't Let Go	Stephen Stills w/ Michael Finnigan	#67
I Cry Just A Little Bit	Shakin' Stevens	#67
Sunshine In The Shade	The Fixx	#69
Love Kills	Freddie Mercury	#69
Edge Of A Dream	Joe Cocker	#69
Encore	Cheryl Lynn	#69
After All	Al Jarreau	#69
Young Thing, Wild Dreams (Rock Me)	Red Rider	#71
When We Make Love	Alabama	#72
Freakshow On The Dance Floor	Bar-Kays	#73
Amnesia	Shalamar	#73
Now It's My Turn	Berlin	#74
All Night Long	Billy Squier	#75
Someone Like You	Michael Stanley Band	#75
Action	Evelyn "Champagne" King	#75
Pretty Mess	Vanity	#75
Supernatural Love	Donna Summer	#75
A Chance For Heaven	Christopher Cross	#76
Let's Go Up	Diana Ross	#77
Body Talk	Deele	#77
I Wanna Go Back	Billy Satellite	#78
Devil In A Fast Car	Sheena Easton	#79
Electric Kingdom	Twilight 22	#79
I Didn't Mean To Turn You On	Cherrelle	#79
Gotta Give A Little Love (Ten Years After)	Timmy Thomas	#80
I Lost On Jeopardy	"Weird Al" Yankovic	#81
Reach Out	Giorgio Moroder w/ Paul Engemann	#81
Sexcrime (Nineteen Eighty-Four)	Eurythmics	#81
Next Love	Deniece Williams	#81
Over My Head	Toni Basil	#81
No Parking (On The Dance Floor)	Midnight Star	#81
Remember What You Like	Jenny Burton	#81
Jimmy Loves Maryann	Josie Cotton	#82
Hurt	Re-Flex	#82
It's Gonna Be Special	Patti Austin	#82

The 80s Music Compendium

KEYBOARDS (cont'd)

Slow Dancin'	Peabo Bryson	#82
Do You Love Me	Andy Fraser	#82
Don't Wait For Heroes	Dennis DeYoung	#83
Theme From "Terms Of Endearment"	Michael Gore	#84
Let It All Blow	Dazz Band	#84
Video!	Jeff Lynne	#85
High Energy	Evelyn Thomas	#85
Sex Shooter	Apollonia 6	#85
Flashes	Tiggi Clay	#86
Anywhere With You	Rubber Rodeo	#86
Such A Shame	Talk Talk	#89
That Was Then But This Is Now	ABC	#89
Bullish	Herb Alpert Tijuana Brass	#90
Don't Do Me	Randy Bell	#90

1985		
Oh Sheila	Ready For The World	#1
Sussudio	Phil Collins	#1
Miami Vice Theme	Jan Hammer	#1
Saving All My Love For You	Whitney Houston	#1
Take On Me	A-Ha	#1
Don't You (Forget About Me)	Simple Minds	#1
Separate Lives	Phil Collins & Marilyn Martin	#1
One More Night	Phil Collins	#1
Heaven	Bryan Adams	#1
Everything She Wants	Wham!	#1
Power Of Love	Huey Lewis & The News	#1
I Want To Know What Love Is	Foreigner	#1
Shout	Tears For Fears	#1
We Are The World	USA For Africa	#1
Say You, Say Me	Lionel Richie	#1
Material Girl	Madonna	#2
All I Need	Jack Wagner	#2
Easy Lover	Philip Bailey w/ Phil Collins	#2
Cherish	Kool & The Gang	#2
Party All The Time	Eddie Murphy	#2
California Girls	David Lee Roth	#3
Head Over Heels	Tears For Fears	#3
If You Love Somebody Set Them Free	Sting	#3
Never Surrender	Corey Hart	#3
Alive & Kicking	Simple Minds	#3
Rhythm Of The Night	Debarge	#3

KEYBOARDS (cont'd)

Axel F	Harold Faltermeyer	#3
Dress You Up	Madonna	#5
Angel	Madonna	#5
Glory Days	Bruce Springsteen	#5
Who's Holding Donna Now	Debarge	#6
Obsession	Animotion	#6
Lay Your Hands On Me	Thompson Twins	#6
Neutron Dance	The Pointer Sisters	#6
Who's Zoomin' Who	Aretha Franklin	#7
In My House	Mary Jane Girls	#7
Voices Carry	Til Tuesday	#8
I Would Die 4 U	Prince	#8
High On You	Survivor	#8
Lovin' Every Minute Of It	Loverboy	#9
Born In The U.S.A.	Bruce Springsteen	#9
All She Wants To Do Is Dance	Don Henley	#9
Fresh	Kool & The Gang	#9
You're Only Human (Second Wind)	Billy Joel	#9
Sugar Walls	Sheena Easton	#9
Be Near Me	ABC	#9
What About Love?	Heart	#10
You Spin Me Round (Like A Record)	Dead Or Alive	#11
Dare Me	The Pointer Sisters	#11
Perfect Way	Scritti Politti	#11
That Was Yesterday	Foreigner	#12
Mr. Telephone Song	New Edition	#12
Just Another Night	Mick Jagger	#12
You Are My Lady	Freddie Jackson	#12
Solid	Ashford & Simpson	#12
Don't Come Around Here No More	Tom Petty And The Heartbreakers	#13
Do What You Do	Jermaine Jackson	#13
People Are People	Depeche Mode	#13
Crazy In The Night (Barking At Airplanes)	Kim Carnes	#15
Call To The Heart	Giuffria	#15
19	Paul Hardcastle	#15
Save A Prayer	Duran Duran	#16
Never Ending Story	Limahl	#17
New Attitude	Patti Labelle	#17
Love Light In Flight	Stevie Wonder	#17
C-I-T-Y	John Cafferty	#18
Operator	Midnight Star	#18
Life In One Day	Howard Jones	#19

KEYBOARDS (cont'd)

Jungle Love	The Time	#20
Shame	The Motels	#21
There Must Be An Angel (Playing With My Heart)	Eurythmics	#22
Tough All Over	John Cafferty	#22
Sunset Grill	Don Henley	#22
Naughty Naughty	John Parr	#23
Object Of My Desire	Starpoint	#25
Take Me With U	Prince	#25
Boy In The Box	Corey Hart	#26
So In Love	Orchestral Manoeuvres In The Dark	#26
Money Changes Everything	Cyndi Lauper	#27
Cannonball	Supertramp	#28
Find A Way	Amy Grant	#29
Possession Obsession	Daryl Hall & John Oates	#30
Invisible	Alison Moyet	#31
This Is Not America	David Bowie/ Pat Metheny Group	#32
Why Can't I Have You	The Cars	#33
Mistake No. 3	Culture Club	#33
I Wonder If I Take You Home	Lisa Lisa & Cult Jam	#34
No Lookin' Back	Michael McDonald	#34
Girls Are More Fun	Ray Parker Jr.	#34
I Wanna Hear It From Your Lips	Eric Carmen	#35
Lost In Love	New Edition	#35
The Bird	The Time	#36
Ooh Ooh Song	Pat Benatar	#36
Let Him Go	Animotion	#39
Forever	Kenny Loggins	#40
Spanish Eddie	Laura Branigan	#40
We Close Our Eyes	Go West	#41
Wild And Crazy Love	Mary Jane Girls	#42
Black Cars	Gino Vannelli	#42
Animal Instinct	Commodores	#43
Hangin' On A String (Contemplating)	Loose Ends	#43
Baby Come And Get It	The Pointer Sisters	#44
Weird Science	Oingo Boingo	#45
You Wear It Well	El Debarge w/ Debarge	#46
Say It Again	Santana	#46
Like A Surgeon	"Weird Al" Yankovic	#47
I'll Be Good	Rene & Angela	#47
After The Fire	Roger Daltrey	#48
Smalltown Boy	Bronski Beat	#48
Born In East L.A.	Cheech & Chong	#48

KEYBOARDS (cont'd)

20/20	George Benson	#48
Treat Her Like A Lady	The Temptations	#48
Do You Wanna Get Away	Shannon	#49
Can't Stop	Rick James	#50
My Toot	Jean Knight	#50
All Of Me For All Of You	9.9	#51
Count Me Out	New Edition	#51
Only For Love	Limahl	#51
Jesse	Julian Lennon	#54
Down On Love	Foreigner	#54
When The Rain Begins To Fall	Jermaine Jackson/ Pia Zadora	#54
Summertime Girls	Y & T	#55
Love & Pride	King	#55
Let's Talk About Me	Alan Parsons Project	#56
Cross My Heart	Eighth Wonder	#56
Hurts To Be In Love	Gino Vannelli	#57
Rain Forest	Paul Hardcastle	#57
Lonely In Love	Giuffria	#57
Yo' Little Brother	Nolan Thomas	#57
Freedom	The Pointer Sisters	#59
Playing To Win	Little River Band	#60
This Is My Night	Chaka Khan	#60
Looking Over My Shoulder	Til Tuesday	#61
Be Your Man	Jesse Johnson	#61
Everyday	James Taylor	#61
Hold Me	Menudo	#62
Kiss And Tell	Isley Jasper Isley	#63
Small Town Girl	John Cafferty	#64
Go For It	Kim Wilde	#65
Dangerous	Loverboy	#65
The Oak Tree	Morris Day	#65
Big In Japan	Alphaville	#66
Abadabadango	Kim Carnes	#67
Some People	Belouis Some	#67
(Closest Thing To) Perfect	Jermaine Jackson	#67
Charm The Snake	Christopher Cross	#68
The Power Of Love (You Are My Lady)	Air Supply	#68
Invitation To Dance	Kim Carnes	#68
Dancin' In The Key Of Life	Steve Arrington	#68
Hard Time For Lovers	Jennifer Holliday	#69
Can You Feel The Beat	Lisa Lisa & Cult Jam	#69
Tired Of Being Blonde	Carly Simon	#70

KEYBOARDS (cont'd)

Holyanna	Toto	#71
Days Are Numbered (The Traveller)	Alan Parsons Project	#71
Test Of Time	The Romantics	#71
Look My Way	The Vels	#72
Eye To Eye	Go West	#73
Mathematics	Melissa Manchester	#74
Lover Come Back To Me	Dead Or Alive	#75
I Was Born To Love You	Freddie Mercury	#76
One Foot Back In Your Door	Roman Holliday	#76
(Come On) Shout	Alex Brown	#76
One Night In Bangkok	Robey	#77
Blue Kiss	Jane Wiedlin	#77
Take No Prisoners (In The Game Of Love)	Peabo Bryson	#78
Bit By Bit	Stephanie Mills	#78
Emotion	Barbra Streisand	#79
Running Back	Urgent	#79
Crazy	Kenny Rogers	#79
Square Rooms	Al Corley	#80
Black Kisses (Never Make You Blue)	Curtie & The Boombox	#81
You Send Me	The Manhattans	#81
A Little Bit Of Heaven	Natalie Cole	#81
Love Resurrection	Alison Moyet	#82
Hold Me	Laura Branigan	#82
Talk To Me	Quarterflash	#83
Shock	The Motels	#84
Fools Like Me	Lorenzo Lamas	#85
Friends	Whodini	#87
Master And Servant	Depeche Mode	#87
Imagination	Belouis Some	#88
Love Grammar	John Parr	#89
Fright Night	J. Geils Band	#91
Heartline	Robin George	#92
Forever Young	Alphaville	#93

1986		
Invisible Touch	Genesis	#1
Live To Tell	Madonna	#1
These Dreams	Heart	#1
Higher Love	Steve Winwood	#1
Holding Back The Years	Simply Red	#1
Venus	Bananarama	#1
Take My Breath Away	Berlin	#1

KEYBOARDS (cont'd)

West End Girls	Pet Shop Boys	#1
Sledgehammer	Peter Gabriel	#1
There'll Be Sad Songs To Make You Cry	Billy Ocean	#1
Addicted To Love	Robert Palmer	#1
Human	Human League	#1
When I Think Of You	Janet Jackson	#1
Glory Of Love	Peter Cetera	#1
How Will I Know	Whitney Houston	#1
Kyrie	Mr. Mister	#1
Rock Me Amadeus	Falco	#1
Greatest Love Of All	Whitney Houston	#1
When The Going Gets Tough, The Tough Get Going	Billy Ocean	#2
Friends And Lovers	Gloria Loring & Carl Anderson	#2
Dancing On The Ceiling	Lionel Richie	#2
Typical Male	Tina Turner	#2
Two Of Hearts	Stacey Q	#3
Who's Johnny	El Debarge	#3
I Can't Wait	Nu Shooz	#3
Nasty	Janet Jackson	#3
Crush On You	The Jets	#3
Mad About You	Belinda Carlisle	#3
Secret Lovers	Atlantic Starr	#3
If You Leave	Orchestral Manoeuvres In The Dark	#4
What Have You Done For Me Lately	Janet Jackson	#4
Take Me Home Tonight	Eddie Money (w/ Ronnie Spector)	#4
Words Get In The Way	Miami Sound Machine	#5
Dreamtime	Daryl Hall	#5
All I Need Is A Miracle	Mike + The Mechanics	#5
The Sweetest Taboo	Sade	#5
Silent Running (On Dangerous Ground)	Mike + The Mechanics	#6
My Hometown	Bruce Springsteen	#6
Word Up	Cameo	#6
Spies Like Us	Paul McCartney	#7
Tonight She Comes	The Cars	#7
Walk Of Life	Dire Straits	#7
Nikita	Elton John	#7
Let's Go All The Way	Sly Fox	#7
A Different Corner	George Michael	#7
Is It Love	Mr. Mister	#8
King For A Day	Thompson Twins	#8
All Cried Out	Lisa Lisa & Cult Jam	#8

KEYBOARDS (cont'd)

Rumors	Timex Social Club	#8
Bad Boy	Miami Sound Machine	#8
Be Good To Yourself	Journey	#9
The Rain	Oran "Juice" Jones	#9
Your Wildest Dreams	The Moody Blues	#9
Love Will Conquer All	Lionel Richie	#9
Modern Woman	Billy Joel	#10
Opportunities (Let's Make Lots Of Money)	Pet Shop Boys	#10
This Could Be The Night	Loverboy	#10
Love Zone	Billy Ocean	#10
Go Home	Stevie Wonder	#10
Baby Love	Regina	#10
I'll Be Over You	Toto	#11
Move Away	Culture Club	#12
Heaven In Your Eyes	Loverboy	#12
Tarzan Boy	Baltimora	#13
Sanctify Yourself	Simple Minds	#14
Man Size Love	Klymaxx	#15
Russians	Sting	#16
Love Is Forever	Billy Ocean	#16
I Think It's Love	Jermaine Jackson	#16
Calling America	Electric Light Orchestra	#18
Sidewalk Talk	Jellybean w/ Catherine Buchanan	#18
(Forever) Live And Die	Orchestral Manoeuvres In The Dark	#19
Never As Good As The First Time	Sade	#20
The Sun Always Shines On T.V.	A-Ha	#20
Earth Angel	New Edition	#21
Digital Display	Ready For The World	#21
Dreams	Van Halen	#22
No Easy Way Out	Robert Tepper	#22
One Step Closer To You	Gavin Christopher	#22
Love Walks In	Van Halen	#22
Everybody Dance	Ta Mara & The Seen	#24
Overjoyed	Stevie Wonder	#24
What About Love	Til Tuesday	#26
Somebody's Out There	Triumph	#27
All The Things She Said	Simple Minds	#28
Money's Too Tight (To Mention)	Simply Red	#28
Night Moves	Marilyn Martin	#28
Sex As A Weapon	Pan Benatar	#28
Point Of No Return	Nu Shooz	#28
Oh, People	Patti Labelle	#29

KEYBOARDS (cont'd)

If She Knew What She Wants	Bangles	#29
You Be Illin'	Run-D.M.C.	#29
I'm Not The One	The Cars	#32
Stick Around	Julian Lennon	#32
For Tonight	Nancy Martinez	#32
Goodbye Is Forever	Arcadia	#33
Goldmine	The Pointer Sisters	#33
Paranoimia	Art Of Noise/ Max Headroom	#34
Velcro Fly	ZZ Top	#35
Welcome To The Boomtown	David & David	#37
Out Of Mind Out Of Sight	Models	#37
Where Do The Children Go	Hooters w/ Patty Smyth	#38
A Little Bit Of Love (Is All It Takes)	New Edition	#38
Walk Like A Man	Mary Jane Girls	#41
Superbowl Shuffle	The Chicago Bears Shufflin' Crew	#41
Can't Wait Another Minute	Five Star	#41
Midas Touch	Midnight Star	#42
Love Always	El Debarge	#43
Right Between The Eyes	Wax	#43
Somewhere	Barbra Streisand	#43
The Finest	The S.O.S. Band	#44
The Big Money	Rush	#45
Restless	Starpoint	#46
Nail It To The Wall	Stacy Lattisaw	#48
With You All The Way	New Edition	#51
I Must Be Dreaming	Giuffria	#52
Headed For The Future	Neil Diamond	#53
Crazay	Jesse Johnson w/ Sly Stone	#53
Call Me	Dennis DeYoung	#54
Under The Influence	Vanity	#56
Don Quichotte	Magazine 60	#56
The Power Of Love	Jennifer Rush	#57
Own The Night	Chaka Khan	#57
Give Me The Reason	Luther Vandross	#57
The Other Side Of Life	The Moody Blues	#58
Let Me Be The One	Five Star	#59
Touch & Go	Emerson, Lake & Powell	#60
Living On Video	Trans-X	#61
All The Kings Horses	The Firm	#61
I Like You	Phyllis Nelson	#61
Secret	Orchestral Manoeuvres In The Dark	#62
Love Comes Quickly	Pet Shop Boys	#62

KEYBOARDS (cont'd)

Mutual Surrender (What A Wonderful World)	Bourgeois Tagg	#62
Your Smile	Rene & Angela	#62
Voice Of America's Sons	John Cafferty	#62
Goin' To The Bank	Commodores	#65
Goin' Crazy!	David Lee Roth	#66
Lead A Double Life	Loverboy	#68
Before I Go	Starship	#68
Baby Talk	Alisha	#68
Headlines	Midnight Star	#69
Say It, Say It	E.G. Daily	#70
Fire With Fire	Wild Blue	#71
More Than Physical	Bananarama	#73
When The Rain Comes Down	Andy Taylor	#73
Feel The Heat	Jean Beauvoir	#73
The Whispers In The Dark	Dionne Warwick	#73
A Good Heart	Feargal Sharkey	#74
You Don't Have To Cry	Rene & Angela	#75
The Heart Is Not So Smart	El Debarge With Debarge	#75
One Way Love	TKA	#75
I Engineer	Animotion	#76
Heart's On Fire	John Cafferty	#76
Lonely Is The Night	Air Supply	#76
Don't Say No Tonight	Eugene Wilde	#76
If You Were A Woman (And I Was A Man)	Bonnie Tyler	#77
No Promises	Icehouse	#79
The Best Of Me	David Foster & Olivia Newton-John	#80
The Men All Pause	Klymaxx	#80
Stereotomy	Alan Parsons Project	#82
Count Your Blessings	Ashford & Simpson	#84
Innocent Eyes	Graham Nash w/ Kenny Loggins	#84
Don't Walk Away	Robert Tepper	#85
This Love	Bad Company	#85
Land Of La La	Stevie Wonder	#86
I'm Your Man	Barry Manilow	#86
No Frills Love	Jennifer Holliday	#87
Hot Water	Level 42	#87
Love In Siberia	Laban	#88
Blame It On The Radio	John Parr	#88
It's Not You, It's Not Me	KBC Band	#89
Am I Forgiven	Isle Of Man	#90
Life's What You Make It	Talk Talk	#90
I Found Someone	Laura Branigan	#90

KEYBOARDS (cont'd)

I'm For Real	Howard Hewett	#90
Once In A Lifetime	Talking Heads	#91
Wood Beez (Pray Like Aretha Franklin)	Scritti Politti	#91
Vanity Kills	ABC	#91
Shelter Me	Joe Cocker	#91
Dancin In My Sleep	Secret Ties	#91
Now And Forever (You And Me)	Anne Murray	#92
This Is The Time	Dennis DeYoung	#93
I Wouldn't Lie	Yarbrough & Peoples	#93
Prove Me Wrong	David Pack	#95
In Between Days (Without You)	The Cure	#99

1987		
I Just Can't Stop Loving You	Michael Jackson	#1
Mony Mony "Live	Billy Idol	#1
Lost In Emotion	Lisa Lisa & Cult Jam	#1
Open Your Heart	Madonna	#1
Head To Toe	Lisa Lisa & Cult Jam	#1
Always	Atlantic Starr	#1
Here I Go Again	Whitesnake	#1
Shake You Down	Gregory Abbott	#1
Bad	Michael Jackson	#1
Lean On Me	Club Nouveau	#1
(I Just) Died In Your Arms	Cutting Crew	#1
I Think We're Alone Now	Tiffany	#1
Didn't We Almost Have It All	Whitney Houston	#1
Nothing's Gonna Stop Us Now	Starship	#1
I Wanna Dance With Somebody (Who Loves Me)	Whitney Houston	#1
Livin' On A Prayer	Bon Jovi	#1
Let's Wait Awhile	Janet Jackson	#2
Somewhere Out There	Linda Ronstadt & James Ingram	#2
Notorious	Duran Duran	#2
I Want Your Sex	George Michael	#2
Is This Love	Whitesnake	#2
Looking For A New Love	Jody Watley	#2
You Got It All	The Jets	#3
In Too Deep	Genesis	#3
Change Of Heart	Cyndi Lauper	#3
Land Of Confusion	Genesis	#4
Shake Your Love	Debbie Gibson	#4
Little Lies	Fleetwood Mac	#4
I Heard A Rumor	Bananarama	#4

KEYBOARDS (cont'd)

Songbird	Kenny G	#4
Touch Me (I Want Your Body)	Samantha Fox	#4
Point Of No Return	Expose	#5
Rhythm Is Gonna Get You	Gloria Estefan/Miami Sound Machine	#5
Come Go With Me	Expose	#5
Control	Janet Jackson	#5
Can't We Try	Dan Hill w/ Vonda Sheppard	#6
Don't You Want Me	Jody Watley	#6
Right On Track	Breakfast Club	#7
Ballerina Girl	Lionel Richie	#7
Rock Steady	The Whispers	#7
Let Me Be The One	Expose	#7
We'll Be Together	Sting	#7
Just To See Her	Smokey Robinson	#8
The Final Countdown	Europe	#8
Catch Me (I'm Falling)	Pretty Poison	#8
The Finer Things	Steve Winwood	#8
It's Not Over ('Til It's Over)	Starship	#9
Love You Down	Ready For The World	#9
Touch Of Grey	Grateful Dead	#9
It's A Sin	Pet Shop Boys	#9
I've Been In Love Before	Cutting Crew	#9
Is This Love	Survivor	#9
Stone Love	Kool & The Gang	#10
Victory	Kool & The Gang	#10
Wot's It To Ya	Robbie Nevil	#10
Lessons In Love	Level 42	#12
Back In The High Life Again	Steve Winwood	#13
Dominoes	Robbie Nevil	#14
The Pleasure Principle	Janet Jackson	#14
I Need Love	L.L. Cool J	#14
Brand New Lover	Dead Or Alive	#15
Stop To Love	Luther Vandross	#15
That Ain't Love	REO Speedwagon	#16
Who Found Who	Jellybean w/ Elisa Fiorillo	#16
Living In A Box	Living In A Box	#17
If She Would Have Been Faithful	Chicago	#17
You Are The Girl	The Cars	#17
Coming Around Again	Carly Simon	#18
I'd Still Say Yes	Klymaxx	#18
The Honeythief	Hipsway	#19
Skeletons	Stevie Wonder	#19

KEYBOARDS (cont'd)

Seven Wonders	Fleetwood Mac	#19
In My Dreams	REO Speedwagon	#19
I Do You	The Jets	#20
Happy	Surface	#20
Endless Nights	Eddie Money	#21
Fascinated	Company B	#21
Serious	Donna Allen	#21
Talk To Me	Chico Debarge	#21
Mary's Prayer	Danny Wilson	#23
As We Lay	Shirley Murdock	#23
Stay The Night	Benjamin Orr	#24
Boys Night Out	Timothy B. Schmit	#25
Fake	Alexander O'Neal	#25
Falling In Love (Uh-Oh)	Miami Sound Machine	#25
Heartbreak Beat	The Psychedelic Furs	#26
Ship Of Fools (Save Me From Tomorrow)	World Party	#27
Facts Of Love	Jeff Lorber w/ Karyn White	#27
Lies	Jonathan Butler	#27
Jimmy Lee	Aretha Franklin	#28
Something Real (Inside Me/ Inside You)	Mr. Mister	#29
Love Will Find A Way	Yes	#30
Two People	Tina Turner	#30
Get That Love	Thompson Twins	#31
True Faith	New Order	#32
I Will Be There	Glass Tiger	#34
Sugar Free	Wa Wa Nee	#35
We Connect	Stacey Q	#35
Don't Need A Gun	Billy Idol	#37
Caught Up In The Rapture	Anita Baker	#37
Notorious	Loverboy	#38
Skin Trade	Duran Duran	#39
Why You Treat Me So Bad	Club Nouveau	#39
Don't Look Down- The Sequel	Go West	#39
Don't Leave Me This Way	Communards	#40
Be There	The Pointer Sisters	#42
Misfit	Curiosity Killed The Cat	#42
Boom Boom (Let's Go Back To My Room)	Paul Lekakis	#43
Say You Really Want Me	Kim Wilde	#44
I Need Your Loving	The Human League	#44
No One In The World	Anita Baker	#44
Show Me	The Cover Girls	#44
Same Old Love (365 Days A Year)	Anita Baker	#44

KEYBOARDS (cont'd)

Beat Patrol	Starship	#46
Silent Morning	Noel	#47
Shattered Glass	Laura Branigan	#48
Back And Forth	Cameo	#50
Cry Wolf	A-Ha	#50
There's Nothing Better Than Love	Luther Vandross w/ Gregory Hines	#50
Dreamin'	Will To Power	#50
How Much Love	Survivor	#51
Ain't So Easy	David & David	#51
Why Can't I Be You	The Cure	#54
You And Me Tonight	Deja	#54
Wild Horses	Gino Vannelli	#55
Still A Thrill	Jody Watley	#56
Living In A Dream	Pseudo Echo	#57
Girlfriend	Bobby Brown	#57
Sexappeal	Georgio	#58
One Lover At A Time	Atlantic Starr	#58
Lover's Lane	Georgio	#59
Variety Tonight	REO Speedwagon	#60
System Of Survival	Earth, Wind & Fire	#60
Satellite	Hooters	#61
Never Enough	Patty Smyth	#61
Hooked On You	Sweet Sensation	#64
The Secret Of My Success	Night Ranger	#64
Holiday	Kool & The Gang	#66
If I Say Yes	Five Star	#67
Hold Me	Sheila E.	#68
I'm Not Perfect (But I'm Perfect For You)	Grace Jones	#69
Have You Ever Loved Somebody	Freddie Jackson	#69
Guaranteed For Life	Millions Like Us	#69
In Love With Love	Debbie Harry	#70
Someone	El Debarge	#70
Suburbia	Pet Shop Boys	#70
Boy Blue	Cyndi Lauper	#71
Don't Give Up	Peter Gabriel/ Kate Bush	#72
Cherokee	Europe	#72
Special Way	Kool & The Gang	#72
Break Every Rule	Tina Turner	#74
You Win Again	Bee Gees	#75
True To You	Ric Ocasek	#75
All I Want	Howard Jones	#76
Strangelove	Depeche Mode	#76

KEYBOARDS (cont'd)

Showing Out (Get Fresh At The Weekend)	Mel & Kim	#78
Someone To Love Me For Me	Lisa Lisa & Cult Jam	#78
Want You For My Girlfriend	4 By Four	#79
Nothing's Gonna Stop Me Now	Samantha Fox	#80
Sweet Rachel	Beau Coup	#80
Don't Tell Me The Time	Martha Davis	#80
Watching Over You	Glenn Medeiros	#80
(I Know) I'm Losing You	Uptown	#80
So The Story Goes	Living In A Box	#81
Rock-A Lott	Aretha Franklin	#82
The Real Thing	Jellybean w/ Steven Dante	#82
Eagles Fly	Sammy Hagar	#82
Running In The Family	Level 42	#83
She Don't Look Back	Dan Fogelberg	#84
Summertime, Summertime	Nocera	#84
Something In My House	Dead Or Alive	#85
Man Against The World	Survivor	#86
Do Ya Do Ya (Wanna Please Me)	Samantha Fox	#87
Dancin' With My Mirror	Corey Hart	#88
So Much For Love	The Venetians	#88
He Wants My Body	Starpoint	#89
Shy Girl	Stacey Q	#89
Hearts Away	Night Ranger	#90
Niagara Falls	Chicago	#91
All I Know Is The Way I Feel	The Pointer Sisters	#93
Solitude Standing	Suzanne Vega	#94
Into My Secret	Alisha	#97
Boy Toy	Tia	#97
Spring Love	The Cover Girls	#98

1988		
Dirty Diana	Michael Jackson	#1
Together Forever	Rick Astley	#1
Red Red Wine	UB40	#1
The Way You Make Me Feel	Michael Jackson	#1
Hold On To The Nights	Richard Marx	#1
Baby, I Love Your Way/ Freebird Medley (Free Baby)	Will To Power	#1
Seasons Change	Expose	#1
So Emotional	Whitney Houston	#1
Bad Medicine	Bon Jovi	#1
Father Figure	George Michael	#1

The 80s Music Compendium

KEYBOARDS (cont'd)

Where Do Broken Hearts Go	Whitney Houston	#1
Groovy Kind Of Love	Phil Collins	#1
Man In The Mirror	Michael Jackson	#1
Get Outta My Dreams, Get Into My Car	Billy Ocean	#1
Anything For You	Gloria Estefan/ Miami Sound Machine	#1
Never Gonna Give You Up	Rick Astley	#1
Look Away	Chicago	#1
One More Try	George Michael	#1
I Don't Wanna Go On With You Like That	Elton John	#2
What Have I Done To Deserve This?	Pet Shop Boys & Dusty Springfield	#2
Shattered Dreams	Johnny Hates Jazz	#2
1-2-3	Gloria Estefan/ Miami Sound Machine	#3
I Don't Wanna Live Without Your Love	Chicago	#3
What's On Your Mind (Pure Energy)	Information Society	#3
Naughty Girls (Need Love Too)	Samantha Fox	#3
Angel	Aerosmith	#3
Everything Your Heart Desires	Daryl Hall & John Oates	#3
Always On My Mind	Pet Shop Boys	#4
Sign Your Name	Terence Trent D'Arby	#4
Hungry Eyes	Eric Carmen	#4
Make It Real	The Jets	#4
When It's Love	Van Halen	#5
One Moment In Time	Whitney Houston	#5
I Don't Want To Live Without You	Foreigner	#5
Girlfriend	Pebbles	#5
I Want Her	Keith Sweat	#5
Pink Cadillac	Natalie Cole	#5
Waiting For A Star To Fall	Boy Meets Girl	#5
Just Like Paradise	David Lee Roth	#6
Don't You Know What The Night Can Do	Steve Winwood	#6
Can't Stay Away From You	Gloria Estefan/ Miami Sound Machine	#6
Candle In The Wind	Elton John	#6
Say You Will	Foreigner	#6
Rocket 2 U	The Jets	#6
Never Tear Us Apart	INXS	#7
Nite And Day	Al B. Sure!	#7
I Saw Him Standing There	Tiffany	#7
Prove Your Love	Taylor Dayne	#7
Electric Blue	Icehouse	#7
Tell It To My Heart	Taylor Dayne	#7
Don't Be Cruel	Bobby Brown	#8
Tunnel Of Love	Bruce Springsteen	#9

KEYBOARDS (cont'd)

Rush Hour	Jane Wiedlin	#9
Some Kind Of Lover	Jody Watley	#10
Just Got Paid	Johnny Kemp	#10
Two Occasions	The Deele	#10
I Found Someone	Cher	#10
Please Don't Go Girl	New Kids On The Block	#10
Another Part Of Me	Michael Jackson	#11
The Promise	When In Rome	#11
There's The Girl	Heart	#12
Chains Of Love	Erasure	#12
Kiss Me Deadly	Lita Ford	#12
I Live For Your Love	Natalie Cole	#13
I Still Believe	Brenda K. Starr	#13
We All Sleep Alone	Cher	#14
Everywhere	Fleetwood Mac	#14
A Nightmare On My Street	D.J. Jazzy Jeff and the Fresh Prince	#15
Spy In The House Of Love	Was (Not Was)	#16
The Twist (Yo, Twist!)	The Fat Boys w/ Chubby Checker	#16
Dreaming	Orchestral Manoeuvres In The Dark	#16
The Colour Of Love	Billy Ocean	#17
Domino Dancing	Pet Shop Boys	#18
Push It	Salt-N-Pepa	#19
You Don't Know	Scarlett & Black	#20
Pop Goes The World	Men Without Hats	#20
My Girl	Suave'	#20
Pamela	Toto	#22
Fishnet	Morris Day	#23
Love Changes (Everything)	Climie Fisher	#23
Honestly	Stryper	#23
What You See Is What You Get	Brenda K. Starr	#24
Small World	Huey Lewis & The News	#25
Not Just Another Girl	Ivan Neville	#26
The Power Of Love	Laura Branigan	#26
Because Of You	The Cover Girls	#27
I Should Be So Lucky	Kylie Minogue	#28
One Good Reason	Paul Carrack	#28
I Know You're Out There Somewhere	The Moody Blues	#30
Sayin' Sorry (Don't Make It Right)	Denise Lopez	#31
Spotlight	Madonna	#32
Thanks For My Child	Cheryl Pepsii Riley	#32
Indestructible	The Four Tops	#35
Trouble	Nia Peeples	#35

KEYBOARDS (cont'd)

Heart Of Mine	Boz Scaggs	#35
When We Kiss	Bardeux	#36
In Your Soul	Corey Hart	#38
Ritual	Dan Reed Network	#38
Symptoms Of True Love	Tracie Spencer	#38
Live My Life	Boy George	#40
Rhythm Of Love	Yes	#40
Promise Me	The Cover Girls	#40
Are You Sure	So	#41
Should I Say Yes?	Nu Shooz	#41
Spring Love (Come Back To Me)	Stevie B.	#43
The Right Stuff	Vanessa Williams	#44
Any Love	Luther Vandross	#44
Yes	Merry Clayton	#45
Little Walter	Tony! Toni! Tone!	#47
I Can't Help It	Bananarama	#47
Love In The First Degree	Bananarama	#48
Boy, I've Been Told	Sa-Fire	#48
She's On The Left	Jeffrey Osborne	#48
I Want You So Bad	Heart	#49
Forgive Me For Dreaming	Elisa Fiorillo	#49
Say It's Gonna Rain	Will To Power	#49
Savin' Myself	Eria Fachin	#50
Summergirls	Dino	#50
Never Can Say Goodbye	The Communards	#51
Boom! There She Was	Scritti Politti w/ Roger	#53
Jackie	Blue Zone U.K.	#54
Hole In My Heart (All The Way To China)	Cyndi Lauper	#54
All I Want Is You	Carly Simon w/ Roberta Flack	#54
Inside Outside	The Cover Girls	#55
Inside A Dream	Jane Wiedlin	#57
Talking Back To The Night	Steve Winwood	#57
Take It While It's Hot	Sweet Sensation	#57
Never Let You Go	Sweet Sensation	#58
Wishing I Was Lucky	Wet Wet Wet	#58
Best Of Times	Peter Cetera	#59
Make It Last Forever	Keith Sweat w/ Jacci McGhee	#59
How Can I Forget You	Elisa Fiorillo	#60
It's Money That Matters	Randy Newman	#60
Dear Mr. Jesus	Powersource (Sharon Batts)	#61
Route 66/ Behind The Wheel	Depeche Mode	#61
The Rumour	Olivia Newton-John	#62

KEYBOARDS (cont'd)

Never Let Me Down Again	Depeche Mode	#63
Hot Thing	Prince	#63
You Have Placed A Chill On My Heart	Eurythmics	#64
Don't Look Any Further	Kane Gang	#64
Stand Up	David Lee Roth	#64
Reason To Live	Kiss	#64
I Want To Be Your Property	Blue Mercedes	#66
Don't Make A Fool Of Yourself	Stacey Q	#66
Like A Child	Noel	#67
Lonely Won't Leave Me Alone	Glenn Medeiros	#67
Blue Monday 1988	New Order	#68
Long And Lasting Love (Once In A Lifetime	Glenn Medeiros	#68
Don't Break My Heart	Romeo's Daughter	#73
Coming Up You	The Cars	#74
Joy	Teddy Pendergrass	#77
Love Struck	Jesse Johnson	#78
Skin Deep	Cher	#79
Something Just Ain't Right	Keith Sweat	#79
My Love	Julio Iglesias w/ Stevie Wonder	#80
Forever Yours	Tony Terry	#80
Get It	Stevie Wonder & Michael Jackson	#80
Killing Me Softly	Al B. Sure!	#80
Dreamin' Of Love	Stevie B.	#80
Magic Carpet Ride	Bardeux	#81
Century's End	Donald Fagen	#83
Turn Off The Lights	The World Class Wreckin Cru	#84
I Heard It Through The Grapevine	California Raisins	#84
Got A New Love	Good Question	#86
Stimulation	Wa Wa Nee	#86
I Believe In You	Stryper	#88
Sendin' All My Love	The Jets	#88
Without You	Peabo Bryson & Regina Belle	#89
Love, Truth & Honesty	Bananarama	#89
Pretty Boys And Pretty Girls	Book Of Love	#90
Theme From S-Express	S-Express	#91
Is It Love	J.J. Fad	#92
When I Fall In Love	Natalie Cole	#95
The Only Way Is Up	Yazz/ Plastic Population	#96
K.I.S.S.I.N.G.	Siedah Garrett	#97
Fat	"Weird Al" Yankovic	#99

KEYBOARDS (cont'd)

1989		
Batdance	Prince	#1
Hangin' Tough	New Kids On The Block	#1
Eternal Flame	Bangles	#1
The Living Years	Mike + The Mechanics	#1
Baby Don't Forget My Number	Milli Vanilli	#1
I'll Be Loving You	New Kids On The Block	#1
Listen To Your Heart	Roxette	#1
My Prerogative	Bobby Brown	#1
Wind Beneath My Wings	Bette Midler	#1
Cold Hearted	Paula Abdul	#1
Girl I'm Gonna Miss You	Milli Vanilli	#1
Forever Your Girl	Paula Abdul	#1
Blame It On The Rain	Milli Vanilli	#1
When I See You Smile	Bad English	#1
Right Here Waiting	Richard Marx	#1
Straight Up	Paula Abdul	#1
Another Day In Paradise	Phil Collins	#1
Cover Girl	New Kids On The Block	#2
Love Song	The Cure	#2
The Lover In Me	Sheena Easton	#2
Soldier Of Love	Donny Osmond	#2
Don't Rush Me	Taylor Dayne	#2
Girl You Know It's True	Milli Vanilli	#2
Express Yourself	Madonna	#2
Real Love	Jody Watley	#2
Born To Be My Baby	Bon Jovi	#3
You Got It (The Right Stuff)	New Kids On The Block	#3
So Alive	Love & Rockets	#3
Heaven Help Me	Deon Estus & George Michael	#5
Shower Me With Your Love	Surface	#5
With Every Beat Of My Heart	Taylor Dayne	#5
Stand	R.E.M.	#6
Surrender To Me	Ann Wilson & Robin Zander	#6
She Wants To Dance With Me	Rick Astley	#6
Secret Rendezvous	Karyn White	#6
All This Time	Tiffany	#6
After All	Cher & Peter Cetera	#6
It's No Crime	Babyface	#7
This Time I Know It's For Real	Donna Summer	#7
This One's For The Children	New Kids On The Block	#7
Lay Your Hands On Me	Bon Jovi	#7

KEYBOARDS (cont'd)

Miss You Like Crazy	Natalie Cole	#7
I Like It	Dino	#7
Kisses On The Wind	Neneh Cherry	#8
Didn't I (Blow Your Mind)	New Kids On The Block	#8
What You Don't Know	Expose	#8
Friends	Jody Watley w/ Eric B. & Rakim	#9
Walking Away	Information Society	#9
Living In Sin	Bon Jovi	#9
Room To Move	Animotion	#9
Don't Tell Me Lies	Breathe	#10
You're Not Alone	Chicago	#10
When I Looked At Him	Expose	#10
Cry	Waterfront	#10
Crazy About Her	Rod Stewart	#11
Keep On Movin'	Soul II Soul	#11
Don't Close Your Eyes	Kix	#11
Electric Youth	Debbie Gibson	#11
Everlasting Love	Howard Jones	#12
Thinking Of You	Sa-Fire	#12
Silhouette	Kenny G	#13
Dial My Heart	The Boys	#13
Sacred Emotion	Donny Osmond	#13
Sincerely Yours	Sweet Sensation w/ Romeo J.D.	#14
A Little Respect	Erasure	#14
Just Because	Anita Baker	#14
I Beg Your Pardon	Kon Kan	#15
Through The Storm	Aretha Franklin & Elton John	#16
No More Rhyme	Debbie Gibson	#17
Hey Baby	Henry Lee Summer	#18
More Than You Know	Martika	#18
Don't Shut Me Out	Kevin Paige	#18
Headed For A Heartbreak	Winger	#19
Don't Make Me Over	Sybil	#20
Cryin'	Vixen	#22
Sunshine	Dino	#23
You're My One And Only (True Love)	Seduction	#23
Orinoco Flow (Sail Away)	Enya	#24
I Feel The Earth Move	Martika	#25
Put Your Mouth On Me	Eddie Murphy	#27
Sugar Daddy	Thompson Twins	#28
She Won't Talk To Me	Luther Vandross	#30
I Only Wanna Be With You	Samantha Fox	#31

KEYBOARDS (cont'd)

I Live By The Groove	Paul Carrack	#31
License To Chill	Billy Ocean	#32
I Wanna Be The One	Stevie B.	#32
Back On Holiday	Robbie Nevil	#34
Let Go	Sharon Bryant	#34
Feels So Good	Van Halen	#35
It's No Secret	Kylie Minogue	#37
In My Eyes	Stevie B.	#37
Downtown	One 2 Many	#37
Giving Up On Love	Rick Astley	#38
My Heart Skips A Beat	The Cover Girls	#38
It Isn't, It Wasn't, It Ain't Never Gonna Be	Aretha Franklin & Whitney Houston	#41
24/7	Dino	#42
Circle	Edie Brickell	#48
Talk To Myself	Christopher Williams	#49
Let The Day Begin	The Call	#51
New Day For You	Basia	#53
I'm Not The Man I Used To Be	Fine Young Cannibals	#54
Congratulations	Vesta	#55
Girl I Am Searching For You	Stevie B.	#56
Closer Than Friends	Surface	#57
Into You	Giant Steps	#58
The Great Commandment	Camouflage	#59
Over And Over	Pajama Party	#59
Right Next To Me	Whistle	#60
The Different Story (World Of Lust And Crime)	Peter Schilling	#61
Praying To A New God	Wang Chung	#63
Round And Round	New Order	#64
I Love To Bass	Bardeux	#68
Got It Made	Crosby, Stills & Nash	#69
Come Home With Me Baby	Dead Or Alive	#69
I Like	Guy	#70
Gonna Make It	Sa-Fire	#71
Hold On	Donny Osmond	#73
Across The Miles	Survivor	#74
Dancing In Heaven (Orbital Be-Bop)	Q-Feel	#75
Repetition	Information Society	#76
I Can't Face The Fact	Gina Go-Go	#78
If You Asked Me To	Patti Labelle	#79
Lay All Your Love On Me	Information Society	#83
Baby Baby	Eighth Wonder	#84
Right Back Where We Started From	Sinitta	#84

KEYBOARDS (cont'd)

Realistic	Shirley Lewis	#84
You Are The One	TKA	#91
Name And Number	Big Noise	#97
Stop!	Erasure	#99

KOTO

SONG	ARTIST	HOT 100 CHART
1981		
Sukiyaki	A Taste Of Honey	#3
Love Light	Yutaka w/Patti Austin	#81

SONG	ARTIST	HOT 100 CHART
1982		
I'll Try Something New	A Taste Of Honey	#41

MANDOLIN

SONG	ARTIST	HOT 100 CHART
1985		
Glory Days	Bruce Springsteen	#5

SONG	ARTIST	HOT 100 CHART
1986		
Day By Day	Hooters	#18
Where Do The Children Go	Hooters w/ Patty Smyth	#38

1987		
Mandolin Rain	Bruce Hornsby and the Range	#4
Back In The High Life Again	Steve Winwood	#13

1989		
Closer To Fine	Indigo Girls	#52

MARIMBA

SONG	ARTIST	HOT 100 CHART
1980		
Wondering Where The Lions Are	Bruce Cockburn	#21
When The Feeling Comes Around	Jennifer Warnes	#45
Who Were You Thinkin' Of	The Doolittle Band	#49
Case Of You	Frank Stallone	#67
Catching The Sun	Spyro Gyra	#68
1982		
Love Plus One	Haircut One Hundred	#37
1983		
Africa	Toto	#1
Love My Way	The Psychedelic Furs	#44
Change	Tears For Fears	#73
1984		
Hold Me Now	Thompson Twins	#3
Blue Jean	David Bowie	#8
Cruel Summer	Bananarama	#9
You Take Me Up	Thompson Twins	#44
1985		
Rhythm Of The Night	Debarge	#3
Born In East L.A.	Cheech & Chong	#48

MELODICA

SONG	ARTIST	HOT 100 CHART
1983		
Mexican Radio	Wall Of Voodoo	#58
1985		
And We Danced	Hooters	#21
Money Changes Everything	Cyndi Lauper	#27

MELODICA (cont'd)

1986		
Where Do The Children Go	Hooters w/ Patty Smyth	#38

1987		
Satellite	Hooters	#61

OBOE

SONG	ARTIST	HOT 100 CHART
1981		
Touch Me (When We're Dancing)	Carpenters	#16
The Cowboy And The Lady	John Denver	#66

1985		
Crazy For You	Madonna	#1

1989		
Jackie Brown	John Cougar Mellencamp	#48

ORGAN

The first list has all the songs that used an organ, not including the songs with an organ solo. The second list includes the songs that featured one organ solo, while the next list includes the songs that had multiple organ solos. The last list shows all the songs with organ solos, but this time they are organized by length of solo.

SONG	ARTIST	HOT 100 CHART
1980		
Biggest Part Of Me	Ambrosia	#3
Master Blaster (Jammin')	Stevie Wonder	#5
Against The Wind	Bob Seger	#5
Don't Do Me Like That	Tom Petty And The Heartbreakers	#10
In America	Charlie Daniels Band	#11
Romeo's Tune	Steve Forbert	#11
You'll Accomp'ny Me	Bob Seger	#14
Jane	Jefferson Starship	#14

ORGAN (cont'd)

Refugee	Tom Petty And The Heartbreakers	#15
Any Way You Want It	Journey	#23
Forever Mine	O'Jays	#28
Let Me Be	Korona	#43
Cry Like A Baby	Kim Carnes	#44
Love That Got Away	Firefall	#50
Is This Love	Pat Travers Band	#50
Solitaire	Peter McLan	#52
Happy Together (A Fantasy)	Captain & Tennille	#53
Girl, Don't Let It Get You Down	The O'Jays	#55
Rock Lobster	B-52s	#56
Here Comes My Girl	Tom Petty And The Heartbreakers	#59
Let's Be Lovers Again	Eddie Money w/Valerie Carter	#65
Alabama Getaway	Grateful Dead	#68
If I Were You	Toby Beau	#70
Desire	The Rockets	#70
Save Me	Dave Mason	#71
Midnight Rain	Poco	#74
Whatever You Decide	Randy Vanwarmer	#77
Shiver And Shake	The Silencers	#81
Say Goodbye To Little Jo	Steve Forbert	#85
You Can Call Me Blue	Michael Johnson	#86

1981		
Keep On Loving You	REO Speedwagon	#1
Slow Hand	The Pointer Sisters	#2
Stop Draggin' My Heart Around	Stevie Nicks w/Tom Petty	#3
There Ain't No Gettin' Over Me	Ronnie Milsap	#5
Tryin' To Live My Life Without You	Bob Seger	#5
This Little Girl	Gary U.S. Bonds	#11
The Waiting	Tom Petty And The Heartbreakers	#19
Love You Like I Never Loved Before	John O'Banion	#24
Ah! Leah!	Donnie Iris	#29
Chloe	Elton John	#34
Who's Making Love	Blues Brothers	#39
Tempted	Squeeze	#49
Triumph	Magic Power	#51
Mercy, Mercy, Mercy	Phoebe Snow	#52
It's My Job	Jimmy Buffett	#57
Fireflies	Fleetwood Mac	#60
Keep This Train A-Rollin'	The Doobie Brothers	#62
I Don't Want To Know Your Name	Glen Campbell	#65

ORGAN (cont'd)

Jole Blon	Gary U.S. Bonds	#65
96 Tears	Garland Jeffreys	#66
Proud	The Joe Chemay Band	#68
Lover	Michael Stanley Band	#68
Michael Damian	She Did It	#69
Shotgun Rider	Delbert McClinton	#70
I Surrender	Arlan Day	#71
Playing With Lightning	Shot In The Dark	#71
Hard Times	James Taylor	#72
Slip Away	Pablo Cruise	#75
Secrets	Mac Davis	#76
Got To Rock On	Kansas	#76
Fire In The Sky	The Dirt Band	#76
All I Need To Know (Don't Know Much)	Bette Midler	#77
A Woman In Love (It's Not Me)	Tom Petty And The Heartbreakers	#79
Love On The Airwaves	Night	#87

1982		
Mickey	Toni Basil	#1
Centerfold	J. Geils Band	#1
Hurts So Good	John Cougar	#2
Always On My Mind	Willie Nelson	#5
Steppin' Out	Joe Jackson	#6
Somebody's Baby	Jackson Browne	#7
Should I Do It	The Pointer Sisters	#13
Personally	Karla Bonoff	#19
Without You (Not Another Lonely Night)	Franke And The Knockouts	#24
Sweet Time	REO Speedwagon	#26
I Found Somebody	Glenn Frey	#31
Sea Of Love	Del Shannon	#33
Hope You Love Me Like You Say You Do	Huey Lewis & The News	#36
I Need You	Paul Carrack	#37
Island Of Lost Souls	Blondie	#37
Stone Cold	Rainbow	#40
He Got You	Ronnie Milsap	#59
Sara	Bill Champlin	#61
Happy Man	Greg Kihn Band	#62
Summer Nights	Survivor	#62
Please Be The One	Karla Bonoff	#63
Lonely Nights	Bryan Adams	#84
How Can You Love Me	Ambrosia	#86

ORGAN (cont'd)

The Longer You Wait	Gino Vannelli	#89
Outlaw	War	#94

1983		
Shame On The Moon	Bob Seger	#2
Dirty Laundry	Don Henley	#3
Straight From The Heart	Bryan Adams	#10
Hot Girls In Love	Loverboy	#11
Even Now	Bob Seger	#12
Lawyers In Love	Jackson Browne	#13
Cuts Like A Knife	Bryan Adams	#15
I've Got A Rock N' Roll Heart	Eric Clapton	#18
This Time	Bryan Adams	#24
I Do	J. Geils Band	#24
Tender Is The Night	Jackson Browne	#25
Roll Me Away	Bob Seger	#27
It Must Be Love	Madness	#33
The Salt Of My Tears	Martin Briley	#36
Looking For A Stranger	Pat Benatar	#39
All Those Lies	Glenn Frey	#41
Bang The Drum All Day	Todd Rundgren	#63
Forever	Little Steven	#63
Too Much Love To Hide	Crosby, Stills & Nash	#69
What If (I Said I Love You)	Unipop	#71
She's A Runner	Billy Squier	#75
Keep It Tight	Single Bullet Theory	#78
Take The Time	Michael Stanley Band	#81
When You Were Mine	Mitch Ryder	#87
Never Tell An Angel (When Your Heart's On Fire)	The Stompers	#88

1984		
Wake Me Up Before You Go-Go	Wham!	#1
Thriller	Michael Jackson	#4
I Want A New Drug	Huey Lewis & The News	#6
Cover Me	Bruce Springsteen	#7
Language Of Love	Dan Fogelberg	#13
A Fine Fine Day	Tony Carey	#22
New Song	Howard Jones	#27
My Ever Changing Moods	The Style Council	#29
Take Me Back	Bonnie Tyler	#46
Tonight	David Bowie w/ Tina Turner	#53
The Allnighter	Glenn Frey	#54

ORGAN (cont'd)

Sweetheart Like You	Bob Dylan	#55
Make My Day	T.G. Sheppard w/ Clint Eastwood	#62
Blue Light	David Gilmour	#62
Can't Wait All Night	Juice Newton	#66
Little Lady	Duke Jupiter	#68
Say Hello To Ronnie	Janey Street	#68
Gloria	The Doors	#71
The Real End	Rickie Lee Jones	#83

1985		
Would I Lie To You?	Eurythmics	#5
Small Town	John Cougar Mellencamp	#6
Private Dancer	Tina Turner	#7
I'm Goin' Down	Bruce Springsteen	#9
I'm Gonna Tear Your Playhouse Down	Paul Young	#13
Sisters Are Doin' It For Themselves	Eurythmics & Aretha Franklin	#18
Til My Baby Comes Home	Luther Vandross	#29
Not Enough Love In The World	Don Henley	#34
Wake Up (Next To You)	Graham Parker w/ The Shot	#39
Centerfield	John Fogerty	#44
Make It Better (Forget About Me)	Tom Petty And The Heartbreakers	#54
Oo-Ee-Diddley-Bop!	Peter Wolf	#61
Information	Eric Martin	#87

1986		
Hip To Be Square	Huey Lewis & The News	#3
Dreamtime	Daryl Hall	#5
Walk Of Life	Dire Straits	#7
War	Bruce Springsteen	#8
Like A Rock	Bob Seger	#12
It's Only Love	Bryan Adams/ Tina Turner	#15
Day By Day	Hooters	#18
Freedom Overspill	Steve Winwood	#20
Jumpin' Jack Flash	Aretha Franklin	#21
Jungle Boy	John Eddie	#52
Everything Must Change	Paul Young	#56
Is That It?	Katrina & The Waves	#70
I Knew The Bride (When She Use To Rock And Roll)	Nick Lowe	#77
Let Me Down Easy	Roger Daltrey	#86
Love And Rock And Roll	Greg Kihn	#92

ORGAN (cont'd)

1987		
Faith	George Michael	#1
Shakedown	Bob Seger	#1
Doing It All For My Baby	Huey Lewis & The News	#6
Something So Strong	Crowded House	#7
Big Time	Peter Gabriel	#8
I Know What I Like	Huey Lewis & The News	#9
Touch Of Grey	Grateful Dead	#9
Walking Down Your Street	Bangles	#11
I Wanna Go Back	Eddie Money	#14
Hourglass	Squeeze	#15
Come As You Are	Peter Wolf	#15
Give To Live	Sammy Hagar	#23
Rock The Night	Europe	#30
Light Of Day	The Barbusters (Joan Jett & The Blackhearts)	#33
Fire	Bruce Springsteen	#46
Johnny B	Hooters	#61
If I Was Your Girlfriend	Prince	#67
Learning To Fly	Pink Floyd	#70
Stand Back	The Fabulous Thunderbirds	#76
What's Too Much	Smokey Robinson	#79

1988		
Father Figure	George Michael	#1
Roll With It	Steve Winwood	#1
Hazy Shade Of Winter	Bangles	#2
Perfect World	Huey Lewis & The News	#3
(Sittin' On) The Dock Of The Bay	Michael Bolton	#11
True Love	Glenn Frey	#13
A Word In Spanish	Elton John	#19
Dance Little Sister (Part One)	Terence Trent D'Arby	#30
Superstitious	Europe	#31
I'm Still Searching	Glass Tiger	#31
Yeah, Yeah, Yeah	Judson Spence	#32
Tomorrow People	Ziggy Marley	#39
Rhythm Of Love	Yes	#40
Baby Can I Hold You	Tracy Chapman	#48
Like The Weather	10,000 Maniacs	#68
I'm Not Your Man	Tommy Conwell	#74
Talkin' Bout A Revolution	Tracy Chapman	#75
What's The Matter Here?	10,000 Maniacs	#80

ORGAN (cont'd)

1989		
Satisfied	Richard Marx	#1
Like A Prayer	Madonna	#1
Love Song	The Cure	#2
Sowing The Seeds Of Love	Tears For Fears	#2
In Your Room	Bangles	#5
What I Am	Edie Brickell	#7
Holding On	Steve Winwood	#11
Angel Of Harlem	U2	#14
That's The Way	Katrina & The Waves	#16
Call It Love	Poco	#18
Veronica	Elvis Costello	#19
I Live By The Groove	Paul Carrack	#31
Need A Little Taste Of Love	The Doobie Brothers	#45
Give Me The Keys (And I'll Drive You Crazy)	Huey Lewis & The News	#47
Gypsy Road	Cinderella	#51
Hearts On Fire	Steve Winwood	#53
Pretending	Eric Clapton w/ Chaka Khan	#55
Somebody Like You	Robbie Nevil	#63
Pride & Passion	John Cafferty	#66
Anchorage	Michelle Schocked	#66
Livin' Right	Glenn Frey	#90
500 Miles	Hooters	#97

SONGS WITH ORGAN SOLOS

Only organ solos that last for ten seconds or longer are listed.

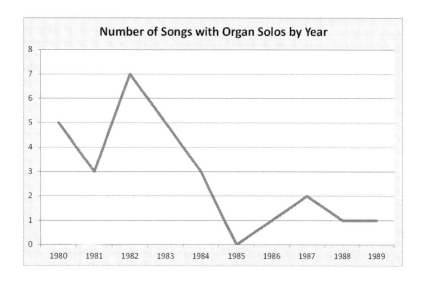

SONGS WITH ORGAN SOLOS (cont'd)

SONG	ARTIST	HOT 100 CHART	LENGTH OF SOLO
1980			
Hungry Heart	Bruce Springsteen	#5	15 seconds
You're The Only Woman (You & I)	Ambrosia	#13	17 seconds
Lady	The Whispers	#28	22 seconds
Walks Like A Lady	Journey	#32	12 seconds
Running Back	Eddie Money	#78	23 seconds
1981			
Miss Sun	Boz Scaggs	#14	11 seconds
In Your Letter	REO Speedwagon	#20	13 seconds
Fade Away	Bruce Springsteen	#20	17 seconds
1982			
Mickey	Toni Basil	#1	19 seconds
Keep The Fire Burnin'	REO Speedwagon	#7	17 seconds
If I Had My Wish Tonight	David Lasley	#36	14 seconds
Angel In Blue	J. Geils Band	#40	34 seconds
Workin' For A Livin'	Huey Lewis & The News	#41	11 seconds
If I Could Get You (Into My Life)	Gene Cotton	#76	19 seconds
1983			
Swingin'	John Anderson	#43	16 seconds
I Can't Stand Still	Don Henley	#48	13 seconds
I Think You'll Remember Tonight	Axe	#94	33 seconds
1984			
I Do'wanna Know	REO Speedwagon	#29	11 seconds
Stop	Sam Brown	#65	19 seconds
Darlin'	Frank Stallone	#81	15 seconds
1986			
Stuck With You	Huey Lewis & The News	#1	24 seconds
1987			
Don't Dream It's Over	Crowded House	#2	23 seconds
If You Let Me Stay	Terence Trent D'Arby	#68	15 seconds

SONGS WITH ORGAN SOLOS (cont'd)

1988			
Better Be Home Soon	Crowded House	#42	29 seconds

1989			
Walk The Dinosaur	Was (Not Was)	#7	16 seconds

SONGS WITH MULTIPLE ORGAN SOLOS

SONG	ARTIST	HOT 100 CHART	LENGTH OF SOLOS
1982			
Freeze-Frame	J. Geils Band	#4	10s,10s

1983			
Industrial Disease	Dire Straits	#75	24s, 12s, 12s, 12s, 38s
Memphis	Joe Jackson	#85	13s, 13s, 13s

THE LONGEST ORGAN SOLOS OF THE 80s

YEAR	SONG	ARTIST	HOT 100 CHART	LENGTH OF SOLO(S)
1983	Industrial Disease	Dire Straits	#75	24, 12, 12, 12, 38 seconds
1982	Angel In Blue	J. Geils Band	#40	34 seconds
1983	I Think You'll Remember Tonight	Axe	#94	33 seconds
1988	Better Be Home Soon	Crowded House	#42	29 seconds
1986	Stuck With You	Huey Lewis & The News	#1	24 seconds
1980	Running Back	Eddie Money	#78	23 seconds
1987	Don't Dream It's Over	Crowded House	#2	23 seconds
1980	Lady	The Whispers	#28	22 seconds
1982	Mickey	Toni Basil	#1	19 seconds
1982	If I Could Get You (Into My Life)	Gene Cotton	#76	19 seconds
1984	Stop	Sam Brown	#65	19 seconds
1980	You're The Only Woman (You & I)	Ambrosia	#13	17 seconds
1981	Fade Away	Bruce Springsteen	#20	17 seconds

THE LONGEST ORGAN SOLOS OF THE 80S (cont'd)

1982	Keep The Fire Burnin'	REO Speedwagon	#7	17 seconds
1983	Swingin'	John Anderson	#43	16 seconds
1989	Walk The Dinosaur	Was (Not Was)	#7	16 seconds
1980	Hungry Heart	Bruce Springsteen	#5	15 seconds
1984	Darlin'	Frank Stallone	#81	15 seconds
1987	If You Let Me Stay	Terence Trent D'Arby	#68	15 seconds
1982	If I Had My Wish Tonight	David Lasley	#36	14 seconds
1983	Memphis	Joe Jackson	#85	13, 13, 13 seconds
1981	In Your Letter	REO Speedwagon	#20	13 seconds
1983	I Can't Stand Still	Don Henley	#48	13 seconds
1980	Walks Like A Lady	Journey	#32	12 seconds
1981	Miss Sun	Biz Scaggs	#14	11 seconds
1982	Workin' For A Livin'	Huey Lewis & The News	#41	11 seconds
1984	I Do'wanna Know	REO Speedwagon	#29	11 seconds
1982	Freeze-Frame	J. Geils Band	#4	10, 10 seconds

PIANO

There are four lists for this section. The first list includes every song that has a piano, excluding the songs that had a piano solo. The second list includes the songs that have a piano solo. The third list contains the songs that had more than one piano solo, while the last list organizes the songs with solos according to the length of the solo.

SONG	ARTIST	HOT 100 CHART
1980		
Lady	Kenny Rogers	#1
The Rose	Bette Midler	#3
Don't Fall In Love With A Dreamer	Kenny Rogers w/Kim Carnes	#4
Cool Change	Little River Band	#10
Don't Do Me Like That	Tom Petty And The Heartbreakers	#10
Into The Night	Benny Mardones	#11
Daydream Believer	Anne Murray	#12
One Fine Day	Carole King	#12
You'll Accomp'ny Me	Bob Seger	#14
Look What You've Done To Me	Boz Scaggs	#14
Love The World Away	Kenny Rogers	#14
Jane	Jefferson Starship	#14
Jojo	Boz Scaggs	#17

PIANO (cont'd)

September Morn'	Neil Diamond	#17
Why Not Me	Fred Knoblock	#18
Wait For Me	Daryl Hall & John Oates	#18
All Night Long	Joe Walsh	#19
Should've Never Let You Go	Neil & Dara Sedaka	#19
Out Here On My Own	Irene Cara	#19
Someone That I Used To Love	Natalie Cole	#21
Fool In The Rain	Led Zeppelin	#21
Heart Hotels	Dan Fogelberg	#21
Deep Inside My Heart	Randy Meisner	#22
How Do I Survive	Amy Holland	#22
Sequel	Harry Chapin	#23
No Night So Long	Dionne Warwick	#23
99	Toto	#26
This Time	John Cougar	#27
Lady	The Whispers	#28
Who'll Be The Fool Tonight	Larsen-Feiten Band	#29
Chiquitita	Abba	#29
Tulsa Time	Eric Clapton	#30
Starting Over Again	Dolly Parton	#36
Kiss Me In The Rain	Barbra Streisand	#37
Ashes By Now	Rodney Crowell	#37
I'd Rather Leave While I'm In Love	Rita Coolidge	#38
(Sartorial Eloquence) Don't Ya Wanna Play This Game No More?	Elton John	#39
Horizontal Bop	Bob Seger	#42
Somethin' 'Bout You Baby I Like	Glen Campbell & Rita Coolidge	#42
Play The Game	Queen	#42
Haven't You Heard	Patrice Rushen	#42
Lucky Me	Anne Murray	#42
Coming Down From Love	Bobby Caldwell	#42
Let Me Be	Korona	#43
Years From Now	Dr. Hook	#51
Autograph	John Denver	#52
One More Time For Love	Billy Preston And Syreeta	#52
I Could Be Good For You	707	#52
Love On A Shoestring	Captain & Tennille	#55
Good Morning Girl/Stay Awhile	Journey	#55
Girl, Don't Let It Get You Down	The O'Jays	#55
Angeline	Allman Brothers Band	#58
Stargazer	Peter Brown	#59
Here Comes My Girl	Tom Petty And The Heartbreakers	#59

PIANO (cont'd)

Breakfast In America	Supertramp	#62
It's Like We Never Said Goodbye	Crystal Gayle	#63
Dancin' In The Streets	Teri Desario w/ K.C. And The Sunshine Band	#66
Brite Eyes	Robbin Thompson Band	#66
True Love Ways	Mickey Gilley	#66
Volcano	Jimmy Buffett	#66
The Good Lord Loves You	Neil Diamond	#67
Who Shot J.R. ?	Gary Burbank	#67
Don't Make Me Over	Jennifer Warnes	#67
Desire	The Rockets	#70
Goodnight My Love	Mike Pinera	#70
Slipstream	Allan Clarke	#70
Shotgun Rider	Joe Sun	#71
Dancin' Like Lovers	Mary Macgregor	#72
Trickle, Trickle	Manhattan Transfer	#73
Blues Power	Eric Clapton	#76
Survive	Jimmy Buffett	#77
The Blue Side	Crystal Gayle	#81
Say Goodbye To Little Jo	Steve Forbert	#85
I Don't Need You Anymore	Jackie Deshannon	#86
You Can Call Me Blue	Michael Johnson	#86
Small Paradise	John Cougar	#87
Where Did We Go Wrong	Frankie Valli & Chris Forde	#90
Trust Me	Cindy Bullens	#90
Mirage	Eric Troyer	#92
One Life To Live	Wayne Massey	#92
The Part Of Me That Needs You Most	Jay Black	#98

1981		
9 To 5	Dolly Parton	#1
The Best Of Times	Styx	#3
Every Little Thing She Does Is Magic	The Police	#3
Oh No	Commodores	#4
Who's Crying Now	Journey	#4
Here I Am (Just When I Thought I Was Over You)	Air Supply	#5
Step By Step	Eddie Rabbitt	#5
Passion	Rod Stewart	#5
Hello Again	Neil Diamond	#6
The Winner Takes It All	Abba	#8
Don't Stop Believin	Journey	#9
Hold On Tight	Electric Light Orchestra	#10

PIANO (cont'd)

This Little Girl	Gary U.S. Bonds	#11
Cool Love	Pablo Cruise	#13
It's Now Or Never	John Schneider	#14
What Are We Doin' In Love	Dottie West w/Kenny Rogers	#14
You Better You Bet	The Who	#18
Sweet Baby	Stanley Clarke/George Duke	#19
Fade Away	Bruce Springsteen	#20
Time Out Of Mind	Steely Dan	#22
Breaking Away	Balance	#22
Seven Year Ache	Roseanne Cash	#22
Since I Don't Have You	Don McLean	#23
Rock And Roll Dreams Come Through	Jim Steinman (Rory Dodd)	#32
You Could Take My Heart Away	Silver Condor	#32
The Party's Over (Hopelessly In Love)	Journey	#34
My Mother's Eyes	Bette Midler	#39
But You Know I Love You	Dolly Parton	#41
Lovin The Night Away	The Dillman Band	#45
Fool That I Am	Rita Coolidge	#46
One More Night	Streek	#47
Let Me Love You Once	Greg Lake	#48
It's All I Can Do	Anne Murray	#53
You Don't Know Me	Mickey Gilley	#55
Hold On	Badfinger	#56
It's My Job	Jimmy Buffett	#57
Stay Awake	Ronnie Laws	#60
Take Me Now	David Gates	#62
Keep This Train A-Rollin'	The Doobie Brothers	#62
Lately	Stevie Wonder	#64
A Lucky Guy	Rickie Lee Jones	#64
Dedicated To The One I Love	Bernadette Peters	#65
Jole Blon	Gary U.S. Bonds	#65
I Don't Want To Know Your Name	Glen Campbell	#65
Pay The Devil (Ooo, Baby, Ooo)	The Knack	#67
Lover	Michael Stanley Band	#68
Still	John Schneider	#69
Set The Night On Fire	Oak	#71
Hard Times	James Taylor	#72
Seduced	Leon Redbone	#72
La La Means I Love You	Tierra	#72
The Woman In Me	Crystal Gayle	#76
Winkin', Blinkin', And Nod	The Doobie Brothers	#76
All I Need To Know (Don't Know Much)	Bette Midler	#77

PIANO (cont'd)

One More Chance	Diana Ross	#79
At This Moment	Billy Vera & The Beaters	#79
American Memories	Shamus M'Cool	#80
Let's Put The Fun Back In Rock N Roll	Freddy Cannon & The Belmonts	#81
It's Just The Sun	Don McLean	#83
Unchained Melody	Heart	#83
Come To Me	Aretha Franklin	#84
Don't Know Much	Bill Medley	#88
I Can't Say Goodbye To You	Helen Reddy	#88
I'm Your Superman	All Sports Band	#93
I'm So Glad I'm Standing Here Today	Crusaders w/ Joe Cocker	#97

1982		
Up Where We Belong	Joe Cocker & Jennifer Warnes	#1
Hard To Say I'm Sorry	Chicago	#1
Chariots Of Fire- Titles	Vangelis	#1
Open Arms	Journey	#2
I've Never Been To Me	Charlene	#3
Hold Me	Fleetwood Mac	#4
Turn Your Love Around	George Benson	#5
Steppin' Out	Joe Jackson	#6
Keep The Fire Burnin'	REO Speedwagon	#7
Take It Away	Paul McCartney	#10
Yesterday's Songs	Neil Diamond	#11
Edge Of Seventeen (Just Like The White Winged Dove)	Stevie Nicks	#11
Blue Eyes	Elton John	#12
Bobbie Sue	The Oak Ridge Boys	#12
Empty Garden (Hey Hey Johnny)	Elton John	#13
Waiting On A Friend	The Rolling Stones	#13
Should I Do It	The Pointer Sisters	#13
You Could Have Been With Me	Sheena Easton	#15
Play The Game Tonight	Kansas	#17
Nobody Said It Was Easy (Lookin' For The Lights)	Le Roux	#18
Take Me Down	Alabama	#18
Run For The Roses	Dan Fogelberg	#18
Out Of Work	Gary U.S. Bonds	#21
She's Got A Way	Billy Joel	#23
(Theme From) Magnum P.I.	Mike Post	#25
My Girl	Donnie Iris	#25
Never Been In Love	Randy Meisner	#28
Be My Lady	Jefferson Starship	#28
Make Believe	Toto	#30

PIANO (cont'd)

More Than Just The Two Of Us	Sneaker	#34
Be Mine Tonight	Neil Diamond	#35
Angel In Blue	J. Geils Band	#40
Shine On	George Duke	#41
Anyone Can See	Irene Cara	#42
Another Sleepless Night	Anne Murray	#44
I'm In Love Again	Pia Zadora	#45
Dreamin'	John Schneider	#45
I Only Want To Be With You	Nicolette Larson	#53
I Will Always Love You	Dolly Parton	#53
(Sittin' On) The Dock Of The Bay	The Reddings	#55
Tonight Tonight	Bill Champlin	#55
Bad Boy/ Having A Party	Luther Vandross	#55
I'll Drink To You	Duke Jupiter	#58
Don't Stop Me Baby (I'm On Fire)	The Boys Band	#61
Summer Nights	Survivor	#62
Only One You	T.G. Sheppard	#68
In The Driver's Seat	John Schneider	#72
So Fine	The Oak Ridge Boys	#76
How Can You Love Me	Ambrosia	#86
I'm Never Gonna Say Goodbye	Billy Preston	#88
Loving You	Chris Rea	#88
Into My Love	Greg Guidry	#92

1983		
Total Eclipse Of The Heart	Bonnie Tyler	#1
King Of Pain	The Police	#3
My Love	Lionel Richie	#5
We've Got Tonight	Kenny Rogers & Sheena Easton	#6
Our House	Madness	#7
You And I	Eddie Rabbitt & Crystal Gayle	#7
Rock The Casbah	The Clash	#8
I Won't Hold You Back	Toto	#10
Far From Over	Frank Stallone	#10
Straight From The Heart	Bryan Adams	#10
Even Now	Bob Seger	#12
How Am I Supposed To Live Without You	Laura Branigan	#12
Faithfully	Journey	#12
Lawyers In Love	Jackson Browne	#13
Allentown	Billy Joel	#17
Breaking Us In Two	Joe Jackson	#18
Rock 'N' Roll Is King	Electric Light Orchestra	#19

PIANO (cont'd)

My Kind Of Lady	Supertramp	#31
No Time For Talk	Christopher Cross	#33
It Must Be Love	Madness	#33
I Won't Stand In Your Way	Stray Cats	#35
I Knew You When	Linda Ronstadt	#37
All My Life	Kenny Rogers	#37
Two Less Lonely People In The World	Air Supply	#38
Memory	Barry Manilow	#39
Miracles	Stacy Lattisaw	#40
So Close	Diana Ross	#40
Hold Me 'Til The Mornin' Comes	Paul Anka w/Peter Cetera	#40
Minimum Love	Mac McAnally	#41
Old Time Rock & Roll	Bob Seger	#48
Stop Doggin' Me Around	Klique	#50
Outstanding	The Gap Band	#51
The Blues	Randy Newman & Paul Simon	#51
I.O.U.	Lee Greenwood	#53
Goodnight Saigon	Billy Joel	#56
Wind Beneath My Wings	Lou Rawls	#65
Save The Overtime (For Me)	Gladys Knight & The Pips	#66
New Frontier	Donald Fagen	#70
I Just Can't Walk Away	The Four Tops	#71
What If (I Said I Love You)	Unipop	#71
American Made	The Oak Ridge Boys	#72
A Little Good News	Anne Murray	#74
Don't Make Me Do It	Patrick Simmons	#75
Industrial Disease	Dire Straits	#75
Where Everybody Knows Your Name (The Theme From "Cheers")	Gary Portnoy	#83
Baby, What About You	Crystal Gayle	#83
Dirty Looks	Juice Newton	#90
Whatever Happened To Old Fashioned Love	B.J. Thomas	#93

1984		
Against All Odds (Take A Look At Me Now)	Phil Collins	#1
Hello	Lionel Richie	#1
I Guess That's Why They Call It The Blues	Elton John	#4
Sister Christian	Night Ranger	#5
If This Is It	Huey Lewis & The News	#6
That's All!	Genesis	#6
They Don't Know	Tracey Ullman	#8
Think Of Laura	Christopher Cross	#9

PIANO (cont'd)

An Innocent Man	Billy Joel	#10
If Ever You're In My Arms Again	Peabo Bryson	#10
The Curly Shuffle	Jump 'N The Saddle	#15
You Can't Get What You Want (Till You Know What You Want)	Joe Jackson	#15
Read 'Em And Weep	Barry Manilow	#18
A Fine Fine Day	Tony Carey	#22
Almost Over You	Sheena Easton	#25
I Do'wanna Know	REO Speedwagon	#29
Nightbird	Stevie Nicks w/ Sandy Stewart	#33
Holding Out For A Hero	Bonnie Tyler	#34
My Oh My	Slade	#37
She Was Hot	The Rolling Stones	#44
High On Emotion	Chris DeBurgh	#44
Love Me In A Special Way	Debarge	#45
Believe In Me	Dan Fogelberg	#48
Had A Dream (Sleeping With The Enemy)	Roger Hodgson	#48
Left In The Dark	Barbra Streisand	#50
Happy Ending	Joe Jackson w/ Elaine Caswell	#57
Make My Day	T.G. Sheppard w/ Clint Eastwood	#62
Turn Around	Neil Diamond	#62
King Of Suede	"Weird Al" Yankovic	#62
Stop	Sam Brown	#65
Say Hello To Ronnie	Janey Street	#68
Cleanin' Up The Town	The Bus Boys	#68
Look At That Cadillac	Stray Cats	#68
Love Has A Mind Of Its Own	Donna Summer w/ Matthew Ward	#70
It's A Hard Life	Queen	#72
The Sun And The Rain	Madness	#72
Perfect Combination	Stacy Lattisaw & Johnny Gill	#75
Somebody Else's Guy	Jocelyn Brown	#75
Tender Years	John Cafferty	#78
Simple	Johnny Mathis	#81
The Real End	Rickie Lee Jones	#83
Thin Line Between Love And Hate	The Pretenders	#83
Theme From "Terms Of Endearment"	Michael Gore	#84
Superstar/Until You Come Back To Me (That's What I'm Gonna Do)	Luther Vandross	#87
Love Has Finally Come At Last	Bobby Womack & Patti Labelle	#88
Each Word's A Beat Of My Heart	Mink Deville	#89
Taxi	J. Blackfoot	#90

PIANO (cont'd)

1985		
Everytime You Go Away	Paul Young	#1
Can't Fight This Feeling	REO Speedwagon	#1
All I Need	Jack Wagner	#2
Sea Of Love	Honeydrippers	#3
The Search Is Over	Survivor	#4
Suddenly	Billy Ocean	#4
Freedom	Wham/George Michael	#4
Pop Life	Prince	#7
Private Dancer	Tina Turner	#7
Valotte	Julian Lennon	#9
Perfect Way	Scritti Politti	#11
Love Theme From St. Elmo's Fire	David Foster	#15
Understanding	Bob Seger	#17
Sunset Grill	Don Henley	#22
Bruce	Rick Springfield	#27
Cannonball	Supertramp	#28
Live Every Moment	REO Speedwagon	#34
Tragedy	John Hunter	#39
Make No Mistake, He's Mine	Barbra Streisand w/ Kim Carnes	#51
Too Young	Jack Wagner	#52
First Night	Survivor	#53
Change	John Waite	#54
Restless Heart	John Waite	#59
I Was Born To Love You	Freddie Mercury	#76
Lady Of My Heart	Jack Wagner	#76
Baby Come Back To Me (The Morse Code Of Love)	The Manhattan Transfer	#83
You're The Only Love	Paul Hyde/ The Payolas	#84
I'm Through With Love	Eric Carmen	#87
Home Sweet Home	Motley Crue	#89

1986		
Glory Of Love	Peter Cetera	#1
Manic Monday	Bangles	#2
What Have You Done For Me Lately	Janet Jackson	#4
To Be A Lover	Billy Idol	#6
A Different Corner	George Michael	#7
Sweet Love	Anita Baker	#8
All Cried Out	Lisa Lisa & Cult Jam	#8
Tender Love	Force M.D.'S	#10
Like A Rock	Bob Seger	#12
American Storm	Bob Seger	#13

PIANO (cont'd)

The Captain Of Her Heart	Double	#16
Jumpin' Jack Flash	Aretha Franklin	#21
For America	Jackson Browne	#30
It's You	Bob Seger	#52
Absolute Beginners	David Bowie	#53
The Heat Of Heat	Patti Austin	#55
Has Anyone Every Written Anything For You	Stevie Nicks	#60
Miami	Bob Seger	#70
Every Little Kiss	Bruce Hornsby and the Range	#72
Working Class Man	Jimmy Barnes	#74
Johnny Come Home	Fine Young Cannibals	#76
Where Are You Now?	Synch	#77
Daydream Believer	The Monkees	#79
I Feel The Magic	Belinda Carlisle	#82
Winter Games	David Foster	#85
Stay True	Sly Fox	#94

1987		
Alone	Heart	#1
Don't Mean Nothing	Richard Marx	#3
Jammin' Me	Tom Petty And The Heartbreakers	#18
Can'tcha Say (You Believe In Me/Still In Love)	Boston	#20
Smoking Gun	Robert Cray Band	#22
Mary's Prayer	Danny Wilson	#23
Ship Of Fools (Save Me From Tomorrow)	World Party	#27
Jimmy Lee	Aretha Franklin	#28
Notorious	Loverboy	#38
Say You Really Want Me	Kim Wilde	#44
Fire	Bruce Springsteen	#46
Coming Up Close	Til Tuesday	#59
Why Can't This Night Go On Forever	Journey	#60
Young Blood	Bruce Willis	#68
Deep River Woman	Lionel Richie w/ Alabama	#71
Don't Give Up	Peter Gabriel/ Kate Bush	#72
Baby Grand	Billy Joel w/ Ray Charles	#75
Black Dog	Newcity Rockers	#80
You're All I Need	Motley Crue	#83

1988		
Father Figure	George Michael	#1
Could've Been	Tiffany	#1
Roll With It	Steve Winwood	#1
Make Me Lose Control	Eric Carmen	#3

PIANO (cont'd)

Giving You The Best That I Got	Anita Baker	#3
Angel	Aerosmith	#3
She's Like The Wind	Patrick Swayze w/ Wendy Fraser	#3
Kissing A Fool	George Michael	#5
Piano In The Dark	Brenda Russell	#6
Candle In The Wind	Elton John	#6
I Found Someone	Cher	#10
Forever Young	Rod Stewart	#12
Don't Know What You Got (Till It's Gone)	Cinderella	#12
Love Overboard	Gladys Knight & The Pips	#13
Be Still My Beating Heart	Sting	#15
Early In The Morning	Robert Palmer	#19
Here With Me	REO Speedwagon	#20
When We Was Fab	George Harrison	#23
Time And Tide	Basia	#26
The Power Of Love	Laura Branigan	#26
Say It Again	Jermaine Stewart	#27
853-5937	Squeeze	#32
I'm Not Your Man	Tommy Conwell	#74
Ever Since The World Began	Tommy Shaw	#75
Jealous Guy	John Lennon	#80
I Believe In You	Stryper	#88
Hey Mambo	Barry Manilow w/ Kid Creole	#90
Broken Land	The Adventures	#95

1989		
If You Don't Know Me By Now	Simply Red	#1
Lost In Your Eyes	Debbie Gibson	#1
Don't Know Much	Linda Ronstadt (w/ Aaron Neville)	#2
Back To Life	Soul II Soul	#4
The End Of The Innocence	Don Henley	#8
The Doctor	The Doobie Brothers	#9
When I Looked At Him	Expose	#10
Keep On Movin'	Soul II Soul	#11
Talk It Over	Grayson Hugh	#19
A Shoulder To Cry On	Tommy Page	#29
The Arms Of Orion	Prince w/ Sheena Easton	#36
We Can Last Forever	Chicago	#55
Oh Daddy	Adrian Belew	#58
Right Next To Me	Whistle	#60
I Don't Want A Lover	Texas	#77
Imagine	Tracie Spencer	#85

PIANO (cont'd)

Falling Out Of Love	Ivan Neville	#91

PIANO SOLOS

Only piano solos that are ten seconds or longer are listed.

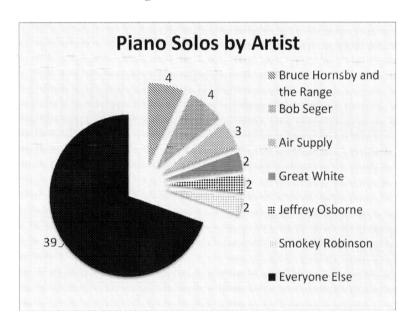

		HOT 100	LENGTH OF
SONG	**ARTIST**	**CHART**	**SOLO**
1980			
Against The Wind	Bob Seger	#5	42 seconds
Romeo's Tune	Steve Forbert	#11	18 seconds
Don't Ask Me Why	Bill Joel	#19	20 seconds
Peanut Butter	Twennynine Feat. Lenny White	#83	16 seconds
1981			
Wasn't That A Party	Rovers	#37	14 seconds
1982			
Even The Nights Are Better	Air Supply	#5	13 seconds
Somewhere Down The Road	Barry Manilow	#21	15 seconds
On The Wings Of Love	Jeffrey Osborne	#29	12 seconds
I'm So Excited	The Pointer Sisters	#30	22 seconds
After The Glitter Fades	Stevie Nicks	#32	12 seconds
Friends In Love	Dionne Warwick & Johnny Mathis	#38	22 seconds

PIANO SOLOS (cont'd)

Young Love	Air Supply	#38	19 seconds
One To One	Carole King	#45	18 seconds
Feel Like A Number	Bob Seger	#48	17 seconds
Ribbon In The Sky	Stevie Wonder	#54	17 seconds
Finally	T.G. Sheppard	#58	16 seconds
Here To Love You	The Doobie Brothers	#65	11 seconds
Shooting Star	Hollywood	#70	15 seconds
Talk Talk	Talk Talk	#75	14 seconds
Route 66	Manhattan Transfer	#78	20 seconds
Seasons Of The Heart	John Denver	#78	16 seconds

1983			
Shame On The Moon	Bob Seger	#2	34 seconds
Making Love Out Of Nothing At All	Air Supply	#2	20 seconds
Does It Make You Remember	Kim Carnes	#36	21 seconds
Just Got Lucky	Joboxers	#36	11 seconds
The Fanatic	Felony	#42	21 seconds
How Do You Keep The Music Playing	James Ingram & Patti Austin	#45	13 seconds
Blame It On Love	Smokey Robinson & Barbara Mitchell	#48	11 seconds
Only You	Commodores	#54	12 seconds
Eenie Meenie	Jeffrey Osborne	#76	34 seconds
Hang On Now	Kajagoogoo	#78	15 seconds

1984			
Head Over Heels	The Go-Go's	#11	34 seconds

1986			
Conga	Miami Sound Machine	#10	31 seconds
Great Gosh A'Mighty (It's A Matter Of Time)	Little Richard	#42	34 seconds

1987			
Mandolin Rain	Bruce Hornsby and the Range	#4	27 seconds
Don't Leave Me This Way	Communards	#40	14 seconds
Sexappeal	Georgio	#58	30 seconds
What's Too Much	Smokey Robinson	#79	30 seconds

1988			
One Good Woman	Peter Cetera	#4	31 seconds
The Promise	When In Rome	#11	12 seconds
Look Out Any Window	Bruce Hornsby and the Range	#35	36 seconds

PIANO SOLOS (cont'd)

Just Like Heaven	The Cure	#40	24 seconds

1989			
Good Thing	Fine Young Cannibals	#1	22 seconds
Right Here Waiting	Richard Marx	#1	22 seconds
Once Bitten Twice Shy	Great White	#5	15 seconds
Healing Hands	Elton John	#13	17 seconds
The Angel Song	Great White	#30	35 seconds
Downtown	One 2 Many	#37	48 seconds

SONGS WITH MULTIPLE PIANO SOLOS

SONG	ARTIST	HOT 100 CHART	LENGTH OF SOLOS
1980			
I Don't Like Mondays	Boomtown Rats	#73	25s, 15s

1981			
Same Old Lang Syne	Dan Fogelberg	#9	17s, 17s

1982			
I Wouldn't Beg For Water	Sheena Easton	#64	18s, 14s

1983			
Roll Me Away	Bob Seger	#27	28s, 45s
Allies	Heart	#83	15s, 11s

1986			
The Way It Is	Bruce Hornsby and the Range	#1	50s, 38s

1987			
Man Against The World	Survivor	#86	19s, 22s

1988			
The Valley Road	Bruce Hornsby and the Range	#5	23s, 64s

THE LONGEST PIANO SOLOS OF THE 80s

YEAR	SONG	ARTIST	HOT 100 CHART	LENGTH OF SOLO
1988	The Valley Road	Bruce Hornsby and the Range	#5	23, 64 seconds
1986	The Way It Is	Bruce Hornsby and the Range	#1	50, 38 seconds
1989	Downtown	One 2 Many	#37	48 seconds
1983	Roll Me Away	Bob Seger	#27	28, 45 seconds
1980	Against The Wind	Bob Seger	#5	42 seconds
1988	Look Out Any Window	Bruce Hornsby and the Range	#35	36 seconds
1989	The Angel Song	Great White	#30	35 seconds
1983	Shame On The Moon	Bob Seger	#2	34 seconds
1983	Eenie Meenie	Jeffrey Osborne	#76	34 seconds
1984	Head Over Heels	The Go-Go's	#11	34 seconds
1986	Great Gosh A'Mighty (It's A Matter Of Time)	Little Richard	#42	34 seconds
1986	Conga	Miami Sound Machine	#10	31 seconds
1988	One Good Woman	Peter Cetera	#4	31 seconds
1987	Sexappeal	Georgio	#58	30 seconds
1987	What's Too Much	Smokey Robinson	#79	30 seconds
1987	Mandolin Rain	Bruce Hornsby and the Range	#4	27 seconds
1980	I Don't Like Mondays	Boomtown Rats	#73	25, 15 seconds
1988	Just Like Heaven	The Cure	#40	24 seconds
1982	I'm So Excited	The Pointer Sisters	#30	22 seconds
1982	Friends In Love	Dionne Warwick & Johnny Mathis	#38	22 seconds
1987	Man Against The World	Survivor	#86	19, 22 seconds
1989	Good Thing	Fine Young Cannibals	#1	22 seconds
1989	Right Here Waiting	Richard Marx	#1	22 seconds
1983	Does It Make You Remember	Kim Carnes	#36	21 seconds
1983	The Fanatic	Felony	#42	21 seconds
1980	Don't Ask Me Why	Bill Joel	#19	20 seconds
1982	Route 66	Manhattan Transfer	#78	20 seconds
1983	Making Love Out Of Nothing At All	Air Supply	#2	20 seconds
1982	Young Love	Air Supply	#38	19 seconds
1982	I Wouldn't Beg For Water	Sheena Easton	#64	18, 14 seconds
1980	Romeo's Tune	Steve Forbert	#11	18 seconds
1982	One To One	Carole King	#45	18 seconds
1982	Feel Like A Number	Bob Seger	#48	17 seconds
1981	Same Old Lang Syne	Dan Fogelberg	#9	17, 17 seconds
1982	Ribbon In The Sky	Stevie Wonder	#54	17 seconds
1989	Healing Hands	Elton John	#13	17 seconds

THE LONGEST PIANO SOLOS OF THE 80s (cont'd)

1980	Peanut Butter	Twennynine Feat. Lenny White	#83	16 seconds
1982	Finally	T.G. Sheppard	#58	16 seconds
1982	Seasons Of The Heart	John Denver	#78	16 seconds
1982	Somewhere Down The Road	Barry Manilow	#21	15 seconds
1983	Allies	Heart	#83	15, 11 seconds
1982	Shooting Star	Hollywood	#70	15 seconds
1983	Hang On Now	Kajagoogoo	#78	15 seconds
1989	Once Bitten Twice Shy	Great White	#5	15 seconds
1981	Wasn't That A Party	Rovers	#37	14 seconds
1982	Talk Talk	Talk Talk	#75	14 seconds
1987	Don't Leave Me This Way	Communards	#40	14 seconds
1982	Even The Nights Are Better	Air Supply	#5	13 seconds
1983	How Do You Keep The Music Playing	James Ingram & Patti Austin	#45	13 seconds
1982	On The Wings Of Love	Jeffrey Osborne	#29	12 seconds
1982	After The Glitter Fades	Stevie Nicks	#32	12 seconds
1983	Only You	Commodores	#54	12 seconds
1988	The Promise	When In Rome	#11	12 seconds
1982	Here To Love You	The Doobie Brothers	#65	11 seconds
1983	Just Got Lucky	Joboxers	#36	11 seconds
1983	Blame It On Love	Smokey Robinson & Barbara Mitchell	#48	11 seconds

SAXOPHONE

The first list has all the songs that used a saxophone, not including the songs with a saxophone solo. The second list includes the songs that featured one saxophone solo, while the next list includes the songs that had multiple saxophone solos. The last list shows all the songs with saxophone solos, but this time they are organized by length of solo.

SONG	ARTIST	HOT 100 CHART
1980		
Little Jeannie	Elton John	#3
Take Your Time (Do It Right) Part 1	S.O.S. Band	#3
On The Radio	Donna Summer	#5
I'm Comin Out	Diana Ross	#5
Off The Wall	Michael Jackson	#10
You're The Only Woman (You & I)	Ambrosia	#13
Why Me	Styx	#26
Gee Whiz	Bernadette Peters	#31
Savannah Nights	Tom Johnston	#34

SAXOPHONE (cont'd)

Live Every Minute	Ali Thomson	#42
Love X Love	George Benson	#61
Breakfast In America	Supertramp	#62
Sherry	Robert John	#70
If I Were You	Toby Beau	#70
The Waiting Game	Swing Out Sister	#86
You Can Call Me Blue	Michael Johnson	#86

1981		
9 To 5	Dolly Parton	#1
Celebration	Kool & The Gang	#1
Being With You	Smokey Robinson	#2
I Don't Need You	Kenny Rogers	#3
Boy From New York City	Manhattan Transfer	#7
Hard To Say	Dan Fogelberg	#7
How 'Bout Us	Champaign	#12
Share Your Love With Me	Kenny Rogers	#14
Just Once	Quincy Jones & James Ingram	#17
Together	Tierra	#18
I Missed Again	Phil Collins	#19
Ai No Corrida	Quincy Jones & James Ingram	#28
Draw Of The Cards	Kim Carnes	#28
No Reply At All	Genesis	#29
I Can Take Care Of Myself	Billy Vera	#39
Love All The Hurt Away	Aretha Franklin & George Benson	#46
Yesterday Once More/Nothing Remains The Same	Spinners	#52
Brooklyn Girls	Robbie Dupree	#54
Mistaken Identity	Kim Carnes	#60
Lover	Michael Stanley Band	#68
I Surrender	Arlan Day	#71
La-Di-Da	Sad Café	#78
Very Special	Debra Laws w/Ronnie Laws	#90
Sharing The Love	Rufus Feat. Chaka Khan	#91

1982		
The Other Woman	Ray Parker Jr.	#4
Get Down On It	Kool & The Gang	#10
One Hundred Ways	Quincy Jones & James Ingram	#14
Daddy's Home	Cliff Richard	#23
I.G.Y. (What A Beautiful World)	Donald Fagen	#26
State Of Independence	Donna Summer	#41
I Know What Boys Like	The Waitresses	#62

SAXOPHONE (cont'd)

Here To Love You	The Doobie Brothers	#65
Standing On The Top- Part 1	The Temptations w/ Rick James	#66
You Got The Power	War	#66
Cross My Heart	Lee Ritenour	#69
Right Away	Kansas	#73
Seasons Of The Heart	John Denver	#78
Don't Stop Trying	Rodway	#83
Steppin' Out	Kool & The Gang	#89

1983		
You Are	Lionel Richie	#4
I Do	J. Geils Band	#24
Poison Arrow	ABC	#25
Tied Up	Olivia Newton-John	#38
So Close	Diana Ross	#40
Nice Girls	Melissa Manchester	#42
After I Cry	Lanier & Co.	#48
Stand By	Roman Holliday	#54
Take Another Picture	Quarterflash	#58
Always	Firefall	#59
Forever	Little Steven	#63
What If (I Said I Love You)	Unipop	#71
You Belong To Me	The Doobie Brothers	#79
Take The Time	Michael Stanley Band	#81
Maybe This Day	Kissing The Pink	#87

1984		
Wake Me Up Before You Go-Go	Wham!	#1
The Glamorous Life	Sheila E.	#7
Blue Jean	David Bowie	#8
Dance Hall Days	Wang Chung	#16
Don't Walk Away	Rick Springfield	#26
Right By Your Side	Eurythmics	#29
Stranger In Town	Toto	#30
Catch My Fall	Billy Idol	#50
Strangers In A Strange World	Jenny Burton & Patrick Jude	#54
The Only Flame In Town	Elvis Costello w/ Daryl Hall	#56
Original Sin	INXS	#58
Someone Like You	Michael Stanley Band	#75
Simple	Johnny Mathis	#81

SAXOPHONE (cont'd)

1985		
Saving All My Love For You	Whitney Houston	#1
The Heat Is On	Glenn Frey	#2
If You Love Somebody Set Them Free	Sting	#3
Election Day	Arcadia	#6
Fortress Around Your Heart	Sting	#8
Love Theme From St. Elmo's Fire	David Foster	#15
Love Is The Seventh Wave	Sting	#17
A Nite At The Apollo Live! The Way You Do The Things You Do/ My Girl	Daryl Hall & John Oates w/ David Ruffin & Eddie Kendrick	#20
Girls Are More Fun	Ray Parker Jr.	#34
Sun City	Artists United Against Apartheid	#38
America	Prince	#46
Your Love Is King	Sade	#54
One Foot Back In Your Door	Roman Holliday	#76
Lady Of My Heart	Jack Wagner	#76
Imagination	Belouis Some	#88

1986		
Danger Zone	Kenny Loggins	#2
Take Me Home Tonight	Eddie Money (w/ Ronnie Spector)	#4
What You Need	INXS	#5
Move Away	Culture Club	#12
The Captain Of Her Heart	Double	#16
Bop	Dan Seals	#42
Love Always	El Debarge	#43
You Can Call Me Al	Paul Simon	#44
I'd Do It All Again	Sam Harris	#52
Absolute Beginners	David Bowie	#53
Love Of A Lifetime	Chaka Khan	#53
Voice Of America's Sons	John Cafferty	#62
Say It, Say It	E.G. Daily	#70
Stranglehold	Paul McCartney	#81
It's Not You, It's Not Me	KBC Band	#89
Gravity	James Brown	#93
This Is The Time	Dennis DeYoung	#93
I Need You	Maurice White	#95
Weatherman	Nick Jameson	#95
One Sunny Day/ Dueling Bikes From Quicksilver	Ray Parker Jr. & Helen Terry	#96

SAXOPHONE (cont'd)

1987		
I Wanna Dance With Somebody (Who Loves Me)	Whitney Houston	#1
C'est La Vie	Robbie Nevil	#2
When Smokey Sings	ABC	#5
Girlfriend	Bobby Brown	#57
System Of Survival	Earth, Wind & Fire	#60
A Trick Of The Night	Bananarama	#76
Dancin' With My Mirror	Corey Hart	#88
Downtown Train	Patty Smyth	#95
Hold Me	Colin James Hay	#99

1988		
Got My Mind Set On You	George Harrison	#1
New Sensation	INXS	#3
I Saw Him Standing There	Tiffany	#7
I Still Believe	Brenda K. Starr	#13
True Love	Glenn Frey	#13
Be Still My Beating Heart	Sting	#15
The Twist (Yo, Twist!)	The Fat Boys w/ Chubby Checker	#16
Staying Together	Debbie Gibson	#22
Missed Opportunity	Daryl Hall & John Oates	#29
Live My Life	Boy George	#40
Promise Me	The Cover Girls	#40
Talking Back To The Night	Steve Winwood	#57
Dancing Under A Latin Moon	Candi	#68
Ooo La La La	Teena Marie	#85
When I Fall In Love	Natalie Cole	#95

1989		
Forever Your Girl	Paula Abdul	#1
Girl I'm Gonna Miss You*	Milli Vanilli	#1
	*Soprano sax	
What You Don't Know	Expose	#8
Everlasting Love	Howard Jones	#12
Back On Holiday	Robbie Nevil	#34
Let Me In	Eddie Money	#60
Baby Come To Me	Regina Belle	#60
We Could Be Together	Debbie Gibson	#71
Way Cool Jr.	Ratt	#75

SONGS WITH SAXOPHONE SOLOS

Only saxophone solos that are ten seconds or longer are listed.

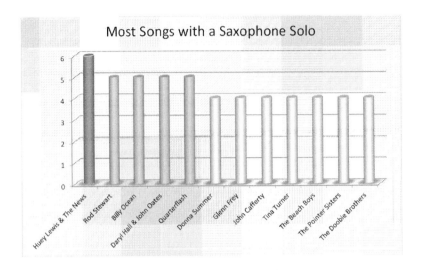

SONG	ARTIST	HOT 100 CHART	LENGTH OF SOLO
1980			
It's Still Rock And Roll To Me	Billy Joel	#1	19 seconds
Funkytown	Lipps, Inc.	#1	14 seconds
Biggest Part Of Me	Ambrosia	#3	11 seconds
Emotional Rescue	The Rolling Stones	#3	20 seconds
Too Hot	Kool & The Gang	#5	35 seconds
Real Love	The Doobie Brothers	#5	21 seconds
You May Be Right	Billy Joel	#7	11 seconds
More Love	Kim Carnes	#10	16 seconds
Let Me Love You Tonight	Pure Prairie League	#10	19 seconds
Cool Change	Little River Band	#10	15 seconds
One Fine Day	Carole King	#12	27 seconds
Heart Hotels	Dan Fogelberg	#21	25 seconds
How Do I Survive	Amy Holland	#22	16 seconds
Carrie	Cliff Richard	#34	15 seconds
Only A Lonely Heart Sees	Felix Cavaliere	#36	29 seconds
Walk Away	Donna Summer	#36	15 seconds
Horizontal Bop	Bob Seger	#42	25 seconds
Let Me Be	Korona	#43	15 seconds
It's For You	Player	#46	28 seconds
I Don't Want To Talk About It	Rod Stewart	#46	30 seconds
Bad Times	Tavares	#47	19 seconds

SONGS WITH SAXOPHONE SOLOS (cont'd)

Solitaire	Peter McIan	#52	32 seconds
First… Be A Woman	Lenore O'Malley	#53	20 seconds
Let's Go 'Round Again	Average White Band	#53	15 seconds
Easy Love	Dionne Warwick	#62	17 seconds
I'm Happy Just To Dance With You	Anne Murray	#64	25 seconds
Trickle, Trickle	Manhattan Transfer	#73	21 seconds
It Hurts Too Much	Eric Carmen	#75	15 seconds
Holdin' On For Dear Love	Lobo	#75	23 seconds
Over You	Roxy Music	#80	22 seconds
Goin' On	The Beach Boys	#83	13 seconds
Only The Lonely (Have A Reason To Be Sad)	La Flavour	#91	23 seconds

1981			
Arthur's Theme (Best That You Can Do)	Christopher Cross	#1	29 seconds
Rapture	Blondie	#1	26 seconds
Urgent	Foreigner	#4	49 seconds
There Ain't No Gettin' Over Me	Ronnie Milsap	#5	19 seconds
Giving It Up For Your Love	Delbert McClinton	#8	19 seconds
Same Old Lang Syne	Dan Fogelberg	#9	43 seconds
This Little Girl	Gary U.S. Bonds	#11	10 seconds
We're In This Love Together	Al Jarreau	#15	27 seconds
Touch Me (When We're Dancing)	Carpenters	#16	22 seconds
Super Freak (Part 1)	Rick James	#16	16 seconds
Ain't Even Done With The Night	John Cougar	#17	14 seconds
Say Goodbye To Hollywood	Billy Joel	#17	30 seconds
Fool In Love With You	Jim Photoglo	#25	20 seconds
Rock And Roll Dreams Come Through	Jim Steinman (Rory Dodd)	#32	21 seconds
Wasn't That A Party	Rovers	#37	17 seconds
One More Night	Streek	#47	33 seconds
Somebody Send My Baby Home	Lenny Leblanc	#55	25 seconds
Stay Awake	Ronnie Laws	#60	55 seconds
Keep This Train A-Rollin'	The Doobie Brothers	#62	20 seconds
I Don't Want To Know Your Name	Glen Campbell	#65	23 seconds
A Heart In New York	Art Garfunkel	#66	19 seconds
The Real Thing	The Brothers Johnson	#67	15 seconds
You're Mine Tonight	Pure Prairie League	#68	19 seconds
Shotgun Rider	Delbert McClinton	#70	17 seconds
La La Means I Love You	Tierra	#72	14 seconds
Want You Back In My Life Again	Carpenters	#72	15 seconds
Winkin', Blinkin', And Nod	The Doobie Brothers	#76	20 seconds
You've Got A Good Love Coming	Van Stephenson	#79	15 seconds
Let's Put The Fun Back In Rock N Roll	Freddy Cannon & The Belmonts	#81	30 seconds

SONGS WITH SAXOPHONE SOLOS (cont'd)

Next Time You'll Know	Sister Sledge	#82	23 seconds
I'm So Glad I'm Standing Here Today	Crusaders w/ Joe Cocker	#97	22 seconds

1982			
Maneater	Daryl Hall & John Oates	#1	42 seconds
I Can't Go For That (No Can Do)	Daryl Hall & John Oates	#1	17 seconds
You Should Hear How She Talks About You	Melissa Manchester	#5	14 seconds
Do You Believe In Love	Huey Lewis & The News	#7	19 seconds
Only The Lonely	The Motels	#9	17 seconds
Love Is In Control (Finger On The Trigger)	Donna Summer	#10	13 seconds
Bobbie Sue	The Oak Ridge Boys	#12	14 seconds
Should I Do It	The Pointer Sisters	#13	29 seconds
Come Go With Me	The Beach Boys	#18	17 seconds
Personally	Karla Bonoff	#19	17 seconds
Big Fun	Kool & The Gang	#21	16 seconds
Out Of Work	Gary U.S. Bonds	#21	17 seconds
Forget Me Nots	Patrice Rushen	#23	17 seconds
Going To A Go-Go	The Rolling Stones	#25	26 seconds
(Theme From) Magnum P.I.	Mike Post	#25	53 seconds
Make Believe	Toto	#30	8 seconds
Your Imagination	Daryl Hall & John Oates	#33	16 seconds
Tell Me Tomorrow- Part 1	Smokey Robinson	#33	10 seconds
Love Plus One	Haircut One Hundred	#37	13 seconds
Tonight Tonight	Bill Champlin	#55	14 seconds
He Got You	Ronnie Milsap	#59	18 seconds
Old Fashioned Love	Smokey Robinson	#60	20 seconds
Every Home Should Have One	Pattie Austin	#62	19 seconds
Back To School Again	The Four Tops	#71	8 seconds
Pledge Pin	Robert Plant	#74	28 seconds
Beechwood 4-5789	Carpenters	#74	12 seconds
This Time	Kiara w/Shanice Wilson	#78	21 seconds
The Longer You Wait	Gino Vannelli	#89	21 seconds
Into My Love	Greg Guidry	#92	20 seconds

1983			
Time (Clock Of The Heart)	Culture Club	#2	17 seconds
She Works Hard For The Money	Donna Summer	#3	12 seconds
Overkill	Men At Work	#3	12 seconds
True	Spandau Ballet	#4	36 seconds
One On One	Daryl Hall & John Oates	#7	15 seconds
Baby Jane	Rod Stewart	#14	14 seconds

SONGS WITH SAXOPHONE SOLOS (cont'd)

Take Me To Heart	Quarterflash	#14	25 seconds
Rio	Duran Duran	#14	42 seconds
Heart To Heart	Kenny Loggins	#15	10 seconds
The Human Touch	Rick Springfield	#18	18 seconds
The Woman In You	Bee Gees	#24	29 seconds
Make Love Stay	Dan Fogelberg	#29	37 seconds
The One Thing	INXS	#30	15 seconds
My Kind Of Lady	Supertramp	#31	50 seconds
No Time For Talk	Christopher Cross	#33	20 seconds
It Must Be Love	Madness	#33	11 seconds
The Border	America	#33	14 seconds
Old Time Rock & Roll	Bob Seger	#48	13 seconds
Land Of A Thousand Dances	J. Geils Band	#60	26 seconds
On The Dark Side	Eddie & The Cruisers	#64	23 seconds
If You Wanna Get Back Your Lady	The Pointer Sisters	#67	17 seconds
Don't Try To Stop It	Roman Holliday	#68	13 seconds
Bread And Butter	Robert John	#68	12 seconds
Every Home Should Have One	Pattie Austin	#69	18 seconds
Ship To Shore	Chris DeBurgh	#71	15 seconds
I Just Can't Walk Away	The Four Tops	#71	24 seconds
Crazy	Manhattans	#72	19 seconds
Keep It Tight	Single Bullet Theory	#78	24 seconds
I Cannot Believe It's True	Phil Collins	#79	22 seconds
Where Everybody Knows Your Name (The Theme From "Cheers")	Gary Portnoy	#83	13 seconds

1984			
Caribbean Queen (No More Love On The Run)	Billy Ocean	#1	33 seconds
Dancing In The Dark	Bruce Springsteen	#2	24 seconds
The Heart Of Rock & Roll	Huey Lewis & The News	#6	27 seconds
Some Guys Have All The Luck	Rod Stewart	#10	15 seconds
It's A Miracle	Culture Club	#13	16 seconds
The Curly Shuffle	Jump 'N The Saddle	#15	9 seconds
Don't Answer Me	Alan Parsons Project	#15	34 seconds
It Ain't Enough	Corey Hart	#17	18 seconds
There Goes My Baby	Donna Summer	#21	17 seconds
She's Mine	Steve Perry	#21	18 seconds
Gold	Spandau Ballet	#29	25 seconds
Alibis	Sergio Mendes	#29	20 seconds
The Kid's American	Matthew Wilder	#33	18 seconds
Only When You Leave	Spandau Ballet	#34	21 seconds
Remember The Nights	The Motels	#36	14 seconds

SONGS WITH SAXOPHONE SOLOS (cont'd)

Tonight	David Bowie w/ Tina Turner	#53	37 seconds
Heart Don't Lie	La Toya Jackson	#56	26 seconds
Happy Ending	Joe Jackson w/ Elaine Caswell	#57	33 seconds
Taxi Dancing	Rick Springfield & Randy Crawford	#59	12 seconds
Walking In My Sleep	Roger Daltrey	#62	20 seconds
I Cry Just A Little Bit	Shakin' Stevens	#67	15 seconds
Look At That Cadillac	Stray Cats	#68	40 seconds
I Pretend	Kim Carnes	#74	17 seconds
You're The Best Thing	The Style Council	#76	28 seconds
I Send A Message	INXS	#77	14 seconds
Tender Years	John Cafferty	#78	18 seconds
Shooting Shark	Blue Oyster Cult	#83	17 seconds
Don't Be My Enemy	Wang Chung	#86	43 seconds
Unfaithfully Yours (One Love)	Stephen Bishop	#87	9 seconds
Love Has Finally Come At Last	Bobby Womack & Patti Labelle	#88	38 seconds

1985			
One More Night	Phil Collins	#1	30 seconds
We Don't Need Another Hero (Thunderdome)	Tina Turner	#2	18 seconds
You Belong To The City	Glenn Frey	#2	18 seconds
Never Surrender	Corey Hart	#3	34 seconds
Smooth Operator	Sade	#5	18 seconds
I'm Goin' Down	Bruce Springsteen	#9	15 seconds
One Of The Living	Tina Turner	#15	18 seconds
Rock And Roll Girls	John Fogerty	#20	27 seconds
A Nite At The Apollo Live! The Way You Do The Things You Do/ My Girl	Daryl Hall & John Oates w/ David Ruffin & Eddie Kendrick	#20	14 seconds
Tough All Over	John Cafferty	#22	14 seconds
Rockin' At Midnight	The Honeydrippers	#25	35 seconds
So In Love	Orchestral Manoeuvres In The Dark	#26	16 seconds
Wake Up (Next To You)	Graham Parker w/ The Shot	#39	18 seconds
Stir It Up	Patti Labelle	#41	18 seconds
Talk To Me	Fiona	#64	23 seconds
Small Town Girl	John Cafferty	#64	24 seconds
Abadabadango	Kim Carnes	#67	15 seconds
(Closest Thing To) Perfect	Jermaine Jackson	#67	27 seconds
Days Are Numbered (The Traveller)	Alan Parsons Project	#71	26 seconds
Eye To Eye	Go West	#73	40 seconds
Mathematics	Melissa Manchester	#74	16 seconds
You Send Me	The Manhattans	#81	26 seconds
Hold Me	Laura Branigan	#82	25 seconds
Talk To Me	Quarterflash	#83	21 seconds

SONGS WITH SAXOPHONE SOLOS (cont'd)

Information	Eric Martin	#87	10 seconds

1986			
How Will I Know	Whitney Houston	#1	17 seconds
When The Going Gets Tough, The Tough Get Going	Billy Ocean	#2	19 seconds
Typical Male	Tina Turner	#2	15 seconds
I'm Your Man	Wham!	#3	13 seconds
Hip To Be Square	Huey Lewis & The News	#3	12 seconds
If You Leave	Orchestral Manoeuvres In The Dark	#4	13 seconds
Talk To Me	Stevie Nicks	#4	16 seconds
Baby Love	Regina	#10	17 seconds
A Love Bizarre	Sheila E.	#11	13 seconds
I Do What I Do (Theme For 9 1/2 Weeks)	John Taylor/Jonathan Elias	#23	10 seconds
Walk Like A Man	Mary Jane Girls	#41	35 seconds
Superbowl Shuffle	The Chicago Bears Shufflin' Crew	#41	17 seconds
So Far So Good	Sheena Easton	#43	20 seconds
Nail It To The Wall	Stacy Lattisaw	#48	14 seconds
Call Me	Dennis DeYoung	#54	32 seconds
California Dreamin'	The Beach Boys	#57	15 seconds
If Your Heart Isn't In It	Atlantic Starr	#57	15 seconds
Let Me Be The One	Five Star	#59	14 seconds
Thorn In My Side	Eurythmics	#68	17 seconds
Miami	Bob Seger	#70	15 seconds
If You Were A Woman (And I Was A Man)	Bonnie Tyler	#77	17 seconds
Stacy	Fortune	#80	19 seconds
I Feel The Magic	Belinda Carlisle	#82	12 seconds
Somebody Somewhere	Platinum Blonde	#82	32 seconds
This Love	Bad Company	#85	16 seconds
I'm For Real	Howard Hewett	#90	18 seconds
Shelter Me	Joe Cocker	#91	15 seconds
Gravity	James Brown	#93	15 seconds
Karen	B.E. Taylor Group	#94	29 seconds
I Want To Make The World Turn Around	The Steve Miller Band	#97	17 seconds
Walk Away Renee	Southside Johnny & The Jukes	#98	10 seconds

1987			
Lost In Emotion	Lisa Lisa & Cult Jam	#1	16 seconds
(I've Had) The Time Of My Life	Bill Medley & Jennifer Warnes	#1	17 seconds
Only In My Dreams	Debbie Gibson	#4	31 seconds
One Heartbeat	Smokey Robinson	#10	21 seconds
Love Power	Dionne Warwick & Jeffrey Osborne	#12	26 seconds

SONGS WITH SAXOPHONE SOLOS (cont'd)

Come As You Are	Peter Wolf	#15	15 seconds
Who Found Who	Jellybean w/ Elisa Fiorillo	#16	16 seconds
Candy	Cameo	#21	35 seconds
Be There	The Pointer Sisters	#42	18 seconds
French Kissin	Debbie Harry	#57	20 seconds
System Of Survival	Earth, Wind & Fire	#60	26 seconds
If I Say Yes	Five Star	#67	17 seconds
Young Blood	Bruce Willis	#68	29 seconds
Should I See	Frozen Ghost	#69	32 seconds
Special Way	Kool & The Gang	#72	45 seconds
Can't Get Started	Peter Wolf	#75	26 seconds
Twistin' The Night Away	Rod Stewart	#80	12 seconds
Rock-A-Lott	Aretha Franklin	#82	17 seconds

1988			
Kokomo	The Beach Boys	#1	17 seconds
Seasons Change	Expose	#1	28 seconds
Get Outta My Dreams, Get Into My Car	Billy Ocean	#1	16 seconds
Roll With It	Steve Winwood	#1	15 seconds
Hands To Heaven	Breathe	#2	14 seconds
I'll Always Love You	Taylor Dayne	#3	23 seconds
She's Like The Wind	Patrick Swayze w/ Wendy Fraser	#3	14 seconds
Hungry Eyes	Eric Carmen	#4	17 seconds
Waiting For A Star To Fall	Boy Meets Girl	#5	23 seconds
Never Tear Us Apart	INXS	#7	16 seconds
Electric Blue	Icehouse	#7	27 seconds
Some Kind Of Lover	Jody Watley	#10	32 seconds
Another Lover	Giant Steps	#13	16 seconds
The Colour Of Love	Billy Ocean	#17	24 seconds
Till I Loved You	Barbra Streisand & Don Johnson	#25	19 seconds
Small World	Huey Lewis & The News	#25	37 seconds
Not Just Another Girl	Ivan Neville	#26	18 seconds
Time And Tide	Basia	#26	15 seconds
Never Knew Love Like This	Alexander O'Neal w/ Cherrelle	#28	13 seconds
Dance Little Sister (Part One)	Terence Trent D'Arby	#30	15 seconds
Going Back To Cali	L.L. Cool J	#31	20 seconds
In Your Soul	Corey Hart	#38	22 seconds
Jackie	Blue Zone U.K.	#54	13 seconds
Darlin' Danielle Don't	Henry Lee Summer	#57	20 seconds
Nice 'N' Slow	Freddie Jackson	#61	17 seconds
Hot Thing	Prince	#63	17 seconds
I Want To Be Your Property	Blue Mercedes	#66	14 seconds

SONGS WITH SAXOPHONE SOLOS (cont'd)

Lonely Won't Leave Me Alone	Glenn Medeiros	#67	14 seconds
Ever Since The World Began	Tommy Shaw	#75	13 seconds
Wait On Love	Michael Bolton	#79	17 seconds
Englishman In New York	Sting	#84	19 seconds
Hands On The Radio	Henry Lee Summer	#85	15 seconds
Reason To Try	Eric Carmen	#87	18 seconds

1989			
The Lover In Me	Sheena Easton	#2	16 seconds
Angelia	Richard Marx	#4	20 seconds
With Every Beat Of My Heart	Taylor Dayne	#5	20 seconds
She Wants To Dance With Me	Rick Astley	#6	16 seconds
Walk The Dinosaur	Was (Not Was)	#7	16 seconds
Dreamin'	Vanessa Williams	#8	24 seconds
I Remember Holding You	Boys Club	#8	11 seconds
The End Of The Innocence*	Don Henley	#8	19 seconds
	*Soprano sax		
When I Looked At Him	Expose	#10	11 seconds
Cry	Waterfront	#10	18 seconds
Get On Your Feet	Gloria Estefan	#11	16 seconds
Crazy About Her	Rod Stewart	#11	14 seconds
Sacred Emotion	Donny Osmond	#13	18 seconds
The Best	Tina Turner	#15	19 seconds
No More Rhyme	Debbie Gibson	#17	30 seconds
License To Chill	Billy Ocean	#32	18 seconds
Radio Romance	Tiffany	#35	13 seconds
Birthday Suit	Johnny Kemp	#36	18 seconds
24/7	Dino	#42	22 seconds
Give Me The Keys (And I'll Drive You Crazy)	Huey Lewis & The News	#47	30 seconds
Congratulations	Vesta	#55	22 seconds
Pride & Passion	John Cafferty	#66	28 seconds
Hold On	Donny Osmond	#73	17 seconds
And The Night Stood Still	Dion	#75	15 seconds
I Can't Face The Fact	Gina Go-Go	#78	19 seconds
Touch The Fire	Icehouse	#84	14 seconds
Right Back Where We Started From	Sinitta	#84	15 seconds
Ain't Too Proud Too Beg	Rick Astley	#89	20 seconds

SONGS WITH SAXOPHONE SOLOS (cont'd)

Livin' Right	Glenn Frey	#90	28 seconds

SONGS WITH MULTIPLE SAXOPHONE SOLOS

SONG	ARTIST	HOT 100 CHART	LENGTH OF SOLOS IN SECONDS
1980			
Ali Thompson	Take A Little Rhythm	#15	14, 11
Jojo	Boz Scaggs	#17	20, 20
Midnight Rocks	Al Stewart	#24	23, 20
I Shoulda Loved Ya	Narada Michael Walden	#66	18, 17
1981			
Just The Two Of Us	Grover Washington Jr. w/Bill Withers	#2	19, 40
One Step Closer	The Doobie Brothers	#24	19, 30, 17
He Can't Love You	Michael Stanley Band	#33	13, 13
Lovin The Night Away	The Dillman Band	#45	11, 12, 22
Fire In The Sky	The Dirt Band	#76	24, 35
At This Moment	Billy Vera & The Beaters	#79	15, 18
Love Light	Yutaka w/Patti Austin	#81	14, 14
1982			
Who Can It Be Now?	Men At Work	#1	13, 30
Harden My Heart	Quarterflash	#3	16, 16,
It's Raining Again	Supertramp	#11	15, 31
Waiting On A Friend	The Rolling Stones	#13	38, 40
The One You Love	Glenn Frey	#15	25, 25, 40
American Music	The Pointer Sisters	#16	13, 16
I Found Somebody	Glenn Frey	#31	20, 19, 25
Let It Be Me	Willie Nelson	#40	15, 17
Right Kind Of Love	Quarterflash	#56	16, 17
Night Shift	Quarterflash	#60	14, 15
Teach Me Tonight	Al Jarreau	#70	13, 33
Piece Of My Heart	Sammy Hagar	#73	21, 24
Every Love Song	Greg Kihn Band	#82	13, 20
Sad Hearts	The Four Tops	#84	16, 18
Running	Chubby Checker	#91	14, 14
Be Mine (Tonight)	Grover Washington, Jr. (Grady Tate)	#92	81, 55

SONGS WITH MULTIPLE SAXOPHONE SOLOS (cont'd)

1983			
Please Mr. Postman	Gentle Persuasion	#82	10, 15

1984			
I Want A New Drug	Huey Lewis & The News	#6	16, 16
A Girl In Trouble (Is A Temporary Thing)	Romeo Void	#35	14, 14, 45, 34

1985			
Careless Whisper	Wham!/George Michael	#1	26, 26, 13
Freeway Of Love	Aretha Franklin	#3	14, 14
Your Love Is King	Sade	#54	20, 20
Willie And The Hand Jive	George Thorogood	#63	24, 20

1986			
Digging Your Scene	The Blow Monkeys	#14	12, 20
You're A Friend Of Mine	Clarence Clemons & Jackson Browne	#18	20, 21
For America	Jackson Browne	#30	10, 10
Taken In	Mike + The Mechanics	#32	15, 13
Where Did Your Heart Go?	Wham!	#50	19, 41

1987			
You Got It All	The Jets	#3	11, 11
I Wanna Go Back	Eddie Money	#14	16, 18
Don't Make Me Wait For Love	Kenny G w/ Lenny Williams	#15	11, 26

1988			
Foolish Beat	Debbie Gibson	#1	20, 19
Endless Summer Nights	Richard Marx	#2	10, 24
I Can't Wait	Deniece Williams	#66	11, 22

1989			
Soul Provider	Michael Bolton	#17	12, 21
We've Saved The Best For Last	Kenny G & Smokey Robinson	#47	19, 19

THE LONGEST SAXOPHONE SOLOS OF THE 80s

YEAR	SONG	ARTIST	HOT 100 CHART	LENGTH OF SOLO(S)
1982	Be Mine (Tonight)	Grover Washington, Jr. (Grady Tate)	#92	81, 55 seconds
1981	Stay Awake	Ronnie Laws	#60	55 seconds
1982	(Theme From) Magnum P.I.	Mike Post	#25	53 seconds
1983	My Kind Of Lady	Supertramp	#31	50 seconds
1981	Urgent	Foreigner	#4	49 seconds
1984	A Girl In Trouble (Is A Temporary Thing)	Romeo Void	#35	45, 34, 14, 14 seconds
1987	Special Way	Kool & The Gang	#72	45 seconds
1981	Same Old Lang Syne	Dan Fogelberg	#9	43 seconds
1984	Don't Be My Enemy	Wang Chung	#86	43 seconds
1982	Maneater	Daryl Hall & John Oates	#1	42 seconds
1983	Rio	Duran Duran	#14	42 seconds
1986	Where Did Your Heart Go?	Wham!	#50	41, 19 seconds
1985	Eye To Eye	Go West	#73	40 seconds
1982	Waiting On A Friend	The Rolling Stones	#13	40, 38 seconds
1982	The One You Love	Glenn Frey	#15	40, 25, 25 seconds
1981	Just The Two Of Us	Grover Washington Jr. w/Bill Withers	#2	40, 19 seconds
1984	Look At That Cadillac	Stray Cats	#68	40 seconds
1984	Love Has Finally Come At Last	Bobby Womack & Patti Labelle	#88	38 seconds
1983	Make Love Stay	Dan Fogelberg	#29	37 seconds
1984	Tonight	David Bowie w/ Tina Turner	#53	37 seconds
1988	Small World	Huey Lewis & The News	#25	37 seconds
1983	True	Spandau Ballet	#4	36 seconds
1986	Walk Like A Man	Mary Jane Girls	#41	35 seconds
1980	Too Hot	Kool & The Gang	#5	35 seconds
1985	Rockin' At Midnight	The Honeydrippers	#25	35 seconds
1987	Candy	Cameo	#21	35 seconds
1981	Fire In The Sky	The Dirt Band	#76	35, 24 seconds
1984	Don't Answer Me	Alan Parsons Project	#15	34 seconds
1985	Never Surrender	Corey Hart	#3	34 seconds
1982	Teach Me Tonight	Al Jarreau	#70	33, 13 seconds
1981	One More Night	Streek	#47	33 seconds
1984	Caribbean Queen (No More Love On The Run)	Billy Ocean	#1	33 seconds
1984	Happy Ending	Joe Jackson w/ Elaine Caswell	#57	33 seconds
1980	Solitaire	Peter McIan	#52	32 seconds
1986	Call Me	Dennis DeYoung	#54	32 seconds

THE LONGEST SAXOPHONE SOLOS OF THE 80s (cont'd)

1986	Somebody Somewhere	Platinum Blonde	#82	32 seconds
1987	Should I See	Frozen Ghost	#69	32 seconds
1988	Some Kind Of Lover	Jody Watley	#10	32 seconds
1982	It's Raining Again	Supertramp	#11	31, 15 seconds
1987	Only In My Dreams	Debbie Gibson	#4	31 seconds
1985	One More Night	Phil Collins	#1	30 seconds
1981	One Step Closer	The Doobie Brothers	#24	30, 19, 17 seconds
1982	Who Can It Be Now?	Men At Work	#1	30, 13 seconds
1980	I Don't Want To Talk About It	Rod Stewart	#46	30 seconds
1981	Say Goodbye To Hollywood	Billy Joel	#17	30 seconds
1981	Let's Put The Fun Back In Rock N Roll	Freddy Cannon & The Belmonts	#81	30 seconds
1989	No More Rhyme	Debbie Gibson	#17	30 seconds
1989	Give Me The Keys (And I'll Drive You Crazy)	Huey Lewis & The News	#47	30 seconds
1980	Only A Lonely Heart Sees	Felix Cavaliere	#36	29 seconds
1981	Arthur's Theme (Best That You Can Do)	Christopher Cross	#1	29 seconds
1982	Should I Do It	The Pointer Sisters	#13	29 seconds
1983	The Woman In You	Bee Gees	#24	29 seconds
1986	Karen	B.E. Taylor Group	#94	29 seconds
1987	Young Blood	Bruce Willis	#68	29 seconds
1980	It's For You	Player	#46	28 seconds
1982	Pledge Pin	Robert Plant	#74	28 seconds
1984	You're The Best Thing	The Style Council	#76	28 seconds
1988	Seasons Change	Expose	#1	28 seconds
1989	Pride & Passion	John Cafferty	#66	28 seconds
1989	Livin' Right	Glenn Frey	#90	28 seconds
1980	One Fine Day	Carole King	#12	27 seconds
1981	We're In This Love Together	Al Jarreau	#15	27 seconds
1984	The Heart Of Rock & Roll	Huey Lewis & The News	#6	27 seconds
1985	Rock And Roll Girls	John Fogerty	#20	27 seconds
1985	(Closest Thing To) Perfect	Jermaine Jackson	#67	27 seconds
1988	Electric Blue	Icehouse	#7	27 seconds
1985	Careless Whisper	Wham!/George Michael	#1	26, 26, 13 seconds
1987	Don't Make Me Wait For Love	Kenny G w/ Lenny Williams	#15	26, 11 seconds
1981	Rapture	Blondie	#1	26 seconds
1982	Going To A Go-Go	The Rolling Stones	#25	26 seconds
1983	Land Of A Thousand Dances	J. Geils Band	#60	26 seconds
1984	Heart Don't Lie	La Toya Jackson	#56	26 seconds
1985	Days Are Numbered (The Traveller)	Alan Parsons Project	#71	26 seconds
1985	You Send Me	The Manhattans	#81	26 seconds
1987	Love Power	Dionne Warwick & Jeffrey Osborne	#12	26 seconds

THE LONGEST SAXOPHONE SOLOS OF THE 80s (cont'd)

1987	System Of Survival	Earth, Wind & Fire	#60	26 seconds
1987	Can't Get Started	Peter Wolf	#75	26 seconds
1985	Hold Me	Laura Branigan	#82	25 seconds
1982	I Found Somebody	Glenn Frey	#31	25, 20, 19 seconds
1980	Heart Hotels	Dan Fogelberg	#21	25 seconds
1980	Horizontal Bop	Bob Seger	#42	25 seconds
1980	I'm Happy Just To Dance With You	Anne Murray	#64	25 seconds
1981	Somebody Send My Baby Home	Lenny Leblanc	#55	25 seconds
1983	Take Me To Heart	Quarterflash	#14	25 seconds
1984	Gold	Spandau Ballet	#29	25 seconds
1982	Piece Of My Heart	Sammy Hagar	#73	24, 21 seconds
1985	Willie And The Hand Jive	George Thorogood	#63	24, 20 seconds
1988	Endless Summer Nights	Richard Marx	#2	24, 10 seconds
1984	Dancing In The Dark	Bruce Springsteen	#2	24 seconds
1983	I Just Can't Walk Away	The Four Tops	#71	24 seconds
1983	Keep It Tight	Single Bullet Theory	#78	24 seconds
1985	Small Town Girl	John Cafferty	#64	24 seconds
1988	The Colour Of Love	Billy Ocean	#17	24 seconds
1989	Dreamin'	Vanessa Williams	#8	24 seconds
1980	Midnight Rocks	Al Stewart	#24	23, 20 seconds
1980	Holdin' On For Dear Love	Lobo	#75	23 seconds
1980	Only The Lonely (Have A Reason To Be Sad)	La Flavour	#91	23 seconds
1981	I Don't Want To Know Your Name	Glen Campbell	#65	23 seconds
1981	Next Time You'll Know	Sister Sledge	#82	23 seconds
1983	On The Dark Side	Eddie & The Cruisers	#64	23 seconds
1985	Talk To Me	Fiona	#64	23 seconds
1988	I'll Always Love You	Taylor Dayne	#3	23 seconds
1988	Waiting For A Star To Fall	Boy Meets Girl	#5	23 seconds
1981	Lovin The Night Away	The Dillman Band	#45	22, 12, 11 seconds
1988	I Can't Wait	Deniece Williams	#66	22, 11 seconds
1980	Over You	Roxy Music	#80	22 seconds
1981	Touch Me (When We're Dancing)	Carpenters	#16	22 seconds
1981	I'm So Glad I'm Standing Here Today	Crusaders w/ Joe Cocker	#97	22 seconds
1983	I Cannot Believe It's True	Phil Collins	#79	22 seconds
1988	In Your Soul	Corey Hart	#38	22 seconds
1989	24/7	Dino	#42	22 seconds
1989	Congratulations	Vesta	#55	22 seconds
1986	You're A Friend Of Mine	Clarence Clemons & Jackson Browne	#18	21, 20 seconds
1989	Soul Provider	Michael Bolton	#17	21, 19 seconds

THE LONGEST SAXOPHONE SOLOS OF THE 80s (cont'd)

1980	Real Love	The Doobie Brothers	#5	21 seconds
1980	Trickle, Trickle	Manhattan Transfer	#73	21 seconds
1981	Rock And Roll Dreams Come Through	Jim Steinman (Rory Dodd)	#32	21 seconds
1982	This Time	Kiara w/Shanice Wilson	#78	21 seconds
1982	The Longer You Wait	Gino Vannelli	#89	21 seconds
1984	Only When You Leave	Spandau Ballet	#34	21 seconds
1985	Talk To Me	Quarterflash	#83	21 seconds
1987	One Heartbeat	Smokey Robinson	#10	21 seconds
1980	Jojo	Boz Scaggs	#17	20, 20 seconds
1985	Your Love Is King	Sade	#54	20, 20 seconds
1988	Foolish Beat	Debbie Gibson	#1	20, 19 seconds
1982	Every Love Song	Greg Kihn Band	#82	20, 13 seconds
1986	Digging Your Scene	The Blow Monkeys	#14	20, 12 seconds
1980	Emotional Rescue	The Rolling Stones	#3	20 seconds
1980	First… Be A Woman	Lenore O'Malley	#53	20 seconds
1981	Fool In Love With You	Jim Photoglo	#25	20 seconds
1981	Keep This Train A-Rollin'	The Doobie Brothers	#62	20 seconds
1981	Winkin', Blinkin', And Nod	The Doobie Brothers	#76	20 seconds
1982	Old Fashioned Love	Smokey Robinson	#60	20 seconds
1982	Into My Love	Greg Guidry	#92	20 seconds
1983	No Time For Talk	Christopher Cross	#33	20 seconds
1984	Alibis	Sergio Mendes	#29	20 seconds
1984	Walking In My Sleep	Roger Daltrey	#62	20 seconds
1986	So Far So Good	Sheena Easton	#43	20 seconds
1987	French Kissin	Debbie Harry	#57	20 seconds
1988	Going Back To Cali	L.L. Cool J	#31	20 seconds
1988	Darlin' Danielle Don't	Henry Lee Summer	#57	20 seconds
1989	Angelia	Richard Marx	#4	20 seconds
1989	With Every Beat Of My Heart	Taylor Dayne	#5	20 seconds
1989	Ain't Too Proud Too Beg	Rick Astley	#89	20 seconds
1989	We've Saved The Best For Last	Kenny G & Smokey Robinson	#47	19, 19 seconds
1989	The End Of The Innocence	Don Henley	#8	19 seconds
1980	It's Still Rock And Roll To Me	Billy Joel	#1	19 seconds
1980	Let Me Love You Tonight	Pure Prairie League	#10	19 seconds
1980	Bad Times	Tavares	#47	19 seconds
1981	There Ain't No Gettin' Over Me	Ronnie Milsap	#5	19 seconds
1981	Giving It Up For Your Love	Delbert McClinton	#8	19 seconds
1981	A Heart In New York	Art Garfunkel	#66	19 seconds
1981	You're Mine Tonight	Pure Prairie League	#68	19 seconds
1982	Do You Believe In Love	Huey Lewis & The News	#7	19 seconds
1982	Every Home Should Have One	Pattie Austin	#62	19 seconds
1983	Crazy	Manhattans	#72	19 seconds

THE LONGEST SAXOPHONE SOLOS OF THE 80s (cont'd)

1986	When The Going Gets Tough, The Tough Get Going	Billy Ocean	#2	19 seconds
1986	Stacy	Fortune	#80	19 seconds
1988	Till I Loved You	Barbra Streisand & Don Johnson	#25	19 seconds
1988	Englishman In New York	Sting	#84	19 seconds
1989	The Best	Tina Turner	#15	19 seconds
1989	I Can't Face The Fact	Gina Go-Go	#78	19 seconds
1980	I Shoulda Loved Ya	Narada Michael Walden	#66	18, 17 seconds
1982	Sad Hearts	The Four Tops	#84	18, 16 seconds
1987	I Wanna Go Back	Eddie Money	#14	18, 16 seconds
1981	At This Moment	Billy Vera & The Beaters	#79	18, 15 seconds
1982	He Got You	Ronnie Milsap	#59	18 seconds
1983	The Human Touch	Rick Springfield	#18	18 seconds
1983	Every Home Should Have One	Pattie Austin	#69	18 seconds
1984	It Ain't Enough	Corey Hart	#17	18 seconds
1984	She's Mine	Steve Perry	#21	18 seconds
1984	The Kid's American	Matthew Wilder	#33	18 seconds
1984	Tender Years	John Cafferty	#78	18 seconds
1985	We Don't Need Another Hero (Thunderdome)	Tina Turner	#2	18 seconds
1985	You Belong To The City	Glenn Frey	#2	18 seconds
1985	Smooth Operator	Sade	#5	18 seconds
1985	One Of The Living	Tina Turner	#15	18 seconds
1985	Wake Up (Next To You)	Graham Parker w/ The Shot	#39	18 seconds
1985	Stir It Up	Patti Labelle	#41	18 seconds
1986	I'm For Real	Howard Hewett	#90	18 seconds
1987	Be There	The Pointer Sisters	#42	18 seconds
1988	Not Just Another Girl	Ivan Neville	#26	18 seconds
1988	Reason To Try	Eric Carmen	#87	18 seconds
1989	Cry	Waterfront	#10	18 seconds
1989	Sacred Emotion	Donny Osmond	#13	18 seconds
1989	License To Chill	Billy Ocean	#32	18 seconds
1989	Birthday Suit	Johnny Kemp	#36	18 seconds
1982	Right Kind Of Love	Quarterflash	#56	17, 16 seconds
1982	Let It Be Me	Willie Nelson	#40	17, 15 seconds
1980	Easy Love	Dionne Warwick	#62	17 seconds
1981	Wasn't That A Party	Rovers	#37	17 seconds
1981	Shotgun Rider	Delbert McClinton	#70	17 seconds
1982	I Can't Go For That (No Can Do)	Daryl Hall & John Oates	#1	17 seconds
1982	Only The Lonely	The Motels	#9	17 seconds
1982	Come Go With Me	The Beach Boys	#18	17 seconds
1982	Personally	Karla Bonoff	#19	17 seconds

THE LONGEST SAXOPHONE SOLOS OF THE 80s (cont'd)

1982	Out Of Work	Gary U.S. Bonds	#21	17 seconds
1982	Forget Me Nots	Patrice Rushen	#23	17 seconds
1983	Time (Clock Of The Heart)	Culture Club	#2	17 seconds
1983	If You Wanna Get Back Your Lady	The Pointer Sisters	#67	17 seconds
1984	There Goes My Baby	Donna Summer	#21	17 seconds
1984	I Pretend	Kim Carnes	#74	17 seconds
1984	Shooting Shark	Blue Oyster Cult	#83	17 seconds
1986	How Will I Know	Whitney Houston	#1	17 seconds
1986	Baby Love	Regina	#10	17 seconds
1986	Superbowl Shuffle	The Chicago Bears Shufflin' Crew	#41	17 seconds
1986	Thorn In My Side	Eurythmics	#68	17 seconds
1986	If You Were A Woman (And I Was A Man)	Bonnie Tyler	#77	17 seconds
1986	I Want To Make The World Turn Around	The Steve Miller Band	#97	17 seconds
1987	(I've Had) The Time Of My Life	Bill Medley & Jennifer Warnes	#1	17 seconds
1987	If I Say Yes	Five Star	#67	17 seconds
1987	Rock-A-Lott	Aretha Franklin	#82	17 seconds
1988	Kokomo	The Beach Boys	#1	17 seconds
1988	Hungry Eyes	Eric Carmen	#4	17 seconds
1988	Nice 'N' Slow	Freddie Jackson	#61	17 seconds
1988	Hot Thing	Prince	#63	17 seconds
1988	Wait On Love	Michael Bolton	#79	17 seconds
1989	Hold On	Donny Osmond	#73	17 seconds
1982	Harden My Heart	Quarterflash	#3	16, 16 seconds
1984	I Want A New Drug	Huey Lewis & The News	#6	16, 16 seconds
1982	American Music	The Pointer Sisters	#16	16, 13 seconds
1981	Super Freak (Part 1)	Rick James	#16	16 seconds
1980	More Love	Kim Carnes	#10	16 seconds
1980	How Do I Survive	Amy Holland	#22	16 seconds
1982	Big Fun	Kool & The Gang	#21	16 seconds
1982	Your Imagination	Daryl Hall & John Oates	#33	16 seconds
1984	It's A Miracle	Culture Club	#13	16 seconds
1985	So In Love	Orchestral Manoeuvres In The Dark	#26	16 seconds
1985	Mathematics	Melissa Manchester	#74	16 seconds
1986	Talk To Me	Stevie Nicks	#4	16 seconds
1986	This Love	Bad Company	#85	16 seconds
1987	Lost In Emotion	Lisa Lisa & Cult Jam	#1	16 seconds
1987	Who Found Who	Jellybean w/ Elisa Fiorillo	#16	16 seconds
1988	Get Outta My Dreams, Get Into My Car	Billy Ocean	#1	16 seconds
1988	Never Tear Us Apart	INXS	#7	16 seconds
1988	Another Lover	Giant Steps	#13	16 seconds

THE LONGEST SAXOPHONE SOLOS OF THE 80s (cont'd)

1989	The Lover In Me	Sheena Easton	#2	16 seconds
1989	She Wants To Dance With Me	Rick Astley	#6	16 seconds
1989	Walk The Dinosaur	Was (Not Was)	#7	16 seconds
1989	Get On Your Feet	Gloria Estefan	#11	16 seconds
1982	Night Shift	Quarterflash	#60	15, 14 seconds
1986	Taken In	Mike + The Mechanics	#32	15, 13 seconds
1983	Please Mr. Postman	Gentle Persuasion	#82	15, 10 seconds
1980	Cool Change	Little River Band	#10	15 seconds
1980	Carrie	Cliff Richard	#34	15 seconds
1980	Walk Away	Donna Summer	#36	15 seconds
1980	Let Me Be	Korona	#43	15 seconds
1980	Let's Go 'Round Again	Average White Band	#53	15 seconds
1980	It Hurts Too Much	Eric Carmen	#75	15 seconds
1981	The Real Thing	The Brothers Johnson	#67	15 seconds
1981	Want You Back In My Life Again	Carpenters	#72	15 seconds
1981	You've Got A Good Love Coming	Van Stephenson	#79	15 seconds
1983	One On One	Daryl Hall & John Oates	#7	15 seconds
1983	The One Thing	INXS	#30	15 seconds
1983	Ship To Shore	Chris DeBurgh	#71	15 seconds
1984	Some Guys Have All The Luck	Rod Stewart	#10	15 seconds
1984	I Cry Just A Little Bit	Shakin' Stevens	#67	15 seconds
1985	I'm Goin' Down	Bruce Springsteen	#9	15 seconds
1985	Abadabadango	Kim Carnes	#67	15 seconds
1986	Typical Male	Tina Turner	#2	15 seconds
1986	California Dreamin'	The Beach Boys	#57	15 seconds
1986	If Your Heart Isn't In It	Atlantic Starr	#57	15 seconds
1986	Miami	Bob Seger	#70	15 seconds
1986	Shelter Me	Joe Cocker	#91	15 seconds
1986	Gravity	James Brown	#93	15 seconds
1987	Come As You Are	Peter Wolf	#15	15 seconds
1988	Roll With It	Steve Winwood	#1	15 seconds
1988	Time And Tide	Basia	#26	15 seconds
1988	Dance Little Sister (Part One)	Terence Trent D'Arby	#30	15 seconds
1988	Hands On The Radio	Henry Lee Summer	#85	15 seconds
1989	And The Night Stood Still	Dion	#75	15 seconds
1989	Right Back Where We Started From	Sinitta	#84	15 seconds
1981	Love Light	Yutaka w/Patti Austin	#81	14, 14 seconds
1982	Running	Chubby Checker	#91	14, 14 seconds
1985	Freeway Of Love	Aretha Franklin	#3	14, 14 seconds
1980	Ali Thompson	Take A Little Rhythm	#15	14, 11 seconds
1980	Funkytown	Lipps, Inc.	#1	14 seconds
1981	Ain't Even Done With The Night	John Cougar	#17	14 seconds

THE LONGEST SAXOPHONE SOLOS OF THE 80s (cont'd)

1981	La La Means I Love You	Tierra	#72	14 seconds
1982	You Should Hear How She Talks About You	Melissa Manchester	#5	14 seconds
1982	Bobbie Sue	The Oak Ridge Boys	#12	14 seconds
1982	Tonight Tonight	Bill Champlin	#55	14 seconds
1983	Baby Jane	Rod Stewart	#14	14 seconds
1983	The Border	America	#33	14 seconds
1984	Remember The Nights	The Motels	#36	14 seconds
1984	I Send A Message	INXS	#77	14 seconds
1985	A Nite At The Apollo Live! The Way You Do The Things You Do/ My Girl	Daryl Hall & John Oates w/ David Ruffin & Eddie Kendrick	#20	14 seconds
1985	Tough All Over	John Cafferty	#22	14 seconds
1986	Nail It To The Wall	Stacy Lattisaw	#48	14 seconds
1986	Let Me Be The One	Five Star	#59	14 seconds
1988	Hands To Heaven	Breathe	#2	14 seconds
1988	She's Like The Wind	Patrick Swayze w/ Wendy Fraser	#3	14 seconds
1988	I Want To Be Your Property	Blue Mercedes	#66	14 seconds
1988	Lonely Won't Leave Me Alone	Glenn Medeiros	#67	14 seconds
1989	Crazy About Her	Rod Stewart	#11	14 seconds
1989	Touch The Fire	Icehouse	#84	14 seconds
1981	He Can't Love You	Michael Stanley Band	#33	13, 13 seconds
1988	Ever Since The World Began	Tommy Shaw	#75	13 seconds
1980	Goin' On	The Beach Boys	#83	13 seconds
1982	Love Is In Control (Finger On The Trigger)	Donna Summer	#10	13 seconds
1982	Love Plus One	Haircut One Hundred	#37	13 seconds
1983	Old Time Rock & Roll	Bob Seger	#48	13 seconds
1983	Don't Try To Stop It	Roman Holliday	#68	13 seconds
1983	Where Everybody Knows Your Name (The Theme From "Cheers")	Gary Portnoy	#83	13 seconds
1986	I'm Your Man	Wham!	#3	13 seconds
1986	If You Leave	Orchestral Manoeuvres In The Dark	#4	13 seconds
1986	A Love Bizarre	Sheila E.	#11	13 seconds
1988	Never Knew Love Like This	Alexander O'Neal w/ Cherrelle	#28	13 seconds
1988	Jackie	Blue Zone U.K.	#54	13 seconds
1989	Radio Romance	Tiffany	#35	13 seconds
1982	Beechwood 4-5789	Carpenters	#74	12 seconds
1983	She Works Hard For The Money	Donna Summer	#3	12 seconds
1983	Overkill	Men At Work	#3	12 seconds
1983	Bread And Butter	Robert John	#68	12 seconds
1984	Taxi Dancing	Rick Springfield & Randy Crawford	#59	12 seconds
1986	Hip To Be Square	Huey Lewis & The News	#3	12 seconds
1986	I Feel The Magic	Belinda Carlisle	#82	12 seconds

THE LONGEST SAXOPHONE SOLOS OF THE 80s (cont'd)

1987	Twistin' The Night Away	Rod Stewart	#80	12 seconds
1987	You Got It All	The Jets	#3	11, 11 seconds
1980	Biggest Part Of Me	Ambrosia	#3	11 seconds
1980	You May Be Right	Billy Joel	#7	11 seconds
1983	It Must Be Love	Madness	#33	11 seconds
1989	I Remember Holding You	Boys Club	#8	11 seconds
1989	When I Looked At Him	Expose	#10	11 seconds
1986	For America	Jackson Browne	#30	10, 10 seconds
1981	This Little Girl	Gary U.S. Bonds	#11	10 seconds
1982	Tell Me Tomorrow- Part 1	Smokey Robinson	#33	10 seconds
1983	Heart To Heart	Kenny Loggins	#15	10 seconds
1985	Information	Eric Martin	#87	10 seconds
1986	I Do What I Do (Theme For 9 1/2 Weeks)	John Taylor/Jonathan Elias	#23	10 seconds
1986	Walk Away Renee	Southside Johnny & The Jukes	#98	10 seconds

SITAR

SONG	ARTIST	HOT 100 CHART
1984		
It Can Happen	Yes	#51

1985		
Don't Come Around Here No More	Tom Petty And The Heartbreakers	#13

1988		
When We Was Fab	George Harrison	#23
Baby Can I Hold You*	Tracy Chapman	#48
	*Electric sitar	

1989		
Talk It Over	Grayson Hugh	#19

STEEL DRUMS

SONG	ARTIST	HOT 100 CHART
1980		
Catching The Sun	Spyro Gyra	#68
1981		
Just The Two Of Us	Grover Washington Jr. w/Bill Withers	#2
1982		
Island Of Lost Souls	Blondie	#37
1983		
I'll Tumble 4 Ya	Culture Club	#9
Ewok Celebration	Meco	#60
Side By Side	Earth, Wind & Fire	#76
1985		
Like To Get To Know You Well	Howard Jones	#49
1986		
Love Touch	Rod Stewart	#6
The Heart Is Not So Smart	El Debarge With Debarge	#75
1988		
Kokomo	The Beach Boys	#1

TAMBORINE

SONG	ARTIST	HOT 100 CHART
1980		
Please Don't Go	KC And Sunshine Band	#1
Too Hot	Kool & The Gang	#5
Stomp!	The Brothers Johnson	#7
Cars	Gary Numan	#9
Off The Wall	Michael Jackson	#10
Deep Inside My Heart	Randy Meisner	#22
How Does It Feel To Be Back	Daryl Hall & John Oates	#30

TAMBORINE (cont'd)

I Can't Let Go	Linda Ronstadt	#31
You Know That I Love You	Santana	#35
King Of The Hill	Rick Pinette & Oak	#36
Happy Together (A Fantasy)	Captain & Tennille	#53
Easy Love	Dionne Warwick	#62
Blues Power	Eric Clapton	#76
Seasons	Grace Slick	#95
The Part Of Me That Needs You Most	Jay Black	#98

1981		
Arthur's Theme (Best That You Can Do)	Christopher Cross	#1
Say Goodbye To Hollywood	Billy Joel	#17
Fire And Ice	Pat Benatar	#17
Hearts On Fire	Randy Meisner	#18
Nobody Wins	Elton John	#21
Find Your Way Back	Jefferson Starship	#29
Castles In The Air	Don McLean	#36
Staying With It	Firefall	#37
Lovers After All	Melissa Manchester & Peabo Bryson	#54
The Cowboy And The Lady	John Denver	#66
Set The Night On Fire	Oak	#71

1982		
Love Will Turn You Around	Kenny Rogers	#13
Make Believe	Toto	#30
After The Glitter Fades	Stevie Nicks	#32
Just Can't Win 'Em All	Stevie Woods	#38
Love Or Let Me Be Lonely	Paul Davis	#40
Should I Stay Or Should I Go	The Clash	#45
Forever Mine	The Motels	#60
All Night With Me	Laura Branigan	#69

1983		
Church Of The Poison Mind	Culture Club	#10
Even Now	Bob Seger	#12
Hand To Hold On To	John Cougar	#19
Change Of Heart	Tom Petty And The Heartbreakers	#21
Roll Me Away	Bob Seger	#27
I Don't Care Anymore	Phil Collins	#39
Forever	Little Steven	#63
Let Me Go	Heaven 17	#74

TAMBORINE (cont'd)

1984		
Wake Me Up Before You Go-Go	Wham!	#1
Pink Houses	John Cougar Mellencamp	#8
Penny Lover	Lionel Richie	#8
Love Will Show Us How	Christine McVie	#30
Music Time	Styx	#40
Turn Around	Neil Diamond	#62
Say Hello To Ronnie	Janey Street	#68
Don't Look Any Further	Dennis Edwards w/Siedah Garrett	#72
Tender Years	John Cafferty	#78
Devil In A Fast Car	Sheena Easton	#79

1985		
Money For Nothing	Dire Straits	#1
Freeway Of Love	Aretha Franklin	#3
If You Love Somebody Set Them Free	Sting	#3
Oh Girl	Boy Meets Girl	#39
Ways To Be Wicked	Lone Justice	#71
Sweet, Sweet Baby (I'm Falling)	Lone Justice	#73
Rebels	Tom Petty And The Heartbreakers	#74

1986		
Walk Like An Egyptian	Bangles	#1
I'm Your Man	Wham!	#3
War	Bruce Springsteen	#8
If Anybody Had A Heart	John Waite	#76

1987		
Faith	George Michael	#1
Lost In Emotion	Lisa Lisa & Cult Jam	#1
Head To Toe	Lisa Lisa & Cult Jam	#1
Notorious	Duran Duran	#2
Paper In Fire	John Cougar Mellencamp	#9
Jammin' Me	Tom Petty And The Heartbreakers	#18

1988		
Groovy Kind Of Love	Phil Collins	#1
Check It Out	John Cougar Mellencamp	#14
Dance Little Sister (Part One)	Terence Trent D'Arby	#30
Twilight World	Swing Out Sister	#31
Feelings Of Forever	Tiffany	#50

TAMBORINE (cont'd)

1989		
Baby Don't Forget My Number	Milli Vanilli	#1
Two Hearts	Phil Collins	#1
Buffalo Stance	Neneh Cherry	#3
In Your Room	Bangles	#5
Hey Baby	Henry Lee Summer	#18
Rock And A Hard Place	The Rolling Stones	#23
My Brave Face	Paul McCartney	#25
Little Jackie Wants To Be A Star	Lisa Lisa & Cult Jam	#29
End Of The Line	Traveling Wilburys	#63
We Could Be Together	Debbie Gibson	#71
And The Night Stood Still	Dion	#75
Never Had A Lot To Lose	Cheap Trick	#75
Similar Features	Melissa Etheridge	#94
This One	Paul McCartney	#94

TIN WHISTLE

SONG	ARTIST	HOT 100 CHART
1980		
The Royal Mile (Sweet Darlin')	Gerry Rafferty	#54

1986		
You Can Call Me Al	Paul Simon	#44

1988		
Broken Land	The Adventures	#95

1989		
Closer To Fine	Indigo Girls	#52

TUBULAR BELLS

SONG	ARTIST	HOT 100 CHART
1980		
Cry Just A Little	Paul Davis	#78

TUBULAR BELLS (cont'd)

The Waiting Game	Swing Out Sister	#86

1981		
Living Inside Myself	Gino Vannelli	#6

1982		
Tonight I'm Yours (Don't Hurt Me)	Rod Stewart	#20
Closer To The Heart	Rush	#69

1983		
Always Something There To Remind Me	Naked Eyes	#8

1984		
They Don't Know	Tracey Ullman	#8
Do They Know It's Christmas?	Band Aid	#13

VIBRAPHONE

SONG	ARTIST	HOT 100 CHART
1980		
Jane	Jefferson Starship	#14
1981		
Can You Feel It	The Jacksons	#77
1983		
You Can't Hurry Love	Phil Collins	#10
1984		
Black Stations/White Stations	M+M	#63
1985		
Freeway Of Love	Aretha Franklin	#3
1988		
Love Will Save The Day	Whitney Houston	#9

VIBRASLAP

SONG	ARTIST	HOT 100 CHART
1980		
Cupid/I've Loved You For A Long Time	Spinners	#4
Take A Little Rhythm	Ali Thompson	#15
Dig The Gold	Joyce Cobb	#42
Is This Love	Pat Travers Band	#50
I Call Your Name	Switch	#83
1981		
Rock And Roll Dreams Come Through	Jim Steinman (Rory Dodd)	#32
1982		
Goin' Down	Greg Guidry	#17
Early In The Morning	The Gap Band	#24
1983		
Just Be Good To Me	The S.O.S. Band	#55
Mexican Radio	Wall Of Voodoo	#58
Get It Right	Aretha Franklin	#61
1986		
Everything In My Heart	Corey Hart	#30
1987		
Fake	Alexander O'Neal	#25
The Right Thing	Simply Red	#27
1988		
Tunnel Of Love	Bruce Springsteen	#9
Dance Little Sister (Part One)	Terence Trent D'Arby	#30
1989		
Friends	Jody Watley w/ Eric B. & Rakim	#9

VIOLIN

Songs in this list feature a single violin. For songs that feature an entire section of violins, see "Violin Section".

SONG	ARTIST	HOT 100 CHART
1980		
Rock With You	Michael Jackson	#1
Lady	Kenny Rogers	#1
Workin My Back To You	Spinners	#2
Cruisin	Smokey Robinson	#4
With You I'm Born Again	Billy Preston & Syreeta	#4
Everybody's Got To Learn Sometime	The Korgis	#18
Hold On	Kansas	#40
Dig The Gold	Joyce Cobb	#42
1981		
I Don't Need You	Kenny Rogers	#3
I Missed Again	Phil Collins	#19
In The Air Tonight*	Phil Collins	#19
	*Very subtle, at the end	
1982		
Wasted On The Way	Crosby, Stills & Nash	#9
Find Another Fool	Quarterflash	#16
Play The Game Tonight	Kansas	#17
Shooting Star	Hollywood	#70
1983		
Come On Eileen	Dexys Midnight Runners	#1
It Must Be Love*	Madness	#33
	*Pizzicato	
I Eat Cannibals	Total Coelo	#66
Shiny Shiny	Haysi Fantayzee	#74
The Celtic Soul Brothers	Dexys Midnight Runners	#86
Bad, Bad Billy	Snuff	#88
Life Gets Better	Graham Parker	#94
1984		
Here Comes The Rain Again	Eurythmics	#4

VIOLIN (cont'd)

Run Runaway*	Slade	#20
	*Electric violin	
Strip	Adam Ant	#42

1985		
Raspberry Beret	Prince	#2

1986		
Papa Don't Preach	Madonna	#1
Stand By Me	Ben E King	#9
Thorn In My Side	Eurythmics	#68

1987		
Paper In Fire	John Cougar Mellencamp	#9
I Don't Mind At All	Bourgeois Tagg	#38

1988		
Cherry Bomb	John Cougar Mellencamp	#8
Check It Out	John Cougar Mellencamp	#14
Baby Can I Hold You*	Tracy Chapman	#48
	*Electric violin	
Rooty Toot Toot	John Cougar Mellencamp	#61
Englishman In New York*	Sting	#84
	*Pizzicato	

1989		
Pop Singer	John Cougar Mellencamp	#15
Jackie Brown	John Cougar Mellencamp	#48
Anchorage	Michelle Schocked	#66
Left To My Own Devices*	Pet Shop Boys	#84
	*Electric	
Crossroads*	Tracy Chapman	#90
	*Pizzicato	

VIOLIN SECTION

Songs in this list feature a violin section. For songs that feature a single violin, see the "Violin" section.

SONG	ARTIST	HOT 100 CHART
1980		
Sexy Eyes	Dr. Hook	#5
Xanadu	Olivia Newton-John/Electric Light Orchestra	#8
Better Love Next Time	Dr. Hook	#12
All Over The World	Electric Light Orchestra	#13
Love The World Away	Kenny Rogers	#14
I'm Alive	Electric Light Orchestra	#16
Jojo	Boz Scaggs	#17
September Morn'	Neil Diamond	#17
Should've Never Let You Go	Neil & Dara Sedaka	#19
I Pledge My Love	Peaches & Herb	#19
Old-Fashion Love	Commodores	#20
Let Me Be Your Angel	Stacy Lattisaw	#21
Someone That I Used To Love	Natalie Cole	#21
Wonderland	Commodores	#25
Forever Mine	O'Jays	#28
Theme From New York, New York	Frank Sinatra	#32
Fire In The Morning	Melissa Manchester	#32
Kiss Me In The Rain	Barbra Streisand	#37
I'd Rather Leave While I'm In Love	Rita Coolidge	#38
Last Train To London	Electric Light Orchestra	#39
I Can't Help Myself (Sugar Pie, Honey Bunch)	Bonnie Pointer	#40
Red Light	Linda Clifford	#41
Haven't You Heard	Patrice Rushen	#42
Power	The Temptations	#43
Let Me Be	Korona	#43
My Heroes Have Always Been Cowboys	Willie Nelson	#44
Us And Love (We Go Together)	Kenny Nolan	#44
All Night Thing	Invisible Man Band	#45
Where Does The Lovin' Go	David Gates	#46
Landlord	Gladys Knight & The Pips	#46
My Prayer	Ray, Goodman & Brown	#47
Bad Times	Tavares	#47
I Wish I Was Eighteen Again	George Burns	#49
Years From Now	Dr. Hook	#51
Can't We Try	Teddy Pendergrass	#52

VIOLIN SECTION (cont'd)

Could I Be Dreaming	The Pointer Sisters	#52
Autograph	John Denver	#52
One More Time For Love	Billy Preston And Syreeta	#52
First... Be A Woman	Lenore O'Malley	#53
Let's Go 'Round Again	Average White Band	#53
Heroes	Commodores	#54
Back Together Again	Roberta Flack & Donny Hathaway	#56
Move Your Boogie Body	The Bar-Kays	#57
Stargazer	Peter Brown	#59
Rebels Are We	Chic	#61
Star	Earth, Wind & Fire	#64
After You	Dionne Warwick	#65
Don't Make Me Over	Jennifer Warnes	#67
The Good Lord Loves You	Neil Diamond	#67
Case Of You	Frank Stallone	#67
Holdin' On For Dear Love	Lobo	#75
Just For The Moment	Ray Kennedy	#82
Love's Only Love	Engelbert Humperdinck	#83
I Love Women	Jim Hurt	#90
One Life To Live	Wayne Massey	#92
Seasons	Grace Slick	#95
The Part Of Me That Needs You Most	Jay Black	#98

1981		
Endless Love	Diana Ross & Lionel Richie	#1
The Tide Is High	Blondie	#1
The One That You Love	Air Supply	#1
Woman In Love	Barbra Streisand	#1
Love On The Rocks	Neil Diamond	#2
Oh No	Commodores	#4
Here I Am (Just When I Thought I Was Over You)	Air Supply	#5
Crying	Don McLean	#5
Hello Again	Neil Diamond	#6
The Sweetest Thing (I've Ever Known)	Juice Newton	#7
America	Neil Diamond	#8
Lady (You Bring Me Up)	Commodores	#8
It's My Turn	Diana Ross	#9
What Kind Of Fool	Barbra Streisand And Barry Gibb	#10
I Made It Through The Rain	Barry Manilow	#10
Her Town Too	James Taylor & J.D. Souther	#11
I Love You	Climax Blues Band	#12
It's Now Or Never	John Schneider	#14

VIOLIN SECTION (cont'd)

Share Your Love With Me	Kenny Rogers	#14
The Old Songs	Barry Manilow	#15
I Could Never Miss You (More Than I Do)	Lulu	#18
Feels So Right	Alabama	#20
That Old Song	Ray Parker Jr. & Raydio	#21
Suddenly	Olivia Newton-John & Cliff Richard	#21
Since I Don't Have You	Don McLean	#23
Smoky Mountain Rain	Ronnie Milsap	#24
Steal The Night	Stevie Woods	#25
Love On A Two Way Street	Stacy Lattisaw	#26
It's A Love Thing	The Whispers	#28
Never Too Much	Luther Vandross	#33
Chloe	Elton John	#34
Castles In The Air	Don McLean	#36
Some Days Are Diamonds (Some Days Are Stone)	John Denver	#36
I Need Your Lovin'	Teena Marie	#37
Twilight	Electric Light Orchestra	#38
My Mother's Eyes	Bette Midler	#39
Too Tight	Con Funk Shun	#40
Lonely Together	Barry Manilow	#45
I've Been Waiting For You All Of My Life	Paul Anka	#48
You Like Me Don't You	Jermaine Jackson	#50
Silly	Deniece Williams	#53
Lovers After All	Melissa Manchester & Peabo Bryson	#54
Full Of Fire	Shalamar	#55
You Don't Know Me	Mickey Gilley	#55
Fly Away	Peter Allen	#55
One Day In Your Life	Michael Jackson	#55
The Sun Ain't Gonna Shine Anymore	Nielsen/Pearson	#56
It's My Job	Jimmy Buffett	#57
And Love Goes On	Earth, Wind & Fire	#59
Stay Awake	Ronnie Laws	#60
I'm Just Too Shy	Jermaine Jackson	#60
Take Me Now	David Gates	#62
Talking Out Of Turn	The Moody Blues	#65
Some Changes Are For Good	Dionne Warwick	#65
The Cowboy And The Lady	John Denver	#66
Aiming At Your Heart	The Temptations	#67
The Real Thing	The Brothers Johnson	#67
Still	John Schneider	#69
Michael Damian	She Did It	#69
Shake It Up Tonight	Cheryl Lynn	#70

VIOLIN SECTION (cont'd)

Somebody Special	Rod Stewart	#71
La La Means I Love You	Tierra	#72
Seasons	Charles Fox	#75
The Woman In Me	Crystal Gayle	#76
Can You Feel It	The Jacksons	#77
All American Girls	Sister Sledge	#79
One More Chance	Diana Ross	#79
Next Time You'll Know	Sister Sledge	#82
Theme From Raging Bull (Cavalleria Rusticana)	Joel Diamond	#82
It's Just The Sun	Don McLean	#83
Come To Me	Aretha Franklin	#84
I Can't Say Goodbye To You	Helen Reddy	#88
Snap Shot	Slave	#91

1982		
Truly	Lionel Richie	#1
I've Never Been To Me	Charlene	#3
Sweet Dreams	Air Supply	#5
It's Gonna Take A Miracle	Deniece Williams	#10
Yesterday's Songs	Neil Diamond	#11
Comin' In And Out Of Your Life	Barbra Streisand	#11
Through The Years	Kenny Rogers	#13
Any Day Now	Ronnie Milsap	#14
Love In The First Degree	Alabama	#15
Somewhere Down The Road	Barry Manilow	#21
And I Am Telling You I'm Not Going	Jennifer Holliday	#22
Love Me Tomorrow	Chicago	#22
Missing You	Dan Fogelberg	#23
My Guy	Sister Sledge	#23
On The Way To The Sky	Neil Diamond	#27
John Denver	Shanghai Breezes	#31
Be Mine Tonight	Neil Diamond	#35
If I Had My Wish Tonight	David Lasley	#36
Route 101	Herb Alpert	#37
Young Love	Air Supply	#38
I Really Don't Need No Light	Jeffrey Osborne	#39
I'm The One	Roberta Flack	#42
Let The Feeling Flow	Peabo Bryson	#42
Anyone Can See	Irene Cara	#42
A Night To Remember	Shalamar	#44
I'm In Love Again	Pia Zadora	#45
A Love Song	Kenny Rogers	#47

VIOLIN SECTION (cont'd)

Memory	Barbra Streisand	#52
Tug Of War	Paul McCartney	#53
(Sittin' On) The Dock Of The Bay	The Reddings	#55
Falling In Love	Balance	#58
Finally	T.G. Sheppard	#58
Perhaps Love	Placido Domingo & John Denver	#59
Loveline	Dr. Hook	#60
Close Enough To Perfect	Alabama	#65
Natural Love	Petula Clark	#66
Teach Me Tonight	Al Jarreau	#70
Fly Away	Stevie Woods	#84
The Very Best In You	Change	#84
Sad Hearts	The Four Tops	#84
I'm Never Gonna Say Goodbye	Billy Preston	#88

1983		
You Are	Lionel Richie	#4
My Love	Lionel Richie	#5
Our House	Madness	#7
I Won't Hold You Back	Toto	#10
You Can't Hurry Love	Phil Collins	#10
Rock 'N' Roll Is King	Electric Light Orchestra	#19
Mornin'	Al Jarreau	#21
Don't You Get So Mad	Jeffrey Osborne	#25
How Many Times Can We Say Goodbye	Dionne Warwick & Luther Vandross	#27
Make Love Stay	Dan Fogelberg	#29
The Border	America	#33
All Time High	Rita Coolidge	#36
All My Life	Kenny Rogers	#37
Memory	Barry Manilow	#39
Miracles	Stacy Lattisaw	#40
Put It In A Magazine	Sonny Charles	#40
The Way He Makes Me Feel	Barbra Streisand	#40
Hold Me 'Til The Mornin' Comes	Paul Anka w/Peter Cetera	#40
How Do You Keep The Music Playing	James Ingram & Patti Austin	#45
I Am Love	Jennifer Holliday	#49
I.O.U.	Lee Greenwood	#53
What's New	Linda Ronstadt	#53
Only You	Commodores	#54
You Can't Run From Love	Eddie Rabbitt	#55
Funny How Time Slips Away	Spinners	#67

VIOLIN SECTION (cont'd)

I Just Can't Walk Away	The Four Tops	#71
Lady Down On Love	Alabama	#76
Eenie Meenie	Jeffrey Osborne	#76
The Sound Of Goodbye	Crystal Gayle	#84
Whatever Happened To Old Fashioned Love	B.J. Thomas	#93

1984		
Hard Habit To Break	Chicago	#3
An Innocent Man	Billy Joel	#10
If Ever You're In My Arms Again	Peabo Bryson	#10
Almost Over You	Sheena Easton	#25
Baby I Lied	Deborah Allen	#26
Hold Me	Teddy Pendergrass w/ Whitney Houston	#46
Believe In Me	Dan Fogelberg	#48
Sail Away	The Temptations	#54
Strangers In A Strange World	Jenny Burton & Patrick Jude	#54
Stop	Sam Brown	#65
You're The Best Thing	The Style Council	#76
Love Again	John Denver & Sylvie Vartan	#85
Superstar/Until You Come Back To Me (That's What I'm Gonna Do)	Luther Vandross	#87

1985		
Sea Of Love	Honeydrippers	#3
You're The Inspiration	Chicago	#3
Suddenly	Billy Ocean	#4
Love Theme From St. Elmo's Fire	David Foster	#15
The Family	The Screams Of Passion	#63
Gotta Get You Home Tonight	Eugene Wilde	#83
I'm Through With Love	Eric Carmen	#87

1986		
There'll Be Sad Songs To Make You Cry	Billy Ocean	#1
Overjoyed	Stevie Wonder	#24
The Heat Of Heat	Patti Austin	#55
Daydream Believer	The Monkees	#79

1987		
Didn't We Almost Have It All	Whitney Houston	#1
Somewhere Out There	Linda Ronstadt & James Ingram	#2
When Smokey Sings	ABC	#5
Ballerina Girl	Lionel Richie	#7

VIOLIN SECTION (cont'd)

Reservations For Two	Dionne Warwick & Kashif	#62
Baby Grand	Billy Joel w/ Ray Charles	#75

1988		
Groovy Kind Of Love	Phil Collins	#1
Sign Your Name	Terence Trent D'Arby	#4
Twilight World	Swing Out Sister	#31
What A Wonderful World	Louis Armstrong	#32
Never Can Say Goodbye	The Communards	#51
Long And Lasting Love (Once In A Lifetime	Glenn Medeiros	#68
Jealous Guy	John Lennon	#80

1989		
Two Hearts	Phil Collins	#1
Don't Know Much	Linda Ronstadt (w/ Aaron Neville)	#2
My Heart Can't Tell You No	Rod Stewart	#4
You Got It	Roy Orbison	#9
A Shoulder To Cry On	Tommy Page	#29
The Arms Of Orion	Prince w/ Sheena Easton	#36
Nature Of Love	Waterfront	#70
All I Want Is You	U2	#83
Hungry	Winger	#85
Edie (Ciao Baby)	The Cult	#93

WHISTLE

SONG	ARTIST	HOT 100 CHART
1980		
Fool In The Rain	Led Zeppelin	#21
All Night Thing	Invisible Man Band	#45

1982		
Love Is In Control (Finger On The Trigger)	Donna Summer	#10

1984		
Right By Your Side	Eurythmics	#29
No Parking (On The Dance Floor)	Midnight Star	#81

WHISTLE (cont'd)

1986		
Bad Boy	Miami Sound Machine	#8
Headlines	Midnight Star	#69

1987		
Shake Your Love	Debbie Gibson	#4

1988		
Cecilia	Times Two	#79

1989		
Hangin' Tough	New Kids On The Block	#1
I Beg Your Pardon	Kon Kan	#15

XYLOPHONE

SONG	ARTIST	HOT 100 CHART
1985		
Do It For Love	Sheena Easton	#29

1986		
Just Another Day	Oingo Boingo	#85

1987		
Keep Your Eye On Me	Herb Alpert	#46

1989		
Wild World	Maxi Priest	#25

MISCELLANEOUS INSTRUMENTS

Ready for something a little different? This is your section.

Songs with autoharps, castanets, and flutophones will be found here. Looking for a song with a hammered dulcimer? John Lennon recorded one. Looking for a song with finger cymbals? Check out Marvin Gaye. What about chimes, gongs, and harpsichords? Check. Songs with all kinds of unusual instruments rarely used in pop music will be found here. Sometimes, the instrument used isn't really even a real instrument, like when Paul McCartney used wine glasses in "This One", from 1989.

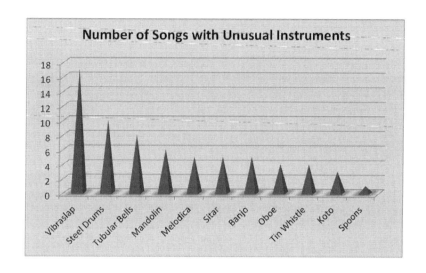

YEAR	SONG	ARTIST	HOT 100 CHART	MISCELLANEOUS INSTRUMENT
1981	Falling In Love Again	Michael Stanley Band	#64	12-String Guitar
1988	Cherry Bomb	John Cougar Mellencamp	#8	Autoharp
1980	Volcano	Jimmy Buffett	#66	Bass Pipe
1989	Closer To Fine	Indigo Girls	#52	Bodhran
1981	Lonely Together	Barry Manilow	#45	Calliope
1988	Family Man	Fleetwood Mac	#90	Castanets
1980	Turning Japanese	The Vapors	#36	Chimes
1981	Hearts	Marty Balin	#8	Cimbalom
1981	Seduced	Leon Redbone	#72	Clarinet
1986	Life In A Northern Town	The Dream Academy	#7	English Horn
1983	Sexual Healing	Marvin Gaye	#3	Finger Cymbals
1986	R.O.C.K. In The U.S.A. (A Salute To 60's Rock)	John Cougar Mellencamp	#2	Flutophone
1982	Truly	Lionel Richie	#1	French Horn
1983	Africa	Toto	#1	Gong

MISCELLANEOUS INSTRUMENTS (cont'd)

1985	Big In Japan	Alphaville	#66	Gong
1981	A Life Of Illusion	Joe Walsh	#34	Guitarron
1981	Watching The Wheels	John Lennon	#10	Hammered Dulcimer
1989	This One	Paul McCartney	#94	Harmonium
1981	Toccata	Sky	#83	Harpsichord
1980	Do That To Me One More Time	Captain & Tennille	#1	Lyricon
1980	Heart Hotels	Dan Fogelberg	#21	Lyricon
1982	Tug Of War	Paul McCartney	#53	Military Snares
1983	Goodnight Saigon	Billy Joel	#56	Military Snares
1982	Steppin' Out	Joe Jackson	#6	Orchestral Bells
1983	Africa	Toto	#1	Recorder
1983	Shiny Shiny	Haysi Fantayzee	#74	Spoons
1982	Rock This Town	Stray Cats	#9	String Bass
1980	Comin Up	Paul McCartney	#1	Varispeed Tape Machine
1989	This One	Paul McCartney	#94	Wine Glasses
1984	Strangers In A Strange World	Jenny Burton & Patrick Jude	#54	Woodwinds

SINGING/VOCAL STYLES AND EFFECTS

Several artists in the 80s used different vocal effects or styles. From singing in falsetto or in the a cappella style (both slightly uncommon, but still used quite a bit), to using a vocoder, talk box, or other "robot-voice" (used more often than you'd guess), to really rare vocal styles (scat and the "chipmunk voice"), they all tried to stand out. And seriously, who wouldn't notice a song that had a chipmunk sing a prominent part?

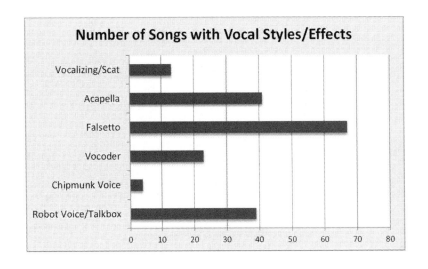

A CAPPELLA

"A cappella" refers to singing without instruments. Some people would argue that a cappella means singing only, with no other sound whatsoever. For this list, I'm defining a cappella as singing without regular instruments, such as the piano, trumpet, guitar, etc.; the presence of finger snaps or hand claps will not disqualify a song from appearing on this list.

We only have one Song from the 80s that was sung entirely a cappella: "Don't Worry, Be Happy" by Bobby McFerrin. It went all the way to number one in 1988. McFerrin produced every sound in the song with his voice or with body percussion.

Most every other song that used the a cappella style used it for just short sections, usually between five and ten seconds. "Super Trouper" by Abba, "Rev It Up" by Newcity Rockers, and "I Want It All" by Queen are fairly typical examples of songs that start with an a cappella section. "65 Love Affair" by Paul Davis, and "Make Me Lose Control" by Eric Carmen are two examples of songs that use an a cappella section to increase the energy later in the song.

SONG	ARTIST	HOT 100 CHART
1980		
Special Lady*	Ray, Goodman & Brown	#5
	*w/finger snaps	
Pilot Of The Airwaves	Charlie Dore	#13
Baby Don't Go	Karla Bonoff	#69
1981		
Seven Bridges Road	Eagles	#21
Super Trouper	Abba	#45
1982		
65 Love Affair	Paul Davis	#6
Shadows Of The Night	Pat Benatar	#13
Whatcha Gonna Do	Chilliwack	#41
So Much In Love*	Timothy B. Schmit	#59
	*Intro w/finger snaps	
Foolin' Yourself	Aldo Nova	#65
When The Radio Is On*	Paul Shaffer	#81
	*End w/finger snaps	
1983		
Pass The Dutchie	Musical Youth	#10
I Do	J. Geils Band	#24
Stand By*	Roman Holliday	#54
	*Towards end w/finger snaps	
Give It Up	Steve Miller Band	#60

189

A CAPPELLA (cont'd)

1984		
Leave It	Yes	#24
So You Ran	Orion The Hunter	#58

1986		
Kyrie	Mr. Mister	#1
Life In A Northern Town	The Dream Academy	#7
If You Were A Woman (And I Was A Man)	Bonnie Tyler	#77
In My Dreams	Dokken	#77
I Knew The Bride (When She Use To Rock And Roll)	Nick Lowe	#77
Dancin In My Sleep	Secret Ties	#91

1987		
Shakedown	Bob Seger	#1
Wipeout	The Fat Boys w/ The Beach Boys	#12
Rev It Up	Newcity Rockers	#86

1988		
Don't Worry Be Happy	Bobby McFerrin	#1
Make Me Lose Control	Eric Carmen	#3
Just Like Paradise	David Lee Roth	#6
Supersonic	J.J. Fad	#30
853-5937	Squeeze	#32
Hot Hot Hot	Buster Poindexter	#45
Little Walter	Tony! Toni! Tone!	#47
Wishing I Was Lucky	Wet Wet Wet	#58
Nice 'N' Slow	Freddie Jackson	#61
Killing Me Softly	Al B. Sure!	#80

1989		
Love In An Elevator	Aerosmith	#5
Who Do You Give Your Love To?	Michael Morales	#15
I Want It All	Queen	#50
Let Me In	Eddie Money	#60
We Could Be Together	Debbie Gibson	#71

CHIPMUNK VOICE

You have to wonder who first heard Alvin and the Chipmunks sing, and thought, "Yeah, that's what I need in my pop/rock song- someone who sings like a chipmunk!" I mean, it's fine for Alvin and co. to sing a Christmas song for an audience of seven-year-olds, but what was Newcleus, an early influential rap group, thinking when they had chipmunks rap all throughout "Jam On It"? Even Michael Jackson gave it a whirl by having chipmunks sing in "P.Y.T. (Pretty Young Thing)". Against all odds, both songs turned out to be two of the best from the decade.

SONG	ARTIST	HOT 100 CHART
1981		
Don't Stop The Music	Yarbrough & Peoples	#19
1982		
Murphy's Law	Cheri	#39
1983		
P.Y.T. (Pretty Young Thing)	Michael Jackson	#10
1984		
Jam On It	Newcleus	#56

FALSETTO

Falsetto, a singing technique unique to the male singer that allows them to sing notes that sound impossibly high, has been a popular singing style throughout the history of popular music in the rock era. A couple of prominent early singers of this style include Brian Wilson of the Beach Boys, and Frankie Valli. Two excellent examples of falsetto from the list below are "Take On Me" by A-Ha, and "She Drives Me Crazy" by Fine Young Cannibals.

SONG	ARTIST	HOT 100 CHART
1980		
Emotional Rescue	The Rolling Stones	#3
Off The Wall	Michael Jackson	#10
All Over The World	Electric Light Orchestra	#13
And The Beat Goes On	The Whispers	#19
Old-Fashion Love	Commodores	#20

FALSETTO (cont'd)

1981		
Let's Groove	Earth, Wind & Fire	#3
What Kind Of Fool	Barbra Streisand & Barry Gibb	#10
Since I Don't Have You	Don McLean	#23

1982		
Let It Whip	Dazz Band	#5
Big Fun	Kool & The Gang	#21
I Believe	Chilliwack	#33
If I Had My Wish Tonight	David Lasley	#36
Shine On	George Duke	#41
Wanna Be With You	Earth, Wind & Fire	#51
The Gigolo	O'Bryan	#57

1983		
Lawyers In Love	Jackson Browne	#13
Heart To Heart	Kenny Loggins	#15
Fall In Love With Me	Earth, Wind & Fire	#17
My Kind Of Lady	Supertramp	#31
I Like It	Debarge	#31
Funny How Time Slips Away	Spinners	#67
Bread And Butter	Robert John	#68

1984		
Time Will Reveal	Debarge	#18
Leave A Tender Moment Alone	Billy Joel	#27
Love Me In A Special Way	Debarge	#45
Sail Away	The Temptations	#54
Without You	David Bowie	#73
Amnesia	Shalamar	#73
Baby, I'm Hooked (Right Into Your Love)	Con Funk Shun	#76

1985		
Take On Me	A-Ha	#1
Easy Lover	Philip Bailey w/ Phil Collins	#2
Head Over Heels	Tears For Fears	#3
I'm On Fire	Bruce Springsteen	#6
Cry	Godley & Crème	#16
Wrap Her Up	Elton John	#20
So In Love	Orchestral Manoeuvres In The Dark	#26
Walking On The Chinese Wall	Phillip Bailey	#46
Smalltown Boy	Bronski Beat	#48

FALSETTO (cont'd)

I'll Be There	Kenny Loggins w/ El Debarge	#88

1986		
Human	Human League	#1
Kiss	Prince	#1
Something About You	Level 42	#7
Nikita	Elton John	#7
Tender Love	Force M.D.'s	#10
Love Comes Quickly	Pet Shop Boys	#62

1987		
Shake You Down	Gregory Abbott	#1
Stone Love	Kool & The Gang	#10
Wipeout	The Fat Boys w/ The Beach Boys	#12
Dominoes	Robbie Nevil	#14
I'd Still Say Yes	Klymaxx	#18
Notorious	Loverboy	#38
Skin Trade	Duran Duran	#39
Don't Leave Me This Way	Communards	#40
I Got The Feelin' (It's Over)	Gregory Abbott	#56
System Of Survival	Earth, Wind & Fire	#60
All I Want	Howard Jones	#76
Want You For My Girlfriend	4 By Four	#79

1988		
Waiting For A Star To Fall	Boy Meets Girl	#5
Rocket 2 U	The Jets	#6
Chains Of Love	Erasure	#12
Say It Again	Jermaine Stewart	#27
Off On Your Own (Girl)	Al B. Sure!	#45
Never Can Say Goodbye	The Communards	#51
Killing Me Softly	Al B. Sure!	#80

1989		
I'll Be Loving You	New Kids On The Block	#1
She Drives Me Crazy	Fine Young Cannibals	#1
This One's For The Children	New Kids On The Block	#7
Didn't I (Blow Your Mind)	New Kids On The Block	#8
Put Your Mouth On Me	Eddie Murphy	#27

RAP

Making a list of rap songs from the 80s was harder than you'd think. First, you have to determine what rap is in the first place. You can find several different definitions, but most will define rap as something along the lines of: "lyrics spoken or chanted in rhythm".

It sounds easy enough, but then you come across a song like 1980's "Money", by Flying Lizards. The lead singer isn't singing. She doesn't seem to be rapping either. It sounds to me that she is simply speaking, or talking. For that reason, I don't classify it as rap. I put it in the "Speaking" category.

What about songs like Pebble's "Girlfriend"? The lead singer raps several different times in the song. It begs the question- Does a song land in the "rap" category just because it has a rap? I say no. I put it in a category that indicates those songs have some rap in them, but the vocalists mostly sing.

My last category for rap is labeled "Mostly or All Rap". Some songs in this list will have some singing, but will be mostly rap. "West End Girls", "Wipeout", and "Brass Monkey" are rap songs that do have some singing, while "Rapper's Delight", "You Be Illin'", and "Colors" are basically 100% rap.

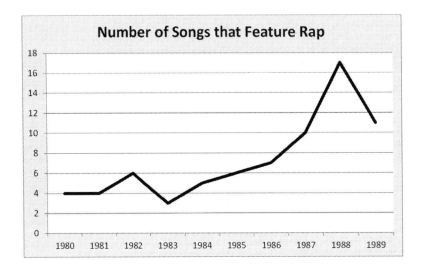

SONGS WITH SPEAKING- NOT RAP

SONG	ARTIST	HOT 100 CHART
1980		
Emotional Rescue	The Rolling Stones	#3
Twilight Zone/Twilight Tone	Manhattan Transfer	#30
Clones (We're All)	Alice Cooper	#40
Money	The Flying Lizards	#50
Rock Lobster	B-52s	#56
Here Comes My Girl	Tom Petty And The Heartbreakers	#59
Merry Christmas In The NFL	Willis "The Guard" & Vigorish	#82

SONGS WITH SPEAKING- NOT RAP (cont'd)

Wango Tango	Ted Nugent	#86
Love On The Phone	Suzanne Fellini	#87

1981		
Take My Heart (You Can Have It If You Want It)	Kool & The Gang	#17
Together	Tierra	#18
Guitar Man	Elvis Presley	#28
Give It To Me Baby	Rick James	#40
Flash's Theme Aka Flash	Queen	#42
Lipstick	Suzi Quatro	#51
Shaddap You Face	Joe Dolce	#53
Skateaway	Dire Straits	#58
Destroyer	The Kinks	#85

1982		
I've Never Been To Me	Charlene	#3
Take Off	Bob & Doug McKenzie w/Geddy Lee	#16
Jump To It	Aretha Franklin	#24
Call Me	Skyy	#26
Valley Girl	Frank Zappa	#32
Words	Missing Persons	#42
Work That Body	Diana Ross	#44
Outlaw	War	#94

1983		
The Girl Is Mine	Michael Jackson & Paul McCartney	#2
Love Is A Battlefield	Pat Benatar	#5
The Look Of Love (Part One)	ABC	#18
The Woman In Me	Donna Summer	#33
Don't Pay The Ferryman*	Chris DeBurgh	#34
	*Shakespeare's "The Tempest" read very quietly during bridge	
Wind Beneath My Wings	Lou Rawls	#65
The Monkey Time	The Tubes	#68
Painted Picture	Commodores	#70
Heat Of The Moment	After 7	#74

1984		
Thriller	Michael Jackson	#4
Panama	Van Halen	#13
Swept Away	Diana Ross	#19

SONGS WITH SPEAKING- NOT RAP (cont'd)

1985		
Sugar Walls	Sheena Easton	#9
Missing You	Diana Ross	#10
Mr. Telephone Song	New Edition	#12
19	Paul Hardcastle	#15
Meeting In The Ladies Room	Klymaxx	#59

1986		
Human	Human League	#1
I'm Your Man	Wham!	#3
The Rain	Oran "Juice" Jones	#9
Yankee Rose	David Lee Roth	#16
Another Night	Aretha Franklin	#22
Saturday Love	Cherrelle w/ Alexander O'Neal	#26
Paranoimia	Art Of Noise/ Max Headroom	#34
Goin' To The Bank	Commodores	#65
The Men All Pause	Klymaxx	#80

1987		
Shake You Down	Gregory Abbott	#1
Control	Janet Jackson	#5
Happy	Surface	#20
Back And Forth	Cameo	#50
I'm Not Perfect (But I'm Perfect For You)	Grace Jones	#69
Tina Cherry	Georgio	#96

1988		
Get Outta My Dreams, Get Into My Car	Billy Ocean	#1
Everything Your Heart Desires	Daryl Hall & John Oates	#3
Please Don't Go Girl	New Kids On The Block	#10
Domino Dancing	Pet Shop Boys	#18
Staying Together	Debbie Gibson	#22
Turn Off The Lights	The World Class Wreckin Cru	#84
You're Not My Kind Of Girl	New Edition	#95

1989		
My Prerogative	Bobby Brown	#1
Miss You Much	Janet Jackson	#1
Kisses On The Wind	Neneh Cherry	#8
Didn't I (Blow Your Mind)	New Kids On The Block	#8
Crazy About Her	Rod Stewart	#11
It Isn't, It Wasn't, It Ain't Never Gonna Be	Aretha Franklin & Whitney Houston	#41

| 24/7 | Dino | #42 |
| Closer Than Friends | Surface | #57 |

SONGS WITH SOME RAP

SONG	ARTIST	HOT 100 CHART
1980		
Stomp!	The Brothers Johnson	#7
1981		
Backfired	Debbie Harry	#43
Square Biz	Teena Marie	#50
1982		
Mickey	Toni Basil	#1
1983		
I'll Tumble 4 Ya	Culture Club	#9
The Clapping Song	Pia Zadora	#36
Candy Girl	New Edition	#46
Should I Love You	Cee Farrow	#82
1984		
I Feel For You	Chaka Khan	#3
Eyes Without A Face	Billy Idol	#4
Breakdance	Irene Cara	#8
Obscene Phone Caller	Rockwell	#35
Strip	Adam Ant	#42
Sex Shooter	Apollonia 6	#85
1985		
Cool It Now	New Edition	#4
Operator	Midnight Star	#18
Wild And Crazy Love	Mary Jane Girls	#42
Count Me Out	New Edition	#51
Oo-Ee-Diddley-Bop!	Peter Wolf	#61
The Oak Tree	Morris Day	#65
Look My Way	The Vels	#72

SONGS WITH SOME RAP (cont'd)

Mathematics	Melissa Manchester	#74
Swear	Sheena Easton	#80
Let's Go Out Tonight*	Nile Rodgers	#88
	*Japanese rap	

1986		
What Have You Done For Me Lately	Janet Jackson	#4
Headlines	Midnight Star	#69

1987		
Looking For A New Love	Jody Watley	#2
Serious	Donna Allen	#21
I Want Action	Poison	#50
(Baby Tell Me) Can You Dance	Shanice Wilson	#50
Shy Girl	Stacey Q	#89
Spring Love	The Cover Girls	#98

1988		
What Have I Done To Deserve This?	Pet Shop Boys & Dusty Springfield	#2
Naughty Girls (Need Love Too)	Samantha Fox	#3
I Don't Want Your Love	Duran Duran	#4
Girlfriend	Pebbles	#5
Rocket 2 U	The Jets	#6
Don't Be Cruel	Bobby Brown	#8
What You See Is What You Get	Brenda K. Starr	#24
Tall Cool One	Robert Plant	#25
Da'Butt	E.U.	#35
Nightime	Pretty Poison	#36
Off On Your Own (Girl)	Al B. Sure!	#45
Cecilia	Times Two	#79

1989		
The Lover In Me	Sheena Easton	#2
On Our Own	Bobby Brown	#2
Roni	Bobby Brown	#3
Every Little Step	Bobby Brown	#3
Secret Rendezvous	Karyn White	#6
Sincerely Yours	Sweet Sensation w/ Romeo J.D.	#14
Don't Shut Me Out	Kevin Paige	#18
Sunshine	Dino	#23
You're My One And Only (True Love)	Seduction	#23
Talk To Myself	Christopher Williams	#49
Puss N' Boots/ These Boots (Are Made For Walkin')	Kon Kan	#58

SONGS WITH SOME RAP (cont'd)

Baby Baby	Eighth Wonder	#84
Heaven Knows	When In Rome	#95

SONGS WITH MOSTLY/ALL RAP

SONG	ARTIST	HOT 100 CHART
1980		
The Legend Of Wooley Swamp	Charlie Daniels Band	#31
Rappers Delight	The Sugarhill Gang	#36
Who Shot J.R. ?	Gary Burbank	#67
The Breaks (Part 1)	Kurtis Blow	#87
1981		
Rapture	Blondie	#1
Double Dutch Bus	Frankie Smith	#30
General Hospi-Tale	The Afternoon Delights	#33
8th Wonder	The Sugarhill Gang	#82
1982		
Planet Rock	Afrika Bambaataa	#48
Apache	The Sugarhill Gang	#53
She Got The Goldmine (I Got The Shaft)	Jerry Reed	#57
The Message	Grand Master Flash	#62
Attack Of The Name Game	Stacy Lattisaw	#70
When The Radio Is On	Paul Shaffer	#81
1983		
Der Kommissar	After The Fire	#5
Posse' On Broadway	Sir Mix-A-Lot	#70
Owwww!	Chunky A	#77
1984		
She's Strange	Cameo	#47
Jam On It	Newcleus	#56
Electric Kingdom	Twilight 22	#79
Rappin' Rodney	Rodney Dangerfield	#83
Beat Street Breakdown - Part 1	Grandmaster Melle Mel	#86

SONGS WITH MOSTLY/ALL RAP (cont'd)

1985		
One Night In Bangkok	Murray Head	#3
Basketball	Kurtis Blow	#71
One Night In Bangkok	Robey	#77
Roxanne, Roxanne	Utfo	#77
Friends	Whodini	#87
Freak-A-Ristic	Atlantic Starr	#90

1986		
West End Girls	Pet Shop Boys	#1
Rock Me Amadeus	Falco	#1
Walk This Way	Run-D.M.C. (w/Aerosmith)	#4
Vienna Calling	Falco	#18
You Be Illin'	Run-D.M.C.	#29
Superbowl Shuffle	The Chicago Bears Shufflin' Crew	#41
Once In A Lifetime	Talking Heads	#91

1987		
Heart And Soul	T'Pau	#4
(You Gotta) Fight For Your Right (To Party!)	Beastie Boys	#7
Wipeout	The Fat Boys w/ The Beach Boys	#12
I Need Love	L.L. Cool J	#14
Me Myself And I	De La Soul	#34
Brass Monkey	Beastie Boys	#48
It's Tricky	Run-D.M.C.	#57
I'm Bad	L.L. Cool J	#84
Go See The Doctor	Kool Moe Dee	#89
Ronnie's Rap	Ron & The D.C Crew	#93

1988		
Parents Just Don't Understand	D.J. Jazzy Jeff and the Fresh Prince	#12
A Nightmare On My Street	D.J. Jazzy Jeff and the Fresh Prince	#15
The Twist (Yo, Twist!)	The Fat Boys w/ Chubby Checker	#16
Push It	Salt-N-Pepa	#19
Supersonic	J.J. Fad	#30
Going Back To Cali	L.L. Cool J	#31
When We Kiss	Bardeux	#36
It Takes Two	Rob Base & D.J. E-Z Rock	#36
Cars With The Boom	L'Trimm	#54
Girls Ain't Nothing But Trouble	D.J. Jazzy Jeff and the Fresh Prince	#57
Way Out	J.J. Fad	#61

SONGS WITH MOSTLY/ALL RAP (cont'd)

Wild, Wild West	Kool Moe Dee	#62
Colors	Ice-T	#70
Mary, Mary	Run-D.M.C.	#75
Louie, Louie	The Fat Boys	#89
Is It Love	J.J. Fad	#92

1989		
Wild Thing	Tone Loc	#2
Girl You Know It's True	Milli Vanilli	#2
Funky Cold Medina	Tone Loc	#3
Buffalo Stance	Neneh Cherry	#3
Bust A Move	Young MC	#7
Friends	Jody Watley w/ Eric B. & Rakim	#9
I'm That Type Of Guy	L.L. Cool J	#15
Me So Horny	The 2 Live Crew	#26
Hey Ladies	Beastie Boys	#36
Joy And Pain	Rob Base/ D.J. E-Z Rock	#58
I Think I Can Beat Mike Tyson	D.J. Jazzy Jeff and the Fresh Prince	#58

ROBOT VOICE/VOCODER/TALKBOX

The vocoder and talk box make the voice sound digitized, or robotic. Many of the songs that use these devices were quite popular; fifteen songs with these vocal effects hit the top ten, with five number ones.

The vocal effects don't always hit you over the head, though. You have to listen quite closely to hear the vocoder in "I Just Called To Say I Love You". It doesn't make an appearance until near the end. Listen for the echo of the chorus. On the other hand, some songs nearly blast you with the vocoder, as in "Let's Groove", by Earth, Wind, and Fire, and "Mr. Roboto", by Styx.

SONG	ARTIST	HOT 100 CHART
1980		
Funkytown	Lipps Inc.	#1
All Over The World	Electric Light Orchestra	#13
On The Rebound	Russ Ballard	#58
I'm Alive	Gamma	#60
Rock It	Lipps, Inc.	#64
More Bounce To The Ounce (Part 1)	Zapp	#86

ROBOT VOICE/VOCODER/TALKBOX (cont'd)

1981		
Let's Groove	Earth, Wind & Fire	#3
In The Air Tonight	Phil Collins	#19
Wrack My Brain	Ringo Starr	#38
I Heard It Through The Grapevine (Part One)	Roger	#79
Let's Dance (Make Your Body Move)	West Street Mob	#88

1982		
Ebony And Ivory	Paul McCartney & Stevie Wonder	#1
Love Is In Control (Finger On The Trigger)	Donna Summer	#10
State Of Independence	Donna Summer	#41
Landslide	Olivia Newton-John	#52
Sing A Simple Song	West Street Mob	#89

1983		
Mr. Roboto	Styx	#3
Puttin' On The Ritz	Taco	#4
P.Y.T. (Pretty Young Thing)	Michael Jackson	#10
Automatic Man	Michael Sembello	#34
Queen Of The Broken Hearts	Loverboy	#34
Papa Was A Rollin' Stone	Wolf	#55
Freak-A-Zoid	Midnight Star	#66
Canvas Of Life	Minor Detail	#92

1984		
I Just Called To Say I Love You	Stevie Wonder	#1
Somebody's Watching Me	Rockwell	#2
Bop 'Til You Drop	Rick Springfield	#20
The Lucky One	Laura Branigan	#20
Catch Me I'm Falling	Real Life	#40
Joystick	Dazz Band	#61
Freakshow On The Dance Floor	Bar-Kays	#73
Body Talk	Deele	#77
Electric Kingdom	Twilight 22	#79
Sexcrime (Nineteen Eighty-Four)	Eurythmics	#81
No Parking (On The Dance Floor)	Midnight Star	#81

1985		
Operator	Midnight Star	#18
Animal Instinct	Commodores	#43
Scientific Love	Midnight Star	#80
You Send Me	The Manhattans	#81

ROBOT VOICE/VOCODER/TALKBOX (cont'd)

Freak-A-Ristic	Atlantic Starr	#90

1986		
Rock Me Amadeus	Falco	#1
I Can't Wait	Nu Shooz	#3
Let's Go All The Way	Sly Fox	#7
One Step Closer To You	Gavin Christopher	#22
Paranoimia	Art Of Noise/ Max Headroom	#34
Living On Video	Trans-X	#61
Headlines	Midnight Star	#69

1987		
Livin' On A Prayer	Bon Jovi	#1
Serious	Donna Allen	#21
Notorious	Loverboy	#38
Silent Morning	Noel	#47
Lover's Lane	Georgio	#59
System Of Survival	Earth, Wind & Fire	#60
Shy Girl	Stacey Q	#89
Ronnie's Rap	Ron & The D.C Crew	#93
Boy Toy	Tia	#97

1988		
I Want To Be Your Man	Roger	#3
Boom! There She Was	Scritti Politti w/ Roger	#53
Something Just Ain't Right	Keith Sweat	#79
(It's Just) The Way That You Love Me	Paula Abdul	#88

1989		
Sowing The Seeds Of Love	Tears For Fears	#2

SHOUTING

SONG	ARTIST	HOT 100 CHART
1980		
All Night Long	Joe Walsh	#19

1980		
Shaddap You Face	Joe Dolce	#53

SHOUTING (cont'd)

1983		
Shoppin' From A To Z	Toni Basil	#77

VOCALIZING/SCAT

Scat- singing nonsense syllables in an improvised manner- is most commonly associated with jazz, not 80s pop. Nonetheless, thirteen songs from the decade used this singing technique. More than half of these songs were from 1980 and 1982.

SONG	ARTIST	HOT 100 CHART
1980		
Give Me The Night	George Benson	#4
Him	Rupert Holmes	#6
Happy Together (A Fantasy)	Captain & Tennille	#53
Breakfast In America	Supertramp	#62
1981		
Love All The Hurt Away	Aretha Franklin & George Benson	#46
1982		
Waiting On A Friend	The Rolling Stones	#13
Jump To It	Aretha Franklin	#24
Under Pressure	Queen & David Bowie	#29
Bad Boy/ Having A Party	Luther Vandross	#55
1983		
Boogie Down	Al Jarreau	#77
1985		
There Must Be An Angel (Playing With My Heart)	Eurythmics	#22
1987		
Lies	Jonathan Butler	#27
1988		
Twilight World	Swing Out Sister	#31

SONGS WITH FOREIGN LANGUAGES

Thirty-three songs from the decade had lyrics that were sung in other languages. To be listed here, a song did not have to be sung entirely in another language. A song only had to have one word from a foreign language to be included in this section. Some songs came close to that minimum standard. "Lost In Emotion" by Lisa Lisa & Cult Jam is sung almost entirely in English, but several times she sings the Spanish phrase "Que Sera".

The most popular foreign languages were French and Spanish. I also included songs in this section if they used nonsense words, or a made-up language. For example, Lionel Richie couldn't find an African language that sounded right for his song, so he made up some African-sounding words for his hit, "All Night Long (All Night)".

Some hit songs used little-known languages as well. According to one of the writers of "Iko Iko", the title is taken from words from a language of Mardi Gras Indians. Swahili and Wolof are two other languages used in hit songs from the decade.

There are two songs that were sung entirely in another language. Both were huge hits. "La Bamba" was a #1 song for Los Lobos in 1987, and "99 Luftballons" hit #2 for Nena in 1984.

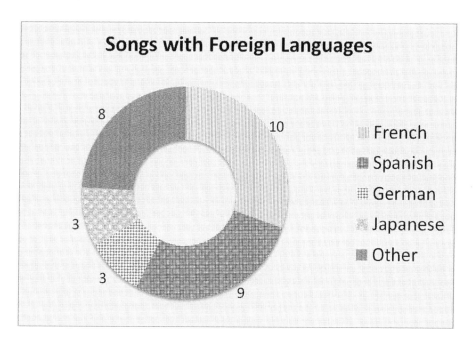

FRENCH

SONG	ARTIST	HOT 100 CHART
1980		
Don't Ask Me Why	Bill Joel	#19
Games Without Frontiers	Peter Gabriel	#48

FRENCH (cont'd)

1981		
Hold On Tight	Electric Light Orchestra	#10
Bon Bon Vie (Gimme The Good Life)	T.S. Monk	#63

1982		
Don't Talk To Strangers	Rick Springfield	#2

1986		
La Bel Age	Pat Benatar	#54
Living On Video	Trans-X	#61

1987		
C'est La Vie	Robbie Nevil	#2
French Kissin	Debbie Harry	#57

1988		
The Right Stuff	Vanessa Williams	#44

SPANISH

SONG	ARTIST	HOT 100 CHART
1983		
Yo No Se'	Pajama Party	#75
1985		
Que Te Quiero	Katrina & The Waves	#71
1986		
Don Quichotte	Magazine 60	#56
1987		
Who's That Girl	Madonna	#1
Lost In Emotion	Lisa Lisa & Cult Jam	#1
La Bamba	Los Lobos	#1
Looking For A New Love	Jody Watley	#2
1988		
Kisses On The Wind	Neneh Cherry	#8
Hot Hot Hot	Buster Poindexter	#45

GERMAN

SONG	ARTIST	HOT 100 CHART
1984		
99 Luftballons	Nena	#2

1986		
Rock Me Amadeus	Falco	#1
Vienna Calling	Falco	#18

JAPANESE

SONG	ARTIST	HOT 100 CHART
1981		
Ai No Corrida	Quincy Jones (Dune)	#28

1983		
Mr. Roboto	Styx	#3

1985		
Let's Go Out Tonight	Nile Rodgers	#88

NONSENSE

SONG	ARTIST	HOT 100 CHART	LANGUAGE
1983			
All Night Long (All Night)*	Lionel Richie	#1	
	*Nonsense- Richie sang made-up words that sound like an African language		
Rock Of Ages*	Def Leppard	#16	
	*Opening countdown "meaningless drivel", according to lead singer		
Ewok Celebration	Meco	#60	

OTHER/UNKNOWN

1984			
Ti Amo	Laura Branigan	#55	Italian

1986			
In Your Eyes	Peter Gabriel	#26	WOLOF (African language)

1987			
Hold Me	Colin James Hay	#99	?

1988			
Don't Look Any Further	Kane Gang	#64	Swahili

1989			
Iko Iko	The Belle Stars	#14	Mardi Gras Indian language

FOR MUSIC EDUCATORS/STUDENTS

Music teachers- Are you getting tired of your students tuning you out when you play yet another piece of Mozart's to explain a certain aspect of music history or music theory? The man wrote some fabulous music, but sometimes your students just don't care. They want to hear some modern music.

Well, why not give them what they want if it will still help them learn what you are teaching? The next time you need musical examples to help explain accelerandos, decelerandos, ostinatos, modulation, syncopation, drones, countermelodies, and call and response, consider using a song from the 80s. Your students will be pleasantly surprised, and more engaged.

ACCELERANDO

An ACCELERANDO is a gradual increase in the tempo of the music. Tempo changes in songs from the 80s are extremely rare. Out of 4172 songs, only nine songs experienced a change in tempo; five songs sped up, and four songs slowed down. It was a stretch to include some of them, however. "Lean On Me", a #1 hit for Club Nouveau in 1987, did not have a gradual increase in tempo. Instead, the change in speed is rather abrupt. "First Night", by Survivor, is notable for having several big changes in tempo.

SONG	ARTIST	HOT 100 CHART
1980		
Seasons	Grace Slick	#95

ACCELERANDO (cont'd)

1983		
Come On Eileen	Dexys Midnight Runners	#1

1985		
First Night	Survivor	#53

1987		
Lean On Me	Club Nouveau	#1

1989		
French Kiss	Lil Louis	#50

DECELERANDO

A DECELERANDO is a gradual decrease in the tempo of the music.

SONG	ARTIST	HOT 100 CHART
1981		
Toccata	Sky	#83

1984		
Left In The Dark	Barbra Streisand	#50

1989		
Batdance	Prince	#1
French Kiss	Lil Louis	#50

OSTINATO

An OSTINATO is a short, repetitive rhythmic or melodic phrase. An ostinato can be an instrument or a vocal part. The key, though, is that it is a short phrase that repeats.

Technically, I probably could've included the drum part of nearly every song in this list, as most drum parts repeat over and over. Instead, I only included songs that had distinctive or especially important ostinatos, or ostinatos that dominated the music.

One of the best examples of an ostinato from the decade comes from "Fool In The Rain" by Led Zeppelin in 1980. The song opens with a short guitar riff (approximately 2 seconds long) that is repeated eighty times (yes, I counted).

The 80s Music Compendium

For an example of a vocal ostinato, listen to "The Borderlines" by Jeffrey Osborne from 1985. The background singers sing the word "borderlines" over and over. Some might argue that a single word is too short to be considered an ostinato, but I would disagree.

For selected songs, I've indicated in the "Notes" column where to find the ostinato. For most other songs, it should be obvious upon listening.

SONG	ARTIST	HOT 100 CHART	NOTES
1980			
Off The Wall	Michael Jackson	//10	
Fool In The Rain	Led Zeppelin	#21	
Savannah Nights	Tom Johnston	#34	
Baby Talks Dirty	The Knack	#38	
Rock Lobster	B-52s	#56	
Computer Game "Theme From The Circus"	Yellow Magic Orchestra	#60	
1981			
Don't Stop The Music	Yarbrough & Peoples	#19	
Heartbreak Hotel	The Jacksons	#22	
My Girl (Gone, Gone, Gone)	Chilliwack	#22	Vocals
A Lucky Guy	Rickie Lee Jones	#64	
Can You Feel It	The Jacksons	#77	
8th Wonder	The Sugarhill Gang	#82	
1982			
Missing You	Dan Fogelberg	#23	
Early In The Morning	The Gap Band	#24	
Call Me	Skyy	#26	Bass part
Get Closer	Linda Ronstadt	#29	
Your Imagination	Daryl Hall & John Oates	#33	
Since You're Gone	The Cars	#41	Percussion
Whatcha Gonna Do	Chilliwack	#41	Keyboard part on chorus
1999	Prince	#44	
Cutie Pie	One Way	#61	
Emotions In Motion	Billy Squier	#68	
1983			
Dirty Laundry	Don Henley	#3	
Wanna Be Startin' Somethin'	Michael Jackson	#5	Bass
Twilight Zone	Golden Earring	#10	Guitar
Ain't Nobody	Rufus/Chaka Khan	#22	Intro
Let's Go Dancin' (Ooh La, La, La)	Kool & The Gang	#30	
I Couldn't Say No	Robert Ellis Orrall w/Carlene Carter	#32	

OSTINATO (cont'd)

You're Driving Me Out Of My Mind	Little River Band	#35	Bass guitar
Betcha She Don't Love You	Evelyn King	#49	
Just Be Good To Me	The S.O.S. Band	#55	
The Metro	Berlin	#58	
This Must Be The Place (Naïve Melody)	Talking Heads	#62	
Bang The Drum All Day	Todd Rundgren	#63	
The Walls Came Down	The Call	#74	
Memphis	Joe Jackson	#85	

1984			
When Doves Cry	Prince	#1	
State Of Shock	Jacksons w/ Mick Jagger	#3	
Thriller	Michael Jackson	#4	
Remember The Nights	The Motels	#36	
Two Tribes	Frankie Goes To Hollywood	#43	Synth bass
Jam On It	Newcleus	#56	Bass
Concealed Weapons	J. Geils Band	#63	
The Gap	Thompson Twins	#69	
Gloria	The Doors	#71	
A Chance For Heaven	Christopher Cross	#76	Keyboard
I Send A Message	INXS	#77	Keyboard
Each Word's A Beat Of My Heart	Mink Deville	#89	Piano

1985			
Don't Lose My Number	Phil Collins	#4	
Born In The U.S.A.	Bruce Springsteen	#9	
No Lookin' Back	Michael McDonald	#34	Keyboard
The Borderlines	Jeffrey Osborne	#38	Vocals- "Borderlines"
Like A Surgeon	"Weird Al" Yankovic	#47	Synth
Freedom	The Pointer Sisters	#59	Keyboard
Swear	Sheena Easton	#80	Guitar
Black Kisses (Never Make You Blue)	Curtie & The Boombox	#81	Bass

1986			
When I Think Of You	Janet Jackson	#1	Bass, keyboard
Let's Go All The Way	Sly Fox	#7	Percussion
Take Me Home	Phil Collins	#7	Percussion
When The Heart Rules The Mind	GTR	#14	
All The Love In The World	The Outfield	#19	
You Be Illin'	Run-D.M.C.	#29	
25 Or 6 To 4	Chicago	#48	
Peter Gunn	Art of Noise	#50	

OSTINATO (cont'd)

I Must Be Dreaming	Giuffria	#52	
Headed For The Future	Neil Diamond	#53	
Goin' To The Bank	Commodores	#65	
Just Another Day	Oingo Boingo	#85	Xylophone
Life's What You Make It	Talk Talk	#90	
Once In A Lifetime	Talking Heads	#91	

1987			
I Knew You Were Waiting (For Me)	Aretha Franklin & George Michael	#1	
Skeletons	Stevie Wonder	#19	
Seven Wonders	Fleetwood Mac	#19	
Fascinated	Company B	#21	
Don't Leave Me This Way	Communards	#40	
Oh Yeah	Yello	#51	Vocals
Sexappeal	Georgio	#58	
Lover's Lane	Georgio	#59	
Satellite	Hooters	#61	
In Love With Love	Debbie Harry	#70	
Crazy World	Big Trouble	#71	
Kiss You (When It's Dangerous)	Eight Seconds	#72	
Jane's Getting Serious	Jon Astley	#77	
The Real Thing	Jellybean w/ Steven Dante	#82	
I'm Bad	L.L. Cool J	#84	Bass line

1988			
Seasons Change	Expose	#1	
Devil Inside	INXS	#2	Guitar
New Sensation	INXS	#3	
Fast Car	Tracy Chapman	#6	Guitar part
Pump Up The Volume	M/A/R/R/S	#13	
Early In The Morning	Robert Palmer	#19	
One Good Reason	Paul Carrack	#28	
Dance Little Sister (Part One)	Terence Trent D'Arby	#30	
Downtown Life	Daryl Hall & John Oates	#31	Vocals- "It feels so..."
Tomorrow People	Ziggy Marley	#39	Vocals- "Tomorrow people"
Are You Sure	So	#41	Keyboard
Never Let Me Down Again	Depeche Mode	#63	Vocals
Nobody's Perfect	Mike + The Mechanics	#63	
Hot Thing	Prince	#63	
Powerful Stuff	The Fabulous Thunderbirds	#65	

OSTINATO (cont'd)

Skin Deep	Cher	#79	
Is It Love	J.J. Fad	#92	
Fat	"Weird Al" Yankovic	#99	

1989			
Miss You Much	Janet Jackson	#1	Background vocals on chorus
Smooth Criminal	Michael Jackson	#7	
Cult Of Personality	Living Colour	#13	
All She Wants Is	Duran Duran	#22	Vocals
Talk To Myself	Christopher Williams	#49	

DRONES

A DRONE is an unchanging pitch that is held for an extended number of beats or seconds. A note that is repeated over and over for an extended amount of time can also be considered a drone. Usually, a drone is a low pitch, but it can also be a high pitch. In classical music, a drone might last for an entire piece.

For an example from classical music, listen to the Prelude to Wagner's "Das Rheingold". You can find several versions on YouTube. The bass instruments play a very low note (a drone) for the entire Prelude.

The bagpipe and several other instruments always produce a drone. For an excellent example of a drone played by bagpipes, listen to "Gravel Walk", by The Rogues (available on YouTube, of course). The very first note you hear is the drone, and it doesn't let up for the whole song.

The 80s pop hit that has a drone last for the entire song is extremely rare. Therefore, I included a song in this list if it had a drone that lasted for "awhile". Rather subjective, I know.

Having said that, 1982's "Eye Of The Tiger" by Survivor has a drone that plays almost the entire song. It's a repeated note played on the guitar. Take a listen to it- the very first sound you hear is the drone.

Expose's 1989 hit "When I Looked At Him" has a more traditional, continuously sounding drone around the middle of the song when they sing, "They say I should be acting cool..."; listen for the high-pitched synthesizer.

For certain songs, I've indicated in the "Notes" section where to hear the drone. For most of the other songs, it should be easy to hear if you listen carefully.

SONG	ARTIST	HOT 100 CHART	NOTES
1980			
Hold On To My Love	Jimmy Ruffin	#10	
Atomic	Blondie	#39	
When The Feeling Comes Around	Jennifer Warnes	#45	High-pitched synth instrument
Don't Misunderstand Me	Rossington Collins Band	#55	Piano on chorus
Desire	The Rockets	#70	Piano
Bounce, Rock, Skate, Roll Pt. 1	Vaughan Mason	#81	Guitar

DRONES (cont'd)

1981			
Theme From "Greatest American Hero (Believe It Or Not)	Joey Scarbury	#2	Synth
The Rambler	Molly Hatchet	#91	Opening

1982			
I Love Rock 'N Roll	Joan Jett & The Blackhearts	#1	Guitar part throughout
Eye Of The Tiger	Survivor	#1	Guitar part
Sweet Dreams	Air Supply	#5	Guitar at end
American Heartbeat	Survivor	#17	Organ at beginning
Voyeur	Kim Carnes	#29	
Shakin'	Eddie Money	#63	Synth throughout
If I Could Get You (Into My Life)	Gene Cotton	#76	Piano on chorus

1983			
Every Breath You Take	The Police	#1	Guitar during verses
Slipping Away	Dave Edmunds	#39	
Cool Places	Sparks & Jane Wiedlin	#49	
Sign Of The Times	The Belle Stars	#75	Bass synth
Keep It Tight	Single Bullet Theory	#78	

1984			
Relax	Frankie Goes To Hollywood	#67	
The Gap	Thompson Twins	#69	Repeated bass

1985			
Party All The Time	Eddie Murphy	#2	
To Live And Die In L.A.	Wang Chung	#41	
Blue Kiss	Jane Wiedlin	#77	Repeated bass note

1986			
Kiss	Prince	#1	
Manic Monday	Bangles	#2	Repeated guitar

1987			
Don't Be Afraid Of The Dark	Robert Cray Band	#74	
Stand Back	The Fabulous Thunderbirds	#76	Repeated notes during verse

1988			
Always On My Mind	Pet Shop Boys	#4	Keyboard at end
Are You Sure	So	#41	
Family Man	Fleetwood Mac	#90	

DRONES (cont'd)

1989			
Miss You Much	Janet Jackson	#1	High drone during chorus
It's No Crime	Babyface	#7	Repeated notes
When I Looked At Him	Expose	#10	
This One	Paul McCartney	#94	

MODULATION

MODULATION is when a song modulates, or changes keys. Usually, this will happen towards the end of a song when the artist wants the song's intensity or level of excitement to increase. Almost all songs that modulate, do it only one time, but a few modulate more than once. Check the next list for songs that modulate multiple times.

SONG	ARTIST	HOT 100 CHART
1980		
Hold On To My Love	Jimmy Ruffin	#10
I Don't Want To Walk Without You	Barry Manilow	#36
Kiss Me In The Rain	Barbra Streisand	#37
Haven't You Heard	Patrice Rushen	#42
Us And Love (We Go Together)	Kenny Nolan	#44
All Night Thing	Invisible Man Band	#45
It's For You	Player	#46
Help Me!	Marcy Levy & Robin Gibb	#50
Computer Game "Theme From The Circus"	Yellow Magic Orchestra	#60
Today Is The Day	Bar-Kays	#60
My Guy/My Girl	Amii Stewart & Johnny Bristol	#63
After You	Dionne Warwick	#65
Holdin' On For Dear Love	Lobo	#75
Inside Of You	Ray, Goodman & Brown	#76
Merry Christmas In The NFL	Willis "The Guard" & Vigorish	#82
Love's Only Love	Engelbert Humperdinck	#83
I Don't Want To Be Lonely	Dana Valery	#87
Where Did We Go Wrong	Frankie Valli & Chris Forde	#90
The Part Of Me That Needs You Most	Jay Black	#98

1981		
Morning Train (Nine To Five)	Sheena Easton	#1
Queen Of Hearts	Juice Newton	#2
Elvira	The Oak Ridge Boys	#5

MODULATION (cont'd)

Hello Again	Neil Diamond	#6
America	Neil Diamond	#8
It's Now Or Never	John Schneider	#14
The Old Songs	Barry Manilow	#15
Is It You	Lee Ritenour w/Eric Tagg	#15
Precious To Me	Phil Seymour	#22
Don't Want To Wait Anymore	The Tubes	#35
Some Days Are Diamonds (Some Days Are Stone)	John Denver	#36
Wasn't That A Party	Rovers	#37
I Need Your Lovin'	Teena Marie	#37
Shine On	L.T.D.	#40
Too Tight	Con Funk Shun	#40
Give A Little Bit More	Cliff Richard	#41
One More Night	Streek	#47
The Sun Ain't Gonna Shine Anymore	Nielsen/Pearson	#56
United Together	Aretha Franklin	#56
It's My Job	Jimmy Buffett	#57
Right Away	Hawks	#63
WKRP In Cincinnati	Steve Carlisle	#65
Run To Me	Savoy Brown	#68
La La Means I Love You	Tierra	#72
One More Chance	Diana Ross	#79
American Memories	Shamus M'Cool	#80
Let's Put The Fun Back In Rock N Roll	Freddy Cannon & The Belmonts	#81
I Can't Say Goodbye To You	Helen Reddy	#88

1982		
Even The Nights Are Better	Air Supply	#5
65 Love Affair	Paul Davis	#6
Break It To Me Gently	Juice Newton	#11
Cool Night	Paul Davis	#11
What's Forever For	Michael Murphey	#19
If The Love Fits Wear It	Leslie Pearl	#28
All Our Tomorrows	Eddie Schwartz	#28
Let's Hang On	Barry Manilow	#32
A Penny For Your Thoughts	Tavares	#33
Oh Julie	Barry Manilow	#38
Shine On	George Duke	#41
I Gotta Try	Michael McDonald	#44
Another Sleepless Night	Anne Murray	#44
Dreamin'	John Schneider	#45
Used To Be	Charlene & Stevie Wonder	#46

MODULATION (cont'd)

If Looks Could Kill	Player	#48
Ribbon In The Sky	Stevie Wonder	#54
Right Here And Now	Bill Medley	#58
Don't Stop Me Baby (I'm On Fire)	The Boys Band	#61
Every Home Should Have One	Pattie Austin	#62
The Only Way Out	Cliff Richard	#64
I Wouldn't Beg For Water	Sheena Easton	#64
Natural Love	Petula Clark	#66
Back To School Again	The Four Tops	#71
Beechwood 4-5789	Carpenters	#74
Too Good To Turn Back Now	Rick Bowles	#77
Opposites Do Attract	All Sports Band	#78
I'm Never Gonna Say Goodbye	Billy Preston	#88
Into My Love	Greg Guidry	#92

1983		
The Girl Is Mine	Michael Jackson & Paul McCartney	#2
Dirty Laundry	Don Henley	#3
Heartbreaker	Dionne Warwick	#10
Don't Forget To Dance	The Kinks	#29
Two Less Lonely People In The World	Air Supply	#38
Memory	Barry Manilow	#39
Candy Girl	New Edition	#46
Blame It On Love	Smokey Robinson & Barbara Mitchell	#48
Always	Firefall	#59
Bad Boys	Wham!	#60
When I'm With You	Sheriff	#61
Every Home Should Have One	Pattie Austin	#69
Crazy	Manhattans	#72
A Little Good News	Anne Murray	#74
Eenie Meenie	Jeffrey Osborne	#76
Keep It Tight	Single Bullet Theory	#78
Where Everybody Knows Your Name (The Theme From "Cheers")	Gary Portnoy	#83
Baby, What About You	Crystal Gayle	#83
Love On My Mind Tonight	The Temptations	#88

1984		
I Just Called To Say I Love You	Stevie Wonder	#1
Jump (For My Love)	The Pointer Sisters	#3
To All The Girls I've Loved Before	Julio Iglesias & Willie Nelson	#5
If Ever You're In My Arms Again	Peabo Bryson	#10

MODULATION (cont'd)

Baby I Lied	Deborah Allen	#26
We're Going All The Way	Jeffrey Osborne	#48
Turn Around	Neil Diamond	#62
A Chance For Heaven	Christopher Cross	#76
Downtown	Dolly Parton	#80

1985		
We Are The World	USA For Africa	#1
Freeway Of Love	Aretha Franklin	#3
You're The Inspiration	Chicago	#3
Getcha Back	The Beach Boys	#26
Lost In Love	New Edition	#35
People Get Ready	Jeff Beck & Rod Stewart	#48
Go For It	Kim Wilde	#65
Gotta Get You Home Tonight	Eugene Wilde	#83
Let's Go Out Tonight	Nile Rodgers	#88
Real Love	Dolly Parton w/ Kenny Rogers	#91
Chain Reaction	Diana Ross	#95

1986		
Invisible Touch	Genesis	#1
Take My Breath Away	Berlin	#1
Don't Forget Me (When I'm Gone)	Glass Tiger	#2
Heartbeat	Don Johnson	#5
Opportunities (Let's Make Lots Of Money)	Pet Shop Boys	#10
I'll Be Over You	Toto	#11
I Think It's Love	Jermaine Jackson	#16
The Whispers In The Dark	Dionne Warwick	#73
The Heart Is Not So Smart	El Debarge With Debarge	#75
Good Music	Joan Jett w/ The Beach Boys	#83
Now And Forever (You And Me)	Anne Murray	#92

1987		
Heaven Is A Place On Earth	Belinda Carlisle	#1
I Wanna Dance With Somebody (Who Loves Me)	Whitney Houston	#1
Livin' On A Prayer	Bon Jovi	#1
Can't We Try	Dan Hill w/ Vonda Sheppard	#6
Breakout	Swing Out Sister	#6
Is This Love	Survivor	#9
Nothing's Gonna Change My Love For You	Glenn Medeiros	#12
Without Your Love	Toto	#38
Don't Leave Me This Way	Communards	#40

MODULATION (cont'd)

Sweet Rachel	Beau Coup	#80

1988		
Seasons Change	Expose	#1
Man In The Mirror	Michael Jackson	#1
I'll Always Love You	Taylor Dayne	#3
Don't Be Cruel	Cheap Trick	#4
Prove Your Love	Taylor Dayne	#7
If It Isn't Love	New Edition	#7
Please Don't Go Girl	New Kids On The Block	#10
I Live For Your Love	Natalie Cole	#13
Spy In The House Of Love	Was (Not Was)	#16
The Colour Of Love	Billy Ocean	#17
You Don't Know	Scarlett & Black	#20
Pop Goes The World	Men Without Hats	#20
Edge Of A Broken Heart	Vixen	#26
The Power Of Love	Laura Branigan	#26
Wishing I Was Lucky	Wet Wet Wet	#58
Dancing Under A Latin Moon	Candi	#68
Long And Lasting Love (Once In A Lifetime	Glenn Medeiros	#68
Samantha (What You Gonna Do?)	Cellarful Of Noise	#69
Always There For You	Stryper	#71
Don't Break My Heart	Romeo's Daughter	#73
Without You	Peabo Bryson & Regina Belle	#89

1989		
I'll Be There For You	Bon Jovi	#1
Listen To Your Heart	Roxette	#1
Cover Girl	New Kids On The Block	#2
Heaven	Warrant	#2
If I Could Turn Back Time	Cher	#3
Shower Me With Your Love	Surface	#5
In Your Room	Bangles	#5
Second Chance	Thirty Eight Special	#6
Put A Little Love In Your Heart	Annie Lennox & Al Green	#9
You're Not Alone	Chicago	#10
When I Looked At Him	Expose	#10
Through The Storm	Aretha Franklin & Elton John	#16
Hey Baby	Henry Lee Summer	#18
License To Chill	Billy Ocean	#32

The 80s Music Compendium

SONGS WITH MULTIPLE INSTANCES OF MODULATION

SONG	ARTIST	HOT 100 CHART
1983		
Lady Love Me (One More Time)	George Benson	#30
1987		
Crazy Crazy Nights	Kiss	#65
1989		
Stand	R.E.M.	#6

SYNCOPATION

SYNCOPATION is when a rhythm in a song accents a beat that is normally weak.

To help understand syncopation, listen to a song and tap your foot to the beat. Any instrument or vocal parts that are between your taps AND stressed are syncopated.

For example, tap your foot and listen to "Material Girl" by Madonna. The verses of this song are syncopated almost the entire way through. They have a herky-jerky feel to them. "Don't Let Him Go" by REO Speedwagon is another great example of a song with lots of syncopation in the vocals.

I've indicated in the "notes" section where to hear the syncopation for some of the songs.

SONG	ARTIST	HOT 100 CHART	NOTES
1980			
Fool In The Rain	Led Zeppelin	#21	
Heartbreaker	Pat Benatar	#23	Guitar
How Does It Feel To Be Back	Daryl Hall & John Oates	#30	Verses
1981			
Too Much Time On My Hands	Styx	#9	Drum part
Time Out Of Mind	Steely Dan	#22	
Don't Let Him Go	REO Speedwagon	#24	Verses
He's A Liar	Bee Gees	#30	Especially verses
Never Too Much	Luther Vandross	#33	Verses
Living Eyes	Bee Gees	#45	Verses

220

SYNCOPATION (cont'd)

Wired For Sound	Cliff Richard	#71	Chorus, some verse

1982			
Did It In A Minute	Daryl Hall & John Oates	#9	
Spirits In The Material World	The Police	#11	Everywhere
Big Fun	Kool & The Gang	#21	"Have some fun"
When All Is Said And Done	Abba	#27	Throughout vocals
The Message	Grand Master Flash	#62	"Don't push me…"

1983			
Waiting For Your Love	Toto	#73	Chorus
Radio Free Europe	Rem	#78	Verses

1984			
Jump (For My Love)	The Pointer Sisters	#3	Vocals on verses
Let's Pretend We're Married	Prince	#52	Vocals
Medicine Song	Stephanie Mills	#65	"Take your Me-di-cine"

1985			
Material Girl	Madonna	#2	Vocals on verses
Lovergirl	Teena Marie	#4	Vocals towards end
Say You're Wrong	Julian Lennon	#21	Horns
Oh Girl	Boy Meets Girl	#39	Vocals on verses

1986			
Angel In My Pocket	One To One	#92	Vocals on verses

1987			
Faith	George Michael	#1	
Coming Around Again	Carly Simon	#18	Vocals on verses

1988			
All Fired Up	Pat Benatar	#19	Vocals

1989			
Rocket	Def Leppard	#12	Vocals- "I can take you through the center of the dark..."

CALL AND RESPONSE

CALL AND RESPONSE is when a vocalist sings a phrase (the call), and another singer or choir answers with a phrase (response). Call and response is usually associated with a solo singer issuing the call, and a choir singing a response, but either part (or both parts) may be voiced with an instrument instead.

Call and response is often used in gospel or blues music, and is very rare in pop music. I could only identify four songs from the 80s that use this technique.

SONG	ARTIST	HOT 100 CHART
1981		
Let's Put The Fun Back In Rock N Roll	Freddy Cannon & The Belmonts	#81
1983		
P.Y.T. (Pretty Young Thing)	Michael Jackson	#10
1985		
Wrap Her Up	Elton John	#20
1988		
Check It Out	John Cougar Mellencamp	#14

COUNTERMELODY

The countermelody, when done well, is one of the most impressive musical devices used in popular music. So what exactly is a countermelody? To put it simply, a COUNTERMELODY is when two different melodies are sung or played at the same time. One of the melodies will usually be more important, or featured, while the other melody is usually more in the background.

Another characteristic of countermelodies is that both of the melodies can be sung separately and they'll sound fine. If it sounds boring, or weird sung by itself, then it probably isn't a countermelody- it's most likely simply a harmony part.

Countermelodies are most commonly associated with classical music. A fantastic example of a countermelody can be found near the end of Joseph Haydn's "Te Deum". To listen to it, just search for it on YouTube. There, you can find numerous examples of this masterpiece.

Back to pop music- Some songs sound like they have a countermelody, when they really don't. At the end of "Lost In Love", by Air Supply, the lead singer is simply improvising over his backup singers, so this would not be considered a countermelody.

"Heart And Soul", by T'Pau, is another song that warrants mention. Most of this song involves two sets of lyrics expressed at the same time. The reason this song is not included on the countermelody list is that while one voice sings the lyrics, the other voice is simply speaking. A countermelody requires two melodies, not one melody and speaking or rapping.

Some songs will have a countermelody, but they are very brief. "Chiquitita" by ABBA is one- its (wonderful) countermelody lasts a mere ten seconds in each of the choruses.

Other songs will have a countermelody that is sadly buried beneath the musical texture, so most people won't even realize it's there. "Head Over Heels" by Tears for Fears is a perfect example of this. Listen to the verse that starts with, "My mother and my brothers used to..." If you listen carefully, you'll hear a great, low countermelody that is easy to miss. I have no idea what he's saying, though.

For songs with countermelodies that are easy to identify, listen to "I Eat Cannibals" by Total Coelo, or "A Trick Of The Night" by Bananarama. For those two examples, like most songs, the countermelody is introduced towards the end.

"Red Red Wine" by UB40 might have the best example of a countermelody from the 80s. It is countermelody is lengthy, easily identifiable, and both melodies are clear and catchy.

I've indicated for some songs the approximate location of the countermelody ("beginning", "end", "chorus", etc.) to make it easier to find.

SONG	ARTIST	HOT 100 CHART	NOTES
1980			
Master Blaster (Jammin')	Stevie Wonder	#5	
Stomp!	The Brothers Johnson	#7	
Ladies Night	Kool & The Gang	#8	End
Off The Wall	Michael Jackson	#10	
All Over The World	Electric Light Orchestra	#13	
Dreamer	Supertramp	#15	
Chiquitita	Abba	#29	Chorus
I Can't Let Go	Linda Ronstadt	#31	
Voices	Cheap Trick	#32	
Keep The Fire	Kenny Loggins	#36	
Stop This Game	Cheap Trick	#48	
Turn It On Again	Genesis	#58	

SONG	ARTIST	HOT 100 CHART	NOTES
1981			
Celebration	Kool & The Gang	#1	
Don't Stand So Close To Me	The Police	#10	End
Don't Stop The Music	Yarbrough & Peoples	#19	
My Girl (Gone, Gone, Gone)	Chilliwack	#22	
Ai No Corrida	Quincy Jones & James Ingram	#28	
Snake Eyes	Alan Parsons Project	#67	End
Don't You Know What Love Is	Touch	#69	
Walking Into The Sunshine	Central Line	#84	End

SONG	ARTIST	HOT 100 CHART	NOTES
1982			
Love Is In Control (Finger On The Trigger)	Donna Summer	#10	
Big Fun	Kool & The Gang	#21	End
Wanna Be With You	Earth, Wind & Fire	#51	Chorus
The Visitors	Abba	#63	End

COUNTERMELODY (cont'd)

Sad Girl	GQ	#93	

1983			
Come On Eileen	Dexys Midnight Runners	#1	
Is There Something I Should Know	Duran Duran	#4	
Our House	Madness	#7	Briefly in middle
Let's Go Dancin' (Ooh La, La, La)	Kool & The Gang	#30	
I Eat Cannibals	Total Coelo	#66	
Shiny Shiny	Haysi Fantayzee	#74	
Side By Side	Earth, Wind & Fire	#76	
Masquerade	Berlin	#82	Towards end

1984			
Runner	Manfred Mann	#22	
Strip	Adam Ant	#42	
Ti Amo	Laura Branigan	#55	
The Ghost In You	The Psychedelic Furs	#59	
Taxi Dancing	Rick Springfield & Randy Crawford	#59	
Black Stations/White Stations	M+M	#63	End
Breaking Up Is Hard On You (A/K/A Don't Take Ma Bell Away From Me)	The American Comedy Network	#70	
Tonight Is What It Means To Be Young	Fire Inc.	#80	

1985			
Head Over Heels	Tears For Fears	#3	
Method Of Modern Love	Daryl Hall & John Oates	#5	
Spanish Eddie	Laura Branigan	#40	End
Let's Talk About Me	Alan Parsons Project	#56	

1986			
Invisible Touch	Genesis	#1	End
True Blue	Madonna	#3	
The Edge Of Heaven	Wham!	#10	
Pleasure And Pain	Divinyls	#76	
It's Alright (Baby's Coming Back)	Eurythmics	#78	
Fall On Me	R.E.M.	#94	

1987			
Don't Leave Me This Way	Communards	#40	
Break Every Rule	Tina Turner	#74	
All I Want	Howard Jones	#76	

COUNTERMELODY (cont'd)

A Trick Of The Night	Bananarama	#76	
Hold Me	Colin James Hay	#99	

1988			
Red Red Wine	UB40	#1	
What Have I Done To Deserve This?	Pet Shop Boys & Dusty Springfield	#2	
The Promise	When In Rome	#11	
Say It Again	Jermaine Stewart	#27	
Spring Love (Come Back To Me)	Stevie B.	#43	
Peek-A-Boo	Siouxsie & The Banshees	#53	
Never Let Me Down Again	Depeche Mode	#63	
It's The End Of The World As We Know It (And I Feel Fine)	R.E.M.	#69	
Englishman In New York	Sting	#84	End

1989			
Sowing The Seeds Of Love	Tears For Fears	#2	
Cherish	Madonna	#2	
Patience	Guns N' Roses	#4	
Heaven Help Me	Deon Estus & George Michael	#5	End
Everlasting Love	Howard Jones	#12	
License To Chill	Billy Ocean	#32	
I Don't Want A Lover	Texas	#77	End
Run To Paradise	Choirboys	#80	Chorus
Now You're In Heaven	Julian Lennon	#93	End

LEAD AND BACKUP SINGER CLASSIFICATION

All songs in this section have backup singers. They are divided into all possible combinations of male, female, and mixed (male AND female) lead singers, and male, female, and mixed backup singers.

This section may be the most useful to cover bands who are looking for songs with a certain combination of male and female singers.

One note- only songs whose backup singers sang at different times than the lead singer are included here. The reason for this stipulation is if they sing the same words at the same time as the lead singer, then all they are likely doing is singing harmony (or, in what would be even less interesting, they'd just be doubling the melody); then this category would basically include every single song of the 80s (just try to find a song without any harmony in the vocals!).

A song in which the backup singers sing at the same time as the lead singer may be included, however, if they are singing a countermelody. For an explanation on countermelodies, see that section.

MALE LEAD WITH MALE BACKUP

SONG	ARTIST	HOT 100 CHART
1980		
Hungry Heart	Bruce Springsteen	#5
Fire Lake	Bob Seger	#6
I'm Alright	Kenny Loggins	#7
Let My Love Open The Door	Pete Townshend	#9
Into The Night	Benny Mardones	#11
This Is It	Kenny Loggins	#11
You're The Only Woman (You & I)	Ambrosia	#13
All Over The World	Electric Light Orchestra	#13
Refugee	Tom Petty And The Heartbreakers	#15
Wait For Me	Daryl Hall & John Oates	#18
And The Beat Goes On	The Whispers	#19
Old-Fashion Love	Commodores	#20
Wondering Where The Lions Are	Bruce Cockburn	#21
Any Way You Want It	Journey	#23
Set Me Free	Utopia	#27
Lady	The Whispers	#28
Forever Mine	O'Jays	#28
Two Places At The Same Time	Ray Parker Jr. & Raydio	#30
Walks Like A Lady	Journey	#32
Back On My Feet Again	The Babys	#33
Carrie	Cliff Richard	#34
Sometimes A Fantasy	Billy Joel	#36
Angel Say No	Tommy Tutone	#38
If You Should Sail	Nielsen/Pearson	#38
Hold On	Kansas	#40
Power	The Temptations	#43
Shandi	Kiss	#47
Fool For Your Loving	Whitesnake	#53
Let's Go 'Round Again	Average White Band	#53
Girl, Don't Let It Get You Down	The O'Jays	#55
A Certain Girl	Warren Zevon	#57
Brite Eyes	Robbin Thompson Band	#66
It's A Night For Beautiful Girls	The Fools	#67
Darlin'	Yipes!!	#68
Too Late	Journey	#70
I Don't Like Mondays	Boomtown Rats	#73
The Very Last Time	Utopia	#76

MALE LEAD WITH MALE BACKUP (cont'd)

Time For Me To Fly	REO Speedwagon	#77
I Can't Stop This Feelin'	Pure Prairie League	#77
Goin' On	The Beach Boys	#83
Peanut Butter	Twennynine feat. Lenny White	#83
Gypsy Spirit	Pendulum	#89
What's Your Hurry Darlin'	Ironhorse	#89

1981		
Private Eyes	Daryl Hall & John Oates	#1
Keep On Loving You	REO Speedwagon	#1
Kiss On My List	Daryl Hall & John Oates	#1
Waiting For A Girl Like You	Foreigner	#2
Let's Groove	Earth, Wind & Fire	#3
The Best Of Times	Styx	#3
A Woman Needs Love (Just Like You Do)	Ray Parker Jr. & Raydio	#4
You Make My Dreams	Daryl Hall & John Oates	#5
Passion	Rod Stewart	#5
Too Much Time On My Hands	Styx	#9
Hold On Tight	Electric Light Orchestra	#10
This Little Girl	Gary U.S. Bonds	#11
I Ain't Gonna Stand For It	Stevie Wonder	#11
When She Was My Girl	The Four Tops	#11
I Love You	Climax Blues Band	#12
It's Now Or Never	John Schneider	#14
Time	Alan Parsons Project	#15
Super Freak (Part 1)	Rick James	#16
Take My Heart (You Can Have It If You Want It)	Kool & The Gang	#17
A Little In Love	Cliff Richard	#17
Together	Tierra	#18
You Better You Bet	The Who	#18
In Your Letter	REO Speedwagon	#20
That Old Song	Ray Parker Jr. & Raydio	#21
Heartbreak Hotel	The Jacksons	#22
She's A Bad Mama Jama (She's Built, She's Stacked)	Carl Carlton	#22
Precious To Me	Phil Seymour	#22
Since I Don't Have You	Don McLean	#23
Living In A Fantasy	Leo Sayer	#23
Juke Box Hero	Foreigner	#26
Twilight	Electric Light Orchestra	#38
Jones Vs. Jones	Kool & The Gang	#39
Straight From The Heart	Allman Brothers Band	#39
Give A Little Bit More	Cliff Richard	#41

MALE LEAD WITH MALE BACKUP (cont'd)

Love T.K.O.	Teddy Pendergrass	#44
Tempted	Squeeze	#49
You Like Me Don't You	Jermaine Jackson	#50
Yesterday Once More/Nothing Remains The Same	Spinners	#52
Nothing Ever Goes As Planned	Styx	#54
Fantastic Voyage	Lakeside	#55
Stay Awake	Ronnie Laws	#60
We Can Get Together	Icehouse	#62
Pay The Devil (Ooo, Baby, Ooo)	The Knack	#67
Aiming At Your Heart	The Temptations	#67
She Did It	Michael Damian	#69
Don't You Know What Love Is	Touch	#69
Wired For Sound	Cliff Richard	#71
La La Means I Love You	Tierra	#72
Hard Times	James Taylor	#72
Slip Away	Pablo Cruise	#75
Fire In The Sky	The Dirt Band	#76
Someday, Someway	Robert Gordon	#76
Secrets	Mac Davis	#76
Watching You	Slave	#78
Let's Put The Fun Back In Rock N Roll	Freddy Cannon & The Belmonts	#81
It's Just The Sun	Don McLean	#83
Walking Into The Sunshine	Central Line	#84
Don't Let Go The Coat	The Who	#84
I'm Gonna Lover Her For Both Of Us	Meatloaf	#84
Heaven In Your Arms	Dan Hartman	#86
Snap Shot	Slave	#91
Ready For Love	Silverado	#92
I'm Your Superman	All Sports Band	#93

1982		
I Can't Go For That (No Can Do)	Daryl Hall & John Oates	#1
Don't Talk To Strangers	Rick Springfield	#2
Freeze-Frame	J. Geils Band	#4
867-5309/Jenny	Tommy Tutone	#4
Shake It Up	The Cars	#4
Let It Whip	Dazz Band	#5
65 Love Affair	Paul Davis	#6
Do You Believe In Love	Huey Lewis & The News	#7
Tainted Love	Soft Cell	#8
Did It In A Minute	Daryl Hall & John Oates	#9
Pac-Man Fever	Buckner & Garcia	#9

MALE LEAD WITH MALE BACKUP (cont'd)

Get Down On It	Kool & The Gang	#10
Man On Your Mind	Little River Band	#14
Time Is Time	Andy Gibb	#15
Play The Game Tonight	Kansas	#17
Let Me Tickle Your Fancy	Jermaine Jackson	#18
Hang Fire	The Rolling Stones	#20
Big Fun	Kool & The Gang	#21
Daddy's Home	Cliff Richard	#23
Without You (Not Another Lonely Night)	Franke And The Knockouts	#24
My Girl	Donnie Iris	#25
Sweet Time	REO Speedwagon	#26
Break It Up	Foreigner	#26
Athena	The Who	#28
Let's Hang On	Barry Manilow	#32
Your Imagination	Daryl Hall & John Oates	#33
I Believe	Chilliwack	#33
Someday, Someway	Marshall Crenshaw	#36
Hope You Love Me Like You Say You Do	Huey Lewis & The News	#36
Love Is Like A Rock	Donnie Iris	#37
Let Me Go	Ray Parker Jr.	#38
Dancing In The Street	Van Halen	#38
Love Or Let Me Be Lonely	Paul Davis	#40
Workin' For A Livin'	Huey Lewis & The News	#41
Since You're Gone	The Cars	#41
Should I Stay Or Should I Go	The Clash	#45
Wanna Be With You	Earth, Wind & Fire	#51
Circle Of Love	Steve Miller Band	#55
She Got The Goldmine (I Got The Shaft)	Jerry Reed	#57
Psychobabble	Alan Parsons Project	#57
So Much In Love	Timothy B. Schmit	#59
Summer Nights	Survivor	#62
Shakin'	Eddie Money	#63
Now Or Never	Axe	#64
Turn On Your Radar	Prism	#64
Dance Wit' Me - Part 1	Rick James	#64
Standing On The Top- Part 1	The Temptations w/ Rick James	#66
Shooting Star	Hollywood	#70
Back To School Again	The Four Tops	#71
Piece Of My Heart	Sammy Hagar	#73
Luanne	Foreigner	#75
Too Good To Turn Back Now	Rick Bowles	#77
When I'm Holding You Tight	Michael Stanley Band	#78

MALE LEAD WITH MALE BACKUP (cont'd)

Don't Talk	Larry Lee	#81
Every Love Song	Greg Kihn Band	#82
Don't Run My Life	Spys	#82
Sad Hearts	The Four Tops	#84
How Can You Love Me	Ambrosia	#86
Steppin' Out	Kool & The Gang	#89
The Longer You Wait	Gino Vannelli	#89
Running	Chubby Checker	#91
Over The Line	Eddie Schwartz	#91
Sad Girl	GQ	#93
Start It All Over	McGuffey Lane	#97

1983		
Every Breath You Take	The Police	#1
Come On Eileen	Dexys Midnight Runners	#1
Let's Dance	David Bowie	#1
Beat It	Michael Jackson	#1
Making Love Out Of Nothing At All	Air Supply	#2
Say It Isn't So	Daryl Hall & John Oates	#2
Mr. Roboto	Styx	#3
King Of Pain	The Police	#3
Hungry Like The Wolf	Duran Duran	#3
Uptown Girl	Billy Joel	#3
Sexual Healing	Marvin Gaye	#3
One Thing Leads To Another	The Fixx	#4
Is There Something I Should Know	Duran Duran	#4
True	Spandau Ballet	#4
My Love	Lionel Richie	#5
Der Kommissar	After the Fire	#5
Family Man	Daryl Hall & John Oates	#6
One On One	Daryl Hall & John Oates	#7
Rock The Casbah	The Clash	#8
She's A Beauty	The Tubes	#10
Pass The Dutchie	Musical Youth	#10
Don't Cry	Asia	#10
Even Now	Bob Seger	#12
Photograph	Def Leppard	#12
Lawyers In Love	Jackson Browne	#13
Heart To Heart	Kenny Loggins	#15
Rock Of Ages	Def Leppard	#16
Fall In Love With Me	Earth, Wind & Fire	#17
The Look Of Love (Part One)	ABC	#18

MALE LEAD WITH MALE BACKUP (cont'd)

Rock 'N' Roll Is King	Electric Light Orchestra	#19
Saved By Zero	The Fixx	#20
Dead Giveaway	Shalamar	#22
Welcome To Heartlight	Kenny Loggins	#24
That's Love	Jim Capaldi	#28
Don't Forget To Dance	The Kinks	#29
Let's Go Dancin' (Ooh La, La, La)	Kool & The Gang	#30
My Kind Of Lady	Supertramp	#31
I Won't Stand In Your Way	Stray Cats	#35
Just Got Lucky	JoBoxers	#36
All My Life	Kenny Rogers	#37
The Closer You Get	Alabama	#38
It's Inevitable	Charlie	#38
Slipping Away	Dave Edmunds	#39
After I Cry	Lanier & Co.	#48
High Time	Styx	#48
The Night	The Animals	#48
Stop Doggin' Me Around	Klique	#50
Shoot For The Moon	Poco	#50
Space Age Whiz Kids	Joe Walsh	#52
Stand By	Roman Holliday	#54
Magnetic	Earth, Wind & Fire	#57
Give It Up	Steve Miller Band	#60
What Love Is	Marty Balin	#63
Europa And The Pirate Twins	Thomas Dolby	#67
Too Much Love To Hide	Crosby, Stills & Nash	#69
Posse' On Broadway	Sir Mix-A-Lot	#70
Reap The Wild Wind	Ultravox	#71
I Just Can't Walk Away	The Four Tops	#71
Let Me Go	Heaven 17	#74
The Walls Came Down	The Call	#74
The One That Really Matters	Survivor	#74
I Didn't Mean To Stay All Night	Starship	#75
Anything Can Happen	Was (Not Was)	#75
The Devil Made Me Do It	Golden Earring	#79
You Belong To Me	The Doobie Brothers	#79
Love Is The Key	Maze feat. Frankie Beverly	#80
State Of The Nation	Industry	#81
Fools Game	Michael Bolton	#82
Where Everybody Knows Your Name (The Theme From "Cheers")	Gary Portnoy	#83
Tonight	The Whispers	#84

MALE LEAD WITH MALE BACKUP (cont'd)

Dancing In The Shadows	After The Fire	#85
Count On Me	Gerard McMahon	#85
The Celtic Soul Brothers	Dexys Midnight Runners	#86
Never Tell An Angel (When Your Heart's On Fire)	The Stompers	#88
Love On My Mind Tonight	The Temptations	#88
Whatever Happened To Old Fashioned Love	B.J. Thomas	#93

1984		
When Doves Cry	Prince	#1
Missing You	John Waite	#1
The Wild Boys	Duran Duran	#2
Joanna	Kool & The Gang	#2
Drive	The Cars	#3
State Of Shock	Jacksons w/ Mick Jagger	#3
Hold Me Now	Thompson Twins	#3
Hard Habit To Break	Chicago	#3
Oh Sherrie	Steve Perry	#3
I Guess That's Why They Call It The Blues	Elton John	#4
Sad Songs (Say So Much)	Elton John	#5
If This Is It	Huey Lewis & The News	#6
I Can Dream About You	Dan Hartman	#6
You Might Think	The Cars	#7
Blue Jean	David Bowie	#8
Penny Lover	Lionel Richie	#8
Breakin' … There's No Stopping Us	Ollie & Jerry	#9
Eat It	Weird Al Yankovic	#12
I Still Can't Get Over Loving You	Ray Parker Jr.	#12
Lights Out	Peter Wolf	#12
Magic	The Cars	#12
Tonight	Kool & The Gang	#13
The Longest Time	Billy Joel	#14
The Curly Shuffle	Jump 'N The Saddle	#15
Are We Ourselves?	The Fixx	#15
Rock Me Tonite	Billy Squier	#15
Who Wears These Shoes?	Elton John	#16
Girls	Dwight Tilley	#16
Stay The Night	Chicago	#16
Torture	Jacksons	#17
It Ain't Enough	Corey Hart	#17
Dancing In The Sheets	Shalamar	#17
Sexy Girl	Glenn Frey	#20
Hello Again	The Cars	#20

MALE LEAD WITH MALE BACKUP (cont'd)

Runner	Manfred Mann	#22
Go Insane	Lindsey Buckingham	#23
Leave It	Yes	#24
We Are The Young	Dan Hartman	#25
I Do'wanna Know	REO Speedwagon	#29
Gold	Spandau Ballet	#29
Bang Your Head (Metal Health)	Quiet Riot	#31
The First Day Of Summer	Tony Carey	#33
Pride (In The Name Of Love)	U2	#33
What Is Love?	Howard Jones	#33
Prime Time	Alan Parsons Project	#34
Boys Do Fall In Love	Robin Gibb	#37
One In A Million	The Romantics	#37
The Whispers To A Scream (Birds Fly)	Icicle Works	#37
Farewell My Summer Love	Michael Jackson	#38
She Was Hot	The Rolling Stones	#44
Body	Jacksons	#47
She's Strange	Cameo	#47
She Don't Know Me	Bon Jovi	#48
(You Can Still) Rock In America	Night Ranger	#51
Sail Away	The Temptations	#54
Looks That Kill	Motley Crue	#54
This Could Be The Right One	April Wine	#58
Original Sin	INXS	#58
The Ghost In You	The Psychedelic Furs	#59
Walking In My Sleep	Roger Daltrey	#62
King Of Suede	"Weird Al" Yankovic	#62
Concealed Weapons	J. Geils Band	#63
Satisfy Me	Billy Satellite	#64
She's Trouble	Musical Youth	#65
I Cry Just A Little Bit	Shakin' Stevens	#67
Cleanin' Up The Town	The Bus Boys	#68
I Wanna Rock	Twisted Sister	#68
Edge Of A Dream	Joe Cocker	#69
Gloria	The Doors	#71
Young Thing, Wild Dreams (Rock Me)	Red Rider	#71
All Night Long	Billy Squier	#75
Baby, I'm Hooked (Right Into Your Love)	Con Funk Shun	#76
A Chance For Heaven	Christopher Cross	#76
Darlin'	Frank Stallone	#81
Simple	Johnny Mathis	#81
Do You Love Me	Andy Fraser	#82

MALE LEAD WITH MALE BACKUP (cont'd)

She Loves My Car	Ronnie Milsap	#84
Such A Shame	Talk Talk	#89
Too Young To Fall In Love	Motley Crue	#90

1985		
Take On Me	A-Ha	#1
Everything She Wants	Wham!	#1
Cherish	Kool & The Gang	#2
Party All The Time	Eddie Murphy	#2
California Girls	David Lee Roth	#3
Nightshift	Commodores	#3
Cool It Now	New Edition	#4
Things Can Only Get Better	Howard Jones	#5
Lovin' Every Minute Of It	Loverboy	#9
Fresh	Kool & The Gang	#9
You're Only Human (Second Wind)	Billy Joel	#9
Somebody	Bryan Adams	#11
You Spin Me Round (Like A Record)	Dead Or Alive	#11
Just A Gigolo/ I Ain't Got Nobody	David Lee Roth	#12
Mr. Telephone Song	New Edition	#12
Jamie	Ray Parker Jr.	#14
Along Comes A Woman	Chicago	#14
Save A Prayer	Duran Duran	#16
Some Things Are Better Left Unsaid	Daryl Hall & John Oates	#18
Emergency	Kool & The Gang	#18
Just As I Am	Air Supply	#19
Jungle Love	The Time	#20
Getcha Back	The Beach Boys	#26
Tenderness	General Public	#27
Turn Up The Radio	Autograph	#29
Possession Obsession	Daryl Hall & John Oates	#30
This Is Not America	David Bowie/ Pat Metheny Group	#32
Why Can't I Have You	The Cars	#33
Mistake No. 3	Culture Club	#33
Communication	The Power Station	#34
Lost In Love	New Edition	#35
The Bird	The Time	#36
The Borderlines	Jeffrey Osborne	#38
In Neon	Elton John	#38
Second Nature	Dan Hartman	#39
The Word Is Out	Jermaine Stewart	#41
Animal Instinct	Commodores	#43

MALE LEAD WITH MALE BACKUP (cont'd)

Say It Again	Santana	#46
Everything I Need	Men At Work	#47
Treat Her Like A Lady	The Temptations	#48
Can't Stop	Rick James	#50
Stand By Me	Maurice White	#50
Count Me Out	New Edition	#51
Only For Love	Limahl	#51
First Night	Survivor	#53
Reaction To Action	Foreigner	#54
Down On Love	Foreigner	#54
Summertime Girls	Y & T	#55
Love & Pride	King	#55
Let's Talk About Me	Alan Parsons Project	#56
Lonely In Love	Giuffria	#57
Restless Heart	John Waite	#59
Playing To Win	Little River Band	#60
Lonely School	Tommy Shaw	#60
Kiss And Tell	Isley Jasper Isley	#63
Dangerous	Loverboy	#65
In And Out Of Love	Bon Jovi	#69
Holyanna	Toto	#71
Days Are Numbered (The Traveller)	Alan Parsons Project	#71
Test Of Time	The Romantics	#71
All Right Now	Rod Stewart	#72
Eye To Eye	Go West	#73
Rebels	Tom Petty And The Heartbreakers	#74
One Foot Back In Your Door	Roman Holliday	#76
You Send Me	The Manhattans	#81
It's Gettin' Late	The Beach Boys	#82
You're The Only Love	Paul Hyde/ The Payolas	#84
Little Sheila	Slade	#86
Janet	Commodores	#87
Master And Servant	Depeche Mode	#87
Follow Your Heart	Triumph	#88
You're In Love	Ratt	#89
Fright Night	J. Geils Band	#91
Heartline	Robin George	#92
Injured In The Game Of Love	Donnie Iris	#92

1986		
You Give Love A Bad Name	Bon Jovi	#1
Kiss	Prince	#1

MALE LEAD WITH MALE BACKUP (cont'd)

Stuck With You	Huey Lewis & The News	#1
Everybody Have Fun Tonight	Wang Chung	#2
Hip To Be Square	Huey Lewis & The News	#3
Living In America	James Brown	#4
If You Leave	Orchestral Manoeuvres In The Dark	#4
Throwing It All Away	Genesis	#4
Dreamtime	Daryl Hall	#5
All I Need Is A Miracle	Mike + The Mechanics	#5
Your Love	The Outfield	#6
Word Up	Cameo	#6
Spies Like Us	Paul McCartney	#7
Tonight She Comes	The Cars	#7
Sweet Freedom	Michael McDonald	#7
Be Good To Yourself	Journey	#9
Opportunities (Let's Make Lots Of Money)	Pet Shop Boys	#10
I'll Be Over You	Toto	#11
Tarzan Boy	Baltimora	#13
Digging Your Scene	The Blow Monkeys	#14
Suzanne	Journey	#17
Girl Can't Help It	Journey	#17
Beat's So Lonely	Charlie Sexton	#17
Calling America	Electric Light Orchestra	#18
Vienna Calling	Falco	#18
All The Love In The World	The Outfield	#19
That Was Then, This Is Now	The Monkees	#20
(How To Be A) Millionaire	ABC	#20
Earth Angel	New Edition	#21
Digital Display	Ready For The World	#21
Press	Paul McCartney	#21
No Easy Way Out	Robert Tepper	#22
Twist And Shout	The Beatles	#23
In Your Eyes	Peter Gabriel	#26
One Hit (To The Body)	The Rolling Stones	#28
I'm Not The One	The Cars	#32
Foolish Pride	Daryl Hall	#33
Feel It Again	Honeymoon Suite	#34
A Kind Of Magic	Queen	#42
Great Gosh A'Mighty (It's A Matter Of Time)	Little Richard	#42
You Can Call Me Al	Paul Simon	#44
Lady Soul	The Temptations	#47
Caravan Of Love	Isley Jasper Isley	#51
Jungle Boy	John Eddie	#52

MALE LEAD WITH MALE BACKUP (cont'd)

Leader Of The Pack	Twisted Sister	#53
Heartache All Over The World	Elton John	#55
California Dreamin'	The Beach Boys	#57
Strength	The Alarm	#61
Goin' Crazy!	David Lee Roth	#66
Rock 'N' Roll To The Rescue	The Beach Boys	#68
Spirit In The Sky	Doctor & The Medics	#69
When The Rain Comes Down	Andy Taylor	#73
Feel The Heat	Jean Beauvoir	#73
Working Class Man	Jimmy Barnes	#74
Don't Say No Tonight	Eugene Wilde	#76
In My Dreams	Dokken	#77
Where Are You Now?	Synch	#77
Eye Of The Zombie	John Fogerty	#81
Just Another Day	Oingo Boingo	#85
Let Me Down Easy	Roger Daltrey	#86
Living In The Background	Baltimora	#87
It's Not You, It's Not Me	KBC Band	#89
I'm For Real	Howard Hewett	#90
This Is The Time	Dennis DeYoung	#93
Fall On Me	R.E.M.	#94
Stay True	Sly Fox	#94
I Want To Make The World Turn Around	The Steve Miller Band	#97

1987		
Bad	Michael Jackson	#1
Is This Love	Whitesnake	#2
Will You Still Love Me?	Chicago	#3
Land Of Confusion	Genesis	#4
I Know What I Like	Huey Lewis & The News	#9
It's Not Over ('Til It's Over)	Starship	#9
Wot's It To Ya	Robbie Nevil	#10
Kiss Him Goodbye	The Nylons	#12
Wipeout	The Fat Boys w/ The Beach Boys	#12
Nobody's Fool	Cinderella	#13
I Won't Forget You	Poison	#13
Dude (Looks Like A Lady)	Aerosmith	#14
Brand New Lover	Dead Or Alive	#15
That Ain't Love	REO Speedwagon	#16
You Are The Girl	The Cars	#17
Animal	Def Leppard	#19
Candy	Cameo	#21

MALE LEAD WITH MALE BACKUP (cont'd)

Ship Of Fools (Save Me From Tomorrow)	World Party	#27
Something Real (Inside Me/ Inside You)	Mr. Mister	#29
Since You've Been Gone	The Outfield	#31
On The Edge Of A Broken Heart	Bon Jovi	#38
Don't Look Down- The Sequel	Go West	#39
Back To Paradise	38 Special	#41
Someone Like You	Daryl Hall	#57
Girlfriend	Bobby Brown	#57
Under The Boardwalk	Bruce Willis	#59
System Of Survival	Earth, Wind & Fire	#60
Rock Me	Great White	#60
The Secret Of My Success	Night Ranger	#64
Holiday	Kool & The Gang	#66
Kick The Wall	Jimmy Davis & Junction	#67
Young Blood	Bruce Willis	#68
If You Let Me Stay	Terence Trent D'Arby	#68
Have You Ever Loved Somebody	Freddie Jackson	#69
Should I See	Frozen Ghost	#69
Happy Together	The Nylons	#75
True To You	Ric Ocasek	#75
Jane's Getting Serious	Jon Astley	#77
Love Is A House	Force M.D.'s	#78
Women	Def Leppard	#80
Sweet Rachel	Beau Coup	#80
Power	Kansas	#84
Dancin' With My Mirror	Corey Hart	#88
So Much For Love	The Venetians	#88
American Dream	Simon F.	#91

1988		
The Way You Make Me Feel	Michael Jackson	#1
Wishing Well	Terence Trent D'Arby	#1
Got My Mind Set On You	George Harrison	#1
Bad Medicine	Bon Jovi	#1
Don't Worry Be Happy	Bobby McFerrin	#1
Every Rose Has Its Thorn	Poison	#1
I Don't Wanna Go On With You Like That	Elton John	#2
Pour Some Sugar On Me	Def Leppard	#2
Simply Irresistible	Robert Palmer	#2
I Want To Be Your Man	Roger	#3
Make Me Lose Control	Eric Carmen	#3
How Can I Fall?	Breathe	#3

MALE LEAD WITH MALE BACKUP (cont'd)

Everything Your Heart Desires	Daryl Hall & John Oates	#3
Don't Be Cruel	Cheap Trick	#4
One Good Woman	Peter Cetera	#4
When It's Love	Van Halen	#5
I Want Her	Keith Sweat	#5
Just Like Paradise	David Lee Roth	#6
Rocket 2 U	The Jets	#6
Never Tear Us Apart	INXS	#7
Nite And Day	Al B. Sure!	#7
Electric Blue	Icehouse	#7
If It Isn't Love	New Edition	#7
Welcome To The Jungle	Guns N' Roses	#7
Walk On Water	Eddie Money	#9
Don't Shed A Tear	Paul Carrack	#9
Hysteria	Def Leppard	#10
Please Don't Go Girl	New Kids On The Block	#10
Do You Love Me	The Contours	#11
The Promise	When In Rome	#11
Chains Of Love	Erasure	#12
Finish What Ya Started	Van Halen	#13
Domino Dancing	Pet Shop Boys	#18
A Word In Spanish	Elton John	#19
Early In The Morning	Robert Palmer	#19
My Girl	Suave'	#20
Strange But True	Times Two	#21
When We Was Fab	George Harrison	#23
Missed Opportunity	Daryl Hall & John Oates	#29
I Know You're Out There Somewhere	The Moody Blues	#30
Downtown Life	Daryl Hall & John Oates	#31
Black And Blue	Van Halen	#34
Indestructible	The Four Tops	#35
Heart Of Mine	Boz Scaggs	#35
Rhythm Of Love	Yes	#40
Spring Love (Come Back To Me)	Stevie B.	#43
Any Love	Luther Vandross	#44
The Dead Heart	Midnight Oil	#53
Wishing I Was Lucky	Wet Wet Wet	#58
Wild, Wild West	Kool Moe Dee	#62
Play That Funky Music	Roxanne	#63
Stand Up	David Lee Roth	#64
Like A Child	Noel	#67
Always There For You	Stryper	#71

MALE LEAD WITH MALE BACKUP (cont'd)

Burning Like A Flame	Dokken	#72
Coming Up You	The Cars	#74
Forever Yours	Tony Terry	#80
She's Fly	Tony Terry	#80
Killing Me Softly	Al B. Sure!	#80
When Will I Be Famous?	Bros	#83
You Make Me Work	Cameo	#85
The Motion Of Love	Gene Loves Jezebel	#87
Reason To Try	Eric Carmen	#87
My Obsession	Icehouse	#88
Let Me Sleep Alone	Cugini	#88
Love Changes Everything	Honeymoon Suite	#91
You're Not My Kind Of Girl	New Edition	#95
Fat	"Weird Al" Yankovic	#99

1989		
Good Thing	Fine Young Cannibals	#1
Rock On	Michael Damian	#1
Hangin' Tough	New Kids On The Block	#1
I'll Be There For You	Bon Jovi	#1
I'll Be Loving You	New Kids On The Block	#1
My Prerogative	Bobby Brown	#1
Two Hearts	Phil Collins	#1
Sowing The Seeds Of Love	Tears For Fears	#2
Heaven	Warrant	#2
Born To Be My Baby	Bon Jovi	#3
You Got It (The Right Stuff)	New Kids On The Block	#3
Armageddon It	Def Leppard	#3
Every Little Step	Bobby Brown	#3
Patience	Guns N' Roses	#4
Heaven Help Me	Deon Estus & George Michael	#5
Love In An Elevator	Aerosmith	#5
Angel Eyes	The Jeff Healey Band	#5
Paradise City	Guns N' Roses	#5
Stand	R.E.M.	#6
Dr. Feelgood	Motley Crue	#6
Second Chance	Thirty Eight Special	#6
Walk The Dinosaur	Was (Not Was)	#7
Poison	Alice Cooper	#7
Rock Wit'cha	Bobby Brown	#7
This One's For The Children	New Kids On The Block	#7
Lay Your Hands On Me	Bon Jovi	#7

MALE LEAD WITH MALE BACKUP (cont'd)

Didn't I (Blow Your Mind)	New Kids On The Block	#8
The Doctor	The Doobie Brothers	#9
You Got It	Roy Orbison	#9
Crazy About Her	Rod Stewart	#11
I Won't Back Down	Tom Petty	#12
Rocket	Def Leppard	#12
It's Not Enough	Starship	#12
Dial My Heart	The Boys	#13
A Little Respect	Erasure	#14
I'm That Type Of Guy	L.L. Cool J	#15
Sunshine	Dino	#23
Cuddly Toy (Feel For Me)	Roachford	#25
What I Like About You	Michael Morales	#28
A Shoulder To Cry On	Tommy Page	#29
Glamour Boys	Living Colour	#31
Feels So Good	Van Halen	#35
The Last Mile	Cinderella	#36
Birthday Suit	Johnny Kemp	#36
In My Eyes	Stevie B.	#37
The Way To Your Heart	Soulsister	#41
Can You Stand The Rain	New Edition	#44
Need A Little Taste Of Love	The Doobie Brothers	#45
I Want It All	Queen	#50
Sold Me Down The River	The Alarm	#50
Tribute (Right On)	The Pasadenas	#52
Girl I Am Searching For You	Stevie B.	#56
Into You	Giant Steps	#58
Don't Say You Love Me	Billy Squier	#58
Moonlight On Water	Kevin Raleigh	#60
My Fantasy	Teddy Riley w/ Guy	#62
End Of The Line	Traveling Wilburys	#63
Got It Made	Crosby, Stills & Nash	#69
I Like	Guy	#70
Smooth Up	Bulletboys	#71
The Mayor Of Simpleton	XTC	#72
Never Had A Lot To Lose	Cheap Trick	#75
(Between A) Rock And A Hard Place	Cutting Crew	#77
Run To Paradise	Choirboys	#80
Shake It Up	Bad Company	#82
Hungry	Winger	#85

MALE LEAD WITH FEMALE BACKUP

SONG	ARTIST	HOT 100 CHART
1980		
(Just Like) Starting Over	John Lennon	#1
Master Blaster (Jammin')	Stevie Wonder	#5
Sexy Eyes	Dr. Hook	#5
Lookin' For Love	Johnny Lee	#5
Hold On To My Love	Jimmy Ruffin	#10
You'll Accomp'ny Me	Bob Seger	#14
Never Be The Same	Christopher Cross	#15
Breakdown Dead Ahead	Boz Scaggs	#15
Jojo	Boz Scaggs	#17
Don't Let Go	Isaac Hayes	#18
Deep Inside My Heart	Randy Meisner	#22
Let Me Be The Clock	Smokey Robinson	#31
Girls Can Get It	Dr. Hook	#34
Years	Wayne Newton	#35
Don't Push It Don't Force It	Leon Haywood	#49
Can't We Try	Teddy Pendergrass	#52
Rock Lobster	B-52s	#56
Honey, Honey	David Hudson	#59
The Good Lord Loves You	Neil Diamond	#67
Goodnight My Love	Mike Pinera	#70
Shotgun Rider	Joe Sun	#71
Blues Power	Eric Clapton	#76
Running Back	Eddie Money	#78
Merry Christmas In The NFL	Willis "The Guard" & Vigorish	#82
Just For The Moment	Ray Kennedy	#82
Love's Only Love	Engelbert Humperdinck	#83
Say Goodbye To Little Jo	Steve Forbert	#85
I've Just Begun To Love You	Dynasty	#87

1981		
Just The Two Of Us	Grover Washington Jr. w/Bill Withers	#2
Tryin' To Live My Life Without You	Bob Seger	#5
Guitar Man	Elvis Presley	#28
You Saved My Soul	Burton Cummings	#37
Give It To Me Baby	Rick James	#40
You're So Easy To Love	Tommy James	#58
You Are Forever	Smokey Robinson	#59

MALE LEAD WITH FEMALE BACKUP (cont'd)

| Bon Bon Vie (Gimme The Good Life) | T.S. Monk | #63 |
| That Didn't Hurt Too Bad | Dr. Hook | #69 |

1982		
The Other Woman	Ray Parker Jr.	#4
Yesterday's Songs	Neil Diamond	#11
Any Day Now	Ronnie Milsap	#14
Hot In The City	Billy Idol	#23
I Really Don't Need No Light	Jeffrey Osborne	#39
Johnny Can't Read	Don Henley	#42
You're My Latest, My Greatest Inspiration	Teddy Pendergrass	#43
Never Give Up On A Good Thing	George Benson	#52
Cat People (Putting Out Fire)	David Bowie	#67
Loving You	Chris Rea	#88
I'm Never Gonna Say Goodbye	Billy Preston	#88
Never Thought I'd Fall In Love	The Spinners	#95

1983		
All Night Long (All Night)	Lionel Richie	#1
Time (Clock Of The Heart)	Culture Club	#2
Far From Over	Frank Stallone	#10
Don't You Get So Mad	Jeffrey Osborne	#25
Mirror Man	The Human League	#30
Everyday I Write The Book	Elvis Costello	#36
Swingin'	John Anderson	#43
Are You Serious	Tyrone Davis	#57
Bad Boys	Wham!	#60
Painted Picture	Commodores	#70
Holiday Road	Lindsey Buckingham	#82
Johnny B. Goode	Peter Tosh	#84
Somebody's Gonna Love You	Lee Greenwood	#96

1984		
Ghostbusters	Ray Parker Jr.	#1
Eyes Without A Face	Billy Idol	#4
Pink Houses	John Cougar Mellencamp	#8
Adult Education	Daryl Hall & John Oates	#8
It's A Miracle	Culture Club	#13
The War Song	Culture Club	#17
Read 'Em And Weep	Barry Manilow	#18
Come Back And Stay	Paul Young	#22
Send Me An Angel	Real Life	#29

MALE LEAD WITH FEMALE BACKUP (cont'd)

Sugar Don't Bite	Sam Harris	#36
Don't Stop	Jeffrey Osborne	#44
Love Of The Common People	Paul Young	#45
We're Going All The Way	Jeffrey Osborne	#48
In The Name Of Love	Ralph MacDonald w/ Bill Withers	#58
Hyperactive	Thomas Dolby	#62
Eat My Shorts	Rick Dees	#75
Something's On Your Mind	"D" Train	#79
Rappin' Rodney	Rodney Dangerfield	#83
Superstar/Until You Come Back To Me (That's What I'm Gonna Do)	Luther Vandross	#87

1985		
Sea Of Love	Honeydrippers	#3
Pop Life	Prince	#7
All She Wants To Do Is Dance	Don Henley	#9
I'm Gonna Tear Your Playhouse Down	Paul Young	#13
Don't Come Around Here No More	Tom Petty And The Heartbreakers	#13
19	Paul Hardcastle	#15
Understanding	Bob Seger	#17
C-I-T-Y	John Cafferty	#18
Life In One Day	Howard Jones	#19
Mystery Lady	Billy Ocean	#24
Celebrate Youth	Rick Springfield	#26
Forever Man	Eric Clapton	#26
Bruce	Rick Springfield	#27
I Wanna Hear It From Your Lips	Eric Carmen	#35
Walking On The Chinese Wall	Phillip Bailey	#46
Make It Better (Forget About Me)	Tom Petty And The Heartbreakers	#54
Change	John Waite	#54
You Look Marvelous	Billy Crystal	#58
Some People	Belouis Some	#67
Dancin' In The Key Of Life	Steve Arrington	#68
Basketball	Kurtis Blow	#71
Take No Prisoners (In The Game Of Love)	Peabo Bryson	#78
Remo's Theme (What If)	Tommy Shaw	#81
Imagination	Belouis Some	#88
Too Much Ain't Enough Love	Jimmy Barnes	#91
Button Off My Shirt	Paul Carrack	#91

1986		
Higher Love	Steve Winwood	#1

MALE LEAD WITH FEMALE BACKUP (cont'd)

Sledgehammer	Peter Gabriel	#1
There'll Be Sad Songs To Make You Cry	Billy Ocean	#1
Human	Human League	#1
Who's Johnny	El DeBarge	#3
To Be A Lover	Billy Idol	#6
Love Touch	Rod Stewart	#6
Tender Love	Force M.D.'s	#10
Heaven In Your Eyes	Loverboy	#12
You Should Be Mine (The Woo Woo Song)	Jeffrey Osborne	#13
Sanctify Yourself	Simple Minds	#14
You're A Friend Of Mine	Clarence Clemons & Jackson Browne	#18
I Do What I Do (Theme For 9 1/2 Weeks)	John Taylor/Jonathan Elias	#23
He'll Never Love You (Like I Do)	Freddie Jackson	#25
All The Things She Said	Simple Minds	#28
Paranoimia	Art Of Noise/ Max Headroom	#34
Bop	Dan Seals	#42
It's You	Bob Seger	#52
I'd Do It All Again	Sam Harris	#52
Crazay	Jesse Johnson w/ Sly Stone	#53
Give Me The Reason	Luther Vandross	#57
Playing With The Boys	Kenny Loggins	#60
Secret	Orchestral Manoeuvres In The Dark	#62
A Good Heart	Feargal Sharkey	#74
Runaway	Luis Cardenas	#83
That's Life	David Lee Roth	#85
I Need You	Maurice White	#95
Walk Away Renee	Southside Johnny & The Jukes	#98

1987		
Mony Mony "Live	Billy Idol	#1
Shake You Down	Gregory Abbott	#1
Don't Disturb This Groove	The System	#4
Right On Track	Breakfast Club	#7
We'll Be Together	Sting	#7
Just To See Her	Smokey Robinson	#8
Big Time	Peter Gabriel	#8
Let's Go	Wang Chung	#9
Dominoes	Robbie Nevil	#14
Stop To Love	Luther Vandross	#15
Living In A Box	Living In A Box	#17
Talk To Me	Chico DeBarge	#21
Day-In Day-Out	David Bowie	#21

MALE LEAD WITH FEMALE BACKUP (cont'd)

Lies	Jonathan Butler	#27
Jam Tonight	Freddie Jackson	#32
Let's Work	Mick Jagger	#39
Misfit	Curiosity Killed The Cat	#42
There's Nothing Better Than Love	Luther Vandross w/ Gregory Hines	#50
These Times Are Hard For Lovers	John Waite	#53
Variety Tonight	REO Speedwagon	#60
We've Only Just Begun (The Romance Is Not Over)	Glenn Jones	#66
I Don't Think That Man Should Sleep Alone	Ray Parker Jr.	#68
Meet El Presidente	Duran Duran	#70
Criticize	Alexander O'Neal	#70
What's Too Much	Smokey Robinson	#79
Twistin' The Night Away	Rod Stewart	#80
So The Story Goes	Living In A Box	#81

1988		
Father Figure	George Michael	#1
Get Outta My Dreams, Get Into My Car	Billy Ocean	#1
Never Gonna Give You Up	Rick Astley	#1
I Don't Want Your Love	Duran Duran	#4
Don't You Know What The Night Can Do	Steve Winwood	#6
Tunnel Of Love	Bruce Springsteen	#9
It Would Take A Strong Strong Man	Rick Astley	#10
(Sittin' On) The Dock Of The Bay	Michael Bolton	#11
One Step Up	Bruce Springsteen	#13
The Twist (Yo, Twist!)	The Fat Boys w/ Chubby Checker	#16
The Colour Of Love	Billy Ocean	#17
Love Changes (Everything)	Climie Fisher	#23
Say It Again	Jermaine Stewart	#27
It Takes Two	Rob Base & D.J. E-Z Rock	#36
Tomorrow People	Ziggy Marley	#39
Are You Sure	So	#41
She's On The Left	Jeffrey Osborne	#48
Darlin' Danielle Don't	Henry Lee Summer	#57
Don't Look Any Further	Kane Gang	#64
I Want To Be Your Property	Blue Mercedes	#66
Thinking Of You	Earth, Wind & Fire	#67
Put This Love To The Test	Jon Astley	#74
Love Struck	Jesse Johnson	#78
Wait On Love	Michael Bolton	#79
Never Die Young	James Taylor	#80

MALE LEAD WITH FEMALE BACKUP (cont'd)

I Heard It Through The Grapevine	California Raisins	#84

1989		
Baby Don't Forget My Number	Milli Vanilli	#1
Girl I'm Gonna Miss You	Milli Vanilli	#1
Blame It On The Rain	Milli Vanilli	#1
So Alive	Love & Rockets	#3
Bust A Move	Young MC	#7
Cry	Waterfront	#10
Hey Baby	Henry Lee Summer	#18
The Last Worthless Evening	Don Henley	#21
Rock And A Hard Place	The Rolling Stones	#23
Me So Horny	The 2 Live Crew	#26
She Won't Talk To Me	Luther Vandross	#30
I Live By The Groove	Paul Carrack	#31
Kiss	Art Of Noise/Tom Jones	#31
Giving Up On Love	Rick Astley	#38
Love Cries	Stage Dolls	#46
Hearts On Fire	Steve Winwood	#53
Oh Daddy	Adrean Belew	#58
Tell Her	Kenny Loggins	#76
Ain't Too Proud Too Beg	Rick Astley	#89

MALE LEAD WITH MIXED BACKUP SINGERS

SONG	ARTIST	HOT 100 CHART
1980		
The Second Time Around	Shalamar	#8
Romeo's Tune	Steve Forbert	#11
Jane	Jefferson Starship	#14
Gimme Some Lovin'	Blues Brothers	#18
Stand By Me	Mickey Gilley	#22
Make A Little Magic	The Dirt Band	#25
(Sartorial Eloquence) Don't Ya Wanna Play This Game No More?	Elton John	#39
Love X Love	George Benson	#61
Trickle, Trickle	Manhattan Transfer	#73
You And Me	Rockie Robbins	#80
Wango Tango	Ted Nugent	#86

MALE LEAD WITH MIXED BACKUP SINGERS (cont'd)

1981		
Celebration	Kool & The Gang	#1
Woman	John Lennon	#2
All Those Years Ago	George Harrison	#2
How 'Bout Us	Champaign	#12
Share Your Love With Me	Kenny Rogers	#14
Say You'll Be Mine	Christopher Cross	#20
Time Out Of Mind	Steely Dan	#22
Smoky Mountain Rain	Ronnie Milsap	#24
Rock And Roll Dreams Come Through	Jim Steinman (Rory Dodd)	#32
Somebody Send My Baby Home	Lenny Leblanc	#55

1982		
Always On My Mind	Willie Nelson	#5
Trouble	Lindsey Buckingham	#9
Take It Away	Paul McCartney	#10
If I Had My Wish Tonight	David Lasley	#36
Angel In Blue	J. Geils Band	#40
1999	Prince	#44
Dreamin'	John Schneider	#45
Tug Of War	Paul McCartney	#53
Right Here And Now	Bill Medley	#58
Younger Days	Joe Fagin	#80
Be Mine (Tonight)	Grover Washington, Jr. (Grady Tate)	#92

1983		
Dirty Laundry	Don Henley	#3
Wanna Be Startin' Somethin'	Michael Jackson	#5
I'm Still Standing	Elton John	#12
All This Love	Debarge	#17
Love In Store	Fleetwood Mac	#22
Try Again	Champaign	#23
I Like It	Debarge	#31
Inside Love (So Personal)	George Benson	#43
Outstanding	The Gap Band	#51
Papa Was A Rollin' Stone	Wolf	#55
Bang The Drum All Day	Todd Rundgren	#63
West Coast Summer Nights	Tony Carey	#64
What You Do To Me	Carl Wilson	#72
Serious Kinda Girl	Christopher Max	#75

MALE LEAD WITH MIXED BACKUP SINGERS (cont'd)

1984		
If Ever You're In My Arms Again	Peabo Bryson	#10
Give It Up	KC	#18
Time Will Reveal	Debarge	#18
No Way Out	Jefferson Starship	#23
So Bad	Paul McCartney	#23
You Take Me Up	Thompson Twins	#44
Love Me In A Special Way	DeBarge	#45
Wet My Whistle	Midnight Star	#61
Layin' It On The Line	Jefferson Starship	#66

1985		
Part-Time Lover	Stevie Wonder	#1
I Want To Know What Love Is	Foreigner	#1
If You Love Somebody Set Them Free	Sting	#3
Alive & Kicking	Simple Minds	#3
Lay Your Hands On Me	Thompson Twins	#6
You Are My Lady	Freddie Jackson	#12
Love Light In Flight	Stevie Wonder	#17
Vox Humana	Kenny Loggins	#29
I Wonder If I Take You Home	Lisa Lisa & Cult Jam	#34
Girls Are More Fun	Ray Parker Jr.	#34
Everyday	James Taylor	#61
Charm The Snake	Christopher Cross	#68
Baby Come Back To Me (The Morse Code Of Love)	The Manhattan Transfer	#83
See What Love Can Do	Eric Clapton	#89
High School Nights	Dave Edmunds	#91

1986		
When The Going Gets Tough, The Tough Get Going	Billy Ocean	#2
Life In A Northern Town	The Dream Academy	#7
King For A Day	Thompson Twins	#8
War	Bruce Springsteen	#8
Your Wildest Dreams	The Moody Blues	#9
Move Away	Culture Club	#12
Tomorrow Doesn't Matter Tonight	Starship	#26
The Love Parade	The Dream Academy	#36
Anotherloverholenyohead	Prince	#63
I'm Your Man	Barry Manilow	#86
Stairway To Heaven	Far Corporation	#89

MALE LEAD WITH MIXED BACKUP SINGERS (cont'd)

1987		
Lean On Me	Club Nouveau	#1
I Want Your Sex	George Michael	#2
C'est La Vie	Robbie Nevil	#2
Don't Mean Nothing	Richard Marx	#3
The Right Thing	Simply Red	#27
I Need Your Loving	The Human League	#44
I Got The Feelin' (It's Over)	Gregory Abbott	#56
If I Was Your Girlfriend	Prince	#67
This Is The World Calling	Bob Geldof	#82
Certain Things Are Likely	KTP	#97
Hold Me	Colin James Hay	#99

1988		
Wild, Wild West	The Escape Club	#1
Man In The Mirror	Michael Jackson	#1
Waiting For A Star To Fall	Boy Meets Girl	#5
Alphabet St.	Prince	#8
Just Got Paid	Johnny Kemp	#10
Another Lover	Giant Steps	#13
Check It Out	John Cougar Mellencamp	#14
Be Still My Beating Heart	Sting	#15
Never Knew Love Like This	Alexander O'Neal w/ Cherrelle	#28
One Good Reason	Paul Carrack	#28
Da'Butt	E.U.	#35
Family Man	Fleetwood Mac	#90

1989		
Batdance	Prince	#1
I Remember Holding You	Boys Club	#8
Sacred Emotion	Donny Osmond	#13
Talk It Over	Grayson Hugh	#19
Put Your Mouth On Me	Eddie Murphy	#27
Cover Of Love	Michael Damian	#31
License To Chill	Billy Ocean	#32
We've Saved The Best For Last	Kenny G & Smokey Robinson	#47
Let Me In	Eddie Money	#60
You Are My Everything	Surface	#84

FEMALE LEAD WITH MALE BACKUP SINGERS

SONG	ARTIST	HOT 100 CHART
1980		
Xanadu	Olivia Newton-John/Electric Light Orchestra	#8
Brass In Pocket (I'm Special)	Pretenders	#14
Gee Whiz	Bernadette Peters	#31
1981		
Draw Of The Cards	Kim Carnes	#28
But You Know I Love You	Dolly Parton	#41
Promises	Barbra Streisand	#48
1982		
Crimson And Clover	Joan Jett & The Blackhearts	#7
It's Gonna Take A Miracle	Deniece Williams	#10
Kids In America	Kim Wilde	#25
Words	Missing Persons	#42
Destination Unknown	Missing Persons	#42
All Night With Me	Laura Branigan	#69
Perfect	Fairground Attraction	#80
1983		
Back On The Chain Gang	Pretenders	#5
The Woman In Me	Donna Summer	#33
Love's Got A Line On You	Scandal	#59
Windows	Missing Persons	#63
Save The Overtime (For Me)	Gladys Knight & The Pips	#66
1984		
Self Control	Laura Branigan	#4
The Lucky One	Laura Branigan	#20
Hands Tied	Scandal Featuring Patty Smyth	#41
Save The Last Dance For Me	Dolly Parton w/ The Jordanaires	#45
Ti Amo	Laura Branigan	#55
Give	Missing Persons	#67
Say Hello To Ronnie	Janey Street	#68
Action	Evelyn "Champagne" King	#75

FEMALE LEAD WITH MALE BACKUP SINGERS (cont'd)

1985		
Material Girl	Madonna	#2
The Goonies 'R' Good Enough	Cyndi Lauper	#10
Crazy In The Night (Barking At Airplanes)	Kim Carnes	#15
Wise Up	Amy Grant	#66
Talk To Me	Quarterflash	#83

1986		
Nail It To The Wall	Stacy Lattisaw	#48
Your Smile	Rene & Angela	#62
Chain Reaction (Special New Mix)	Diana Ross	#66
Fire With Fire	Wild Blue	#71
Divided Heart	Kim Carnes	#79
Good Music	Joan Jett w/ The Beach Boys	#83
Dancin In My Sleep	Secret Ties	#91

1987		
I Wanna Dance With Somebody (Who Loves Me)	Whitney Houston	#1
Touch Me (I Want Your Body)	Samantha Fox	#4
Rhythm Is Gonna Get You	Gloria Estefan/Miami Sound Machine	#5
Falling In Love (Uh-Oh)	Miami Sound Machine	#25
Don't Tell Me The Time	Martha Davis	#80
Rock-A-Lott	Aretha Franklin	#82

1988		
Naughty Girls (Need Love Too)	Samantha Fox	#3
Love Overboard	Gladys Knight & The Pips	#13
We All Sleep Alone	Cher	#14
Thanks For My Child	Cheryl Pepsii Riley	#32
Heart Don't Fail Me Now	Holly Knight w/ Daryl Hall	#59
How Can I Forget You	Elisa Fiorillo	#60
Breakaway	Big Pig	#60
I Feel Free	Belinda Carlisle	#88
The Only Way Is Up	Yazz/ Plastic Population	#96
Lead Me On	Amy Grant	#96

1989		
The Way You Love Me	Karyn White	#7
I Wanna Have Some Fun	Samantha Fox	#8
Friends	Jody Watley w/ Eric B. & Rakim	#9
Get On Your Feet	Gloria Estefan	#11
Dressed For Success	Roxette	#14

FEMALE LEAD WITH MALE BACKUP SINGERS (cont'd)

That's The Way	Katrina & The Waves	#16
Little Liar	Joan Jett & the Blackhearts	#19
You're My One And Only (True Love)	Seduction	#23
Little Jackie Wants To Be A Star	Lisa Lisa & Cult Jam	#29
The Right Stuff	Vanessa Williams	#44

FEMALE LEAD WITH FEMALE BACKUP SINGERS

SONG	ARTIST	HOT 100 CHART
1980		
One Fine Day	Carole King	#12
No Night So Long	Dionne Warwick	#23
I Can't Help Myself (Sugar Pie, Honey Bunch)	Bonnie Pointer	#40
Red Light	Linda Clifford	#41
Could I Be Dreaming	The Pointer Sisters	#52
Sweet Sensation	Stephanie Mills	#52
Scandal	RCR	#94
1981		
Woman In Love	Barbra Streisand	#1
Slow Hand	The Pointer Sisters	#2
The Winner Takes It All	Abba	#8
Tell It Like It Is	Heart	#8
Touch Me (When We're Dancing)	Carpenters	#16
It's All I Can Do	Anne Murray	#53
United Together	Aretha Franklin	#56
Dedicated To The One I Love	Bernadette Peters	#65
Come To Me	Aretha Franklin	#84
Where's Your Angel	Lani Hall	#88
Once A Night	Jackie English	#94
1982		
Gloria	Laura Branigan	#2
You Should Hear How She Talks About You	Melissa Manchester	#5
Muscles	Diana Ross	#10
Edge Of Seventeen (Just Like The White Winged Dove)	Stevie Nicks	#11
Should I Do It	The Pointer Sisters	#13

FEMALE LEAD WITH FEMALE BACKUP SINGERS (cont'd)

Nobody	Sylvia	#15
Love Come Down	Evelyn King	#17
My Guy	Sister Sledge	#23
Jump To It	Aretha Franklin	#24
Get Closer	Linda Ronstadt	#29
I'm So Excited	The Pointer Sisters	#30
This Man Is Mine	Heart	#33
Work That Body	Diana Ross	#44
If I Were You	Lulu	#44
Beechwood 4-5789	Carpenters	#74

1983		
Flashdance… What A Feeling	Irene Cara	#1
Sweet Dreams (Are Made Of This)	Eurythmics	#1
Stand Back	Stevie Nicks	#5
Ain't Nobody	Rufus/Chaka Khan	#22
How Many Times Can We Say Goodbye	Dionne Warwick & Luther Vandross	#27
Can't Shake Loose	Agnetha Faltskog	#29
So Close	Diana Ross	#40
Nice Girls	Melissa Manchester	#42
It's Raining Men	The Weather Girls	#46
I Need You	The Pointer Sisters	#48
I Am Love	Jennifer Holliday	#49
Get It Right	Aretha Franklin	#61
Got To Be There	Chaka Khan	#67
Sign Of The Times	The Belle Stars	#75
No One Can Love You More Than Me	Melissa Manchester	#78
Please Mr. Postman	Gentle Persuasion	#82
Shy Boy (Don't It Make You Feel Good)	Bananarama	#83

1984		
Let's Hear It For The Boy	Deniece Williams	#1
Girls Just Want To Have Fun	Cyndi Lauper	#2
Here Comes The Rain Again	Eurythmics	#4
Lucky Star	Madonna	#4
Automatic	The Pointer Sisters	#5
They Don't Know	Tracey Ullman	#8
Cruel Summer	Bananarama	#9
Borderline	Madonna	#10
Head Over Heels	The Go-Go's	#11
Holiday	Madonna	#16
Swept Away	Diana Ross	#19

FEMALE LEAD WITH FEMALE BACKUP SINGERS (cont'd)

Turn To You	The Go-Go's	#32
Holding Out For A Hero	Bonnie Tyler	#34
Take Me Back	Bonnie Tyler	#46
Left In The Dark	Barbra Streisand	#50
Just The Way You Like It	The S.O.S. Band	#64
Medicine Song	Stephanie Mills	#65
Stop	Sam Brown	#65
Straight From The Heart (Into Your Life)	Coyote Sisters	#66
Encore	Cheryl Lynn	#69
Break-A-Way	Tracey Ullman	#70
I Pretend	Kim Carnes	#74
You Were Made For Me	Irene Cara	#78
I Didn't Mean To Turn You On	Cherrelle	#79
Anywhere With You	Rubber Rodeo	#86
Robert Deniro's Waiting	Bananarama	#95

1985		
Crazy For You	Madonna	#1
Freeway Of Love	Aretha Franklin	#3
You Give Good Love	Whitney Houston	#3
I Miss You	Klymaxx	#5
Would I Lie To You?	Eurythmics	#5
In My House	Mary Jane Girls	#7
New Attitude	Patti LaBelle	#17
Sisters Are Doin' It For Themselves	Eurythmics & Aretha Franklin	#18
Find A Way	Amy Grant	#29
Running Up That Hill	Kate Bush	#30
Wild And Crazy Love	Mary Jane Girls	#42
Cross My Heart	Eighth Wonder	#56
Freedom	The Pointer Sisters	#59
All Fall Down	Five Star	#65
Hard Time For Lovers	Jennifer Holliday	#69
Tired Of Being Blonde	Carly Simon	#70
Sweet, Sweet Baby (I'm Falling)	Lone Justice	#73
Mathematics	Melissa Manchester	#74
Frankie	Sister Sledge	#75
(Come On) Shout	Alex Brown	#76
Bit By Bit	Stephanie Mills	#78

1986		
These Dreams	Heart	#1
How Will I Know	Whitney Houston	#1

FEMALE LEAD WITH FEMALE BACKUP SINGERS (cont'd)

Manic Monday	Bangles	#2
Two Of Hearts	Stacey Q	#3
I Can't Wait	Nu Shooz	#3
Mad About You	Belinda Carlisle	#3
True Blue	Madonna	#3
Sweet Love	Anita Baker	#8
Bad Boy	Miami Sound Machine	#8
Nothin' At All	Heart	#10
Baby Love	Regina	#10
I Can't Wait	Stevie Nicks	#16
If She Knew What She Wants	Bangles	#29
For Tonight	Nancy Martinez	#32
Goldmine	The Pointer Sisters	#33
Private Number	The Jets	#47
Love Of A Lifetime	Chaka Khan	#53
Let Me Be The One	Five Star	#59
Jimmy Mack	Sheena Easton	#65
Thorn In My Side	Eurythmics	#68
Headlines	Midnight Star	#69
Female Intuition	Mai Tai	#71
More Than Physical	Bananarama	#73
It's Alright (Baby's Coming Back)	Eurythmics	#78
The Men All Pause	Klymaxx	#80
I Feel The Magic	Belinda Carlisle	#82
Your Personal Touch	Evelyn "Champagne" King	#86
No Frills Love	Jennifer Holliday	#87

1987		
Who's That Girl	Madonna	#1
You Keep Me Hangin' On	Kim Wilde	#1
I Think We're Alone Now	Tiffany	#1
Change Of Heart	Cyndi Lauper	#3
Only In My Dreams	Debbie Gibson	#4
La Isla Bonita	Madonna	#4
I Heard A Rumor	Bananarama	#4
Point Of No Return	Expose	#5
Come Go With Me	Expose	#5
Control	Janet Jackson	#5
Let Me Be The One	Expose	#7
Walking Down Your Street	Bangles	#11
What's Going On	Cyndi Lauper	#12

FEMALE LEAD WITH FEMALE BACKUP SINGERS (cont'd)

Who Found Who	Jellybean w/ Elisa Fiorillo	#16
Coming Around Again	Carly Simon	#18
Jimmy Lee	Aretha Franklin	#28
Two People	Tina Turner	#30
Say You Really Want Me	Kim Wilde	#44
No One In The World	Anita Baker	#44
Same Old Love (365 Days A Year)	Anita Baker	#44
Still A Thrill	Jody Watley	#56
French Kissin	Debbie Harry	#57
Why Should I Cry?	Nona Hendryx	#58
Hooked On You	Sweet Sensation	#64
If I Say Yes	Five Star	#67
Show Me The Way	Regina Belle	#68
In Love With Love	Debbie Harry	#70
Break Every Rule	Tina Turner	#74
A Trick Of The Night	Bananarama	#76
Heartache	Pepsi & Shirlie	#78
Shy Boys	Ana	#94

1988		
Seasons Change	Expose	#1
Hazy Shade Of Winter	Bangles	#2
Out Of The Blue	Debbie Gibson	#3
Giving You The Best That I Got	Anita Baker	#3
Circle In The Sand	Belinda Carlisle	#7
There's The Girl	Heart	#12
All Fired Up	Pat Benatar	#19
Staying Together	Debbie Gibson	#22
Time And Tide	Basia	#26
Trouble	Nia Peeples	#35
Nightime	Pretty Poison	#36
Symptoms Of True Love	Tracie Spencer	#38
Promise Me	The Cover Girls	#40
Love In The First Degree	Bananarama	#48
Feelings Of Forever	Tiffany	#50
Inside Outside	The Cover Girls	#55
Take It While It's Hot	Sweet Sensation	#57
Way Out	J.J. Fad	#61
I Can't Wait	Deniece Williams	#66
Don't Walk Away	Toni Childs	#72
Skin Deep	Cher	#79
Sendin' All My Love	The Jets	#88

FEMALE LEAD WITH FEMALE BACKUP SINGERS (cont'd)

1989		
Eternal Flame	Bangles	#1
Straight Up	Paula Abdul	#1
Miss You Much	Janet Jackson	#1
Express Yourself	Madonna	#2
If I Could Turn Back Time	Cher	#3
Back To Life	Soul II Soul	#4
In Your Room	Bangles	#5
With Every Beat Of My Heart	Taylor Dayne	#5
Dreamin'	Vanessa Williams	#8
What You Don't Know	Expose	#8
When I Looked At Him	Expose	#10
Leave A Light On	Belinda Carlisle	#11
Keep On Movin'	Soul II Soul	#11
Just Because	Anita Baker	#14
Iko Iko	The Belle Stars	#14
Be With You	Bangles	#30
I Only Wanna Be With You	Samantha Fox	#31
Let Go	Sharon Bryant	#34
Radio Romance	Tiffany	#35
Don't Ask Me Why	Eurythmics	#40
Trouble Me	10,000 Maniacs	#44
Over And Over	Pajama Party	#59
I Can't Face The Fact	Gina Go-Go	#78
Imagine	Tracie Spencer	#85

FEMALE LEAD WITH MIXED BACKUP SINGERS

SONG	ARTIST	HOT 100 CHART
1980		
Sara	Fleetwood Mac	#7

1981		
Boy From New York City	Manhattan Transfer	#7
Don't Stop The Music	Yarbrough & Peoples	#19
House Of The Rising Sun	Dolly Parton	#77
Paradise	Change	#80

FEMALE LEAD WITH MIXED BACKUP SINGERS (cont'd)

1982		
Make A Move On Me	Olivia Newton-John	#5
Love's Been A Little Bit Hard On Me	Juice Newton	#7
Love Is In Control (Finger On The Trigger)	Donna Summer	#10
Find Another Fool	Quarterflash	#16
Anyone Can See	Irene Cara	#42
Could It Be Love	Jennifer Warnes	#47
Those Good Old Dreams	Carpenters	#63
Natural Love	Petula Clark	#66

1983		
Total Eclipse Of The Heart	Bonnie Tyler	#1
Why Me?	Irene Cara	#13
Heart Of The Night	Juice Newton	#25
Everyday People	Joan Jett & The Blackhearts	#37
Spice Of Life	Manhattan Transfer	#40
Juicy Fruit	Mtume	#45
Young Love	Janet Jackson	#64
Shoppin' From A To Z	Toni Basil	#77
Touch A Four Leaf Clover	Atlantic Starr	#87

1984		
Got A Hold On Me	Christine McVie	#10
Who's That Girl	Eurythmics	#21
Baby I Lied	Deborah Allen	#26
Flashes	Tiggi Clay	#86

1985		
Dress You Up	Madonna	#5
Who's Zoomin' Who	Aretha Franklin	#7
Missing You	Diana Ross	#10
Love Resurrection	Alison Moyet	#82

1986		
Nasty	Janet Jackson	#3
Like Flames	Berlin	#82
Now And Forever (You And Me)	Anne Murray	#92

1987		
Lost In Emotion	Lisa Lisa & Cult Jam	#1
Little Lies	Fleetwood Mac	#4
I'd Still Say Yes	Klymaxx	#18
Seven Wonders	Fleetwood Mac	#19

FEMALE LEAD WITH MIXED BACKUP SINGERS (cont'd)

As We Lay	Shirley Murdock	#23
Hold Me	Sheila E.	#68
Montego Bay	Amazulu	#90

1988		
The Loco-Motion	Kylie Minogue	#3
I'll Always Love You	Taylor Dayne	#3
I Live For Your Love	Natalie Cole	#13
Everywhere	Fleetwood Mac	#14
I Want You So Bad	Heart	#49
Don't Break My Heart	Romeo's Daughter	#73
(It's Just) The Way That You Love Me	Paula Abdul	#88

1989		
Listen To Your Heart	Roxette	#1
Like A Prayer	Madonna	#1
Sincerely Yours	Sweet Sensation w/ Romeo J.D.	#14
As Long As You Follow	Fleetwood Mac	#43
We Could Be Together	Debbie Gibson	#71

MIXED LEAD WITH MALE BACKUP SINGERS

SONG	ARTIST	HOT 100 CHART
1983		
I Couldn't Say No	Robert Ellis Orrall w/Carlene Carter	#32

1985		
Hangin' On A String (Contemplating)	Loose Ends	#43
Freak-A-Ristic	Atlantic Starr	#90

1989		
Tell Me I'm Not Dreaming	Robert Palmer w/ B.J. Nelson	#60

MIXED LEAD WITH FEMALE BACKUP SINGERS

SONG	ARTIST	HOT 100 CHART
1980		
Dancin' In The Streets	Teri DeSario w/ K.C. And The Sunshine Band	#66
1987		
Don't Leave Me This Way	Communards	#40
1989		
Love Shack	The B-52s	#3

MIXED LEAD WITH MIXED BACKUP SINGERS

SONG	ARTIST	HOT 100 CHART
1982		
Hot Fun In The Summertime	Dayton	#58
1983		
(Keep Feeling) Fascination	The Human League	#8
Winds of Change	Jefferson Starship	#39
Side By Side	Earth, Wind & Fire	#76
1984		
Tell Me If You Still Care	The S.O.S. Band	#65
Tonight Is What It Means To Be Young	Fire Inc.	#80
1985		
We Are The World	USA For Africa	#1
Sun City	Artists United Against Apartheid	#38
1986		
Saturday Love	Cherrelle w/ Alexander O'Neal	#26
Hands Across America	Voices Of America	#65
You Don't Have To Cry	Rene & Angela	#75
I Engineer	Animotion	#76

MIXED LEAD WITH MIXED BACKUP SINGERS (cont'd)

1987		
Holiday	The Other Ones	#29
Dreamin'	Will To Power	#50

1989		
Put A Little Love In Your Heart	Annie Lennox & Al Green	#9

DUETS

Every song in this section has two lead singers, or a lead singer with a backup singer who plays such a prominent role that it sounds as if there were two lead singers. For example, in the song "Tell Me If You Still Care," by the S.O.S. Band in 1984, the male singer has most of the lead. The female voice isn't featured near as long, but does carry the lead in the middle of the song. Because of this, I've classified this song as a duet.

Songs won't be included just because it's performed by a duo. If it sounds as though only one singer is singing the lead, then it won't be included in this section. That's why many songs by Hall & Oates, the Pet Shop Boys, and Eurythmics, among others, aren't listed here, even though those groups are technically duos.

MALE/FEMALE DUETS

SONG	ARTIST	HOT 100 CHART
1980		
You Are My Heaven	Roberta Flack & Donny Hathaway	#47
Help Me!	Marcy Levy & Robin Gibb	#50
One More Time For Love	Billy Preston And Syreeta	#52
Don't Misunderstand Me	Rossington Collins Band	#55
That Lovin' You Feelin' Again	Roy Orbison & Emmylou Harris	#55
Back Together Again	Roberta Flack & Donny Hathaway	#56
My Guy/My Girl	Amii Stewart & Johnny Bristol	#63
Let's Be Lovers Again	Eddie Money w/Valerie Carter	#65
Private Idaho	The B-52s	#74
Where Did We Go Wrong	Frankie Valli & Chris Forde	#90
1981		
Everlasting Love	Rex Smith & Rachel Sweet	#32
Staying With It	Firefall	#37
Two Hearts	Stephanie Mills & Teddy Pendergrass	#40
Lovers After All	Melissa Manchester & Peabo Bryson	#54
Full Of Fire	Shalamar	#55

262

MALE/FEMALE DUETS (cont'd)

Jole Blon	Gary U.S. Bonds	#65
Love Light	Yutaka w/Patti Austin	#81
Very Special	Debra Laws w/Ronnie Laws	#90

1982		
Up Where We Belong	Joe Cocker & Jennifer Warnes	#1
I Keep Forgettin' (Every Time You're Near)	Michael McDonald	#4
Leather And Lace	Stevie Nicks w/ Don Henley	#6
Key Largo*	Bertie Higgins	#8
	*Small part for female at end	
Yesterday's Songs	Neil Diamond	#11
A Penny For Your Thoughts	Tavares	#33
Friends In Love	Dionne Warwick & Johnny Mathis	#38
Used To Be	Charlene & Stevie Wonder	#46
Street Corner	Ashford & Simpson	#56
Make Up Your Mind	Aurra	#71
Baby, Come To Me	Pattie Austin w/ James Ingram	#73
This Time	Kiara w/Shanice Wilson	#78
Ain't Nothing Like The Real Thing/ You're All I Need To Get By	Chris Christian w/ Amy Holland	#88
Into My Love	Greg Guidry	#92

1983		
Total Eclipse Of The Heart	Bonnie Tyler	#1
Islands In The Stream	Kenny Rogers & Dolly Parton	#1
Never Gonna Let You Go	Sergio Mendes	#4
We've Got Tonight	Kenny Rogers & Sheena Easton	#6
You And I	Eddie Rabbitt & Crystal Gayle	#7
Tonight, I Celebrate My Love	Peabo Bryson/ Roberta Flack	#16
How Many Times Can We Say Goodbye	Dionne Warwick & Luther Vandross	#27
I Couldn't Say No	Robert Ellis Orrall w/Carlene Carter	#32
Take The Short Way Home	Dionne Warwick w/Barry Gibb	#41
How Do You Keep The Music Playing	James Ingram & Patti Austin	#45
Midnight Blue	Louise Tucker w/Charlie Skarbek	#46
Blame It On Love	Smokey Robinson & Barbara Mitchell	#48
Cool Places	Sparks & Jane Wiedlin	#49
Smiling Islands	Robbie Patton	#52
Sex (I'm A…)	Berlin	#62
Ricky	"Weird Al" Yankovic	#63
The Monkey Time	The Tubes	#68
Bread And Butter	Robert John	#68
Shiny Shiny	Haysi Fantayzee	#74

MALE/FEMALE DUETS (cont'd)

All The Right Moves	Jennifer Warnes/ Christ Thompson	#85

1984		
Almost Paradise… Love Theme From Footloose	Mike Reno & Ann Wilson	#7
Torture	Jacksons	#17
All Of You	Julio Iglesias & Diana Ross	#29
The Last Time I Made Love	Joyce Kennedy & Jeffrey Osborne	#40
Hold Me	Teddy Pendergrass w/ Whitney Houston	#46
Don't Waste Your Time	Yarbrough & Peoples	#48
Tonight	David Bowie w/ Tina Turner	#53
Strangers In A Strange World	Jenny Burton & Patrick Jude	#54
Happy Ending	Joe Jackson w/ Elaine Caswell	#57
You're Looking Like Love To Me	Peabo Bryson/ Roberta Flack	#58
Taxi Dancing	Rick Springfield & Randy Crawford	#59
The Lebanon	The Human League	#64
Tell Me If You Still Care	The S.O.S. Band	#65
Fading Away	Will To Power	#65
Love Has A Mind Of Its Own	Donna Summer w/ Matthew Ward	#70
Don't Look Any Further	Dennis Edwards w/Siedah Garrett	#72
Perfect Combination	Stacy Lattisaw & Johnny Gill	#75
The Greatest Gift Of All	Kenny Rogers & Dolly Parton	#81
You, Me And He	Mtume	#83
Love Again	John Denver & Sylvie Vartan	#85
Love Has Finally Come At Last	Bobby Womack & Patti Labelle	#88

1985		
Separate Lives	Phil Collins & Marilyn Martin	#1
Obsession	Animotion	#6
Solid	Ashford & Simpson	#12
Never Ending Story	Limahl	#17
I Got You Babe	UB40 w/ Chrissie Hynde	#28
I'll Be Good	Rene & Angela	#47
When The Rain Begins To Fall	Jermaine Jackson/ Pia Zadora	#54
The Family	The Screams Of Passion	#63
Look My Way	The Vels	#72
I'll Be There	Kenny Loggins w/ El Debarge	#88
Real Love	Dolly Parton w/ Kenny Rogers	#91

1986		
The Next Time I Fall	Peter Cetera w/ Amy Grant	#1
On My Own	Patti Labelle & Michael McDonald	#1

MALE/FEMALE DUETS (cont'd)

Friends And Lovers	Gloria Loring & Carl Anderson	#2
Secret Lovers	Atlantic Starr	#3
Take Me Home Tonight	Eddie Money (w/ Ronnie Spector)	#4
All Cried Out	Lisa Lisa & Cult Jam	#8
A Love Bizarre	Sheila E.	#11
I Wanna Be A Cowboy	Boys Don't Cry	#12
It's Only Love	Bryan Adams/ Tina Turner	#15
Never As Good As The First Time	Sade	#20
Saturday Love	Cherrelle w/ Alexander O'Neal	#26
Needles And Pins	Tom Petty w/ Stevie Nicks	#37
If Your Heart Isn't In It	Atlantic Starr	#57
You Don't Have To Cry	Rene & Angela	#75
The Best Of Me	David Foster & Olivia Newton-John	#80
Count Your Blessings	Ashford & Simpson	#84
Good Friends*	Joni Mitchell	#85
	*w/Michael McDonald	
Love In Siberia	Laban	#88
I Wouldn't Lie	Yarbrough & Peoples	#93
One Sunny Day/ Dueling Bikes From Quicksilver	Ray Parker Jr. & Helen Terry	#96

1987		
(I've Had) The Time Of My Life	Bill Medley & Jennifer Warnes	#1
Always	Atlantic Starr	#1
I Knew You Were Waiting (For Me)	Aretha Franklin & George Michael	#1
Nothing's Gonna Stop Us Now	Starship	#1
Somewhere Out There	Linda Ronstadt & James Ingram	#2
U Got The Look*	Prince	#2
	*w/Sheena Easton	
Can't We Try	Dan Hill w/ Vonda Sheppard	#6
Love Power	Dionne Warwick & Jeffrey Osborne	#12
Serious	Donna Allen	#21
Holiday	The Other Ones	#29
Flames Of Paradise	Jennifer Rush w/ Elton John	#36
Why You Treat Me So Bad	Club Nouveau	#39
You And Me Tonight	Deja	#54
Reservations For Two	Dionne Warwick & Kashif	#62
Don't Give Up	Peter Gabriel/ Kate Bush	#72
Someone To Love Me For Me	Lisa Lisa & Cult Jam	#78

1988		
What Have I Done To Deserve This?	Pet Shop Boys & Dusty Springfield	#2
She's Like The Wind	Patrick Swayze w/ Wendy Fraser	#3

MALE/FEMALE DUETS (cont'd)

Piano In The Dark*	Brenda Russell	#6
	*w/Joe Esposito	
Till I Loved You	Barbra Streisand & Don Johnson	#25
Never Knew Love Like This	Alexander O'Neal w/ Cherrelle	#28
Make It Last Forever	Keith Sweat w/ Jacci McGhee	#59
Turn Off The Lights	The World Class Wreckin Cru	#84
Without You	Peabo Bryson & Regina Belle	#89
I Wasn't The One (Who Said Goodbye)	Agnetha Faltskog & Peter Cetera	#93

1989		
The Look	Roxette	#1
Forever Your Girl	Paula Abdul	#1
Baby, I Love Your Way/ Freebird Medley (Free Baby)	Will To Power	#2
Don't Know Much	Linda Ronstadt (w/ Aaron Neville)	#2
Love Shack	The B-52s	#3
Surrender To Me	Ann Wilson & Robin Zander	#6
After All	Cher & Peter Cetera	#6
Close My Eyes Forever	Lita Ford w/ Ozzy Osbourne	#8
Put A Little Love In Your Heart	Annie Lennox & Al Green	#9
Sincerely Yours	Sweet Sensation w/ Romeo J.D.	#14
Through The Storm	Aretha Franklin & Elton John	#16
The Arms Of Orion	Prince w/ Sheena Easton	#36
Bring Down The Moon	Boy Meets Girl	#49
Tell Me I'm Not Dreaming	Robert Palmer w/ B.J. Nelson	#60
The Different Story (World Of Lust And Crime)	Peter Schilling	#61

FEMALE/FEMALE DUETS

SONG	ARTIST	HOT 100 CHART
1984		
Nightbird	Stevie Nicks w/ Sandy Stewart	#33
1985		
Sisters Are Doin' It For Themselves	Eurythmics & Aretha Franklin	#18
Make No Mistake, He's Mine	Barbra Streisand w/ Kim Carnes	#51

The 80s Music Compendium

FEMALE/FEMALE DUETS (cont'd)

1987		
Making Love In The Rain*	Herb Alpert w/ Lisa Keith	#35
	*Janet Jackson technically a backup singer here, but it could easily be considered a duet	

1989		
It Isn't, It Wasn't, It Ain't Never Gonna Be	Aretha Franklin & Whitney Houston	#41
I Love To Bass	Bardeux	#68

MALE/MALE DUETS

SONG	ARTIST	HOT 100 CHART
1981		
The Sun Ain't Gonna Shine Anymore	Nielsen/Pearson	#56

1982		
Don't Fight It	Kenny Loggins w/Steve Perry	#17
Under Pressure	Queen & David Bowie	#29
Young Love	Air Supply	#38
Just To Satisfy You	Waylon Jennings & Willie Nelson	#52
The Gigolo	O'Bryan	#57
Perhaps Love	Placido Domingo & John Denver	#59

1983		
Say Say Say	Paul McCartney & Michael Jackson	#1
The Girl Is Mine	Michael Jackson & Paul McCartney	#2
Hold Me 'Til The Mornin' Comes	Paul Anka w/Peter Cetera	#40
The Blues	Randy Newman & Paul Simon	#51

1984		
To All The Girls I've Loved Before	Julio Iglesias & Willie Nelson	#5
Yah Mo B There	James Ingram w/ Michael McDonald	#19
Ebony Eyes	Rick James w/ Smokey Robinson	#43
Can't Let Go	Stephen Stills w/ Michael Finnigan	#67

1985		
Easy Lover	Philip Bailey w/ Phil Collins	#2
Dancing In The Street	Mick Jagger/ David Bowie	#7
Wrap Her Up	Elton John	#20

MALE/MALE DUETS (cont'd)

1986		
You're A Friend Of Mine	Clarence Clemons & Jackson Browne	#18
Crazay	Jesse Johnson w/ Sly Stone	#53

1987		
There's Nothing Better Than Love	Luther Vandross w/ Gregory Hines	#50
Baby Grand	Billy Joel w/ Ray Charles	#75

1988		
My Love	Julio Iglesias w/ Stevie Wonder	#80
Get It	Stevie Wonder & Michael Jackson	#80

1989		
Joy And Pain	Rob Base/ D.J. E-Z Rock	#58
When Love Comes To Town	U2 w/ B.B. King	#68

FAMOUS BACKUP SINGERS

It's always refreshing to me to discover that a famous singer agreed to sing backup for another artist. Sure, their motives aren't always 100% pure, as they realize they'll gain some exposure from singing in the song (especially if it becomes a hit), but still, it's nice to imagine them doing it as a favor for a lesser-known artist.

SONG	ARTIST	HOT 100 CHART	BACKUP SINGER
1980			
Fire Lake	Bob Seger	#6	Glenn Frey, Don Henley, Timothy B. Schmit
This Is It	Kenny Loggins	#11	Michael McDonald
Deep Inside My Heart	Randy Meisner	#22	Kim Carnes
Make A Little Magic	The Dirt Band	#25	Nicolette Larson
Too Late	Journey	#70	Backed By The Temptations
Save Me	Dave Mason	#71	Michael Jackson

1981			
Super Freak (Part 1)	Rick James	#16	The Temptations
Tempted	Squeeze	#49	Elvis Costello
Square Biz	Teena Marie	#50	Rick James
Jole Blon	Gary U.S. Bonds	#65	Bruce Springsteen
Paradise	Change	#80	Luther Vandross

FAMOUS BACKUP SINGERS (cont'd)

1982			
Love Is In Control (Finger On The Trigger)	Donna Summer	#10	James Ingram
Take Off	Bob & Doug McKenzie w/Geddy Lee	#16	Geddy Lee
Personally	Karla Bonoff	#19	Don Henley, Timothy B. Schmitt
If I Had My Wish Tonight	David Lasley	#36	Bonnie Raitt
Angel In Blue	J. Geils Band	#40	Cissy Houston, Luther Vandross
State Of Independence	Donna Summer	#41	James Ingram, Michael Jackson, Kenny Loggins, Lionel Richie, Dionne Warwick, Stevie Wonder
I Gotta Try	Michael McDonald	#44	Kenny Loggins
Emotions In Motion	Billy Squier	#68	Freddy Mercury, Roger Taylor

1983			
Wanna Be Startin' Somethin'	Michael Jackson	#5	James Ingram
P.Y.T. (Pretty Young Thing)	Michael Jackson	#10	James Ingram, Latoya Jackson, Janet Jackson
Heartbreaker	Dionne Warwick	#10	Barry Gibb
The Woman In Me	Donna Summer	#33	James Ingram
Papa Was A Rollin' Stone	Wolf	#55	Michael Jackson

1984			
Somebody's Watching Me	Rockwell	#2	Michael Jackson
State Of Shock	Jacksons w/ Mick Jagger	#3	Mick Jagger
If Ever You're In My Arms Again	Peabo Bryson	#10	Richard Marx
Girls	Dwight Tilley	#16	Tom Petty
This Woman	Kenny Rogers	#23	Barry Gibb
Centipede	Rebbie Jackson	#24	Michael Jackson, The Weather Girls
Heart Don't Lie	La Toya Jackson	#56	Janet Jackson, Musical Youth
The Only Flame In Town	Elvis Costello w/ Daryl Hall	#56	Daryl Hall
Eyes That See In The Dark	Kenny Rogers	#79	Barry Gibb

1985			
Money For Nothing	Dire Straits	#1	Sting
Party All The Time	Eddie Murphy	#2	Rick James
California Girls	David Lee Roth	#3	Carl Wilson, Christopher Cross
All She Wants To Do Is Dance	Don Henley	#9	Patty Smyth
Eaten Alive	Diana Ross	#77	Michael Jackson
Chain Reaction	Diana Ross	#95	Barry Gibb

1986			
Higher Love	Steve Winwood	#1	Chaka Khan

FAMOUS BACKUP SINGERS (cont'd)

Don't Forget Me (When I'm Gone)	Glass Tiger	#2	Bryan Adams
I'll Be Over You	Toto	#11	Michael McDonald
Sidewalk Talk	Jellybean w/ Catherine Buchanan	#18	Madonna
You're A Friend Of Mine	Clarence Clemons & Jackson Browne	#18	Daryl Hannah
Where Do The Children Go	Hooters w/ Patty Smyth	#38	Patty Smyth
Chain Reaction (Special New Mix)	Diana Ross	#66	Bee Gees
Love Is The Hero	Billy Squier	#80	Freddy Mercury
Good Music	Joan Jett w/ The Beach Boys	#83	The Beach Boys
Innocent Eyes	Graham Nash w/ Kenny Loggins	#84	Kenny Loggins
Good Friends	Joni Mitchell	#85	Michael McDonald

1987			
Back In The High Life Again	Steve Winwood	#13	James Taylor
Making Love In The Rain	Herb Alpert w/ Lisa Keith	#35	Janet Jackson
Deep River Woman	Lionel Richie w/ Alabama	#71	Alabama
Graceland	Paul Simon	#81	The Everly Brothers

1988			
The Right Stuff	Vanessa Williams	#44	Johnny Gill
All I Want Is You	Carly Simon w/ Roberta Flack	#54	Roberta Flack
Heart Don't Fail Me Now	Holly Knight w/ Daryl Hall	#59	Daryl Hall

1989			
Pretending	Eric Clapton w/ Chaka Khan	#55	Chaka Khan
Falling Out Of Love	Ivan Neville	#91	Bonnie Raitt

SONGS WITH A CHILDREN'S CHOIR

SONG	ARTIST	HOT 100 CHART
1980		
Another Brick In The Wall (Part II)	Pink Floyd	#1
Voice Of Freedom	Jim Kirk/ Tm Singers	#71

SONG	ARTIST	HOT 100 CHART
1981		
Can You Feel It	The Jacksons	#77

SONGS WITH A CHILDREN'S CHOIR (cont'd)

1982		
It's Raining Again	Supertramp	#11

1983		
Unconditional Love	Donna Summer w/Musical Youth	#43

1984		
I'm Free (Heaven Helps The Man)	Kenny Loggins	#22

1985		
We Don't Need Another Hero (Thunderdome)	Tina Turner	#2
We Belong	Pat Benatar	#5

1986		
School's Out	Krokus	#67

1988		
Dear Mr. Jesus	Powersource (Sharon Batts)	#61

1989		
Toy Soldiers	Martika	#1
The Living Years	Mike + The Mechanics	#1
This One's For The Children	New Kids On The Block	#7

SONGS WITH AN ADULT CHOIR

It's worth noting the amazing performances of songs that use an adult choir. There were twelve such songs in the 80s- five of them hit #1. Maybe more artists should've used adult choirs.

SONG	ARTIST	HOT 100 CHART
1980		
Seasons	Grace Slick	#95
1981		
Can You Feel It	The Jacksons	#77
1982		
State Of Independence	Donna Summer	#41

SONGS WITH AN ADULT CHOIR (cont'd)

1984		
Do They Know It's Christmas?	Band Aid	#13

1985		
I Want To Know What Love Is	Foreigner	#1
We Are The World	USA For Africa	#1

1986		
Hands Across America	Voices Of America	#65
Stairway To Heaven	Far Corporation	#89

1988		
Man In The Mirror	Michael Jackson	#1

1989		
The Living Years	Mike + The Mechanics	#1
Like A Prayer	Madonna	#1
Closer To Fine	Indigo Girls	#52

SONGS THAT SAMPLE OTHER CREATIVE WORKS

Several songs from the 80s sampled or borrowed from another work of art. Usually, the work of art was another song. Charles Fox reworked Pachabel's "Canon in D", while Tony! Toni! Tone! borrowed from the spiritual "Wade In The Water" for "Little Walter", for example. Some songs borrowed dialogue from a movie ("Batdance", by Prince), however, or from Shakespeare ("Don't Pay The Ferryman" by Chris DeBurgh). Details for each song are listed below.

SONG	ARTIST	HOT 100 CHART	NOTES
1980			
I Don't Want To Walk Without You	Barry Manilow	#36	Sings "Singing in the Rain" melody at the end
Rappers Delight	The Sugarhill Gang	#36	Borrows bass riff from Chic's "Good Times"
I Like To Rock	April Wine	#86	Uses "Satisfaction" and "Daytripper" guitar riff at end
1981			
Same Old Lang Syne	Dan Fogelberg	#9	Ends w/"Auld Lang Syne"
It's Now Or Never	John Schneider	#14	Melody from "O Sole Mio" by di Capua
La La Means I Love You	Tierra	#72	Fragments of "Didn't I Blow Your Mind This Time"
Seasons	Charles Fox	#75	Pachabel's "Canon in 'D'"

SONGS THAT SAMPLE OTHER CREATIVE WORKS (cont'd)

1982			
It's Raining Again	Supertramp	#11	English nursery rhyme at end

1983			
Down Under	Men At Work	#1	Flute plays "Kookaburra" snippet
Don't Pay The Ferryman	Chris DeBurgh	#34	Shakespeare's "The Tempest" read very low during bridge
Midnight Blue	Louise Tucker w/Charlie Skarbek	#46	Uses Beethoven "Pathetique" sonata melody

1984			
Say Hello To Ronnie	Janey Street	#68	Starts w/"Auld Lang Syne"

1987			
Brass Monkey	Beastie Boys	#48	Samples "Bring It Here" by Wild Sugar

1988			
Tall Cool One	Robert Plant	#25	Short (very short) bits of various Led Zeppelin tunes
Little Walter	Tony! Toni! Tone!	#47	Borrows from spiritual "Wade In The Water"
Girls Ain't Nothing But Trouble	D.J. Jazzy Jeff and the Fresh Prince	#57	Theme from "I Dream Of Jeannie"

1989			
Batdance	Prince	#1	Many bits of dialogue from "Batman"
Puss N' Boots/ These Boots (Are Made For Walkin')	Kon Kan	#58	Borrows from Led Zeppelin
Doctorin' The Tardis	The Timelords	#66	Borrows from "Rock And Roll Part 2" and theme from "Doctor Who"

SONGS WITH FAKE ENDINGS

SONG	ARTIST	HOT 100 CHART
1980		
(Just Like) Starting Over	John Lennon	#1
Stop This Game	Cheap Trick	#48
1982		
Love Is Alright Tonight	Rick Springfield	#20

SONGS WITH FAKE ENDINGS (cont'd)

1985		
Born In The U.S.A.	Bruce Springsteen	#9
Emotion	Barbra Streisand	#79

1987		
Faith	George Michael	#1
Animal	Def Leppard	#19
Fire	Bruce Springsteen	#46

1988		
True Love	Glenn Frey	#13

SONGS THAT TELL STORIES

Each of the songs listed below tells a story. Some of the stories involve the supernatural ("(Ghost) Riders In The Sky", "The Legend Of Wooley Swamp"), some are reviews of television shows ("Who Shot J.R. ?", "General Hospi-Tale"), some tell fairly standard love stories ("Sequel", "Same Old Lang Syne"), while the plots in other songs can only be described as ridiculous ("I Lost On Jeopardy", "I Think I Can Beat Mike Tyson").

SONG	ARTIST	HOT 100 CHART
1980		
Ride Like The Wind	Christopher Cross	#2
Coward Of The County	Kenny Rogers	#3
Fool In The Rain	Led Zeppelin	#21
Sequel	Harry Chapin	#23
The Legend Of Wooley Swamp	Charlie Daniels Band	#31
Who Shot J.R. ?	Gary Burbank	#67

1981		
Same Old Lang Syne	Dan Fogelberg	#9
Don't Stand So Close To Me	The Police	#10
(Ghost) Riders In The Sky	Outlaws	#31
General Hospi-Tale	The Afternoon Delights	#33
American Memories	Shamus M'Cool	#80

1982		
It's My Party	Dave Stewart & Barbara Gaskin	#72

SONGS THAT TELL STORIES (cont'd)

1983		
Don't Pay The Ferryman	Chris DeBurgh	#34
Wind Him Up	Saga	#64

1984		
Jam On It	Newcleus	#56
I Lost On Jeopardy	"Weird Al" Yankovic	#81

1989		
18 And Life	Skid Row	#4
I Think I Can Beat Mike Tyson	D.J. Jazzy Jeff and the Fresh Prince	#58

SONGS WITH SOUND EFFECTS

SONG	ARTIST	HOT 100 CHART	SOUND EFFECT
1980			
Answering Machine	Rupert Holmes	#32	Telephone/Answering machine

1981			
Walk Right Now	The Jacksons	#73	Siren

1982			
Pac-Man Fever	Buckner & Garcia	#9	Pac-Man
Call Me	Skyy	#26	Phone Beeps

1984			
Joystick	Dazz Band	#61	Video Games

1986			
Don Quichotte	Magazine 60	#56	Telephone Ring

LAYERING

Here's a list that I wish had fifty times as many songs in it. Layering is when an artist begins a musical section with just a few instruments. After a short amount of time, another instrument is added. A few more seconds go by, and another instrument enters the mix. This continues for anywhere from a few seconds to entire sections of songs.

For an excellent example of this technique, listen to the very beginning of Hall & Oates' song, "I Can't Go For That (No Can Do)".

For an example of layering from a song from the 80s that did NOT make the Hot 100 chart, listen to "Double Life" by The Cars. They spend the first minute and a half slowly bringing in guitars, drums, and percussion until they sing the first chorus.

SONG	ARTIST	HOT 100 CHART
1980		
Take Your Time (Do It Right) Part 1	S.O.S. Band	#3
I Shoulda Loved Ya	Narada Michael Walden	#66
1982		
I Can't Go For That (No Can Do)	Daryl Hall & John Oates	#1
Shine On	George Duke	#41
The Visitors	Abba	#63
1985		
Axel F	Harold Faltermeyer	#3
1986		
Face The Face	Pete Townshend	#26

SONGS WITH WHISTLING

SONG	ARTIST	HOT 100 CHART
1980		
Games Without Frontiers	Peter Gabriel	#48
1982		
Centerfold	J. Geils Band	#1
(Sittin' On) The Dock Of The Bay	The Reddings	#55
1983		
Love Is A Battlefield	Pat Benatar	#5
1986		
Walk Like An Egyptian	Bangles	#1

SONGS WITH WHISTLING (cont'd)

Like Flames	Berlin	#82

1987		
Never Let Me Down	David Bowie	#27

1988		
Don't Worry Be Happy	Bobby McFerrin	#1
Jealous Guy	John Lennon	#80

1989		
Patience	Guns N' Roses	#4

HAND-CLAPS

SONG	ARTIST	HOT 100 CHART
1980		
Rock With You	Michael Jackson	#1
Crazy Little Thing Called Love	Queen	#1
Another One Bites The Dust	Queen	#1
Stomp!	The Brothers Johnson	#7
Ladies Night	Kool & The Gang	#8
Let's Get Serious	Jermaine Jackson	#9
Jesse	Carly Simon	#11
You've Lost That Lovin' Feelin'	Daryl Hall & John Oates	#12
All Over The World	Electric Light Orchestra	#13
Do You Love What You Feel	Rufus & Chaka	#30
You're Supposed To Keep Your Love For Me	Jermaine Jackson	#34
Rappers Delight	The Sugarhill Gang	#36
Help Me!	Marcy Levy & Robin Gibb	#50
Fool For A Pretty Face (Hurt By Love)	Humble Pie	#52
Let's Go 'Round Again	Average White Band	#53
Borrowed Time	Styx	#64
I Shoulda Loved Ya	Narada Michael Walden	#66
Midnight Rendezvous	The Babys	#72
Just Can't Wait	J. Geils Band	#78
My Mistake	The Kingbees	#81
Bounce, Rock, Skate, Roll Pt. 1	Vaughan Mason	#81

HAND-CLAPS (cont'd)

1981		
I Love A Rainy Night	Eddie Rabbitt	#1
Private Eyes	Daryl Hall & John Oates	#1
Rapture	Blondie	#1
Morning Train (Nine To Five)	Sheena Easton	#1
Start Me Up	The Rolling Stones	#2
Too Much Time On My Hands	Styx	#9
Ain't Even Done With The Night	John Mellencamp	#17
Just Once	Quincy Jones & James Ingram	#17
Winning	Santana	#17
Our Lips Our Sealed	The Go-Go's	#20
Seven Year Ache	Roseanne Cash	#22
Ai No Corrida	Quincy Jones & James Ingram	#28
No Reply At All	Genesis	#29
I'm In Love	Evelyn King	#40
The Real Thing	The Brothers Johnson	#67
It Hurts To Be In Love	Dan Hartman	#72
Can You Feel It	The Jacksons	#77
Watching You	Slave	#78
I Heard It Through The Grapevine (Part One)	Roger	#79
All American Girls	Sister Sledge	#79
8th Wonder	The Sugarhill Gang	#82

1982		
Jack & Diane	John Cougar Mellencamp	#1
Mickey	Toni Basil	#1
I Love Rock 'N Roll	Joan Jett & The Blackhearts	#1
We Got The Beat	The Go-Go's	#2
Hurts So Good	John Cougar	#2
Freeze-Frame	J. Geils Band	#4
Should I Do It	The Pointer Sisters	#13
Forget Me Nots	Patrice Rushen	#23
Let's Hang On	Barry Manilow	#32
Someday, Someway	Marshall Crenshaw	#36
Angel In Blue	J. Geils Band	#40
I Only Want To Be With You	Nicolette Larson	#53
Street Corner	Ashford & Simpson	#56
I Predict	Sparks	#60
Happy Man	Greg Kihn Band	#62
Don't Let Me In	Sneaker	#63
Dance Wit' Me - Part 1	Rick James	#64
Can't Hold Back (Your Loving)	Kano	#89

HAND-CLAPS (cont'd)

1983		
Everyday People	Joan Jett & The Blackhearts	#37
Don't Make Me Do It	Patrick Simmons	#75
Red Hot	Herb Alpert	#77
Never Tell An Angel (When Your Heart's On Fire)	The Stompers	#88

1984		
Pink Houses	John Cougar Mellencamp	#8

1985		
Party All The Time	Eddie Murphy	#2
I'm Goin' Down	Bruce Springsteen	#9

1987		
True To You	Ric Ocasek	#75

1988		
Desire	U2	#3
I Could Never Take The Place Of Your Man	Prince	#10

1989		
Good Thing	Fine Young Cannibals	#1
This One's For The Children	New Kids On The Block	#7
Dressed For Success	Roxette	#14

FINGER-SNAPS

SONG	ARTIST	HOT 100 CHART
1980		
Special Lady	Ray, Goodman & Brown	#5
Let's Get Serious	Jermaine Jackson	#9
You're Supposed To Keep Your Love For Me	Jermaine Jackson	#34

1981		
I Love A Rainy Night	Eddie Rabbitt	#1
My Girl (Gone, Gone, Gone)	Chilliwack	#22
Still Cruisin'	The Beach Boys	#93

FINGER-SNAPS (cont'd)

1982		
Rosanna	Toto	#2
Muscles	Diana Ross	#10
Come Go With Me	The Beach Boys	#18
Under Pressure	Queen & David Bowie	#29
This Man Is Mine	Heart	#33
So Much In Love	Timothy B. Schmit	#59
When The Radio Is On	Paul Shaffer	#81

1984		
The Longest Time	Billy Joel	#14

1985		
Ooh Ooh Song	Pat Benatar	#36

1986		
A Kind Of Magic	Queen	#42

1987		
I Just Can't Stop Loving You	Michael Jackson	#1
What's Going On	Cyndi Lauper	#12

1988		
Man In The Mirror	Michael Jackson	#1
Make Me Lose Control	Eric Carmen	#3
Promise Me	The Cover Girls	#40

1989		
Cherish	Madonna	#2

SONGS WITH AN ORCHESTRA

You have to admire the ambition of pop stars that say they want their next song to be backed, not by a few extra musicians, or a string quartet, or even a boys choir, but by an entire orchestra.

As you can imagine, there weren't many songs that employed an orchestra, but there were several. They were all fairly popular- three of them made the top ten.

SONGS WITH AN ORCHESTRA (cont'd)

SONG	ARTIST	HOT 100 CHART	NOTES
1981			
Time	Alan Parsons Project	#15	The Orchestra of the Munich Chamber Opera
1982			
Hooked On Classics	Royal Philharmonic Orchestra	#10	Royal Philharmonic Orchestra
Hooked On Big Bands	Frank Barber Orchestra	#61	
1985			
One Night In Bangkok	Murray Head	#3	London Symphony Orchestra
1989			
Sowing The Seeds Of Love	Tears For Fears	#2	
The Arms Of Orion	Prince w/ Sheena Easton	#36	The Clare Fischer Orchestra

SONGS OF EXTREME DURATION

Where is "Rapper's Delight", by The Sugarhill Gang? Good question. The long version is <u>really</u> long. It's over fourteen minutes. They also released a "short" version, clocking in at 6 1/2 minutes. For these lists though, I go by the single version whenever possible. The single for "Rapper's Delight" was just under five minutes long, so it doesn't make the list.

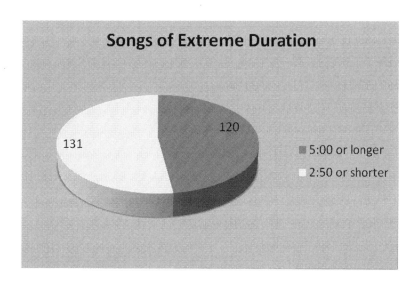

THE LONGEST SONGS OF THE 80s

(5:00 OR LONGER)

YEAR	SONG	ARTIST	HOT 100 CHART	LENGTH
1989	One	Metallica	#35	7:23
1989	Paradise City	Guns N' Roses	#5	6:46
1980	Sequel	Harry Chapin	#23	6:36
1981	Rapture	Blondie	#1	6:29
1985	Sunset Grill	Don Henley	#22	6:28
1981	Rock And Roll Dreams Come Through	Jim Steinman (Rory Dodd)	#32	6:25
1980	Brite Eyes	Robbin Thompson Band	#66	6:24
1985	We Are The World	USA For Africa	#1	6:22
1984	Left In The Dark	Barbra Streisand	#50	6:12
1986	In Your Eyes	Peter Gabriel	#26	6:11
1980	Fool In The Rain	Led Zeppelin	#21	6:08
1983	Mama	Genesis	#73	6:07
1989	The Last Worthless Evening	Don Henley	#21	6:03
1989	Radar Love	White Lion	#59	6:02
1981	Walking On Thin Ice	Yoko Ono	#58	5:58
1989	Lay Your Hands On Me	Bon Jovi	#7	5:58
1988	Sweet Child O' Mine	Guns N' Roses	#1	5:55
1985	Rockin' At Midnight	The Honeydrippers	#25	5:54
1985	All You Zombies	Hooters	#58	5:54
1986	Like A Rock	Bob Seger	#12	5:53
1989	Patience	Guns N' Roses	#4	5:53
1987	Don't Give Up	Peter Gabriel/ Kate Bush	#72	5:52
1983	Industrial Disease	Dire Straits	#75	5:50
1986	Superbowl Shuffle	The Chicago Bears Shufflin' Crew	#41	5:50
1988	One More Try	George Michael	#1	5:50
1985	You Belong To The City	Glenn Frey	#2	5:49
1985	Freeway Of Love	Aretha Franklin	#3	5:49
1983	Goodnight Saigon	Billy Joel	#56	5:48
1982	The Visitors	Abba	#63	5:47
1988	Love Bites	Def Leppard	#1	5:46
1980	Don't Say Goodnight (It's Time For Love)	The Isley Brothers	#39	5:45
1986	Stairway To Heaven	Far Corporation	#89	5:45
1987	Jimmy Lee	Aretha Franklin	#28	5:44
1987	Women	Def Leppard	#80	5:43
1989	I'll Be There For You	Bon Jovi	#1	5:43
1989	Sowing The Seeds Of Love	Tears For Fears	#2	5:43

THE LONGEST SONGS OF THE 80s (cont'd)

1989	I'm A Believer	Giant	#56	5:43
1983	True	Spandau Ballet	#4	5:39
1983	Dirty Laundry	Don Henley	#3	5:38
1983	Just Be Good To Me	The S.O.S. Band	#55	5:37
1988	Father Figure	George Michael	#1	5:37
1988	When It's Love	Van Halen	#5	5:37
1989	It Isn't, It Wasn't, It Ain't Never Gonna Be	Aretha Franklin & Whitney Houston	#41	5:37
1980	Emotional Rescue	The Rolling Stones	#3	5:35
1981	Passion	Rod Stewart	#5	5:35
1983	Eminence Front	The Who	#68	5:35
1986	The Big Money	Rush	#45	5:35
1986	Absolute Beginners	David Bowie	#53	5:35
1984	Medley: Love Songs Are Back Again	Band Of Gold	#64	5:33
1983	Total Eclipse Of The Heart	Bonnie Tyler	#1	5:31
1986	Welcome To The Boomtown	David & David	#37	5:31
1984	Love Has Finally Come At Last	Bobby Womack & Patti Labelle	#88	5:30
1986	Everything Must Change	Paul Young	#56	5:30
1989	The Living Years	Mike + The Mechanics	#1	5:30
1989	Open Letter (To A Landlord)	Living Colour	#82	5:30
1985	Everything She Wants	Wham!	#1	5:27
1980	Chiquitita	Abba	#29	5:26
1987	I've Been In Love Before	Cutting Crew	#9	5:26
1989	Listen To Your Heart	Roxette	#1	5:26
1982	Electricland	Bad Company	#74	5:25
1989	Dreamin'	Vanessa Williams	#8	5:25
1984	Read 'Em And Weep	Barry Manilow	#18	5:24
1985	Alive & Kicking	Simple Minds	#3	5:24
1980	Biggest Part Of Me	Ambrosia	#3	5:23
1989	Armageddon It	Def Leppard	#3	5:21
1989	Once Bitten Twice Shy	Great White	#5	5:21
1989	Love Has Taken Its Toll	Saraya	#64	5:21
1982	I.G.Y. (What A Beautiful World)	Donald Fagen	#26	5:20
1984	Take Me Back	Bonnie Tyler	#46	5:20
1983	Who's Behind The Door?	Zebra	#61	5:19
1984	In The Mood	Robert Plant	#39	5:19
1989	Like A Prayer	Madonna	#1	5:19
1981	Same Old Lang Syne	Dan Fogelberg	#9	5:18
1984	Hold Me	Teddy Pendergrass w/Whitney Houston	#46	5:18
1988	Don't Know What You Got (Till It's Gone)	Cinderella	#12	5:18
1984	An Innocent Man	Billy Joel	#10	5:16

THE LONGEST SONGS OF THE 80s (cont'd)

1984	Olympia	Sergio Mendes	#58	5:16
1984	Tonight Is What It Means To Be Young	Fire Inc.	#80	5:16
1985	Freedom	Wham!	#3	5:16
1980	Little Jeannie	Elton John	#3	5:15
1982	Planet Rock	Afrika Bambaataa	#48	5:15
1983	I Cannot Believe It's True	Phil Collins	#79	5:14
1988	Without You	Peabo Bryson & Regina Belle	#89	5:14
1989	The End Of The Innocence	Don Henley	#8	5:14
1982	That Girl	Stevie Wonder	#4	5:13
1985	Just Another Night	Mick Jagger	#12	5:13
1988	Be Still My Beating Heart	Sting	#15	5:13
1989	In My Eyes	Stevie B	#37	5:12
1981	Medley II	Stars On 45	#67	5:11
1980	Even It Up	Heart	#33	5:10
1986	For America	Jackson Browne	#30	5:10
1987	Every Little Kiss	Bruce Hornsby and the Range	#14	5:10
1988	Parents Just Don't Understand	D.J. Jazzy Jeff and the Fresh Prince	#12	5:10
1988	The Dead Heart	Midnight Oil	#53	5:10
1989	My Heart Can't Tell You No	Rod Stewart	#4	5:10
1985	Sun City	Artists United Against Apartheid	#38	5:09
1988	Devil Inside	INXS	#2	5:09
1984	Wrapped Around Your Finger	The Police	#8	5:08
1986	War	Bruce Springsteen	#8	5:08
1983	She Blinded Me With Science	Thomas Dolby	#5	5:07
1984	Here Comes The Rain Again	Eurythmics	#4	5:07
1987	Heat Of The Night	Bryan Adams	#6	5:07
1987	Wanted Dead Or Alive	Bon Jovi	#7	5:07
1988	Tunnel Of Love	Bruce Springsteen	#9	5:07
1989	Right Next To Me	Whistle	#60	5:07
1980	Power	The Temptations	#43	5:05
1986	The Rain	Oran "Juice" Jones	#9	5:05
1988	Angel	Aerosmith	#3	5:05
1985	Careless Whisper	Wham!/George Michael	#1	5:04
1983	Big Log	Robert Plant	#20	5:03
1985	I Want To Know What Love Is	Foreigner	#1	5:03
1987	Didn't We Almost Have It All	Whitney Houston	#1	5:03
1980	Lady	The Whispers	#28	5:02
1981	I'm So Glad I'm Standing Here Today	Crusaders w/Joe Cocker	#97	5:02
1981	Who's Crying Now	Journey	#4	5:01
1982	Do I Do	Stevie Wonder	#13	5:01
1988	Broken Land	The Adventures	#95	5:01
1986	Sledgehammer	Peter Gabriel	#1	5:00

THE LONGEST SONGS OF THE 80s (cont'd)

| 1986 | Dreamtime | Daryl Hall | #1 | 5:00 |
| 1988 | Here With Me | REO Speedwagon | #20 | 5:00 |

THE SHORTEST SONGS OF THE 80s

(2:50 OR SHORTER)

YEAR	SONG	ARTIST	HOT 100 CHART	LENGTH
1988	Hippy Hippy Shake	Georgia Satellites	#45	1:45
1981	I Love My Truck	Glen Campbell	#94	1:50
1980	Theme From The Dukes of Hazzard (Good Ol' Boys)	Waylon Jennings	#21	2:06
1982	Come Go With Me	The Beach Boys	#18	2:06
1987	Come On, Let's Go	Los Lobos	#21	2:09
1981	Almost Saturday Night	Dave Edmunds	#54	2:11
1983	Holiday Road	Lindsey Buckingham	#82	2:11
1982	Oh Julie	Barry Manilow	#38	2:13
1982	Wake Up Little Susie	Simon & Garfunkel	#27	2:16
1986	In Between Days (Without You)	The Cure	#99	2:16
1981	Dedicated To The One I Love	Bernadette Peters	#65	2:17
1982	So Much In Love	Timothy B. Schmit	#59	2:17
1988	What A Wonderful World	Louis Armstrong	#32	2:17
1983	War Games	Crosby, Stills & Nash	#45	2:18
1980	How Do I Make You	Linda Ronstadt	#10	2:19
1981	Mister Sandman	Emmylou Harris	#37	2:20
1983	Bad Boys	Wham!	#60	2:20
1982	Hang Fire	The Rolling Stones	#20	2:22
1981	It's Just The Sun	Don McLean	#83	2:25
1988	Alphabet St.	Prince	#8	2:25
1980	Daydream Believer	Anne Murray	#12	2:26
1981	Someday, Someway	Robert Gordon	#76	2:26
1984	Sunshine In The Shade	The Fixx	#69	2:26
1984	Breaking up Is Hard On You (a/k/a Don't Take Ma Bell Away From Me)	The American Comedy Network	#70	2:26
1985	Miami Vice Theme	Jan Hammer	#1	2:26
1984	Are We Ourselves?	The Fixx	#15	2:27
1981	Running Scared	The Fools	#50	2:28
1982	Get Closer	Linda Ronstadt	#29	2:28
1980	One Fine Day	Carole King	#12	2:29
1981	Mercy, Mercy, Mercy	Phoebe Snow	#52	2:29

THE SHORTEST SONGS OF THE 80s (cont'd)

1981	The Woman In Me	Crystal Gayle	#74	2:29
1986	That's Life	David Lee Roth	#85	2:29
1982	We Got The Beat	The Go-Go's	#2	2:30
1982	In The Driver's Seat	John Schneider	#72	2:30
1986	Needles And Pins	Tom Petty w/ Stevie Nicks	#37	2:30
1980	On The Road Again	Willie Nelson	#20	2:31
1982	Sea Of Love	Del Shannon	#33	2:31
1986	Twist And Shout	The Beatles	#23	2:31
1981	Since I Don't Have You	Don McLean	#23	2:32
1981	Fashion	David Bowie	#70	2:32
1982	I Get Excited	Rick Springfield	#32	2:32
1980	Gee Whiz	Bernadette Peters	#31	2:33
1987	I Don't Mind At All	Bourgeois Tagg	#38	2:33
1983	I'll Tumble 4 Ya	Culture Club	#9	2:34
1984	On The Wings Of A Nightingale	The Everly Brothers	#50	2:34
1984	Break-A-Way	Tracey Ullman	#70	2:34
1985	I'm On Fire	Bruce Springsteen	#6	2:34
1981	All I Have To Do Is Dream	Andy Gibb & Victoria Principal	#51	2:35
1981	Teacher Teacher	Rockpile	#51	2:35
1982	She Looks A Lot Like You	Clocks	#67	2:35
1983	Ricky	"Weird Al" Yankovic	#63	2:35
1980	Looks Like Love Again	Dann Rogers	#41	2:36
1982	Workin' For A Livin'	Huey Lewis & The News	#41	2:36
1982	(You're So Square) Baby, I Don't Care	Joni Mitchell	#47	2:36
1983	Where Everybody Knows Your Name (Theme From "Cheers")	Gary Portnoy	#83	2:36
1980	Whip It	Devo	#14	2:37
1981	Blaze Of Glory	Kenny Rogers	#66	2:37
1983	Delirious	Prince	#8	2:37
1982	Tainted Love	Soft Cell	#8	2:38
1983	Everyday People	Joan Jett & The Blackhearts	#37	2:38
1988	Talkin' Bout A Revolution	Tracy Chapman	#75	2:38
1980	Think About Me	Fleetwood Mac	#20	2:39
1981	Elvira	The Oak Ridge Boys	#5	2:39
1981	Blessed Are The Believers	Anne Murray	#34	2:39
1982	Be Mine Tonight	Neil Diamond	#35	2:39
1983	American Made	The Oak Ridge Boys	#72	2:39
1980	Don't Do Me Like That	Tom Petty And The Heartbreakers	#10	2:40
1981	Seduced	Leon Redbone	#72	2:40
1982	I Want Candy	Bow Wow Wow	#62	2:40
1980	First Time Love	Livingston Taylor	#38	2:41
1983	On The Dark Side	Eddie & The Cruisers	#64	2:41

THE SHORTEST SONGS OF THE 80s (cont'd)

1984	On The Dark Side	John Cafferty	#7	2:41
1986	Wrap It Up	The Fabulous Thunderbirds	#50	2:41
1980	Let My Love Open the Door	Pete Townshend	#9	2:42
1980	I Can't Let Go	Linda Ronstadt	#31	2:42
1981	I've Done Everything For You	Rick Springfield	#8	2:42
1981	You're My Girl	Franke And The Knockouts	#27	2:42
1981	Ch Ch Cherie	Johnny Average Band	#53	2:42
1982	Take Off	Bob & Doug McKenzie w/ Geddy Lee	#16	2:42
1983	Baby, What About You	Crystal Gayle	#83	2:42
1989	I Only Wanna Be With You	Samantha Fox	#31	2:42
1983	Favorite Waste Of Time	Bette Midler	#78	2:43
1987	Come As You Are	Peter Wolf	#15	2:43
1980	Crazy Little Thing Called Love	Queen	#1	2:44
1981	Our Lips Are Sealed	The Go-Go's	#20	2:44
1981	It Hurts To Be In Love	Dan Hartman	#72	2:44
1982	Dreamin'	John Schneider	#45	2:44
1982	Happy Band	Greg Kihn Band	#62	2:44
1983	Safety Dance	Men Without Hats	#3	2:44
1983	Shoot For The Moon	Poco	#50	2:44
1983	Stand By	Roman Holliday	#54	2:44
1980	Let Me Love You Tonight	Pure Prairie League	#10	2:45
1980	I'm Almost Ready	Pure Prairie League	#34	2:45
1980	Somethin' 'Bout You Baby I Like	Glen Campbell & Rita Coolidge	#42	2:45
1981	Guitar Man	Elvis Presley	#28	2:45
1981	Flash's Theme aka Flash	Queen	#42	2:45
1982	I Love Rock 'N Roll	Joan Jett & The Blackhearts	#1	2:45
1982	A World Without Heroes	Kiss	#56	2:46
1982	He Could Be The One	Josie Cotton	#74	2:46
1989	Pop Singer	John Cougar Mellencamp	#15	2:46
1981	Hearts On Fire	Randy Meisner	#19	2:47
1981	Working In The Coal Mine	Devo	#43	2:47
1982	I Need You	Paul Carrack	#37	2:47
1982	So Fine	The Oak Ridge Boys	#76	2:47
1985	California Girls	David Lee Roth	#3	2:47
1987	Happy Together	The Nylons	#75	2:47
1982	Yesterday's Songs	Neil Diamond	#11	2:48
1986	R.O.C.K. In The U.S.A. (A Salute To 60's Rock)	John Cougar Mellencamp	#2	2:48
1982	Bobby Sue	The Oak Ridge Boys	#12	2:49
1982	What's Forever For	Michael Murphey	#19	2:49
1982	Someday, Someway	Marshall Crenshaw	#36	2:49
1983	The Other Guy	Little River Band	#11	2:49

THE SHORTEST SONGS OF THE 80s (cont'd)

1985	Radioactive	The Firm	#28	2:49
1986	Fall On Me	R.E.M.	#94	2:49
1980	Hit Me With Your Best Shot	Pat Benatar	#9	2:50
1980	Clones (We're All)	Alice Cooper	#40	2:50
1981	The Breakup Song (They Don't Write 'Em)	Greg Kihn Band	#15	2:50
1981	Precious To Me	Phil Seymour	#22	2:50
1981	Heart Like A Wheel	The Steve Miller Band	#24	2:50
1981	I've Been Waiting For You All My Life	Paul Anka	#48	2:50
1981	It's All I Can Do	Anne Murray	#53	2:50
1981	Bet Your Heart On Me	Johnny Lee	#54	2:50
1981	That Didn't Hurt Too Bad	Dr. Hook	#69	2:50
1981	Pay You Back With Interest	Gary O'	#70	2:50
1982	Just To Satisfy You	Waylon Jennings & Willie Nelson	#52	2:50
1982	Voice On The Radio	Conductor	#63	2:50
1982	If I Could Get You (Into My Life)	Gene Cotton	#76	2:50
1983	Sign Of The Times	The Belle Stars	#75	2:50
1985	Baby Come Back To Me (The Morse Code Of Love)	The Manhattan Transfer	#83	2:50
1986	Velcro Fly	ZZ Top	#35	2:50
1988	Way Out	J.J. Fad	#61	2:50

THE 189 BEST SONGS OF THE 80s

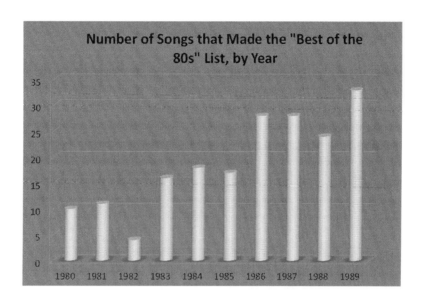

So here we have the first chart that may make some of you curse my name and tear my book in two. Not coincidently, this is also the first chart that is purely subjective. Here are what I consider to be the best 189 songs of the 1980s. Why 189 songs? As I listened to each of the 4,172 hit songs from the 80s, I kept a separate list of what I deemed to be the best songs. I had no pre-conceived notion of how many songs were great, or how many songs deserved to be on such a list. If I decided it was a great song, it made the list.

There are a few things you should know before you peruse the list. First, my guilty pleasures of the 80s, musically speaking, include Debbie Gibson, Wham!, and Milli Vanilli. So heads up.

Second, I'm not a huge U2, Rolling Stones, or rap fan. So if you're looking for tons of songs by those bands, or in that genre, you'll be disappointed. I will say that "Sunday, Bloody Sunday" is definitely one of the best songs of the 80s. Had it made the Hot 100 chart, it would be very high on my list. How it never cracked the Hot 100 chart, I'll never know.

Third- A song did not have to be a "huge" hit to make my list. Sure, quite a few number one hits did make my list, but there are also 17 songs that didn't even rise above #40. And usually, those low-charting songs are the best things about lists like these.

I mean, everybody has heard "Take On Me", by A-Ha, even people who aren't fans of 80s music. Likewise for "Drive", by The Cars, and "Jump", by Van Halen. Those songs still receive regular airplay. And they should- they're great songs. But when was the last time you heard "Jam On It", "Jealous Guy", or "Just Be Good To Me"? Have you ever heard, "No One Can Love You More Than Me", by Melissa Manchester? That one peaked at #78, but it sounds like a top ten hit to me. What about "I Eat Cannibals", by Total Coelo? That one only made it to #66. Listen to it and I think you'll agree it's one of the best pop songs ever with the word "cannibals" in the title.

So find the songs you're not familiar with on my list, and give them a listen. I hope that you discover some great songs you never heard before, or re-discover some old classics that you forgot were so good.

The 80s Music Compendium

And hey, if you don't like my list, you can always make your own. Just be sure to listen to every single hit from the decade. You know, so you can be fair to all the songs and artists. All 4,172 songs are waiting...

One note- if a song hit the Hot 100 chart twice, ("When I'm With You", by Sheriff, for example) I listed the chart position and year for its first appearance.

RANK	YEAR	SONG	ARTIST	HOT 100 CHART
#1	1985	Take On Me	A-Ha	#1
#2	1988	Sweet Child O' Mine	Guns N' Roses	#1
#3	1985	One Night In Bangkok	Murray Head	#3
#4	1984	When Doves Cry	Prince	#1
#5	1986	Word Up	Cameo	#6
#6	1985	Would I Lie To You?	Eurythmics	#5
#7	1988	The Promise	When In Rome	#11
#8	1986	Let's Go All The Way	Sly Fox	#7
#9	1988	Foolish Beat	Debbie Gibson	#1
#10	1984	Strut	Sheena Easton	#7
#11	1988	Love Bites	Def Leppard	#1
#12	1984	Drive	The Cars	#3
#13	1980	Fool In The Rain	Led Zeppelin	#21
#14	1981	Don't Let Him Go	REO Speedwagon	#24
#15	1984	Jam On It	Newcleus	#56
#16	1985	Everything She Wants	Wham!	#1
#17	1989	Sowing The Seeds Of Love	Tears For Fears	#2
#18	1981	In The Air Tonight	Phil Collins	#19
#19	1988	Dirty Diana	Michael Jackson	#1
#20	1988	The Way You Make Me Feel	Michael Jackson	#1
#21	1984	Missing You	John Waite	#1
#22	1988	Candle In The Wind	Elton John	#6
#23	1981	Ah! Leah!	Donnie Iris	#29
#24	1985	Careless Whisper	Wham!/George Michael	#1
#25	1986	Every Little Kiss	Bruce Hornsby and the Range	#72
#26	1988	Jealous Guy	John Lennon	#80
#27	1989	Like A Prayer	Madonna	#1
#28	1989	Send Me An Angel '89	Real Life	#26
#29	1983	Uptown Girl	Billy Joel	#3
#30	1983	Photograph	Def Leppard	#12
#31	1984	Magic	The Cars	#12
#32	1986	You Can Call Me Al	Paul Simon	#44
#33	1987	Only In My Dreams	Debbie Gibson	#4
#34	1984	Do They Know It's Christmas?	Band Aid	#13
#35	1983	Come On Eileen	Dexys Midnight Runners	#1
#36	1983	Every Breath You Take	The Police	#1
#37	1984	Jump	Van Halen	#1

THE 189 BEST SONGS OF THE 80s (cont'd)

#38	1984	Wrapped Around Your Finger	The Police	#8
#39	1986	The Way It Is	Bruce Hornsby and the Range	#1
#40	1987	Keep Your Hands To Yourself	Georgia Satellites	#2
#41	1983	Just Be Good To Me	The S.O.S. Band	#55
#42	1989	Closer To Fine	Indigo Girls	#52
#43	1988	Red Red Wine	UB40	#1
#44	1983	No One Can Love You More Than Me	Melissa Manchester	#78
#45	1988	Simply Irresistible	Robert Palmer	#2
#46	1986	Don't Forget Me (When I'm Gone)	Glass Tiger	#2
#47	1988	Father Figure	George Michael	#1
#48	1987	La Isla Bonita	Madonna	#4
#49	1989	Be With You	Bangles	#30
#50	1989	The End Of The Innocence	Don Henley	#8
#51	1985	Material Girl	Madonna	#2
#52	1983	When I'm With You	Sheriff	#61
#53	1984	I Can Dream About You	Dan Hartman	#6
#54	1989	Love In An Elevator	Aerosmith	#5
#55	1984	Head Over Heels	The Go-Go's	#11
#56	1985	Freedom	Wham/George Michael	#4
#57	1988	Peek-A-Boo	Siouxsie & The Banshees	#53
#58	1989	In Your Room	Bangles	#5
#59	1986	Conga	Miami Sound Machine	#10
#60	1987	Mandolin Rain	Bruce Hornsby and the Range	#4
#61	1980	Sara	Fleetwood Mac	#7
#62	1989	Veronica	Elvis Costello	#19
#63	1989	The Living Years	Mike + The Mechanics	#1
#64	1984	Hello Again	The Cars	#20
#65	1983	Beat It	Michael Jackson	#1
#66	1987	Heart And Soul	T'Pau	#4
#67	1980	Train In Vain (Stand By Me)	The Clash	#23
#68	1989	A Little Respect	Erasure	#14
#69	1988	Wishing Well	Terence Trent D'Arby	#1
#70	1986	Sledgehammer	Peter Gabriel	#1
#71	1986	All I Need Is A Miracle	Mike + The Mechanics	#5
#72	1988	One More Try	George Michael	#1
#73	1987	Holiday	The Other Ones	#29
#74	1980	Chiquitita	Abba	#29
#75	1986	Rock Me Amadeus	Falco	#1
#76	1984	The Longest Time	Billy Joel	#14
#77	1986	Addicted To Love	Robert Palmer	#1
#78	1983	Wanna Be Startin' Somethin'	Michael Jackson	#5
#79	1984	Thriller	Michael Jackson	#4

THE 189 BEST SONGS OF THE 80s (cont'd)

#80	1989	One	Metallica	#35
#81	1984	Wake Me Up Before You Go-Go	Wham!	#1
#82	1985	Axel F	Harold Faltermeyer	#3
#83	1985	St. Elmo's Fire (Man In Motion)	John Parr	#1
#84	1988	Make It Real	The Jets	#4
#85	1987	Faith	George Michael	#1
#86	1989	What You Don't Know	Expose	#8
#87	1987	Point Of No Return	Expose	#5
#88	1986	Two Of Hearts	Stacey Q	#3
#89	1988	What Have I Done To Deserve This?	Pet Shop Boys & Dusty Springfield	#2
#90	1989	Girl I'm Gonna Miss You	Milli Vanilli	#1
#91	1989	We Didn't Start The Fire	Billy Joel	#1
#92	1981	Don't Stand So Close To Me	The Police	#10
#93	1983	Billie Jean	Michael Jackson	#1
#94	1981	You Better You Bet	The Who	#18
#95	1987	Land Of Confusion	Genesis	#4
#96	1985	You Spin Me Round (Like A Record)	Dead Or Alive	#11
#97	1985	Weird Science	Oingo Boingo	#45
#98	1980	Into The Night	Benny Mardones	#11
#99	1989	Sincerely Yours	Sweet Sensation w/ Romeo J.D.	#14
#100	1989	Leave A Light On	Belinda Carlisle	#11
#101	1988	Chains Of Love	Erasure	#12
#102	1984	Ti Amo	Laura Branigan	#55
#103	1984	That's All!	Genesis	#6
#104	1982	Steppin' Out	Joe Jackson	#6
#105	1983	Africa	Toto	#1
#106	1987	Open Your Heart	Madonna	#1
#107	1987	Fascinated	Company B	#21
#108	1983	Drop The Pilot	Joan Armatrading	#78
#109	1989	Girl You Know It's True	Milli Vanilli	#2
#110	1988	She's Like The Wind	Patrick Swayze w/ Wendy Fraser	#3
#111	1989	Toy Soldiers	Martika	#1
#112	1981	Every Little Thing She Does Is Magic	The Police	#3
#113	1982	Should I Stay Or Should I Go	The Clash	#45
#114	1985	And She Was	Talking Heads	#54
#115	1986	West End Girls	Pet Shop Boys	#1
#116	1981	Ai No Corrida	Quincy Jones (Dune)	#28
#117	1989	Secret Rendezvous	Karyn White	#6
#118	1986	Mad About You	Belinda Carlisle	#3
#119	1987	Brand New Lover	Dead Or Alive	#15
#120	1987	Touch Of Grey	Grateful Dead	#9
#121	1987	True Faith	New Order	#32

THE 189 BEST SONGS OF THE 80s (cont'd)

#122	1985	Money For Nothing	Dire Straits	#1
#123	1986	I Didn't Mean To Turn You On	Robert Palmer	#2
#124	1980	Breakfast In America	Supertramp	#62
#125	1980	All Over The World	Electric Light Orchestra	#13
#126	1981	Woman	John Lennon	#2
#127	1987	Kiss Him Goodbye	The Nylons	#12
#128	1980	(Just Like) Starting Over	John Lennon	#1
#129	1987	Big Time	Peter Gabriel	#8
#130	1989	Express Yourself	Madonna	#2
#131	1982	I Can't Go For That (No Can Do)	Daryl Hall & John Oates	#1
#132	1983	In A Big Country	Big Country	#17
#133	1989	Miss You Much	Janet Jackson	#1
#134	1988	Push It	Salt-N-Pepa	#19
#135	1987	Nobody's Fool	Cinderella	#13
#136	1986	Walk Of Life	Dire Straits	#7
#137	1986	Tonight She Comes	The Cars	#7
#138	1986	Walk Like An Egyptian	Bangles	#1
#139	1984	Against All Odds (Take A Look At Me Now)	Phil Collins	#1
#140	1986	I'm Not The One	The Cars	#32
#141	1986	In Your Eyes	Peter Gabriel	#26
#142	1981	Twilight	Electric Light Orchestra	#38
#143	1983	I Eat Cannibals	Total Coelo	#66
#144	1988	Naughty Girls (Need Love Too)	Samantha Fox	#3
#145	1987	Come Go With Me	Expose	#5
#146	1987	Heaven Is A Place On Earth	Belinda Carlisle	#1
#147	1988	Make Me Lose Control	Eric Carmen	#3
#148	1980	Atomic	Blondie	#39
#149	1987	Alone	Heart	#1
#150	1989	This Time I Know It's For Real	Donna Summer	#7
#151	1983	Always Something There To Remind Me	Naked Eyes	#8
#152	1981	Let's Groove	Earth, Wind & Fire	#3
#153	1980	Master Blaster (Jammin')	Stevie Wonder	#5
#154	1986	Opportunities (Let's Make Lots Of Money)	Pet Shop Boys	#10
#155	1989	Cold Hearted	Paula Abdul	#1
#156	1985	Centerfield	John Fogerty	#44
#157	1989	My Prerogative	Bobby Brown	#1
#158	1986	Nikita	Elton John	#7
#159	1986	No Easy Way Out	Robert Tepper	#22
#160	1989	Buffalo Stance	Neneh Cherry	#3
#161	1987	Big Love	Fleetwood Mac	#5
#162	1986	These Dreams	Heart	#1
#163	1986	Glory Of Love	Peter Cetera	#1

THE 189 BEST SONGS OF THE 80s (cont'd)

#164	1987	Lost In Emotion	Lisa Lisa & Cult Jam	#1
#165	1986	Russians	Sting	#16
#166	1986	Tarzan Boy	Baltimora	#13
#167	1989	Second Chance	Thirty Eight Special	#6
#168	1989	Dr. Feelgood	Motley Crue	#6
#169	1985	Fortress Around Your Heart	Sting	#8
#170	1987	Livin' On A Prayer	Bon Jovi	#1
#171	1987	It's A Sin	Pet Shop Boys	#9
#172	1986	Your Wildest Dreams	The Moody Blues	#9
#173	1987	U Got The Look	Prince	#2
#174	1989	Poison	Alice Cooper	#7
#175	1988	Just Like Heaven	The Cure	#40
#176	1985	Remo's Theme (What If)	Tommy Shaw	#81
#177	1989	Angel Of Harlem	U2	#14
#178	1983	Sexual Healing	Marvin Gaye	#3
#179	1982	It's Raining Again	Supertramp	#11
#180	1987	The Final Countdown	Europe	#8
#181	1989	18 And Life	Skid Row	#4
#182	1988	Everywhere	Fleetwood Mac	#14
#183	1981	Same Old Lang Syne	Dan Fogelberg	#9
#184	1989	Bust A Move	Young MC	#7
#185	1985	We Are The World	USA For Africa	#1
#186	1987	Lean On Me	Club Nouveau	#1
#187	1987	(You Gotta) Fight For Your Right (To Party!)	Beastie Boys	#7
#188	1989	Glamour Boys	Living Colour	#31
#189	1988	Don't Worry Be Happy	Bobby McFerrin	#1

THE 65 WORST SONGS OF THE 80s

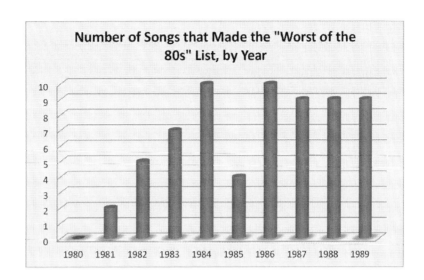

First, I just want to say that I have no agenda here. I'm not out to "get" any particular artist because I don't like their music. I am including this section because I realized that, though this is my favorite musical decade, there are a lot of lousy songs from the 80s. I mean, these songs are real bad. So I thought, if I'm keeping a "Best of" list, I should also keep a "Worst of" list- you know, to balance things out.

The songs on this list are spread out pretty evenly among the artists, for the most part. Only three artists have more than one song on the list (We're looking at you, Culture Club, Klymaxx, and New Kids On The Block.).

I suppose many of the artists on the list should not be a surprise. For example, I think we're all pretty much aware that the music of New Kids On The Block has not stood the test of time very well at all. Several artists on the "Worst" list might come as a surprise, though. Some of them are well-respected and established musicians. Such artists include Diana Ross, Eurythmics, Madonna, Paul McCartney, The Police, and Queen. Hey, no artist is safe- put out a bad song that somehow became a hit, and it'll make the list.

What would earn a song a place on this less-than-desirable list? Many times, it is the lyrics. A shining example of such lyrics can be found in Cliff Richard's hit song, "Wired For Sound" from 1981. The main message of this song is that Cliff absolutely loves the technology that allows him to listen to music. He loves cassette tapes. He loves record players. AM and FM radio stations make him feel "so ecstatic". Oh, don't forget speakers. He sings, "I like small speakers, I like tall speakers..." You get the idea that if there was another kind of speaker that ended with "-all", he'd like it, too. So there you have it, a song that extolls the virtue of severely outdated audio equipment. No thanks.

Another reason a song makes this list is that it is a poor cover of a great old song. "Dedicated To The One I Love", "Don't Stand So Close To Me '86", and "Cecilia" are examples of this type.

One last reason a song might be on this list- Sometimes, I simply can't stand the way a song sounds.

Although there aren't any number one hits on this list, there are six songs that peaked inside the top ten. Over half of the songs didn't make it inside the top fifty, however.

So here you go, 65 of the worst songs of the decade. Enjoy. Well, you won't. But you know what I mean.

THE 65 WORST SONGS OF THE 80s (cont'd)

SONG	ARTIST	HOT 100 CHART
1981		
Dedicated To The One I Love	Bernadette Peters	#65
Wired For Sound	Cliff Richard	#71
1982		
Body Language	Queen	#11
Valley Girl	Frank Zappa	#32
Murphy's Law	Cheri	#39
Work That Body	Diana Ross	#44
I Know What Boys Like	The Waitresses	#62
1983		
Do You Really Want To Hurt Me	Culture Club	#2
The Clapping Song	Pia Zadora	#36
Space Age Whiz Kids	Joe Walsh	#52
All Touch	Rough Trade	#58
Shoppin' From A To Z	Toni Basil	#77
For The Love Of Money	Bulletboys	#78
Keep It Confidential	Nona Hendryx	#91
1984		
Obscene Phone Caller	Rockwell	#35
My Oh My	Slade	#37
Boys Do Fall In Love	Robin Gibb	#37
Vitamin L	B.E. Taylor Group	#66
Remember What You Like	Jenny Burton	#81
Sexcrime (Nineteen Eighty-Four)	Eurythmics	#81
You, Me And He	Mtume	#83
Rappin' Rodney	Rodney Dangerfield	#83
She Loves My Car	Ronnie Milsap	#84
Sex Shooter	Apollonia 6	#85
1985		
Private Dancer	Tina Turner	#7
Mistake No. 3	Culture Club	#33
Meeting In The Ladies Room	Klymaxx	#59
Roxanne, Roxanne	Utfo	#77

THE 65 WORST SONGS OF THE 80s (cont'd)

1986		
Spies Like Us	Paul McCartney	#7
Sidewalk Talk	Jellybean w/ Catherine Buchanan	#18
Somewhere	Barbra Streisand	#43
Don't Stand So Close To Me '86	The Police	#46
Nail It To The Wall	Stacy Lattisaw	#48
The Heat Of Heat	Patti Austin	#55
Headlines	Midnight Star	#69
The Men All Pause	Klymaxx	#80
Runaway	Luis Cardenas	#83
Living In The Background	Baltimora	#87

1987		
Living In A Box	Living In A Box	#17
Happy	Surface	#20
Beat Patrol	Starship	#46
Girlfriend	Bobby Brown	#57
Love Is Contagious	Taja Sevelle	#62
Go See The Doctor	Kool Moe Dee	#89
Tina Cherry	Georgio	#96
Certain Things Are Likely	KTP	#97
Boy Toy	Tia	#97

1988		
Please Don't Go Girl	New Kids On The Block	#10
Fishnet	Morris Day	#23
Spotlight	Madonna	#32
Cars With The Boom	L'Trimm	#54
Samantha (What You Gonna Do?)	Cellarful Of Noise	#69
Cecilia	Times Two	#79
Century's End	Donald Fagen	#83
Ooo La La La	Teena Marie	#85
Jack The Lad	3 Man Island	#94

1989		
This One's For The Children	New Kids On The Block	#7
Didn't I (Blow Your Mind)	New Kids On The Block	#8
All She Wants Is	Duran Duran	#22
Me So Horny	The 2 Live Crew	#26
Little Jackie Wants To Be A Star	Lisa Lisa & Cult Jam	#29
Radio Romance	Tiffany	#35
French Kiss	Lil Louis	#50

THE 65 WORST SONGS OF THE 80s (cont'd)

Oh Daddy	Adrean Belew	#58
New Thing	Enuff Z'Nuff	#67

99 SONGS THAT DESERVED TO MAKE THE TOP-40

There are a number of gems that, for whatever reason, couldn't sustain any momentum to break inside the top 40 of the Hot 100. Keep in mind that if a song makes this list, I'm not saying it's one of the best songs of the decade (although that is true for a few of them). Usually, it just means that the song was good enough that it deserved a better fate than to stall out in the lower half of the chart.

Several of these songs are fantastic and undeniably catchy- I'll never understand how some of them couldn't make the top 40. If you decide you only have time to listen to one song from each year on this list, then allow me to choose them for you: from 1980, "Breakfast In America"; from 1981, "Can You Feel It"; from 1982, "Since You're Gone"; from 1983, ""Just Be Good To Me"; from 1984, "Jam On It"; from 1985, "Remo's Theme (What If)"; from 1986, "Every Little Kiss"; from 1987, "Suburbia"; from 1988, "Peek-A-Boo"; from 1989, "This One".

You should also pay extra attention to the 1983 list in this section. Almost every one of those songs should've been a top ten hit.

So if you've been a fan of 80s music for years, and think you've heard it all, you probably haven't. Set some time aside and explore this list. I bet you'll discover some brand new favorite songs from the 80s for yourself.

SONG	ARTIST	HOT 100 CHART
1980		
The Spirit Of Radio	Rush	#51
Breakfast In America	Supertramp	#62
Say Goodbye To Little Jo	Steve Forbert	#85
1981		
Give A Little Bit More	Cliff Richard	#41
Tempted	Squeeze	#49
Playing With Lightning	Shot In The Dark	#71
Can You Feel It	The Jacksons	#77
Don't Let Go The Coat	The Who	#84
1982		
Since You're Gone	The Cars	#41
1999	Prince	#44
My Kinda Lover	Billy Squier	#45
Should I Stay Or Should I Go	The Clash	#45
Enough Is Enough	April Wine	#50
The Gigolo	O'Bryan	#57

99 SONGS THAT DESERVED TO MAKE THE TOP-40 (cont'd)

I'll Drink To You	Duke Jupiter	#58
The Only Way Out	Cliff Richard	#64
Goodbye To You	Scandal	#65
You Got The Power	War	#66
Standing On The Top- Part 1	The Temptations w/ Rick James	#66
Nowhere To Run	Santana	#66
Don't Run My Life	Spys	#82

1983		
Stand By	Roman Holliday	#54
Just Be Good To Me	The S.O.S. Band	#55
Sharp Dressed Man	ZZ Top	#56
Sex (I'm A…)	Berlin	#62
On The Dark Side	Eddie & The Cruisers	#64
I Eat Cannibals	Total Coelo	#66
Shiny Shiny	Haysi Fantayzee	#74
Drop The Pilot	Joan Armatrading	#78
No One Can Love You More Than Me	Melissa Manchester	#78
Johnny B. Goode	Peter Tosh	#84
Four Little Diamonds	Electric Light Orchestra	#86

1984		
Strip	Adam Ant	#42
High On Emotion	Chris DeBurgh	#44
On The Wings Of A Nightingale	The Everly Brothers	#50
Ti Amo	Laura Branigan	#55
Jam On It	Newcleus	#56
The Ghost In You	The Psychedelic Furs	#59
Just The Way You Like It	The S.O.S. Band	#64
Say Hello To Ronnie	Janey Street	#68
Edge Of A Dream	Joe Cocker	#69
Break-A-Way	Tracey Ullman	#70
Gloria	The Doors	#71

1985		
Centerfield	John Fogerty	#44
Weird Science	Oingo Boingo	#45
America	Prince	#46
And She Was	Talking Heads	#54
Restless Heart	John Waite	#59
Sweet, Sweet Baby (I'm Falling)	Lone Justice	#73
Eaten Alive	Diana Ross	#77

99 SONGS THAT DESERVED TO MAKE THE TOP-40 (cont'd)

Remo's Theme (What If)	Tommy Shaw	#81
Baby Come Back To Me (The Morse Code Of Love)	The Manhattan Transfer	#83
Home Sweet Home	Motley Crue	#89
See What Love Can Do	Eric Clapton	#89
Heartline	Robin George	#92

1986		
A Kind Of Magic	Queen	#42
Great Gosh A'Mighty (It's A Matter Of Time)	Little Richard	#42
You Can Call Me Al	Paul Simon	#44
25 Or 6 To 4	Chicago	#48
It's You	Bob Seger	#52
Absolute Beginners	David Bowie	#53
Say It, Say It	E.G. Daily	#70
Every Little Kiss	Bruce Hornsby and the Range	#72
Heart's On Fire	John Cafferty	#76
Love Is The Hero	Billy Squier	#80
Just Another Day	Oingo Boingo	#85
Stairway To Heaven	Far Corporation	#89

1987		
Ain't So Easy	David & David	#51
Satellite	Hooters	#61
Johnny B	Hooters	#61
In Love With Love	Debbie Harry	#70
Learning To Fly	Pink Floyd	#70
Suburbia	Pet Shop Boys	#70
You Win Again	Bee Gees	#75
Happy Together	The Nylons	#75
True To You	Ric Ocasek	#75
Right Next Door (Because Of Me)	Robert Cray Band	#80
Graceland	Paul Simon	#81
Strap Me In	The Cars	#85
Battleship Chains	Georgia Satellites	#86
The Boy In The Bubble	Paul Simon	#86

1988		
Hot Hot Hot	Buster Poindexter	#45
Little Walter	Tony! Toni! Tone!	#47
Baby Can I Hold You	Tracy Chapman	#48
Peek-A-Boo	Siouxsie & The Banshees	#53
Blue Monday 1988	New Order	#68

99 SONGS THAT DESERVED TO MAKE THE TOP-40 (cont'd)

It's The End Of The World As We Know It (And I Feel Fine)	R.E.M.	#69
Don't Be Afraid Of The Dark	Robert Cray Band	#74
I'm Not Your Man	Tommy Conwell	#74
Jealous Guy	John Lennon	#80

1989		
The Way To Your Heart	Soulsister	#41
Fascination Street	The Cure	#46
Talk To Myself	Christopher Williams	#49
Closer To Fine	Indigo Girls	#52
Don't Say You Love Me	Billy Squier	#58
The Different Story (World Of Lust And Crime)	Peter Schilling	#61
End Of The Line	Traveling Wilburys	#63
All I Want Is You	U2	#83
This One	Paul McCartney	#94

BONUS CHART!

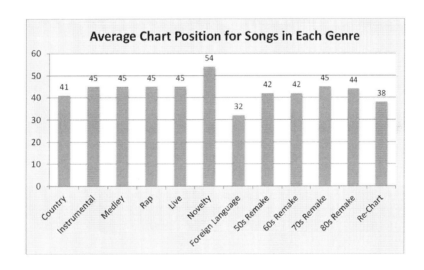

A NOTE FROM THE AUTHOR

Thanks for reading! I hope you found "The 80s Compendium" useful and interesting. If you haven't already, please leave a review at your favorite online book retailer. This book is also available for purchase as an ebook at most online retailers. If you've already purchased the softcover edition, and would like to also purchase the ebook version, email me, and I'll send you a discount coupon.

Don't forget to email me at davekinzerbooks@gmail.com if you have any questions, corrections, or comments. Remember, if you'd like to voice your opinion on which decade I should cover for my next compendium, email me.

The following resources made this project much easier:

www.allmusic.com An amazing resource when you want to look up a particular singer, song, band, album, or anything related to popular music.

"Joel Whitburn's Pop Annual 1955-2011"- This book lists every single song that hit Billboard's Hot 100 charts. A fairly expensive book, but very useful. The index, which lists every song included in the book, is 139 pages alone.

YouTube- Listen to every song ever written. Except for Prince or Bob Seger. They don't like YouTube.

www.discogs.com This website is primarily intended for collectors of records and other musical recordings. What I found extremely useful was that some of the pages on this site include the liner notes of albums, which will tell you what instruments were played on the record.

Thanks for purchasing "The 80s Compendium"!

Dave Kinzer

Printed in Poland
by Amazon Fulfillment
Poland Sp. z o.o., Wrocław

52530015R00175